Walter Benjamin and
the Antinomies of Tradition

WALTER BENJAMIN AND THE ANTINOMIES OF TRADITION

JOHN McCOLE

Cornell University Press

ITHACA AND LONDON

First published 1993 by Cornell University Press.

International Standard Book Number 0-8014-2465-8 (cloth)
International Standard Book Number 0-8014-9711-6 (paper)
Library of Congress Catalog Card Number 92-21431
Printed in the United States of America
Librarians: Library of Congress cataloging information
appears on the last page of the book.

FOR SOPHIE

Contents

Preface

In this book I explore the origins and tensions of Walter Benjamin's dealings with tradition. Few thinkers in this century have been as perceptive about the workings of tradition, as acutely aware of their own relation to it, and as convinced of the necessity of recovering the past in order to redeem the present; of those, no other was at the same time so ready to face up to the complicity of culture in injustice and conclude that humanity would have to "prepare itself to survive culture, if need be." Benjamin at once mourned and celebrated what he took to be an inevitable liquidation of traditional culture, persistently trying to find the right way of salvaging what was useful. His refusal to surrender either of these attitudes and his determination to think both through to their conclusions lend his dealings with tradition their peculiar honesty.

At the same time, this is also a book about how to make sense of this tension in Benjamin's work. It cannot, I argue, be reduced to psychological ambiguity or ambivalence about his social role, nor did it derive from a conception of tradition that can be traced to some intellectual influence. Rather, it was the consequence of a sustained argument with the entrenched orthodoxies of German intellectual culture, an argument through which Benjamin sought to keep faith with the experience of all that was "untimely, sorrowful, and unsuccessful" or, as he came to put it, to vindicate the oppressed of history. The Benjamin who appears here is not (or not just) a virtuoso reader, a micrological investigator of culture, or a master of mimetic interaction with his objects, though at times he could be all of those. The hallmark of his work lies in its paradoxical, antinomial coherence. This coherence, I argue, can best be explained by taking him at his word—"the critic is a strategist in the literary struggle"—and reconstructing his pursuit of long-term intellectual strategies. These strategies originated in choices he made at the time of his break with the youth movement and were clearly articulated in his immanent critique of German early romanticism. While his strategies continued to develop in response to new circumstances, the formative influence of this early constellation can still be traced in his dealings with baroque *Trauerspiel*, technology, and aestheticism in his later work.

To reconstruct Benjamin's strategies, I call on Pierre Bourdieu's concept of the intellectual field to propose an approach to doing intellectual history that goes beyond documentary and reductive approaches. An intellectual field is a historically specific structure of orthodoxies and heterodoxies, and Benjamin's project can best be understood as an immanent critique of a specifically German intellectual culture dominated by the peculiar constellation of idealism and historicism that constituted what Fritz Ringer calls the mandarin orthodoxy. My study is not another intellectual biography of Benjamin, though I do hope to establish criteria for one that would be truly rigorous. Rather, it focuses attention on a particular issue, a crucial and previously under-illuminated aspect of his work—what I call his construction of the antinomies of tradition.

My work has been generously supported, in various ways, by a research grant from the Deutscher Akademischer Austauschdienst; the Graduate School of Boston University; the John Lax Fellowship of Brown University, and Peter and Anneli Lax; Harvard University; the Jaroslaw and Helena Stroczan Foundation of Mainz-Mombach; and, of course, my parents. I thank all of them.

Parts of Chapter 7 appeared as "Benjamin's *Passagen-Werk:* A Guide to the Labyrinth," *Theory and Society* 14 (1985), 497–509; reprinted by permission.

My debts to individuals are far-reaching, as they must be with a project of this nature. Two are particularly important. Fritz Ringer has been an incomparable mentor. He did not just introduce me to the study of German intellectual culture; he also imparted a vision of intellectual history, why it is important, and how to do it. He was the first to make me realize that I had to argue for my views, and he even succeeded in getting me to do it at times. As a reader, he has never settled for anything less than lucidity; throughout this long project, he managed the wondrous feat of being both a tenacious and a tactful critic. Nancy Lyman Roelker has helped to sustain my work on many levels for many years now; she has been unstinting and resourceful in providing sound advice, thoughtful criticism, and needed encouragement. I value both of them as teachers and as friends. My work would not have been possible without them.

Carl Chiarenza was the first to encourage me to write on Benjamin; it was in his seminar on the history of photography that this project began. In Frankfurt, Lloyd Spencer generously led me into the maze of Benjamin's texts and the arcane worlds of Benjamin scholarship and left his indelible imprint on my image of Benjamin. Conversations and seminars with Burkhardt Lindner helped encourage my early work in Frankfurt as well. Irving Wohlfarth provided an incisive critique of the manuscript at an important point in its development. If our ways of reading differ, I nevertheless hope that my debt to and respect for his unsurpassed work on Benjamin will be evident throughout this book. At various stages of the work I have also had particularly helpful readings from Michael Bernstein, Donald Fleming, Mary Gluck, Mark Kishlansky, Charles Maier, Michael McKeon, Simon Schama, Kasia Stroczan, and Sophie Volpp; David J. Schoetz provided indispensable technical assistance with the footnotes. Tom Gleason, of Brown University, has genially presided over some of my pivotal passages. My editor at Cornell, John Ackerman, has shown extraordinary patience, and John Thomas's meticulous copy editing has saved me much embarrassment. My thanks to all of them. Finally, I thank my colleagues at Social Studies and at the History Department at Harvard University, and particularly my students, whose gift for dialogue and dispute amazes and sustains me.

My father did not live to see the completion of this book. I can only hope it would have given him pleasure.

JOHN McCOLE

Cambridge, Massachusetts

A Note on Translations
and Citations

All translations of Benjamin's texts in this book are my own.

References to Benjamin's works are included parenthetically within the text. Figures in parentheses beginning with a roman numeral refer to Benjamin's *Gesammelte Schriften:* the roman numeral (I–VII) designates the volume, followed by an arabic numeral designating the page number (see the Bibliography for a list of the individual volumes). Figures in parentheses beginning with a "B" refer to the German edition of Benjamin's letters, *Briefe.*

Walter Benjamin and
the Antinomies of Tradition

These days the revolutionary will contains the conservative within itself, dialectically: at present this is the only way to those things of which the bourgeoisie has so long—unjustly—seen itself as the guardian.

(III 68)

Introduction

Benjamin's Construction of the Antinomies of Tradition

1. Benjamin on Tradition

Readers of Walter Benjamin's essays in cultural criticism from the 1930s will have noticed his remarkable ambivalence toward the decay of tradition and experience which he took to be the hallmark of his times. Benjamin did not doubt that he was living through a crisis whose manifestations had first broken into the open during the lifetime of his own generation, which "between 1914 and 1918 had one of the most monstrous experiences in world history. . . . A generation that had gone to school with the horse-drawn streetcar now stood under the open sky in a landscape where nothing remained unchanged but the clouds, and beneath these clouds, in a force field of destructive torrents and explosions, was the tiny, fragile human body" (II 214). It was certainly the political experience of his generation that created this sense of crisis—the "gruesome and chaotic renaissance in which so many place their hopes," as he described it in 1933 during the first months of his exile following the Nazi seizure of power in Germany (II 215). Yet beneath the political crisis he sensed an epochal upheaval in the organization of the human sensorium, the very structure of perception and experience. The vertigo induced by the political experiences of the generation of 1914, he was convinced, was also grounded in the vertiginous, disorienting acceleration of the pace of social and technological change in the opening decades of the twentieth century. The "structure of experience has changed," Benjamin contended, and he cited Paul Valéry's observation that, "for the past twenty years, neither matter, nor space, nor time have been what they had been since time immemorial" (I 608, 472). For him, these changes in the structure of experience were both part of the explanation for the political and human catastrophes of the interwar period and a key to the possibility of bringing them under control.

Benjamin examined many aspects of this crisis in the structure of perception and experience, but in his overarching formulations he often referred to it as a crisis of tradition: "a shattering blow to all that has been handed down—a shattering of tradition, which is the obverse of the present crisis and renewal of humanity" (I 477–478). What he meant by "tradition" was less a particular canon of texts or values than the very coherence, communicability, and thus the *transmissibility* of experience. "For experience is a matter of tradition, in collective as in private life. It is built up less out of individual facts firmly fixed in memory than of accumulated, often unconscious data that flow together in memory" (I 608). Benjamin's accounts of the decay of experience and tradition often sound the lamenting, elegiac tones usually associated with cultural conservatives. This note becomes perceptible in the way he contrasts the two German terms for experience, *Erfahrung* and *Erlebnis*. The individual's ability to assimilate sensations, information, and events to an integrated stock of experience (*Erfahrung*) was being stunted, he felt, with the result that experience was reduced to a series of atomized, unarticulated moments merely lived through (*Erlebnis*). When perception was sealed off from experience in this way, the result was both a decay of tradition and the helpless perplexity of the isolated individual. It became "a matter of chance whether the individual gets an image of himself, whether he can take hold of his experience" (I 610–611).

But Benjamin was too astute to acquit traditional culture of complicity in the political barbarism of the 1930s. To him, many central concepts of traditional culture "such as creativity and genius, eternal value and mystery," seemed bound to promote "the processing of factual materials in the fascist sense" (I 473). Since the modes of perception underlying this culture were shot through with atavistic elements, they could provide no viable alternative—let alone effective resistance—to the new political barbarism. In this light, the imperative was not to lament the decay of tradition but to affirm, defiantly, the new "poverty of experience." We have seen too much of what this culture can bring, he insisted, "not to consider it honorable to own up to our poverty. . . . Poverty of experience: this need not be understood to mean that people yearn for new experience. No, they yearn to get free of experiences, they yearn for an environment in which they can bring their poverty—outer, and ultimately inner poverty as well—to bear so purely and clearly that something upright comes of it" (II 215, 218). The task at hand was not to grasp at the last straws of a dying culture but to get ready "to survive culture, if need be" (II 219).

Benjamin's mature work thus seems to oscillate between celebrating and mourning the destruction of tradition and traditional culture. It would be easy to dismiss this radical ambivalence as evidence of changing moods, of opportunism, or even more simply as an unnoticed inconsistency in his thought. Among the things that force us to take it seriously, however, is his attempt to bundle these diverse elements into a single concept—that of the aura of an object of perception. Benjamin's theory of the aura was first and foremost an aesthetic theory, but he was convinced that aesthetic phenomena provide especially sensitive anticipations of broader perceptual and social trends.[1] For him the decay of the aura, a "crisis of artistic reproduction," exemplified a much more general "crisis of perception" (I 645). The human sensorium, he assumed, was not naturally and immutably given but underwent fundamental historical transformations. And the changing structure of perception—the "formal signature" of an age, which the best art historians had sometimes succeeded in portraying— could in turn be related to underlying social transformations. The destruction of the aura was "a symptomatic process whose significance points beyond the realm of art" to the social transformations of advanced capitalist society (I 477–478). He saw the aura as the juncture at which connections between a broad network of social and historical processes could be identified. In his own work, it served an analogous function: like a catalyst added to a chemical solution approaching saturation, it crystallized his implicit theory of experience and tradition. For us, it can provide a microcosm in which the puzzles and antinomies of Benjamin's mature work appear in condensed form.

Benjamin never gave a definitive, discursive analysis of his concept of the aura. Instead, he evoked an image of what it is like to experience an object auratically. His fundamental account of auratic perception, to which he referred back in all his explicit discussions of the aura, appeared in his "Small History of Photography" (1931). The aura sometimes appears as the "atmosphere" that seems to envelop an object, a scene, or a moment. Benjamin glosses this experience with an apparently unremarkable account of experiencing nature as an aesthetic phenomenon:[2]

[1] For instance, see the suggestions (I 500–501, n.26) that condense the lines of thought he was developing at the time in his notes for the "Arcades" project. The prototype of such anticipatory phenomena in his work was the temporal inversion of the déjà vu phenomenon described in "A Death Notice," in *Berlin Childhood around 1900* (IV 251–252).

[2] Wolfgang Kemp traces this passage to closely related formulations in the work of the art historian Alois Riegl. Benjamin explicitly referred to Riegl's studies of the changing "formal signature" of perception in "The Work of Art in the Age of Its Technical Reproducibility." See Kemp, "Fernbilder: Benjamin und die Kunstwissenschaft," 224–240. Benjamin's conception of the aura was fed by many sources, a point usually missed by attempts to isolate a single, definitive origin. For a sustained examination, see Marlene Stoessel, *Aura: Das vergessene Menschliche*. I return to this phenomenology in discussing Ludwig Klages's phenomenology of dream consciousness as the trace of an archaic mode of perception in Chapter 5, Section 4.

> What is aura, actually? An extraordinary weave of space and time: the
> unique appearance of a distance, however close it may be. While resting
> on a summer afternoon, to trace the crest of a mountain range against the
> horizon or a branch that casts its shadow on the beholder, until the mo-
> ment or the hour becomes part of its appearance—that is what it means to
> breathe the aura of these mountains, this branch. (II 378)

On closer inspection, this seemingly casual gloss turns out to be a
concise, surprisingly dense description of contemplation and the conditions that make it possible. To begin with, the subject must assume a
position of repose in order to establish the necessary distance from the
object. Contemplation, "intent attentiveness" (*gespanntes Aufmerken*)
then depends on a paradoxical tension between distance and closeness. Contemplation is ordinarily thought of and experienced as absorption in the object: "One who concentrates before a work of art
immerses himself in it. He enters into this work of art like the legend-
ary Chinese painter as he viewed his finished painting" (I 504). Yet, as
Benjamin's description makes clear, contemplative immersion simultaneously requires distance: one breathes the atmosphere of the mountain range, but the mountain range itself is unapproachable; the shadow of the branch is cast on the observer but will vanish if he moves to
grasp the branch. This paradox is captured in the terse formulation
that the aura is the "appearance of a distance, however close it may
be."

Furthermore, the aura has a temporal aspect: time ("a summer after-
noon") merges with the spatial dimensions of distance and closeness
"until the moment or the hour becomes part of the appearance." The
entwinement of space and time thus makes the aura the *unique* appearance of a distance. The result is that peculiar phenomenon whereby certain appearances seem permeated by an atmosphere one can
"breathe," despite—or indeed because of—its insubstantiality. For
Benjamin, the aura that arises from such attentiveness is a hallmark not
only of visual or aesthetic perception but of cognitive processes as
such: the aura "applies, in thinking, to the intentional gaze of attentiveness as it does to a gaze in the literal sense" (I 646). In nonvisual
contemplation, temporal distance or disinterested detachment may replace spatial distance as the constituent dimension of the aura. Abandonment to the structure of the object and its unique otherness calls
forth a play of association in the beholder, saturating the atmosphere
that seems to envelop it with a "mood."

Benjamin unfolds the implications of this fundamental account of
auratic perception in several directions. For instance, the "unique appearance of a distance, however close it may be," as described on the

basis of natural objects, can be read as an account of contemplative immersion in a work of art. In "The Work of Art in the Age of Its Technical Reproducibility," Benjamin uses this translation of the concept of the aura into aesthetic terms to make the cultic character of the work of art apparent. To breathe the aura of an object means to experience its unique presence and its essential unapproachability, both of which are hallmarks of the "cultic image" (I 480, n. 7; I 647). The fleeting, elusive weave of space and time which constitutes the aura lends the object an air of secrecy and mystery, of inviolability. Yet the auratically perceived object seems to cast a spell that binds and absorbs the observer; in the thrall of this spell, one may even begin to sense that the object looks back. This spell lends the cultic object its authority. In other words, auratic perception has something literally atavistic about it. "As we know," Benjamin observes, "the earliest works of art originated in the service of a ritual"; and "it is of decisive importance that the work of art's auratic mode of existence never entirely separates from its ritual function." The modern, post-Renaissance mode of aesthetic perception as an appreciation of beauty "is still recognizable as secularized ritual even in the most profane forms of the cult of beauty" (I 480). And since aesthetic phenomena have symptomatic value, this suggests that atavistic, mythic compulsions continue, unrecognized, to dominate the forms of perception and experience throughout modern society.

The auratic mode of perception lends objects a "cult value," a fetishistic character, and thereby a mystifying authority. To disperse the aura would therefore be a liberating achievement. The work of art, for instance, can be "emancipated from its parasitic dependence on ritual, for the first time in world history." The "shattering of the aura" can "pry the object from its shell," "actualize it"; the object ceases to cast a spell on the beholder, who can then get at it directly and assert control over it. The "formal signature" of a mode of perception in which this takes place would be one in which distance and uniqueness are overcome by the desire to "bring things closer" and a "feeling for the uniformity of things" (I 477–480).

Crucial to Benjamin's argument is the idea that a nonauratic mode of perception is not an abstract program to be imposed on reality but a tangible potential inherent in the new, rapidly proliferating media of photomechanical reproduction, photography, and film. What these media share is the ability to "reproduce" objects technically and "bring them closer," thereby placing them into new contexts and submitting them to "perceptual tests" that liquidate the cultic authority built on distance and uniqueness. Reproductions, for instance, remove an object from its exclusive presence in its original setting and enable "the original to meet the beholder halfway"; although the original itself remains untouched, "nevertheless the quality of its presence, its 'here and now', is always depreciated"—that is, the mode of its reception is altered irrevocably (I 476–477). Photography "can bring out those aspects of reality which are unattainable to the naked eye yet accessible to the lens," penetrating the formerly inviolable surface of the visible world. Film brings an even more extensive technical penetration of reality: the film's surface of appearances is a deliberate technical construction by means of montage. With film, the media of technical reproduction go beyond altering the mode of reception of traditional works of art to establish a new mode of aesthetic production and reception. The new media do not signal the vulgarization and degeneration of ideal, eternal values, as their cultured detractors were claiming; rather, they may foster a more critical, testing attitude toward mystifying authority. In this mode, Benjamin's rhetoric is exuberant, defiant, and militant. The "liquidation of the traditional value of the cultural inheritance" has a "cathartic side" (I 478). It creates a "clean slate," a "drawing board" for those "constructors" ready to own up to the "poverty of experience" (II 215). Benjamin's account of the aura as an atavism, a mystifying haze, and his advocacy of the technical instruments of its destruction constitute a moment in his work which can aptly be termed liquidationist.

When Benjamin turns to consider the aura of historical objects, however, the implications are quite different. Once again, he begins from the unique presence of the auratically perceived object:

> the "here and now" of the work of art—its unique presence at the place where it is located. The "here and now" of the original constitutes the essence of its authenticity . . . a core more sensitive . . . than that of any natural object. (I 475–477)

Once again, the aura consists in the uniqueness of the object and the presence it seems to radiate; together, these constitute its authenticity. But this historical presence is not simply some enthralling, charismatic immediacy. Instead, it is the appearance of historical depth inherent in the object: "On this unique presence, however, and on nothing else was enacted the history to which it was submitted in the course of its existence. . . . This is its authenticity. The authenticity of a thing is the quintessence of all that is transmissible about it from its very beginning onward, ranging from its material duration to its historical testimony." The authenticity of the object, its uniqueness, rests in its *full* historical testimony, that is, in the entire range of contexts it has passed through, not just in its singular, documentary testimony to its origins. For instance, successive phases in the reception of a work are shaped by the contexts in which they take place; and each of these phases in turn becomes part of the context for the subsequent reception. In effect, the transmission of a work inscribes this history on it, so that "the uniqueness of the work of art is identical with its embeddedness in the context of tradition." This accrual of historical testimony—authenticity—lends the object a certain authority, but an authority that is by no means fixed and dictatorial: "Tradition itself is something thoroughly alive and extraordinarily changeable" (I 480). Authoritative meanings may even be radically reversed; but they can be challenged and overthrown only if they are passed along at all. The aura of the object thus harbors and guarantees the transmissibility of its history. It provides the "web" of tradition, the medium of transmission.

If the destruction of the aura threatened the transmissibility of culture, Benjamin came to see the very ability to have coherent experience being eroded as well. Both tradition and experience were rooted in memory, and for him memory too was an auratic phenomenon. In other essays of the 1930s, he explored the implications of the fact that the kind of memory that can lend coherence to ongoing, accumulating experience depends on associative richness rather than mechanical precision in recalling discrete facts. Traces of older experience must be hauled up from the depths of memory to be rearranged and reassociated with new, incoming stimuli if experience is to develop at all. The source material of memory consists in "the associations that . . . tend to cluster around the object of perception," the aura of the object. These unconscious associations are the traces left by experience, much as the practiced hand of the experienced artisan leaves its traces on the object of use (I 644). Memory itself, then, involves both "the ability to interpolate endlessly into what has been" (VI 476) and a "process of assimilation, which takes place in the depths" (II 447). In "The Storyteller" (1936), Benjamin described this process of assimilating events to a stock of experience in order to pass them along as the essence of the culture of storytelling. Storytelling "sinks the matter into the life of the teller, in order to bring it out of him again"; for "telling stories is always the art of telling them further" (II 446–447). What stories pass along is "counsel" or "wisdom," though "counsel is less the answer to a question than a suggestion about the continuation of an ongoing story." But "to seek this counsel one would first have to be able to tell the story." Cut off from the perceptual and mnemonic coherence bestowed by auratic perception, the individual is "solitary, unable to express himself about his most important concerns in an exemplary fashion, is himself uncounseled and can give no counsel to others" (II 442–443). For lack of counsel (*Rat*), he lapses into perplexity (*Ratlosigkeit*). Benjamin does not even hesitate to identify the forms in which an intact memory provides the basis for coherent perception as cultic. But as part of the web of transmissibility and memory, the aura does not appear as the trace of a dangerous atavism. On the contrary: the destruction of the aura would be a dangerous leap in the dark; to advocate its liquidation would be to surrender the possibility of making sense of the world. On these matters, Benjamin intones accents characteristic of the cultural conservative.

Thus, while Benjamin's phenomenological descriptions of auratic perception cluster around a common center, he draws diverse and often apparently contradictory implications from the aura and its destruction. Just as he asserts that the decay of the aura signals broader tendencies, so his analysis of the phenomenon captures the radical ambivalence that provides the generative tension of so much of his mature work. Benjamin's work celebrates and mourns, by turns, the liquidation of tradition.

In some passages, the conflicting moments of this ambivalence lie so close together that Benjamin seems to call himself to order and reverse direction. "The Storyteller," for instance, strikes an unmistakably elegiac note from the outset. The figure of the storyteller "is something already remote from us and is getting ever more remote. . . . It is as if an ability that seemed inalienable to us, the most secure of our securities, were taken from us" (I 438–439). But when the elegiac tones threaten to slip over into nostalgia, he checks the progress of the argument with a fierce disclaimer:

> The storyteller is a man who has counsel for his hearers. But if "having counsel" is beginning to have an old-fashioned ring these days, this is due to the fact that the communicability of experience is decreasing. As a result, we have no counsel, either for ourselves or for others. . . . Counsel woven into the fabric of lived experience is wisdom. The art of storytelling is drawing to an end because the epic side of truth—wisdom—is dying out. But this is a process that goes a long way back. And nothing would be more foolish than to want to see in it merely a "symptom of decay," let alone a "modern" phenomenon. Rather, it is only a concomitant symptom of secular, historical forces of production, which have quite gradually removed storytelling from the realm of living speech and at the same time make it possible to sense a new beauty in what is vanishing. (II 442)

The abrupt reversal in this passage begins when Benjamin pins the accusation of foolishness on a somewhat shadowy opponent. As his theories of the aura and of experience show, Benjamin himself was by no means averse to constructing theories of decay. In fact, the reversal in this passage seems to be triggered by uneasiness at the drift of his own language toward the conservative, antimodernist version of the lament over the decay of experience. The defiant, progressive-sounding assurances about secular, historical forces of production with which he seeks to justify this reversal sound like whistling in the dark here. Real support for such assurances comes only from the theory that the optical testing fostered by the reception of film is the signature of a new, critical mode of perception, as sketched in "The Work of Art in the Age of Its Technical Reproducibility." It is instructive to note that "The Storyteller" was Benjamin's next major project after months of intensive work on the first version of the "Work of Art" theses. This pair of essays seems to be governed by an inner law of complementarity, however tense and paradoxical. In his essays of the 1930s, Benjamin composed an intricate counterpoint of works in which he successively developed the liquidationist and culturally conservative implications of his basic insights.[3]

A dialectic of these perspectives unfolds in Benjamin's mature work: the more insistent his demands for liquidation and his identification with the forces of destruction, the deeper his permeation of vanishing forms of experience. This counterpoint, which took many forms, was nowhere more arresting than when fixed in the image of a single figure. As he observed admiringly of his friend Franz Hessel,

> One must not think that a pious gaze, which remains fixed on the museum-like, is enough to discover the whole antiquity of the "Old West" into which Hessel leads his readers. Only a man in whom the new announces itself so clearly, however quietly, can throw such an original and early gaze on what has just become old. (III 197)

The "Old West," the Berlin neighborhood of their bourgeois childhood which Benjamin credited Hessel with having helped him to (re)discover, was also an allegory for the precincts of an aging Western tradition which, Benjamin felt sure, was likewise approaching obsolescence. In describing Hessel's virtues as a guide, Benjamin cryptically referred to the mainsprings of his own work. He certainly sought to "let the new announce itself" in his work more emphatically than Hessel had, but the dialectical optic ascribed to Hessel was obviously his own. By extension, the figure named Benjamin united an experience of tradition more profound than that of its conservative guardians

---

[3] Along with the "Work of Art" theses and "The Storyteller" (1935/36), the most dramatic examples are "Unpacking My Library" and "The Destructive Character" (1931; IV 388–398) as well as "Doctrine of the Similar"/"On the Mimetic Ability" and "Experience and Poverty" (1933; II 204–219). Of course, Benjamin did not mechanically alternate between these moments, and it can be dubious to single out a text as evidence of optimism or pessimism at any given time.

with a commitment to transcending it more emphatic than that of most radicals. Benjamin refused to surrender either of these attitudes toward the past. He found them equally compelling, though their consequences appeared to conflict; together, they form the figure of an antinomy in his thinking. His seeming ambivalence was not mere oscillation but, rather, an ongoing experiment: in allowing perspectives usually juxtaposed as "radical" and "conservative," "Enlightened" and "traditionalist," to converge in his work, he challenged the accepted paradigms of cultural criticism. His work constructs and explores the antinomies of a tradition understood as being in decay, antinomies whose force had emerged in the concrete historical situation of interwar Europe. This counterpoint constituted one of the most productive tensions in Benjamin's thought; it also underlies his relevance for us. It must be heeded and read properly if we are to go to the heart of his work.

2. The Reception of Benjamin's Work

The practice of identifying conflicting tendencies in Benjamin's mature works is in itself nothing new. In one way or another it has always been central to the controversies generated by their reception. The difficulties begin when we ask how to spell out the issues involved and, equally important, how to come to grips with a body of work in which paradoxes and reversals provide so much of the animating force.

Benjamin found himself faced with these questions during his own lifetime and took an explicit stand on them in his letters. As has often been noted, each of his major intellectual partners—Gershom Scholem, Theodor W. Adorno, and Bertolt Brecht—claimed to be in tune with the true sources of his inspiration and warned him against the baneful influence of the others.[4] Brecht, greeting a convert to the idea of the author as producer, viewed Benjamin as an ally for his own increasingly isolated position in the debates over Marxist aesthetics in the 1930s. Insofar as the "Work of Art" theses addressed the problem

---

[4] These controversies, particularly what is sometimes called the Benjamin-Adorno debate, have been written up many times now. For more detailed summaries, see Martin Jay, *The Dialectical Imagination: A History of the Frankfurt School and the Institute of Social Research, 1923–1950*, chap. 6; Burkhardt Lindner, "Brecht/Benjamin/Adorno: Über Veränderungen der Kunstproduktion im wissenschaftlich-technischen Zeitalter"; Susan Buck-Morss, *The Origin of Negative Dialectics: Theodor W. Adorno, Walter Benjamin, and the Frankfurt Institute*, chap. 9; Richard Wolin, *Walter Benjamin: An Aesthetic of Redemption*, chap. 6; and Eugene Lunn, *Marxism and Modernism: An Historical Study of Lukács, Brecht, Benjamin, and Adorno*, pt. 3.

of fostering more critical, testing habits of perception among audiences, Brecht found them congenial. But Benjamin's conception of the aura, even as an analytical category, seemed to Brecht a relapse into obscurantism: "all so much mysticism, coupled with an antimystical stance. in such a form is the materialist conception of history adapted! it is pretty awful."[5] Scholem, whose own project of recovering the Jewish mystical tradition had received a decisive impetus from the young Benjamin's philosophies of language and history,[6] regarded Benjamin's overtures to any sort of Marxism as a poisoning of the wellsprings of his metaphysical genius, which Scholem saw in a theologically inspired metaphysics of language. The attempt to force his insights into a Marxist "phraseology," he admonished, was self-deception and, still worse, "a singularly intensive kind of self-betrayal"; the "bewildering estrangement and disjointedness . . . between your [Benjamin's] *true* and your *pretended* thought process" created an "ambiguity" that was eventually bound to erode "the morality of your insights, one of your most precious possessions." Never one to pull punches, Scholem warned Benjamin against what he could only see as flirting with disaster: "Self-deception too easily veers into suicide" (B 525–527, 533). Adorno, who could also count Benjamin's early work among his decisive formative influences, believed himself to be mediating the conflict in suggesting that Benjamin might best contribute to the dialectical Critical Theory being developed by the Institut für Sozialforschung by remaining faithful to his early, immediately theological conceptions. Instead of Scholem's emphatic either/or, Adorno thus offered him a both/and option, but at the same price—a renunciation of Brecht's revolutionary hopes. He deplored the "sublimated remnant of certain Brechtian motifs" he detected in Benjamin's presentation of the concept of the aura, which he held responsible for a tendency to ascribe an unambiguously counterrevolutionary function to the autonomous work of art. The remedy could only be "more dialectics," which meant "the thorough liquidation of Brechtian motifs." Not without condescension, Adorno declared it "my task . . . to hold your arm steady until Brecht's sun has once again sunk into exotic waters" (I 1002-1006). Personal allegiances and animosities were thus woven together with substantive issues, and the implicit message always turned out to be that Benjamin was in danger of falling between all possible stools.

Benjamin responded to these challenges, for all his well-known discretion, by making it clear that he deliberately sought simultaneously

[5] Brecht, *Arbeitsjournal: Erster Band, 1938 bis 1942*, 16.
[6] This point has also been made by David Biale, *Gershom Scholem: Kabbalah and Counter-History*, 136.

to maintain positions that his most important intellectual partners found irreconcilable.[7] With great persistence, he fought off any suggestion that he faced a mutually exclusive choice between his earlier and later orientations. Under pressure from Scholem, he felt forced at one point to protest that the "alternatives that evidently underlie your worries"—theological metaphysics and Marxist materialism as mutually exclusive credos—"don't possess a shadow of vitality for me" (B 605). Instead, it had "become clearer and clearer" to him "that between my very particular position on the philosophy of language and the dialectical materialist way of considering things there is a mediation, however tense and problematic" (B 523). At other times even such talk of a mediation between positions often seemed too weak to him. Benjamin had an astonishing inclination (it might better be called a compulsion) to formulate alternatives in radical terms and then to pose his work as the medium in which they might be united. Truth, he felt sure, lies in extremes. And so his ultimate response to his partners was to assert the paradoxical *identity* of positions that they insisted were irreconcilable alternatives.

> I will not admit to a quintessential difference between these two [religious and political] observances. But just as little to a mediation. I am speaking here of an identity that manifests itself solely in the paradoxical reversal of the one into the other (in whichever direction) and only under the indispensible precondition that each observance be carried out ruthlessly enough and radically in its own sense. The task here, therefore, is to decide, not once and for all, but in every moment. But to *decide*. . . . To proceed always radically, never consistently in the most important matters . . . (B 425)

Benjamin's insistence on the identity of opposed positions revealed by paradoxical reversals was to have been vindicated in his master project on nineteenth-century Paris; not accidentally, it was never finished. He attributed the interminable delays in coming to grips with it to the arduous process of transforming "the mass of conceptions and images from the period, now long past, of my immediately metaphysical, indeed theological thought" into a form that would "nourish my present constitution with full force" (B 659). In other words, the project was literally an experiment. The accusations of his intellectual partners at

---

[7] Scholem referred to Benjamin's "Chinese courtesy," which he found contradicted by his "personal radicalism" of manner. Benjamin's discretion often verged on secrecy mongering; for instance, he often refrained from referring to his acquaintances by name. This enabled him to keep his contacts so isolated from one another that Scholem sometimes only much later discovered that they had common acquaintances. See Scholem, *Walter Benjamin: Die Geschichte einer Freundschaft,* 35, 47, 57. Clearly, such tactics would have well served the intellectual strategy described here.

times undoubtedly hindered this experiment by generating unnecessary friction; but sometimes they actually served it as well: Scholem, Adorno, and Brecht, to name just three, served as sounding boards, as Benjamin developed his position by playing each off against the others. This is clearest in his correspondence, where he employed a sensitive counterpoint of tact and tactics, as Irving Wohlfarth has aptly put it.[8] Similarly, many of his essays can be read as having had virtual addressees.

The fronts established among Benjamin's intellectual partners during his lifetime were reestablished among his postwar readers.[9] His writings were first assembled for a wider readership in the posthumous two-volume edition entitled *Schriften*, published in 1955; the spectacular, embittered controversies over them arose only later, in the context of the German student movement of the mid-to-late 1960s. These controversies generated what might now be called the classical interpretations of Benjamin. They bear the imprint of postwar German intellectual culture and in some respects, therefore, they deserve to be seen as more than just secondary literature or outdated, esoteric wrangling.

The reintroduction of Benjamin's texts was initiated and supervised by Adorno, whom Benjamin had named as the executor of his literary estate. Quite understandably, Adorno continued to promote the view that Benjamin's work lay squarely within the tradition of Critical Theory being developed by the now-repatriated Institut. His introductions to successive publications of Benjamin's works, together with the authority that inhered in their personal association, gave the postwar reception its first orientation. Adorno's position was further consolidated by the publication of a dissertation by his student Rolf Tiedemann, *Studien zur Philosophie Walter Benjamins* (1965), the first unified, "Adornian" interpretation.[10] Against this background, the intensity of

[8] See Wohlfarth, " 'Die eigene, bis zum Verschwinden reife Einsamkeit': Zu Walter Benjamins Briefwechsel mit Gershom Scholem," 170–171. Wohlfarth has given us the most incisive portrayals of this side of Benjamin.

[9] This homology has been pointed out by Jürgen Habermas, "Bewußtmachende oder rettende Kritik? Die Aktualität Walter Benjamins," 175, as well as by Wohlfarth, "No-Man's-Land: On Walter Benjamin's 'Destructive Character'," 56. A reliable survey of the controversy through 1978 has been provided by Burkhardt Lindner, "Werkbiographie und kommentierte Bibliographie (bis 1970)" and "Benjamin-Bibliographie (1971–1978)." The most comprehensive account of the reception of Benjamin's works is Klaus Garber, "Stationen der Benjamin-Rezeption 1940–1985," in *Rezeption und Rettung: Drei Studien zu Walter Benjamin*.

[10] Benjamin's papers in turn became part of Adorno's literary estate, now forming the "Benjamin-Archiv Theodor W. Adorno" in Frankfurt. The history of this portion of his papers is described in the "Editorischer Bericht" to the *Gesammelte Schriften* (I 751–762). Adorno's prefaces to various postwar editions of Benjamin's individual works, along with his "Charakteristik Walter Benjamins," are collected in Adorno et al., *Über Walter*

the reception Benjamin's writings found in the German student movement is not surprising. His reflections on the revolutionary potential
latent in culture and the new communications media provided access
to "repressed debates" of the 1930s which had simply been paved over
by the postwar West German "restoration." What was more, Adorno
was now accused of tailoring Benjamin's image and even censoring his
texts to suit his own purposes; under the circumstances, this was seen
as tantamount to collaborating in the repression. The "new left" Benjamin was thus a "Brechtian" Benjamin, whose revolutionary élan provided leverage against the resignation into which Adorno seemed to
have lapsed.[11] Scholem, from his position in Israel, must have been
struck by how little had changed in this respect since the 1930s. He
continued to insist on the theological roots of Benjamin's insights while
acerbically noting the propensity of young Marxists to "cite Benjamin
like Holy Writ."[12] And as if to round out the cycle, Hannah Arendt,
who had met Benjamin in Paris exile circles during the 1930s, pronounced a plague on all these houses. She defended Benjamin as an
homme de lettres, a cultivated, old-fashioned private scholar (*Privatgelehrter*), who "was ready, or thought he was, to do many things: to
study Hebrew for three hundred marks a month if the Zionists thought
it would do them some good, or to think dialectically, with all the
mediating trimmings, for one thousand French francs if there was no
other way of doing business with the Marxists."[13]

These controversies began to ease by the mid-1970s, inaugurating a
new phase in the reception of Benjamin's works, a phase that in many

---

Benjamin. Tiedemann has now supplemented his dissertation with *Dialektik im Stillstand,*
a collection of his own prefaces and afterwords to editions of Benjamin's individual
works. Among more recent works that adopt the Adornian position on most issues, see
Wolin, *Walter Benjamin.*

[11] The controversy is reconstructed in Lindner, "Werkbiographie und kommentierte
Bibliographie," 108–111. An excellent retrospective account by one then involved in the
disputes is Ansgar Hillach, "Walter Benjamin: Korrektiv Kritischer Theorie oder revolu-
tionäre Handhabe? Zur Rezeption Benjamins durch die Studentenbewegung." See also
Andreas Huyssen, "The Cultural Politics of Pop," in *After the Great Divide: Modernism,
Mass Culture, Postmodernism,* especially 152–156.

[12] Gershom Scholem, "Walter Benjamin und sein Engel," 87. A translation of this
essay, along with his earlier "Walter Benjamin," appeared in Scholem, *On Jews and
Judaism in Crisis: Selected Essays.* Scholem contributed a great deal to the recovery and
reconstruction of Benjamin's life and works from the 1960s to the 1980s. See his *Walter
Benjamin,* the collection of his numerous essays under the title *Walter Benjamin und sein
Engel,* and above all his collected correspondence with Benjamin from the 1930s, *Walter
Benjamin/Gershom Scholem Briefwechsel, 1933–1940.*

[13] Hannah Arendt, "Walter Benjamin, 1892–1940," 24–28. Published as the introduction to *Illuminations,* the first (and for a long time the only) collection of Benjamin's essays
in English, this essay has had an extraordinary influence on the American reception of
Benjamin outside post-new left circles. See Susan Sontag's incisive portrayal of Benjamin
as the melancholy exemplar of a vanishing species, "The Last Intellectual."

respects continues into the present. On the one hand, the apparent urgency of the issues declined as the political dust thrown up by the student movement settled. Some participants now moved on into academic careers of their own; to many, it seemed time to take stock. "Naive identification wishes,"[14] demands for immediate relevance, and attempts to appropriate Benjamin's works for particular theoretical schools no longer seemed the order of the day. Meanwhile, publication of the first volumes of the *Gesammelte Schriften* was putting the entire debate on a new footing. Accusations of doctoring or suppressing texts gradually lost their object. An incomparably broader range of texts now became available, calling for a long process of digestion. These changes by no means signaled a declining interest in Benjamin. On the contrary, they unleashed a tidal wave of scholarly literature whose sheer volume testifies to a fascination comparable to the passions of the Benjamin revival. This new literature was often disparagingly referred to as "Benjamin philology" in order to criticize the depoliticization of his work seen as resulting from scholarly neglect of its relevance.[15] Equally conspicuous, however, were its almost ritualistic pledges of allegiance to Benjamin's own principle of *Aktualität*, or contemporary relevance.[16]

These new readings have provided us with a far more differentiated image of Benjamin. The earlier practice of breaking loose individual themes, essays, or periods in his work in the interest of shoring up other positions has gradually given way to an integral view of his work. Above all, the strict polarities that once governed the Benjamin revival—early/late work, theology/Marxism, metaphysics/materialism—have lost their compelling force. Instead, the numerous lines of continuity running through all phases of his work increasingly receive their due. The new philological sobriety has produced close readings of a much broader range of texts. At the same time, Benjamin's identity has come to be seen precisely in his ambivalences and his attempt to make them productive. In this respect, the most important develop-

[14] The formulation is from Burkhardt Lindner, "Positives Barbarentum—aktualisierte Vergangenheit," 130.

[15] See, for instance, the issue of *alternative* entitled "Faszination Benjamin" (vol. 23 [June/August 1980]).

[16] Peter Bürger attributes this paradox to the bad faith of left intellectuals from the student movement who went on to academic careers: "One wants to be simultaneously *in* the institution and *not in it*. The illusory resolution of this paradox is the Benjamin cult. For Benjamin is the outsider, the revolutionary, who is also recognized by traditional German studies" ("Literaturwissenschaft heute," 790). Bürger's argument becomes far more drastic, tracing the "Benjamin cult" back to an identity crisis and narcissistic ego weakness on the part of its proponents. Aside from its sheer implausibility, this debunking strategy, which attempts to invalidate opponents' responses in advance, tends to cut off rational argument rather then promote it. Nevertheless, the extraordinary fascination with Benjamin does call for explanation.

ment was the long-awaited publication of the manuscripts of his unfinished master project, the *Passagen-Werk,* or "Arcades" project, which
appeared as Volume V of the *Gesammelte Schriften* in 1982. Benjamin himself saw the "Arcades" project as an attempt to mobilize the metaphysically and theologically founded stock of thoughts and images from his
early work to enrich his later conceptions. The labor of assimilating this
mass of new materials has helped to delay the emergence of a new set of
interpretive fronts comparable to those of the Benjamin revival.[17]

Nevertheless, one trend can be identified with certainty: the differ-
entiation of Benjamin's image from the schools that once laid claim to
him has led to a stress on his utter incommensurability. Unlocking the
secret architecture of his work exercises a powerful fascination, and
doing so undoubtedly vindicates intentions misunderstood during his
own lifetime. Our interest in vindicating such a position may be the
signature of a time in which ideologies seem once more to have failed.
No one has done more to establish Benjamin's incommensurability as
the hallmark of his work than Wohlfarth, whose essays on Benjamin
are the consummate achievement of this phase of the reception. Wohlfarth's studies have four cardinal virtues. First, he demonstrates beyond any doubt that Benjamin saw himself as pursuing the "secret
strategy" of exploiting the generative tension between extreme alternatives such as politics and theology, but "without sitting on the
fence." As a result, his work became, in Wohlfarth's image, a "crossing
in no-man's-land," exposing him to the danger of "crossfire" from his
would-be allies.[18] Second, and equally important, Wohlfarth shows
that this effort was by no means restricted to the late phase of Benjamin's work; rather, it permeated the early, "theological" work as
well.[19] Both contradiction and continuity have their place in
Wohlfarth's image of Benjamin. In a sense, he acts as the executor of
Benjamin's insistence on those paradoxical reversals that reveal the
unsuspected identity of extreme alternatives. Third, what helps make

[17] The *Passagen-Werk* and Baudelaire essays were subsequently supplemented by
manuscripts found among Georges Bataille's papers in the Bibliothèque Nationale; see
the report by Michael Espagne and Michael Werner, "Vom Passagen-Projekt zum
'Baudelaire'": Neue Handschriften zum Spätwerk Walter Benjamins." The volume *Passagen: Walter Benjamins Urgeschichte des XIX. Jahrhunderts,* edited by Norbert Bolz and
Bernd Witte, provides a sampling of first efforts to evaluate the "Arcades" project in
colloquia held in Berlin and Paris in 1983. Contributions to the Paris colloquium are
gathered in Heinz Wismann, ed., *Walter Benjamin et Paris.* In English, see Susan Buck-
Morss, *The Dialectics of Seeing,* for an ambitious attempt to reconstruct and even extend
Benjamin's project.
[18] See especially Wohlfarth, " 'Die eigene, bis zum Verschwinden reife Einsamkeit,' "
172–173, 179–185; and "No-Man's-Land," 49–50. A list of his essays to date can be found
in the Bibliography.
[19] Especially pointedly in Wohlfarth, "The Politics of Prose and the Art of Awakening:
Walter Benjamin's Version of a German Romantic Motif," 142–143.

this argument so compelling is Wohlfarth's unparalleled mastery of Benjamin's rhetorical rhythms and metaphorical figures. His essays are so saturated by creative citation that to read them is, seemingly, to read Benjamin to the second power—assuming, of course, that the reader already has a secure command of Benjamin's texts (the penalty incurred by this virtue is to amplify Benjamin's already formidable esotericism). Finally, Wohlfarth insists that Benjamin's productive confrontation of apparent opposites presupposes a nonpsychological conception of character, a "deconstructed subjectivity." While citing with philological precision Benjamin's own characterizations of his work as a medium, he points out how Benjamin also uncannily anticipated many central themes in contemporary poststructuralism.[20] Insofar as such "latent parallels (and divergences)" help guide his reading, Wohlfarth simultaneously fulfills Benjamin's own commandment of a productive encounter with the past.

The strengths of Wohlfarth's work epitomize the solid gains of what I have called the second phase of the reception. Yet in one respect the spirit of the 1960s Benjamin revival lives on. For, despite the broad consensus that Benjamin staged his work as a confrontation between extreme positions, the nature of these contradictions has escaped rigorous examination. Too often in the literature of Benjamin, his positions have been simplified to the point of caricature by the continued use of such labels as "metaphysical," "theological," "materialist," and "political." Benjamin himself often employed such shorthand notations, but the vital distinction between what he said (and even thought) he was doing and what he really did has too long been neglected. Attention to his shorthand has been necessary and often productive in the second phase of the reception, which went back to the texts to take Benjamin at his word. But the labels themselves can obscure the issues by evoking stereotyped, reflex loyalties. It is sometimes rather hard for the outsider to see just what might be at stake in the alternative between politics and theology or theology and materialism. The response to such difficulties surely cannot be to recommend that this outsider undergo a process of initiation into the arcane rites of Benjamin scholarship.

With the unpacking of Benjamin's concept of tradition at the beginning of this chapter I address this question by directing sustained attention to a particular, central tension in his mature work. The dialectical tension within the concept of aura—between what I call its liquidationist and its culturally conservative moments—provides a microcosm of ambivalences that surfaced in the cultural criticism of the

---

[20] Explicitly in Wohlfarth, "No-Man's-Land," 48.

"middle" works, from 1926 to 1935. My first hypothesis is that Benjamin's encounter with modernist and avant-garde culture during these years was what first crystallized his awareness of the antinomies of tradition. The moments of the antinomy strikingly exemplify the unique constellation of modernist approaches to tradition which preoccupied him. First, there was the attempt to liquidate an oppressive tradition as such, and not just the previous style, as a step toward mobilizing the socially organizing function of culture. For Benjamin, the figure of Brecht was particularly important; but it should also be remembered that the French surrealists, after their own fashion, likewise hoped that an "end of art" would bring a liberating release of energies. Benjamin's response to these liquidationist currents represents the vein of tough talk in his work. Another family of modernists penetrated the surface of everyday experience to reveal atavistic, mythic elements in a social world that had allegedly been rationalized. Kafka and the surrealists, for instance, pursued this goal in their own, very different ways. Finally, there were those modernists who may, however ironically, be called conservative in the sense described above. Their method was to hold to traditional forms and genres but to explode them from within, pushing them to their limits by confronting them with modern, often urban experience. Proust's narratives of memory, Baudelaire's urban lyric poetry, and Kafka's parables and paradoxes all worked in this way. The quality of Benjamin's language when he is handling the latter themes is always decidedly more tender, even elegiac.

Works employing these modernist and avant-garde methods were Benjamin's favored objects of commentary, and he returned to them repeatedly. But he never simply borrowed ideas and constructed a montage of them; his relationship to modernism cannot be reduced to a question of simple intellectual influences. Working through these modernist paradigms from the particular standpoint provided by his early work, he discovered both unsuspected correspondences among them and unexpected contradictions within them. The yield was a theory of images and a conception of history structured around the tension between liquidationist and culturally conservative moments, a tension whose emergence he ascribed to the catastrophic, accelerating decay of bourgeois culture in his own time. My focus, in other words, lies on the specific increment in his conception of tradition produced by his engagement with modernism, rather than on the abstract identity of early and late works, or "theology" and "materialism."

The use of the term "conservative" to designate one moment of the antinomy is bound to provoke misunderstanding and therefore calls for special comment at the outset. My exegesis of Benjamin's passages on aura is meant to distill a particular aspect of conservatism: the cultural conservative's concern with the phenomenon of tradition as such, that is, with the transmissibility of culture and with what happens in the process of transmission.[21] Tradition, in this sense, is the medium of cultural transmission, within which patterns of perception, concepts, and values may be formulated *and* contested. Indeed, liquidationists also presuppose the existence of a tradition, one that has become an oppressive burden and is therefore fit for destruction, in the words of Benjamin's "destructive character" (IV 397).[22] To single out Benjamin's concern with tradition is by no means to imply that his radicalism was a mere façade. Scholem called attention to the deep-seated "element of personal radicalism, even personal ruthlessness," in him.[23] The conservative moment at issue here is distinct from those substantive values typically defended by conservatives, such as authority, hierarchy, and resistance to change. The difficulty in freeing the term from its associations has helped create a taboo against coming to terms with this moment in Benjamin's work, which is not surprising in light of the high ideological stakes that have always been placed on the debate.[24]

But there are more differentiated, productive attitudes to conservatism than to place it under a taboo. In a comment on the relationship between the Frankfurt School's cultural criticism and the antimodernist cultural pessimism of the German mandarins, Jürgen Habermas once

---

[21] It may be objected that Benjamin sought not the preservation of an intact cultural heritage but its emphatic actualization, a point stressed by Lindner, "Positives Barbarentum." This is true, but actualization itself depends on a medium of transmission that is in *some* sense intact.

[22] The liquidationist temperament itself has a tradition reaching back to the radical humanists of the Enlightenment. Benjamin himself made a moving appeal to this counter-tradition during the 1930s, most pointedly in the last of his essays to be published during his lifetime, his preface to Carl Gustav Jochmann's "The Regression of Poetry."

[23] Scholem, "Walter Benjamin," 174.

[24] Habermas once launched a minor controversy by characterizing Benjamin's method as "redemptive criticism" (*rettende Kritik*) in order to distinguish it from the Frankfurt School's conception of ideology critique, and by calling this procedure conservative ("Bewußtmachende oder rettende Kritik?," 185–186). Bürger, insisting that the term "conservative" be reserved for the historicist conceptions Benjamin unambiguously opposed, countered by suggesting that the term "preservative" (*bewahrend*) would have been more appropriate ("Benjamin's 'rettende Kritik'. Vorüberlegungen zum Entwurf einer kritischen Hermeneutik," 163). Habermas's distinction and Bürger's qualification are helpful, yet the exchange seems to me to miss the point in two important ways. First, the discussion of Benjamin's philosophy of history has always been fixated on the explicit position he sketched in "On the Concept of History." I argue that his working conception of history moves on many levels, not all of which were presented on the level of his explicit theory. Second, to suggest that Benjamin incorporated the experience of the cultural conservative into his own sense of history is by no means to suggest that he was a closet conservative. And if we do not acknowledge that he did so, important motifs in his work are bound to appear as mere lapses into nostalgia.

proposed that "hidden in the German mandarins' culturally conservative frame of reference there might be experiences worked through and questions posed which, in an appropriate frame of reference, could be reformulated and claim systematic interest."[25] Habermas's suggestion might be read as the seed of an intellectual strategy: to replace the simplistic enemy-image of conservatism, not for purposes of détente or compromise, but to locate the unredeemed utopian potential of a tradition and thereby to criticize cultural conservatism from within. I suggest that Benjamin's modernist cultural criticism operated in just this way. He conducted an experimental, immanent critique of both the idealist and the vitalist (*lebensphilosphische*) varieties of conservatism so deeply rooted in the German tradition. Indeed, he had to contend with a conservatism that was not comfortably established but was becoming increasingly anxious, shrill, and radical in its own fashion.

The idea that a penetration of the experience of tradition could be turned toward a critical understanding of modern experience was actually stated by Benjamin himself. This is how he came to see Kafka:

> Kafka's work is an ellipse whose foci lie far apart and are determined, on the one hand, by mystical experience (which is above all the experience of tradition) and, on the other, by the experience of the modern big-city dweller. . . . What is actually, in a very literal sense, wild in Kafka is that this most recent world of experience was conveyed to him precisely by the mystical tradition. This, of course, would not have been possible without devastating processes . . . within this tradition. The long and the short of it is that clearly an appeal had to be made to the forces of this tradition if an individual (by the name of Franz Kafka) was to be confronted with this reality of ours. (B 760–762)

In this passage it becomes clear that the foci of Benjamin's own work were essentially those he attributed to Kafka: a mystical experience of tradition and the experience of the modern big-city dweller. The indi-

---

[25] Habermas, "Die deutschen Mandarine," 249. This formulation comes from his review of Ringer's *The Decline of the German Mandarins: The German Academic Community, 1890–1933*. Habermas argued that this was how Horkheimer and Adorno had dealt with conservatism, and that Ringer failed to see this because the historical sociology of knowledge necessarily reduces positions to the interests they express and cannot redeem their distorted truth claims. But Habermas overlooks the distinction between orthodox and modernist mandarins which lies at the center of Ringer's argument: what distinguished the modernists was precisely their attempt to salvage part of the critical potential of an increasingly ideological, socially confirmative tradition of *Bildung*. At their best, the modernists pursued just the kind of strategy Habermas described, if not always as radically or effectively as one might wish. His description of this procedure *as* a strategy, however, suggests the linkage between the intellectual field and the individual intellectual project that I propose in Section 3, below.

vidual by the name of Franz Kafka might just as well have been named Walter Benjamin. Observing that "Kafka listened intently to tradition," Benjamin distanced himself only subtly by noting that "Kafka's experience was founded *solely* on tradition, to which he surrendered himself . . . and he who strains to listen intently does not see" (B 762, emphasis added). Benjamin wanted to listen attentively to tradition without letting it blind him. Tradition was not a source of ready answers; on the contrary, "Kafka's work represents a sickness of tradition" (B 763). The dialectic of liquidationist and conservative moments provides the productive tension in Benjamin's mature work, and the complementarity of his images of Kafka and Hessel captures that tension perfectly: no insight into the new without a profound experience of tradition, no penetration of tradition without a clear perception of the new.

3. Benjamin's Project and the Intellectual Field

To Benjamin himself it was clear that "my life, as well as my work, moves in extreme positions. The breadth it thereby claims, the freedom to move into conjunction things and thoughts that are considered incompatible," provides its generative tension (II 1369). With this observation in mind, I would first suggest that to gauge the breadth of Benjamin's mature work we must begin by redescribing the lines of tension that govern it: the antinomies of tradition provide its moving force as much as do the paradoxical reversals of theology into politics.

My second concern involves the origin of these productive tensions. Can we explain how Benjamin came to operate in this way, or must we simply accept it as the mark of his genius? The accounts of Scholem, Adorno, and Arendt, all of whom knew Benjamin, stress the utter originality of his method and insights. Adorno was impressed by "his capacity for continually bringing out new aspects of things, not by exploding conventions through criticism, but rather by organizing himself so as to be able to relate to his subject matter in a way that seemed beyond all convention"; "the thesis that where knowledge is concerned the most individual is the most general," Adorno found, "fits him perfectly."[26] Arendt considered him (in Hofmannsthal's words) "absolutely incomparable," one of "the unclassifiable ones . . . whose work neither fits the existing order nor introduces a new genre that lends itself to future classification." The fact that "everything Benjamin wrote . . . always turned out to be *sui generis*" was among the

[26] Theodor W. Adorno, "A Portrait of Walter Benjamin," 229.

sources of his misfortune, because it was bound to provoke misunderstandings; at the same time, however, it provided the basis for his posthumous recognition.[27] On the latter point, at least, Arendt has been proved right: our awareness of Benjamin's uniqueness has been renewed, and perhaps even heightened, in the course of the recent reception. Benjamin, the incommensurable, uncompromising outsider, has won the reputation of somehow having seen through all the ideological stereotypes of his age. This image forms no small part of the fascination he exercises. But how did he come to do this? If his encounter with modernist culture yielded a concept of tradition that challenges the conventional paradigms of cultural criticism, why did it prove so fruitful? After all, Benjamin was not the only critic of modernism in his times.

The implicit answer to this question in most of the literature seems to be that the productivity of Benjamin's project cannot be explained; to do so would be to explain it away by setting aside its truth claims. By now few would deny the necessity of reading Benjamin in context, but the uniqueness of his procedures and the force of the insights they generated are still treated as uncaused causes that cannot really be accounted for. The result of this resistance, willy-nilly, is a drift (nevertheless condemned in the following breath) toward the canonization of Benjamin as a great thinker whose texts are paid the painstaking philological reverence due his stature. The danger is clear: the fascination with his uniqueness tends, by lending his image charisma, to seal off his work against productive appropriation; and this is what Benjamin's present-day readers can wish for least of all. Wohlfarth warns us against hagiography, pointing out that "it is not by chance that Benjamin's theory of the aura aimed at its demolition. . . . He thereby decreed that his heirs should not practice an ancestor cult."[28] But how is such worship to be averted?

One of the most direct measures has been to point out that Benjamin pursued his strategy of juxtapositions as part of a rejection of the ideal of the unified personality. As Burkhardt Lindner observes, "Benjamin never indulged himself in the image of a harmoniously self-realizing personality"; instead, he arranged his work "as an enacting of contradictions," of "constellations, which themselves in turn replicated larger constellations." In doing so he anticipated important themes in contemporary poststructuralism: "In his own way, he practiced what is nowadays discussed as the decentering of the subject." Benjamin's polyvalence "explains" the uniqueness of his intellectual strategy; at

[27] Arendt, "Walter Benjamin," 3.
[28] Wohlfarth, " 'Die eigene, bis zum Verschwinden reife Einsamkeit,' " 189.

the same time, it seems to guarantee that his works are programmed for a productive reception. We cannot seek to restore to his texts a unified consistency which they never had to begin with; rather, they must be read "for the sake of the unresolved historical constellation."[29] The result is what has been called "political" Benjamin interpretation by some of its proponents. And this approach, in turn, can be legitimated by referring to Benjamin's own critical maxim of *Aktualität*—a mode of reception that activates its object by recognizing the unique temporal constellation between the critic's present and a specific moment in the past.[30] Benjamin's strategy is explained just enough to immunize him against canonization as a great thinker, but without running the risk of neutralizing his work.

But are the principles of poststructuralism or *Aktualität* really enough to ensure a critical reception? Are they the only way to explain Benjamin's position and strategy while staying clear of a reductive reading? The difficulty of pursuing these issues points to the more general problem of how to account for intellectual projects. Providing such accounts has traditionally been the business of intellectual history, which relates texts to contexts. But intellectual history, many feel, amounts at best to a pedestrian documentation of discrete intellectual influences (whereas what is really interesting is what Benjamin made of them); at worst, it attempts to trace works to external, "underlying" psychological or sociological causes and ends by denying their truth

[29] These citations are from Lindner, "Positives Barbarentum," 138–139, and from his introduction to the volume *"Links hatte alles noch sich zu enträtseln,"* 8. Wohlfarth makes this case in his own way in "No-Man's-Land," 48, 50–51, and in "Die einzige, bis zum Verschwinden reife Einsamkeit.'"
An awareness of convergences between Critical Theory and French poststructuralism has grown rapidly in recent years, providing the basis for these new readings of Benjamin; see Martin Jay, *Adorno,* 21–22. Among the first signals of a reception of poststructuralism in Germany was the volume edited by Friedrich A. Kittler and Horst Turk, *Urszenen: Literaturwissenschaft als Diskursanalyse und Diskurskritik,* which included essays both on Benjamin and by prominent interpreters of Benjamin. For an incisive account of the origins of these trends in Benjamin's and Adorno's readings of the *Frühromantik,* see Jochen Hörisch, "Herrscherwort, Geld und geltende Sätze: Adornos Aktualisierung der Frühromantik und ihre Affinität zur poststrukturalistischen Kritik des Subjekts."
[30] Norbert Bolz defends this intention as the hallmark of "young academics . . . who neither resign themselves to the business of scholarship nor let themselves be bargained out of the political claims of their theoretical practice"; see Bolz, "Einleitung: Walter Benjamin und seine Totengräber," 8. In the foreword to this collection, coeditor Richard Faber underscores the point with reference to Benjamin: "This volume does not plead for a Benjamin-orthodoxy. It not only creates further (and questionable) heresies, it also consciously addresses the task of a productive Benjamin reception. Benjamin should be treated as he himself proceeded: critically redeeming [*rettend*]. . . . the editors in particular understand their reception of Benjamin politically" (5–6). Since one can insist on *Aktualität* by citing Benjamin's own principles, philological scrupulousness receives a self-transcending bonus: you can have your philological cake and eat it too.

claims.[31] Although intellectual history may be able to illuminate lesser works, it is thought, it must stop at the threshold of complex, "first-rate" texts, those that transcend categories and schools, challenge unquestioned assumptions, and thus remain intrinsically interesting or relevant. These aversions result from real causes: too often, intellectual history *has* been simply documentary or reductive. The dominance of documentary and reductive approaches has led to widespread disillusionment with intellectual history and thus helped fuel the self-doubting demoralization in which it has often languished.[32] Studies of Benjamin have sometimes reflected such (healthy) skepticism: their authors limit the treatment of historical context to reconstructing positions and exchanges in past controversies, thus clarifying the issues Benjamin was addressing. These efforts are certainly necessary; they have been essential in freeing our view of Benjamin from the identifications that dominated the revival of interest in the 1960s. My pointer toward the role played by modernism in his formulation of the antinomies of tradition proposes such a corrective of context.

Yet, however valuable they may be, such correctives of context do not exhaust the possibilities of intellectual history. To open up these possibilities, we would have to begin to rethink some of intellectual history's fundamental conceptions, starting with a more rigorous definition of ideational context. Pierre Bourdieu provides an especially promising way to do this with his concept of the "intellectual field."[33] Briefly, an intellectual field is a systematic and historically specific structure of orthodoxies and heterodoxies, a structure of discourse that imposes choices not always logically apparent to those who argue

[31] This objection was behind Critical Theory's dismissal of Karl Mannheim's conception of the sociology of knowledge; see Martin Jay, "The Frankfurt School's Critique of Karl Mannheim and the Sociology of Knowledge." One of the first attempts to give a comprehensive account of Benjamin's early work has been criticized on just these grounds—for being both documentary (sometimes arbitrarily) and reductive: Bernd Witte, *Walter Benjamin: Der Intellektuelle als Kritiker.*

[32] On the revival of intellectual history in the 1980s and the methodological debates set off by proposals to incorporate new perspectives from recent literary and cultural theory, see among a growing body of work Dominick LaCapra and Steven L. Kaplan, eds., *European Intellectual History: Reappraisals and New Perspectives*; James Kloppenberg, "Deconstruction and Hermeneutic Strategies for Intellectual History: The Recent Work of Dominick LaCapra and David Hollinger"; and David Harlan, "Intellectual History and the Return of Literature," and David Hollinger's response, "The Return of the Prodigal: The Persistence of Historical Knowing."

[33] For accounts in English, see Pierre Bourdieu, "Intellectual Field and Creative Project," and "The Genesis of the Concepts of *Habitus* and of Field." Fritz Ringer's "The Intellectual Field, Intellectual History, and the Sociology of Knowledge" is an important statement of Bourdieu's significance for intellectual history. The following discussion is indebted to Ringer's adaptation of Bourdieu.

within its range. Positions within a field tend to be defined in terms of one another, whether as complements or opposites. This means that doctrines, seen in terms of the field, have what Bourdieu calls positional properties: in particular, established orthodoxies prestructure the possibilities of heterodoxy, or at least the conventional ones.[34] The field metaphor is thus not simply topographic ("within these boundaries one may move freely in any direction") but, rather, magnetic; an intellectual field is a force field in which the poles not only are specified but have a specific force of attraction and repulsion as well. The positions intellectuals take are affected by such forces whether or not they are conscious of them. The effects show themselves in the way their works function publicly (or "objectively") in the field, but they also enter into the very formulation of their ideas.

These conditions do not determine the content of positions within the field in any simple sense. Rather, the structure of orthodoxies and heterodoxies objectively *constrains* the discourse it supports by giving doctrines, concepts, and images a positional value. But the field always leaves room for more or less conscious manipulation and maneuvering. As Fritz Ringer puts it, "just as a line of color will look different when placed against a changed background, so a proposition may be altered by a transformation of the surrounding field. The artist is by no means helpless in the face of this phenomenon; but he must change the color of his line to achieve an equivalent effect against an altered ground."[35] Finally, Bourdieu also stresses that the positional properties of doctrines that are logically identical may differ radically according to the field in which they operate. Ideas that appear as challenging, critical heterodoxies in a given field may well become entrenched as orthodoxies that legitimate vested interests in another.[36] An intellectual history sensitive to these factors must take an interest in the positional value a given doctrine acquires in various fields.

The concepts of field and positional value can sharpen our awareness of a broad range of phenomena that elude a more conventional history of ideas. Ringer points out their usefulness for comparing intellectual cultures. For instance, they help to illuminate the puzzling circumstance that positivism could have become the academic orthodoxy in France around the turn of the twentieth century while serving

---

[34] Bourdieu, "Intellectual Field and Creative Project," 89; see also the section on "Doxa, Orthodoxy, Heterodoxy" in *Outline of a Theory of Practice*, 159–171.

[35] Ringer, "The German Mandarins Reconsidered," 5.

[36] Bourdieu, "Intellectual Field and Creative Project," 89. As this suggests, though fields have a relatively autonomous logic of their own, they are bound up with institutionalized power.

as a left-wing heresy in German intellectual culture during the same period.[37] Moreover, within a given field positional values may come into play in interesting ways as that field changes through time. Thus, as Ringer's *Decline of the German Mandarins* demonstrates, the doctrine of *Bildung* central to German humanism and idealism around the turn of the nineteenth century possessed an "optimistic, socially universal, and even utopian" dimension in proposing that cultivation and merit replace birth as the standards for distributing social power, opportunity, and rewards. This critical moment gradually evaporated, however, in the changing social environment of the nineteenth century, as *Bildung* increasingly came to signify exclusionary standards that served to defend the privileges and rescue the self-image of the educated strata. German idealism became a constituent of the orthodox academic culture in the course of the nineteenth century, and the neo-idealist revival in the *Geisteswissenschaften* that began in the latter part of the century had a pronounced apologetic bearing. One consequence of this positional shift was quite startling: the small minority of academicians whom Ringer calls modernist mandarins, those who hoped to rescue some of the critical thrust of the mandarin tradition under changed circumstances, recognized that "one could not truly represent Wilhelm von Humboldt one hundred years after his time without actually changing his words."[38]

These examples illustrate two important implications of the field concept for intellectual history. Considered as contexts, intellectual fields are grounded in social and institutional conditions that must be reconstructed by a historical sociology of knowledge; and such reconstruction involves a great deal more than documenting discrete linkages and influences.[39] Yet, at the same time, the variable, positional quality of ideas implies that the texts themselves speak with different voices in different contexts; and this strongly suggests a conception of texts (or at least some texts) as inherently multivalent and complex. The contextual and textual implications of the field concept are thus interdependent: skillfully applied, the concept of intellectual field can

[37] Ringer, "The Intellectual Field," 272. Ringer systematically compares the fields of French and German academic culture around the turn of twentieth century in his *Fields of Knowledge: French Academic Culture in Comparative Perspective, 1890–1920*.

[38] Ringer, "The German Mandarins Reconsidered," 5–8. Many of the commonplace misunderstandings of this argument are addressed in Ringer, "Differences and Cross-National Similarities among Mandarins."

[39] This stress on the social and institutional anchorage of the habitus distinguishes Bourdieu's conception of fields from conceptions of discourse as relatively free-floating "languages," but some versions of the latter may be compatible with it. On the reconstruction of discourses, see J. G. A. Pocock, "Introduction: The State of the Art," in *Virtue, Commerce, and History*.

guide close readings of texts, readings that are sensitive to the presence of polarities, tensions, and ambiguities.

Clearly, then, the concept of the intellectual field is eminently relevant to our comprehension of individual intellectual projects as well. It focuses our attention on the various ways the pull of a field enters into an argument, quite independent of the author's conscious intentions, whether in the formulation of an argument or in its reception. This tends to be true even of an outsider who argues within its bounds. A field is constantly replicated by the habitual, unconscious reproduction of the problems and rhetoric of an intellectual culture, its system of "unconscious intellectual choices."[40] To opt for the heterodox may be no more than to move to another, though perhaps more precarious, position within the field. Quite apart from the morality of such choices, which we may often admire, heterodoxy in itself does not necessarily produce incisive criticism. Instead, the most incisive thinking tends to be that which emerges from the habitus by making unconscious assumptions explicit, assumptions that may be shared by orthodox and heterodox alike.[41] The concept of emergence can help to demystify the originality of the innovative critic and innoculate us against the kind of intellectual hero worship that so easily results from seeing "the new idea as an uncaused cause."[42] The challenge is to conceive of the relations between field and text in a way that is supple enough to account for those intellectual projects that do not simply typify positions within the field but transcend and transform it creatively.

With this in mind, I would like to posit the characteristics of a particular type of critical emergence that Benjamin's intellectual project demonstrates with special clarity. A critique may be especially powerful if undertaken by someone whose original intellectual commitments are heavily saturated by the orthodoxies of a field. In this case, the critique of those orthodoxies may take the special form of an *immanent critique*—a critique "from within" that intervenes in the dynamics of a tradition by playing off certain of its moments against others.[43] Such a critic will be sensitive to what Hans-Georg Gadamer calls *Wirkungsgeschichte*, or "effective-history," the way the traditions one criticizes are already integral to one's own position. But in the exemplary case, he or

[40] Bourdieu, "Intellectual Field and Creative Project," 115.

[41] Bourdieu, *Outline of a Theory of Practice*, 168–169.

[42] Ringer, "The Intellectual Field," 273.

[43] As my comments here are meant to suggest, I am not using the concept of immanent critique in the strictly early romantic sense, which pertains to the unfolding of formal elements of the work, but in an extended sense akin to Benjamin's own later hermeneutic, which includes the conditions and interests that guide its transmission and reception. See my discussion in Chapter 7, Section 3, and Heinrich Kaulen, *Rettung und Destruktion: Untersuchungen zur Hermeneutik Walter Benjamins*.

she will also be particularly alert to selective readings of tradition and to the interests that guide them—that is, to *reception* history. Bourdieu refers to the way the structure of a field "refracts" any outside influences passing through it, and this holds for ideas recovered from the submerged past of a tradition as well.[44] Finally, the persistent and consequential pursuit of such an immanent critique may involve a long-term *strategy* for an individual intellectual project, setting an implicit agenda and guiding the dynamics of its development. My argument in this book is that Benjamin's productive ambivalence about the decay of tradition, the dialectic of liquidationist and culturally conservative moments in his work, calls for a special kind of historical reading. We can best illuminate Benjamin's project by understanding it as an immanent critique of a rather specifically German intellectual culture whose traditions were dominated by that peculiar constellation of idealism and historicism which constituted the mandarin orthodoxy.[45] By paying closer attention to his pursuit of the long-term intellectual strategies this critique called for, we can shed a great deal of light on the dynamics of his project.

Benjamin was undoubtedly among the twentieth century's quintessentially marginal and extraterritorial figures, and it may seem unusually perverse to bring him "into" any field in the way I am proposing here. In part, this perversity has its methodological point. Benjamin represents a borderline case for testing the limits of the concept of the intellectual field: if it can help illuminate his project, it is bound to be fruitful for more conventional cases. But I have also found that the perspective of the field throws crucial yet neglected aspects of his project into relief—above all, the formative influence of the youth movement, the tenacity of his critique of idealist aesthetics, and the importance of his immanent critique of romanticism. It may also seem that my emphasis on the early origins of the long-term strategy that unifies his project willfully curtails a body of work notable for its diversity. Indeed, throughout his life Benjamin was extraordinarily willing to continue opening himself to new contexts and impulses. An intellectual biography (which this study, focused on the issue of tradition,

[44] Bourdieu, "Intellectual Field and Creative Project," 118.

[45] The essential foundations for the construction of this field have been laid by Ringer's *Decline of the German Mandarins*. Of course, subfields and adjacent fields have their own particular structures and codes. This is true of the semi- or nonacademic literary and publicistic fields in which, for instance, the meaning of idealism was somewhat different and *Lebensphilosophie* was far more significant than in academic culture. To an extent, this was also true of the prewar German youth movement, although as Chapter 1 shows the youth movement uncannily reproduced a version of the dominant field. Benjamin constantly crossed borders in his life and his work. I explore the implications of his move to the larger field of Weimar cultural politics in Chapter 4, Section 2.

does not aspire to be) would have to do justice to this diversity. But in his very openness Benjamin succeeded—pace Scholem and Adorno—in remaining true to himself, and this too must be explained.

Finally, it should be kept in mind throughout that what is in question are implicit strategies and virtual agendas rather than any detailed, explicit blueprint Benjamin developed. The philological caution of taking Benjamin at his word should not recklessly be thrown overboard; nevertheless, many aspects of his work may be clearer to us than they were to him. Too often, perhaps, his works have been exempted from his own critical maxim that "only the future has developers strong enough to bring out the image in all its details" (I 1238, V 603). The fact remains that Benjamin often showed himself strikingly sensitive to what I call field relationships, positional values, and strategies. He never deceived himself about his own debt to the German intellectual tradition. But he was painfully aware of how debased that tradition had become; moreover, he recognized that this sickness undeniably had deep roots within the tradition itself, and that it had proliferated with the full complicity of its would-be guardians. For all these reasons, he was perfectly clear about the dubiousness of piously conserving this tradition as a priceless heritage.

Benjamin's remarkable perspicuity in these matters often emerged in his exchanges with Scholem. Particularly when Scholem accused him of flirting with lethal ambiguities by provocatively declaring his sympathies with dialectical materialism, Benjamin felt forced to protest. What Scholem failed to see, Benjamin countered, was that he was compelled to work within a specific ideological force field: "That means: I am determined to pursue my cause under all circumstances, but this cause is not identical in every circumstance . . . and to meet false circumstances correctly—i.e., with something 'correct'—that is not granted to me" (B 530). To stress the need to "listen intently" to tradition, or to lament its unraveling all too loudly, would be to run the risk of a far more lethal misunderstanding than Scholem's—that of being identified with those regressive forces Benjamin always clearly understood as his enemies. "There is the question of neighborhood," he admonished:

Even if one's writings are "counterrevolutionary"—as you quite correctly characterize mine from the party point of view—should one explicitly put them at the service of the counterrevolution as well? Shouldn't one rather denature them, like spirits, making them definitely and reliably unpalatable for it, at the risk that they become unpalatable for anyone? Can the clarity with which one distinguishes oneself from the pronouncements, the language of people one continually learns to avoid in life, ever be too great? (B 531)

Benjamin himself loved the strategic metaphor, above all in its military version, and he used it repeatedly, in ever-new modulations. "The critic is a strategist in the literary struggle," he once declared (IV 108). The strategic conception was not merely a militant affectation of his middle and later periods; as I hope to show, it was an operative maxim of his work from the time of his break with the youth movement. It meant far more than simply adjusting the presentation of his arguments to the way they might be received; rather, his strategic sensibility entered into the very formulation of his positions. Benjamin's method of working through paradoxical reversals and juxtapositions, I argue, can be more sensibly and productively understood as the expression of such an intellectual strategy than as a genial anticipation of the poststructuralist deconstruction of subjectivity. The results of Benjamin's project, such as his construction of the antinomies of tradition, must ultimately be understood as the discovery of unsuspected fault lines in the German intellectual tradition itself.

4. The Argument

In Chapter 1, I show how a passionate, idiosyncratic engagement in the prewar German youth and student movements set Benjamin's initial ideological coordinates. He declared himself a partisan of the idea of an autonomous youth culture as a regenerative alternative to the philistinism and routinized practicality of the adult world. Youth, Benjamin wrote, is a "steadily pulsating feeling for the abstractness of pure *Geist*" (B 93). As a university student, he translated this program into a defense of the idea of the university as a "community of the knowing" (*Erkennenden*) that shapes the totality of the learner. In both cases, the idea of youth was a counter to the predominance of "empty, general utility" and "mechanical duty" as cultural standards (II 76–81). By evoking such principles, Benjamin was adopting the language and assumptions of a specific idealist code,[46] which he saw as the sole guarantee of uncompromising opposition to the adult world. He seems to have been unaware, as yet, of the objective ambiguity with which any appeal to idealism was necessarily burdened in his situation. For, at the same time, orthodox mandarin academics were also calling for

[46] Accordingly, whenever Benjamin uses the term "idea" it carries a range of associations that go far beyond the commonplace meaning of a thought or conception. In the German intellectual culture of his time, an idea was commonly understood to be not just a subjective notion but something transcendent, absolute, and timeless; in ethical terms, it suggested a value higher than mere utilitarian interests. Later, in his doctoral dissertation on early romanticism, he referred to ideas in the more formal and technical sense of post-Kantian philosophical idealism; and in the prologue to the *Trauerspiel* book he invoked an explicitly Platonic sense of "ideas" for reasons I discuss in Chapter 3, Section 5.

the revival of an idealism that would elevate the totality of learning and scholarship above the utilitarian, materialistic vulgarization they found rampant in the society of imperial Germany. *Their* idealism was the ideological and socially confirmative decay product of a German idealist tradition that had once included decidedly utopian strains. From the very beginning, Benjamin's conception of youth placed him in a contradictory, precarious position within the dominant intellectual field.

He was equally vehement in denouncing tendencies that exerted a great influence within the youth movement but looked, from his idealist perspective, like false forms of opposition. He saw the vitalism of the Wandervogel, their nature worship and their cult of charismatic leadership, as evidence of what he called unmastered natural forces and thus a threat to the autonomy of *Geist*. Nor was Benjamin more favorably inclined toward the progressive social and political engagement advocated in his own circles. The attempt to combine activism with study was bound to lead to an instrumentalization of thought and action—and thus to an unacknowledged complicity with the adult world. The would-be heterodoxies of vitalism and activism were ineffectual at best and pernicious at worst. Both threatened the autonomy of youth culture and *Geist*, whereas for Benjamin only an unadulterated dedication to the idea could undergird the regenerative autonomy of youth.

Against this background, the outbreak of World War I was a traumatic shock for Benjamin. Although he never confused "the ideas of 1914" with the regenerative power of the idea he meant to advocate, he was forced to recognize the slippages that made a murderous abuse of idealist rhetoric so easy. In Chapter 2 I show that at this point he made a crucial choice. Instead of abandoning idealism in disillusionment and shifting his ground to one of the available heterodoxies, he undertook to salvage the critical potential of his earlier idealism. Rather than disavow his allegiances, he sought to vindicate them. This meant carrying the ideological configuration that had defined his position in the youth movement into his further work. In a sense, he now faced a triangular configuration—instrumentalism, vitalism, and a debauched, corrupted idealism—and wanted to affirm his distance from all three while remaining within an idealist framework. Benjamin's commitments in the youth and student movements and the way he came to reckon with them set the coordinates of his intellectual project to an extent that has seldom been appreciated.[47] To attempt to rescue the critical potential of

---

[47] A notable exception is Michael Jennings, "The Mortification of the Text: The Development of Walter Benjamin's Literary Criticism, 1912–1924." For my own awareness of the crucial and ongoing role played by Benjamin's commitments in the youth movement, I am indebted to Lloyd Spencer.

idealism in the face of these pressures was to choose the path of greatest resistance, and it was bound to expose him to constant misunderstandings. One of the most productive veins he struck at the beginning of this project lay in the texts of early German romanticism, the *Frühromantik*, above all those of Friedrich Schlegel and Novalis, which he examined in his doctoral dissertation. Their works furnished him with an epistemologically founded concept of critique and a messianic conception of history with which to innoculate idealism against its affirmative tendencies. But the romantic tradition, too, was subject to ideological abuse, as his experience in the youth movement had made him recognize. Benjamin responded to this pull of the field by adopting a long-term critical strategy—to reactivate the critical potential of the *Frühromantik* in defiance of an overwhelmingly conservative reception. His encounter with the *Frühromantik* thus became an immanent critique of romanticism as well.

Benjamin's project constantly required fresh supplies of what he called antitoxins to innoculate his work against the affirmative moments in the idealist tradition. In Chapter 3, I show how Benjamin's *Origin of German Trauerspiel* furthered his original strategy by mobilizing the destructive energies of baroque allegory against the harmonizing biases of the classical and romantic conceptions of the symbol. In the work's preface he elaborated a revised concept of criticism that can only be called hyperidealist. But, while holding fast to a concept of transcendence, he relentlessly argued against any claim that a material form can incarnate and stabilize the absolute, a claim that is essential to idealist classicism. The allegorical form, with its dizzying proliferation of codes of signification, denied the very possibility of stable embodiments of absolute meaning. Benjamin thus continued the immanent critique of romanticism he had begun in his dissertation on the early romantics: the baroque allegorical form provided a more definitive, more resilient corrective to the affirmative idealism of classical aesthetics than romanticism alone was capable of. As Benjamin pursued these explorations, moreover, something new emerged. His theory of allegory spelled out an uncompromisingly radical modernist aesthetic in all but the name. This implicit modernism was no miraculous coincidence: he had won it through a rigorous, independent recourse to the romantic sources of cultural modernism, before undertaking any extensive, direct encounter with modernist works. I argue that Benjamin's theory of allegory, as well as its implicit modernism, must be understood as responses to the personal and intellectual traumas he had faced in 1914.

In Chapters 4–6 I explore Benjamin's direct encounter with modernist culture, his turn to politics, and his adoption of what he sometimes called a materialist stance toward cultural and political issues. In Chap-

ter 4 the next phase of his work—the middle years from 1925 to 1933—
is placed against a broader intellectual field of debates over culture and
politics in the Weimar Republic. Benjamin found in certain forms of
radical modernist culture a fitting counterpart to the liquidationist tendencies which, in his own earlier work, he had couched in the language of eradicating the bonds of ensnarement in mythic compulsions.
On the face of it, his identification with the "back to the drawing
board" spirit of radical constructivism may seem a self-denying gesture
coming from one who had so long been engaged in an intimate critique
and reconstruction of traditions. But as I show in the previous chapters, this is where the inherent logic of his immanent critique of romanticism was already leading him.

Yet Benjamin's long-term strategy also continued to develop in response to the larger field. Particularly in this new context, the accenting
of the liquidationist and nihilist moments of his work forced the issue
of clarifying his relationship to the nihilism of the radical conservatives. Benjamin responded by articulating a philosophical anthropology of his own—an "anthropological materialism" allied, but not identical, with Marxism—in which his distinctive conception of the progressive potential of technology was crucial. Through his association
with the "destructive character" of Brecht, Benjamin decisively furthered all these constructivist strategies. Yet Brecht also provided him
with pointers back to the question of a legitimate recourse to tradition.

Chapters 5 and 6 then bring us to Benjamin's encounter with French
cultural modernism in the two forms that yielded the most productive
impulses for his own project: surrealism and the prose of Proust. The
essays in which Benjamin came to terms with them prove that his own
observations on the identity of his early and late work can be just as
misleading as the notion of a radical discontinuity that guided the
classical interpretations discussed above. By no means did he simply
transform critical principles already won from his previous work; what
he accomplished was neither a mediation of extremes nor a demonstration of their paradoxical identity. Instead, he continued his immanent
critique of idealism and romanticism by pursuing his reflections on the
historical dimension of critique. His theory of images as phantasmagoria and his reflections on the temporal rhythms in which historical images become legible provided fresh antitoxins against the
latent affirmative moments in idealism and romanticism. In Chapter 5 I
explore his critical appropriation of the surrealist figures of dream images and of awakening as a rupture with entranced delusions. In
Chapter 6 I work through his transformation of Proust's dialectic of
involuntary memory images.

Chapter 7 is an examination of the provisional synthesis of Benjamin's antinomial dialectic of tradition that was beginning to emerge

in his unfinished master project on the culture of modernity in nineteenth-century Paris. The conception of dialectical images that lies at the heart of the project has long been known from his précis "Paris, Capital of the Nineteenth Century." But his extensive working notes for the project show that his encounter with modernist and avant-garde culture was vitally important in formulating this conception. The antinomies of tradition take their most precise form in this theory of critique. Yet the productivity of Benjamin's critical appropriation of modernist influences can be fully appreciated, I argue, only as the culmination of a long-term strategy of immanent critique established in his early work.

In the conclusion, I assess the distance traveled and reconstruct what Benjamin had to say, directly and indirectly, about some particularly German intellectual and cultural traditions. Readers of Benjamin's "On the Concept of History" (often known as "Theses on the Philosophy of History") have long been familiar with his identification of the historian's task as that of redeeming unfulfilled hopes: Benjamin admonished the historian, as the executor of a "*weak* messianic power," to "brush history against the grain" in order to recover both suppressed counter-traditions and the subversive moments embedded within established traditions. I examine what he accomplished to this end for the traditions with which he himself was saturated. In the end, I hope to have shown that we can best unriddle Benjamin's construction of the antinomies of tradition by specifying it historically.

Chapter One

Benjamin and the Idea of Youth

Benjamin was an ardent, intellectually demanding, melancholy adolescent; in fact, the grand passion of his adolescence was the idea of youth itself. Often publishing under the pseudonym Ardor, he proclaimed youth to be a "steady, pulsating feeling for the abstractness of pure *Geist*" (B 93) and styled his private reflections a "metaphysics of youth" (II 91–104). In his writings before the outbreak of World War I, Benjamin traded in an idiom that exalts adolescent idealism, an idiom pervasive in European culture since the beginnings of the romantic movement at the turn of the nineteenth century. These texts represent his first gropings toward clarity rather than any articulate intellectual identity. As such, the notions they expound were to play no explicit role in his later works. But it would be wrong simply to write them off as tokens of enthusiasms he outgrew. Read carefully against their historical context, Benjamin's early works can be seen to invoke a particular form of this code, a historically specific set of formulations of adolescent idealism: they speak the idiom of an autonomous youth culture whose mission is to act as the agent of a general cultural renewal; recent studies have provided a good deal of evidence to suggest that this version of youth ideology was specific to Wilhelmine Germany in the decade before the war.[1] Moreover, in order to distance himself from the garden varieties of the Wandervogel ideology that set the tone in the German youth movement at large, Benjamin invoked a second code by identifying with Gustav Wyneken's call for youth to lead a

[1] Comparative studies suggest that this identification of youth as the agent of a general cultural regeneration was the specifically German variant of a generational consciousness that was on the rise across Europe at the time. See Robert Wohl, *The Generation of 1914*, 45–48, and Hans Mommsen, "Generationskonflikt und Jugendrevolte in der Weimarer Republik," 53–54.

renewal of *Geist*. Wyneken attempted to wed the idea of a leadership role for an autonomous youth culture with a diagnosis of cultural crisis in many ways typical of a rather orthodox form of German mandarin idealism; when combined with the visionary pose he attempted to strike, the result was an ideology shot through with ambiguities characteristic of prewar neoconservatives, the so-called conservative revolutionaries.

Benjamin's trial identifications with the youth movement came to an abrupt, traumatic end with the outbreak of the war: Wyneken, along with the overwhelming majority of the youth movement, saw the mobilization as the very incarnation of the idealistic spirit they had been striving for, while Benjamin rejected the war root and branch as its nightmarish, barbaric opposite. Feeling embittered and betrayed, he abandoned the cause and the rhetoric of youth. Nevertheless, it was to remain his decisive, formative intellectual identification. His engagement had been both passionate and concrete enough to set the coordinates of his future intellectual strategy: while remaining firmly convinced of the need for fundamental cultural renewal and intensely committed to metaphysical imperatives seen as utterly transcending the present order of things, he was left profoundly suspicious of all the idioms in which calls for renewal had been issued—the vitalism of the Wandervogel, the social engagement of his politically minded fellow students, and the rhetoric of German idealism in both its orthodox and radical conservative variants.

1. The Topography of the German Youth Movement

The middle-class German youth movement, which first flourished between the turn of the century and the outbreak of World War I, was an extremely variegated phenomenon, far more differentiated in its scope and aims than is commonly assumed.[2] Although often simply identified with the Wandervogel tendency, which formed its conspicuous mainstream, it included a whole range of subcurrents whose adherents often defined themselves by contrast with the Wandervogel. The common denominator of all these groups was the notion that youth must lead a general cultural and social regeneration, a mission it could fulfill only by striving to create an autonomous youth culture.

[2] On the middle-class origins of the Wandervogel and the strong participation of boys from families of the *Bildungsbürgertum*, see Ulrich Aufmuth, *Die deutsche Wandervogelbewegung unter soziologischem Aspekt*, and Otto Neuloh and Wilhelm Zilius, *Die Wandervögel: Eine empirisch-soziologische Untersuchung der frühen deutschen Jugendbewegung*.

The topography of the movement can be charted by distinguishing the variety of ways these notions of youth autonomy and cultural regeneration were played out. The importance of this topography, for our purposes, is that within these currents the young Walter Benjamin first took his bearings.[3]

The Wandervogel groups provided the original form of the youth movement and, before the war, its largest contingent by far. Spontaneously formed by their urban, middle-class, overwhelmingly male participants, they enabled youth to get out of the cities in order to experience nature free of the supervision and constraints of school and parents. Hiking, singing folksongs around a bonfire, and sleeping in the hay provided the key symbols of a common identity that fused the "vital" experiences of nature and the bonds of male community. Their aim was not to rebel against authority as such; typically, each group chose a leader who was to provide a source of healthy, natural authority. To the Wandervogel, youth autonomy meant escaping from an oppressive, unhealthy adult world to create a refuge where contact with such sources of vitality, ideals, and natural community could be renewed. There was also a Jewish counterpart to the Wandervogel, the Blau-Weiss.[4] Though formed as a secession from the increasingly anti-Semitic Wandervogel and nominally Zionist in character, the Blau-Weiss groups were remarkably similar to them; the members of both groups were rebelling against what they felt to be the stifling respectability of their parents. These similarities found striking expression in the early philosophy of Martin Buber, who became something of an unofficial spiritual guide to the movement. In his *Drei Reden über das Judentum,* Buber espoused a Jewish version of *Lebensphilosophie* which stressed the Jews' need to cast off the fetters of an alien, "Western" rationality and return to the primordial sources of Jewish community rooted in their "Oriental" identity.[5] The Wandervogel and the Blau-

[3] On the youth movement in general, see Walter Laqueur, *Young Germany;* Peter D. Stachura, *The German Youth Movement, 1900–1945;* and Winfried Mogge, "Wandervogel, Freideutsche Jugend und Bünde: Zum Jugendbild der bürgerlichen Jugendbewegung." Many fundamental documents are gathered in Werner Kindt, ed., *Grundschriften der deutschen Jugendbewegung.* The editorial notes to Benjamin's *Gesammelte Schriften* also contain a wealth of valuable information on the context of Benjamin's involvement, including extensive citations from autobiographical accounts by numerous participants (II 824–918). The editors' insistence on the irrelevance of Benjamin's involvement in the youth movement, a position they appear to have taken over from Adorno, is, however, anything but the last word on the subject.

[4] On the Blau-Weiss, see Hermann Meier-Cronemeyer, "Jüdische Jugendbewegung."

[5] Martin Buber, *Drei Reden über das Judentum,* 48, 55, 79. The development of Buber's views from his early, asocial mysticism to the later, dialogic philosophy of *I and Thou* is traced by Paul Mendes-Flohr, *From Mysticism to Dialogue: Martin Buber's Transformation of German Social Thought.*

Weiss were thus curiously parallel versions of a youth secession pro-posing a return to natural sources of vitality.[6]

By 1913, these impulses took a new direction among those groups who banded together to form an umbrella organization under the name Freideutsche Jugend (Free German Youth).[7] The Freideutsche Jugend began as a coalition set up for the specific purpose of organiz-ing a youth festival, the Free German Youth Day, on the Meißner Mountain as an alternative to the official centennial commemorations of the German victory over Napoleon at the battle of Leipzig. This undertaking in itself indicates a shift in orientation; for these groups, youth autonomy meant more than the Wandervogel's withdrawal from adult society. Just what form a confrontation should take, however, was hotly disputed among the Freideutsche Jugend. Some advocated principles of lifestyle reform, such as abstinence; others focused on school reforms that would give pupils the right to a certain measure of self-administration, for which they used the slogan of a "school com-munity." The great majority thought in terms of a rather limited mea-sure of responsible self-government, not unlike student councils in high schools in the United States. But a small, vocal group associated with the Freideutsche Jugend held out for the uncompromising ideal of a comprehensive, autonomous youth culture that would be much more than a mere adjunct of the school administration. These were the radicals of the youth movement, who distinguished themselves from the rest by adopting the label "youth culture movement."[8]

Despite their limited numbers, the radicals managed to achieve noto-riety. Their effort to cultivate a tone of high intellectual seriousness was an important part of what marked them off from the rest. They es-poused the ideas of Wyneken, an ambitious, maverick educational re-former, and attracted the attention of a circle of independent, left-wing literary intellectuals in Berlin centered around the expressionist journal *Die Aktion* and its editor, Franz Pfemfert. Wyneken's sponsorship and Pfemfert's support enabled them to publish a journal of their own, *Der Anfang* (The Beginning), which provided a platform for the radicals' program and was meant to open a channel of communication between

[6] See George Mosse, "The Influence of the Volkish Idea on German Judaism," in *Germans and Jews*, 94–102.

[7] The Freideutsche Jugend and the events surrounding the Meißner festival, particu-larly with respect to Wyneken's role, are summarized well by Heinrich Kupffer, *Gustav Wyneken*, 85–91.

[8] On the youth culture movement, the *Anfang* circle, and the Academic Committee for School Reform, see Ulrich Hermann, "Die Jugendkulturbewegung: Der Kampf um die höhere Schule"; Kupffer, *Gustav Wyneken*, 74–80; Ulrich Linse, "Die Jugendkultur-bewegung"; Philip Lee Utley, "Radical Youth: Generational Conflict in the *Anfang* Move-ment, 1912–January 1914"; and Utley's dissertation, "Siegfried Bernfeld: Left-wing Youth Leader, Psychoanalyst, and Zionist, 1910–1918."

isolated, disaffected secondary pupils and the university students who edited and ran it. Even among the radicals, however, there was a further, fundamental split. Siegfried Bernfeld, for instance, a Viennese student who was among the moving spirits on the editorial board, understood the youth culture movement as a social and political movement whose autonomy could be grounded only in an organizational and publicity network of its own. He founded the Academic Committee for School Reform, which, in tandem with *Der Anfang*, conducted surveys of the activities of secondary pupils and helped promote the founding of regular discussion groups, so-called *Sprechsäle*, in which pupils and students met to discuss the issues of the youth movement. Bernfeld thought in terms of fostering social work by and for youth and hoped that a youth movement of this sort would develop in the direction of socialist politics. The other wing of the radical faction rejected any and all such political gestures, envisioning the revolutionary potential of youth in purely cultural terms. Its advocates insisted that an autonomous youth community could only be grounded on *Geist* alone, keeping clear of any practical or political entanglements whatsoever. They regarded the *Sprechsaal* as a forum for autonomous intellectual development, an academy or educational community (*Erziehungsgemeinschaft*) in which the intellectual elite of the new youth would quite literally educate itself. Their most prominent spokesperson was Walter Benjamin.

The Freideutsche Jugend, however, were utterly uninterested in such internal struggles among the radicals: the leaders of its constituent organizations met at Marburg in March 1914 to expel all groups associated with Wyneken. There seem to have been numerous motives for the expulsion. The immediate occasion was a political scandal in which *Der Anfang* and Bernfeld's Academic Committee for School Reform came into conflict with the Bavarian and Prussian educational authorities, and even with the police in Vienna, over the alleged propagation of subversive ideas among secondary school pupils. The mainstream groups, worried that the Freideutsche Jugend might come to be associated in the public mind with Wyneken and *Der Anfang*, saw their chances of achieving moderate reforms endangered; they were seeking to repair the damage by publicly dissociating themselves from the radicals.[9] Behind this motive lurked the suspicion that Wyneken, enamored of posing as the prophet of youth, had been making a power play to set himself up as the leader of the youth movement. More fundamentally, however, the members of the *Anfang* group were dis-

---

[9] The *Anfang* controversy is related by Klaus Laermann, "Der Skandal um den *Anfang*: Ein Versuch jugendlicher Gegenöffentlichkeit im Kaiserreich," and by Kupffer, *Gustav Wyneken*, 91–96.

tinguished from the rest of the youth movement by their political sympathies and their family backgrounds. Their political orientation was left-liberal, socialist, and in some cases anarchist, which put them at odds with the *völkisch* nationalism to which the majority inclined. Moreover, the radicals' most prominent representatives, particularly in Berlin and Vienna, were children of the Jewish *Bildungsbürgertum*. As a result, they met with the typically anti-Semitic charge that their emphasis on social organization (Bernfeld) and intellectuality (Benjamin) corroded the vital experience of nature and the group, in which the majority saw the cardinal virtues of the youth movement.[10]

The radicals' expulsion, however, only contributed to a shift in the focus of their energies which was already under way. By the spring of 1914, most of them had long since become university students; accordingly, their sights were shifting away from the youth movement at large and upward from the secondary schools to the universities. The Berlin radicals, in particular, tried to convert the Freie Studentenschaft (Independent Student Association, an umbrella organization for non-fraternity groups) into a vehicle for their aims. Benjamin, fully engaged in these efforts, was elected president of the Berlin Freie Studentenschaft in the spring semester of 1914, a position he held until the outbreak of the war. The Independents' debates continued to center on the issue of youth autonomy and the creation of new forms to express, secure, and propagate it. There was a great deal of continuity in the emerging fronts: in the radicals' debates, the Corps students stood in for the Wandervogel's flight from responsibility into male camaraderie and ultranationalist sentiments, while the radicals themselves divided over the question of which combination of lifestyle reform, engaged social work with overtures toward socialist politics, and dedication to *Geist* would best serve the regeneration of culture, which to them unquestionably remained the mission of youth. With the declaration of war in August 1914, these seemed to become moot issues.

2. Gustav Wyneken's Ideological Ambiguities

The guiding spirit for the radicals in general—and particularly for Benjamin—was the maverick pedagogical activist Gustav Wyneken.

[10] The numerical preponderance was pointed out by Bernfeld, who later estimated that the radicals numbered 3,000 in 1914, of whom "certainly" one-third were Jews; of the 500 Viennese members of his Academic Committee, 450 were Jews (II 848). Conditions in Berlin were probably much like those in Vienna. An extremely perceptive study of the radical groups within the Jewish youth movements of the time, which also sheds light on Jews who, like Benjamin, participated in the non-Jewish movements, is Gert Mattenklott, " 'Nicht durch Kampfesmacht und nicht durch Körperkraft . . . ': Alternativen Jüdischer Jugendbewegung in Deutschland vom *Anfang* bis 1933."

Wyneken cut a peculiar figure on the educational scene in late Wilhelmine Germany.[11] In the first decade of the century, he played the leading role in establishing an experimental private school at Wickersdorf based on the notion of a free school community (*Freie Schulgemeinde*) which encouraged pupil self-government and autonomy; this won him a reputation as a progressive educator. By 1910, however, personal rivalries with his colleagues and conflicts with the state educational authorities cost him his teacher's license; embittered, Wyneken set out to vindicate himself by promulgating his pedagogical principles in a series of lectures and pamphlets. During these years, he broadened his conception of the free school community into a more general notion of youth culture, partly in an attempt to set himself up as the leader of the youth movement. His initial overtures were successful enough to convince the Freideutsche Jugend to adopt his version of the proclamation of the Meißner festival as the official invitation; but this success was reversed the following spring when, as we have seen, they expelled all the groups affiliated with him. In 1913 he also published a collection of articles under the title *Schule und Jugendkultur* (School and Youth Culture) in which he attempted to suggest that his program had systematic philosophical foundations. In fact, Wyneken's entire program is a brew of often bewilderingly diverse tendencies. It must be understood more as woolly ideology than as rigorous, formal thought; indeed, its most striking feature is its ideological ambiguity. The *nature* of this ambiguity, however, would prove crucially important for Benjamin and can be spelled out precisely, in terms of the intellectual field.

Wyneken's clashes with the authorities and his reputation for radicalism should not deceive us about the fact that his notions were thoroughly grounded in the orthodox idealism of mandarin academic culture. Wyneken faithfully echoed the orthodox lament over a cultural crisis that allegedly resulted from the egoistic, materialistic, and utilitarian degradation of higher, ideal values. He sounded this keynote right at the outset of *Schule und Jugendkultur* by invoking objective *Geist*, in a strong sense of the term, as his orienting concept. Objective *Geist*, he reminded his readers, is not a sum of individual intellects, nor a mere abstraction from them; rather, it is a higher-level entity, a whole that is greater than the sum of its parts. But for him it was also more than just collective culture; in fact, he tended to regard it as a metaphysical entity in its own right. He then used this notion to set certain priorities straight: objective *Geist* is not the reflection of society; on the contrary, society "is only the means for *Geist* to unfold itself." Thus "the fundamental axiom of all human action should be: serve *Geist*." In

---

[11] The best study of Wyneken is Kupffer, *Gustav Wyneken*; also see Lewis D. Wurgaft, *The Activists: Kurt Hiller and the Politics of Action on the German Left, 1914–1933*, 29–31.

the moral realm, the counterpart of objective *Geist* is the objective will, as incorporated by the state. By consequence, the state is "not an association of individuals, not a general business transaction . . . but rather . . . a new individual of a higher sort, which only uses individuals in order to unfold itself on them and through them." A year before the war, Wyneken left no room for doubt about his view of what it might mean to serve the state: "We see with astonishment how the state . . . sends its citizens by the thousands to their deaths, of whom not a single one wishes to die; and we sense something of the fearful force of the objective will . . . . *that there is such a thing*, that is what counts, that is the important thing."[12] In such formulations, service to *Geist* and the state comes to sound like the observance of a ritual cult that calls for human sacrifice. To his way of thinking, however, the cultural crisis could be overcome only by a renewal of such idealism; and the key to this renewal, for Wyneken as for the mandarins, was education. Education must not be practically oriented: it was not "fitness training for the economic struggle for existence," nor should it promote an "individualistic economic perversion of true purposes"; since calculating, instrumental action itself was the problem, this would only deepen the crisis. Instead, education must inculcate idealistic devotion to those agencies that stood above all merely partial, selfish "interests": objective *Geist* and the state. "The task of the school . . . is to guarantee the continuity of *Geist*."[13] In its mandarin inflection, the call for an idealistic revival often amounted to a demand for the restoration of the mandarins' own spiritual leadership; the edge of anxiety in their prophecies of cultural demise spoke more directly about their fear of increasing irrelevance than about the objective social situation.[14] Wyneken, however marginal to the established academic culture, shared fully in the mandarins' pseudo-diagnosis of the cultural crisis. In this respect, his variety of protest was utterly orthodox.

It was in the consequences he drew from such run-of-the-mill orthodox themes that Wyneken earned his reputation for radicalism. Most important was his view that autonomous youth, not the mandarin elite, was destined to be the agent of cultural renewal. For him, this conclusion followed logically from his diagnosis of the cultural crisis: youth was "the natural time of idealism," when receptivity to "absolute values" and the calling of objective *Geist* was keenest.[15] Wyneken tended to portray the general revival of idealism to be led by

---

[12] Gustav Wyneken, *Schule und Jugendkultur*, 6–7, 10–11.
[13] Ibid., 56.
[14] This response has been analyzed by Ringer, *Decline of the German Mandarins*, especially chap. 5, "The Origins of the Cultural Crisis, 1890–1920."
[15] Wyneken, *Schule und Jugendkultur*, 46, 69.

youth in the inflated rhetoric of a new religiosity: "Youth strives for the unconditional. It aims for the ultimate value without beating around the bush. It is the period of passions and love, of the capacity for belief and enthusiasm, and those are goods whose inestimable value will be grasped again by the adult generation only once a new religion has come over it."[16] If youth meant unconditional idealism, then it followed that youth culture could not be defined in any specific terms, but only as "an idea, a task, an ideal . . . a geometric locus, so to speak."[17] However elusive Wyneken may have been about a positive definition, he had no trouble deducing what a pedagogical program geared to these notions must exclude. First of all, the free school community challenged the family's role: education in the family was a stopgap measure at best, because "it cannot even provide the most elementary precondition" of autonomy, "the company of peers." Parents who refused to allow the "coziness" of their private sphere to be blown open by "the fresh air of greater, more general interests" were condemned as "hostile to culture" and "backward."[18] His position on religious education was equally likely to provoke Wilhelmine sensibilities: religious education must cease to serve the reproduction of existing social institutions, meaning the established confessional churches, in order to promote acts "performed in consciousness of their absolute and eternal value and for the sake of their eternal value" alone.[19] And when frustrated in his attempt to institutionalize these notions in his experimental schools, Wyneken turned outside the school to pose as the prophet and leader of an extrainstitutional movement. At his most adventurous, he went so far as to describe the state as "only formal, only a tool" for the self-realization of *Geist*.[20] Though an orthodox historian of philosophy might well have said something of the sort in a scholarly exegesis of Hegel's philosophy, any such relativization of the state would have been strictly avoided in a more open context, where it might easily be "misunderstood."

The general tendency of Wyneken's departures from the orthodox mandarin diagnosis of the cultural crisis is clear: he spoke as if ready to jettison the fundamental institutions of the empire in the interest of ideal tasks. Virtually no mandarin, orthodox or modernist, would have countenanced any such threat to order. In all this, his program was typical of the neoconservative or conservative revolutionary ideologies emerging at the time. What distinguished such neoconservatives from

---

[16] Ibid., 43.
[17] Gustav Wyneken, *Was ist "Jugendkultur"?*, 18.
[18] Wyneken, *Schule und Jugendkultur*, 17–18.
[19] Ibid., 66.
[20] Ibid., 11.

the mandarins was their conviction that the elites, the institutions, and the official culture of Wilhelmine Germany were too compromised to lead the necessary cultural renewal; still, as elitists, the neoconservatives rejected the antiintellectual populism of the *völkisch* nationalists. Wyneken preached a revolution of *Geist*, but not as a means of promoting individual cultivation; rather, the notion was to generate a new elite of leaders and thereby inaugurate a new age in world history. His rhetoric of spiritual leadership intones the entire scale of neoconservative doctrines of genius and submission. Education, he insisted, must root out the obsolete superstition of the well-rounded, individual personality. Instead, it must aim at producing a new species of bearers of culture—the creative genius, the productive "hero of *Geist*." But since the objectivity of *Geist* calls for the submission of the subject, the genius must also learn "to allow truth to command him, that is, to submit himself to *Geist*." Thus, the creative genius must also be inculcated with the receptive ideal of service, as exemplified in the school community by free submission to self-chosen leaders. Wyneken proposed this synthesis of genius with the "aristocratic" virtue of unconditional loyalty as a counter to the democratization of the bourgeois ideal of personality, which he disparaged as a "despicable, ridiculous fiction—as if the sovereignty of the genius were everybody's property and goal."[21] Finally, as we have already seen, he cast the mission of this new spiritual elite as a new religiosity; the dawning of the new religion was portrayed in eschatalogical, almost chiliastic, terms. In the new age whose onset he claimed to glimpse, the created world itself would be redeemed: "The development of *Geist* is nature's rousing itself from the deep, deathly sleep of creation. He who serves *Geist*, who tends and enhances it, works along, as far as a worldly creature can, on the salvation of the world."[22]

Given all this, Wyneken's appeal to the radical wing of the youth movement may seem puzzling; but we must consider how his program was likely to appear to students like Bernfeld and Benjamin. First and foremost, Wyneken seemed to offer the most stringent, uncompromising guarantees of the autonomy of youth and youth culture, which he grounded in the absolute autonomy of objective *Geist*. Nor was he averse to couching these arguments in a purple rhetoric that must have flattered his young admirers: "The history of human culture has been the stations of the cross of youth."[23] Of course, each follower read this program somewhat selectively: for Bernfeld, its social and institutional

---

21 Ibid., 26–30.
22 Ibid., 10, 169.
23 Ibid., 33.

side—as exemplified by the free school community—was central; for Benjamin, the demand for an unconditional pursuit of intellectual culture free of any and all practicality—the idea of youth—was at the heart of the issue. In either case, Wyneken's conjunction of *Geist* and radical school reform seemed to provide a clear-cut, programmatic alternative to the Wandervogel. These issues of principle were reinforced by concrete political and tactical considerations: Wyneken's clashes with the school authorities had led him into a pragmatic alliance with political opposition groups, and he was known to be sympathetic to the progressive liberals and the Social Democrats, despite the worlds that separated his program from theirs. Finally, the sincerity of his personal commitment appeared beyond doubt; deprived of his license to teach, Wyneken seemed something of a martyr to his convictions. Few things promote unity more effectively than the consciousness of having common enemies—"reactionary officials and philistine parents," as Bernfeld later put it.[24] Thus, Wyneken's position was charged through and through with ideological ambiguities, ambiguities that were in turn absorbed and then confronted by his most ardent partisans—above all, by Walter Benjamin.

3. Wyneken's "Strict and Fanatical Pupil"

In the years before the war, Benjamin often stressed that the foundation of his intellectual identity, which was built on his engagement in the youth movement, was an unconditional devotion to Wyneken's program: "My thinking proceeds again and again from my first teacher, Wyneken, and always returns to him" (B 59). In 1912—he was already twenty-one years old—he unabashedly stressed that his identification was unqualified: his encounter with Wyneken, whose pupil he had been at the Landeserziehungsheim in Haubinda in 1905/6, had been his "decisive spiritual [*geistiges*] experience" (II 836); and he confessed that "on the school question . . . I have no positive views of my own but am the strict and fanatical pupil of G. Wyneken" (II 896). He signed his regular contributions to *Der Anfang* with the pseudonym Ardor and worked "in Wyneken's mission" to spread the word by setting up discussion groups to propagate his notions, first among fellow pupils at the Kaiser Friedrich Gymnasium in Berlin and later, as a student, at the universities in Berlin and Freiburg (B 52). In fact, in conceiving of youth as a harbinger of a radical renewal of *Geist*, he

---

[24] Siegfried Bernfeld, *Die Schulgemeinde und ihre Funktion im Klassenkampf*, cited in the editors' commentary in the *Gesammelte Schriften* (II 846).

stood closer to Wyneken's conception of youth culture than any other of his followers—including the editors of *Der Anfang* who, like Bernfeld, advocated concrete social engagement.[25] Not only did he adopt particular ideas and a certain elevated rhetorical tone from Wyneken; much more important, he also absorbed the ideological ambiguities of Wyneken's brand of idealism, and along with them a specific orientation in the intellectual field.

It was first and foremost in his diagnosis of a cultural crisis and the call for a renewal of idealism and *Geist* that the young Benjamin followed Wyneken's lead. Like Wyneken, he recast the orthodox mandarin lament so as to portray an autonomous youth culture as the sole locus of energies that could generate a general cultural revival. This idealistic diagnosis undergirded his definition of a new youth: "This steady, pulsating feeling for the abstractness of pure *Geist* is what I would like to call youth" (B 93). To Benjamin, *Geist*—"the necessity of the idea" (B 95)—was above all an ethical imperative: it required conscious, unconditional adherence to absolute values and principles for their own sake, as opposed to action on the basis of calculated interest or practical utility. Like Wyneken, he occasionally referred to Kant's doctrine of the ethical will, with its distinction between morality and legality, as the basis for this view (II 48); but it would be wrong to treat Benjamin's invocation of *Geist* as a formal, rigorously logical philosophical doctrine. Rather, by way of a broad system of affinities and analogies, it provided him with a series of demarcations on the issues that animated the youth movement.

For instance, Benjamin insisted that the demand for an autonomous youth culture and for school reform was not to be misunderstood as a commonplace social reform movement in the interest of a limited group; properly understood, it was an objective expression of the ethical situation of the age and as such stood above mere interests. For him, the imperatives of *Geist* utterly transcended those of politics, just as the idea represented a sphere of values that could never be reached by any calculated pursuit of what was merely useful. On the basis of this idealism, Benjamin argued relentlessly for a conception of education which—no doubt unwittingly—echoed many standard mandarin themes with astonishing faithfulness. True education, he insisted, must be kept clear of practical or vocational training of any sort; the universities must root out "that falsification of creative spirit [*Schöpfergeist*] into the spirit of profession [*Berufsgeist*], which we see at work everywhere" and overthrow "the secret reign of the professional idea" which was eating away at their substance (II 81, 83). Rather, education

---

25 Kupffer, *Gustav Wyneken*, 79.

must be "the propagation of spiritual values [*Fortpflanzung geistiger Werte*]" (II 13). Instead of promoting the pursuit of an "empty, general utility" (II 79), learning must aim to shape the totality of the learner and inculcate a certain kind of universality. This would redound to the benefit of learning as well, by restoring the totality of a metaphysical orientation to an academic culture that had been fragmented by narrow specialization; philosophy would be returned to its rightful place as the queen of the disciplines (II 81–83). The university itself must be restored to its rightful identity as a "community of creators," a "community of the knowing [*Erkennenden*]" (II 76). And the leaders of this regeneration must be youth, with their "steady, pulsating feeling for the abstractness of pure *Geist.*" In Benjamin's vision, students imbued with this spirit of youth culture were to serve as "the great transformer, which is to transmit the new ideas . . . into scholarly [*wissenschaftliche*] questions through a philosophical orientation" (II 83). Thus, Benjamin's diagnosis of the cultural crisis and his prescription for renewal, in their essential outlines, followed Wyneken's recasting of orthodox mandarin idealism in terms of an autonomous youth culture and youth leadership.

If the mission of youth was founded in its unique receptivity to the imperatives of *Geist,* then it was logical that Benjamin insist on the converse as well: only an undivided devotion to *Geist* could guarantee the autonomy of youth culture. His identification with Wyneken thus provided the touchstone for criticizing inauthentic currents within the youth movement. Benjamin was no uncritical enthusiast of youth; he found false, ineffectual, and even dangerous forms of opposition to the adult world to be all too pervasive in the German youth movement.

The first of these spurious advocates for youth were the Wandervogel, who, with their cult of nature and vitality, seem never to have held any fascination for Benjamin. His commentary on the Meißner festival, published in *Die Aktion,* scathingly criticized the chauvinistic atmosphere and anti-Semitic incidents for which certain of the Wandervogel contingents and their adult sympathizers had been responsible. The charge Benjamin leveled at them, however, was not very illuminating at first sight: their chauvinism lacked "youthfulness," because "hiking, festive garments, and folk dances are not the last word and—in 1913—still nothing spiritual [*Geistiges*]"; he reduced his dissatisfaction with the Meißner festival to the polemical formula "youth was silent" (II 67–68). He seems not to have taken the Wandervogel seriously enough to argue against them directly, but in other contexts he made clear what disturbed him. Benjamin was profoundly suspicious of what he once called "unmastered natural forces" (II 84). This was more than just a city child's indifference toward nature: he went so far as to assert that "a horror of nature is the test of a true sense for nature. He who feels no horror for nature has no idea what to make of it" (B 83). Interestingly, he credited the romantics with having discovered "the night-side of nature: it is not basically good; it is strange, dreadful, terrible, loathsome—vile" (II 22). It may not be possible to explain this revulsion any further than to point out that it was the obverse of his reverence for *Geist:* reaching, as he so often did, for a religious idiom, he even spoke of "the deadly sin of making *Geist* natural" (II 32); vitalism violated the "strictly dualistic conception" of *Geist* and nature (II 837). Benjamin had an acute sense of the demonic in nature, a feeling that natural forces would somehow wreak vengeance on those who either failed to acknowledge the heteronomy of nature and *Geist* or submitted to the power of inauthentic conventions. To him, the Wandervogel's cult of nature and male camaraderie was a narcotic that enabled them to remain oblivious to the solitude and isolation they might be forced into by an honest, direct confrontation with the adult world. It was an inauthentic attempt to maintain the fiction of youthful innocence: "The greatest obstacle today's youth must overcome [is] its assessment as—an animal, that is, a remorseless innocent, driven by instinct" (B 86–88). Benjamin saw this false innocence as far more than irresponsibility: the vitalism of the Wandervogel courted the retribution of forces whose demonic power was being denied.

Nevertheless, Benjamin's deep-seated rejection of the Wandervogel did not dispose him to make common cause with his neighbors in the radical wing of the youth movement, the advocates of social engagement so influential on the editorial board of *Der Anfang* and among the leaders of the Freie Studentenschaft in Berlin. On the contrary, he took them seriously enough to carry on a running polemic against them. His political sympathies in these years lay somewhere between left liberalism and social democracy, but this—like politics itself—represented only "the choice of the lesser evil" (II 842–843). Benjamin's decisive objection to orienting youth culture and student life toward practical social engagement was that the "totality of the will finds no expression" in it; the "authenticity [*Ursprünglichkeit*]" (II 61) of the person was necessarily rent asunder by the instrumental pursuit of calculated interests. Purposive-rational action, in his view, reduced humanity to "a working machine for ends, each of which is always conditioned by another in an endless series," resulting in "the degradation of all work into something technical" (II 20). He applied this argument to social engagement in particular, which to his way of thinking "serves, for the average person, as a repression of the authentic and undiverted strivings of the inner person" (II 78–79). He often seemed to limit this objection to youth, as the period of life in which the striving for *Geist* could find its purest expression; but at times he broadened the case to human nature as such, demanding "a break with the degrading lie that man can achieve perfect fulfillment in the service of society—as if society, in which we do indeed live, were the ultimate determinant of the person" (II 25–26).

Once again, Benjamin leveled what he took to be his most devastating charge at his opponents—"unyouthfulness." "The symptomatic significance of the ventures of the Independent Students, the Christian Social groups, and many others, is that they reproduce the discord between the university and the state as a whole microcosmically within the university" (II 79). Student social engagement, as a kind of training in instrumental, purposive-rational action, unwittingly reproduced the university's own falsification of *Geist* in attempting to mix vocational training with the pursuit of *Wissenschaft*; and student politics, too, necessarily "strays onto the smoothed course of liberal politics . . . towed along by public opinion, the flattered and spoiled child of the parties and associations." Benjamin's polemic climaxed in the provocative charge that "progressive" free students, by "laying claim to the reputation of fighters and liberators in university life," were actually "almost more dangerous than the fraternities, because more deceptive and misleading" (II 80). He castigated the activists, as he did the Wandervogel, as perpetrators of a mendacious, inauthentic compromise, the victims of bad faith: "Social work . . . is not the ethical heightening of a spiritual [*geistiges*] life but a fearful reaction to it," a flight into "empty general utility" and a "mechanical" feeling of duty (II 78).

Benjamin allowed one qualification of his argument: social work could indeed engage the totality of the person, but only if pursued in the "Tolstoyan spirit," "the truly serious spirit of social work that arose in the ideas of the profoundest of anarchists and in the Christian monastic communities." Such a utopian all-or-nothing commitment, however, was irreconcilable with youth and student life, which called for an undivided pursuit of *Geist*. Social engagement as a part-time occupation for students could end only as a grotesque and unwitting rehearsal for the duplicity of adult life, with its dishonest compromise between feelings of duty and the pursuit of self-interest. For youth, only an unconditional pursuit of *Geist* could produce "the deepest bond between profession and life—to be sure, a deeper life" (II 82).

Benjamin's devotion to Wyneken's program was strong enough to channel his sense of Jewish identity as well. In 1912 his letters referred to discussions of political and cultural Zionism "as a possibility and perhaps as a duty" (B 44), and the issue was forced when an acquaintance, Ludwig Strauß, wrote to solicit his help in founding a journal devoted to German-Jewish culture.[26] Benjamin rejected the approach, stressing that his "decisive spiritual experience" had been his encounter with Wyneken while a pupil at Haubinda, before the issue of his Jewishness became "important or problematic," and that he saw no room for two formative commitments in his life (II 836–837). The universalism of his orientation foreclosed any path to cultural particularism: "For me Judaism is in no way an end in itself but rather a most eminent bearer and representative of *Geist*" (II 839).[27] He could only regard nationalism as "a dangerous force of inertia." The only form of Zionism accessible to him was a "culture-Zionism, which sees Jewish values *everywhere*," including in non-Jewish cultures, "and works for them"; European culture would find itself in a sorry state if the Jews withdrew their energies from it (II 838). But any identification with Zionism at the time was also blocked by the particular form in which it presented itself. Strauß was devoted to Buber's vision of Judaism, whose vitalism was deeply suspect to Benjamin. Buber's mystical philosophy of a primordial Jewish experience (*Erlebnis*) appeared to him a dangerous surrender to demonic, natural forces.[28] He saw evidence of its inability to produce a binding cultural impulse in the failings of the Blau-Weiss variety of Zionism; in most Zionist students he had encountered, "the Jewish was a natural impulse, Zionism a matter of political organization. The inner core of their personality was by no means determined by Jewishness: they propagate Palestine and drink like Germans. . . . they least of all may speak of the Jewish experience" (II 838). Yet Benjamin conceded to Strauß the relevance of his Jewish identity. He noted that those who were working for the Wickersdorf idea with the most genuine devotion were "for the most part Jews."[29] And although he asserted that he could best express his Jewishness through his devotion to Wyneken's ideas, at the same time he had no assimilationist illusions and affirmed his sense of cultural difference: "I am a Jew and if I live as a conscious human being, then as a conscious

[26] Anson Rabinbach explores the background to Strauß's request and provides a sensitive, extended reading of the correspondence in "Between Enlightenment and Apocalypse: Benjamin, Bloch, and Modern German Jewish Messianism," 88–99. He rightly stresses that Benjamin had already formed a clear attitude toward Jewish issues by 1912, three years before meeting Scholem.

[27] Benjamin also insisted that it was illegitimate in principle "ever to limit the concept of culture to any *part* of humanity" and alluded to a tension between this ideal and Wyneken's conception of an aristocracy of *Geist* (II 840–841). This tension was to play a crucial role in his disillusionment with Wyneken.

[28] See Scholem, *Walter Benjamin*, 42. In conversation at the time, Benjamin parodied Buber's philosophy by reducing it to the question "Have you had the Jewish experience yet?"

[29] In fact, Benjamin noted, "I am extraordinarily glad when I encounter a German in matters of *Geist*" (II 839).

Jew" (II 837).[30] Before the war, then, Benjamin assessed the possibilities of his Jewish identity through the lens of his orientation within the youth movement. But if his solution was clear for the moment, it
was also liable to become unstable should his commitment to Wyneken's program be called into question.

Idealism as the touchstone for the mission of an autonomous youth
culture; a distaste for populist, antiintellectual vitalism; a deep-seated
distrust of instrumental action and politics: in all these respects, Benjamin's early orientation bore the stamp of Wyneken's variations on
mandarin orthodoxy. And just like Wyneken, where Benjamin did
overstep the bounds of the orthodox rhetoric of cultural crisis, he often
verged toward the idealist variety of neoconservatism. His insistence
on the absolute irreconcilability of *Geist* and convention, of the idea
and practicality, shared much of Wyneken's profound hostility to the
official institutions of the German empire. In itself, this hostility was
compatible with a broad range of ideological tendencies; but Benjamin
inclined to place it in the service of a quasi-religious will to decision as
the fulcrum for establishing new values. His polemic against the humanistic gymnasium was a case in point. He began from a rather
standard orthodox attack on the modernist justification of the classical
curriculum in terms of its utility for future professional life; instead, he
affirmed that the conception of the classical gymnasium might suit the
autonomy of youth culture insofar as it "has maintained a noble composure and been spared the Darwinistic frenzy of purpose that otherwise afflicts our pedagogy." But he then went on to denounce
orthodox, idealist classicism itself as "washed-out humanism." Disparaging its facile portrayal of classical Greek culture as "a fabled realm
of 'harmonies' and 'ideals'," he jeered at "the intimacy of philistinism
and the humanistic gymnasium," whose end result was "the
phlegmatic sentimentality with which, forty years later, the first verses
of the *Odyssey* are intoned at the dinner table (between the fish and the
roast)." Invoking Nietzsche, Benjamin demanded that pupils be confronted instead with "the misogynistic, homophilic, aristocratic Greek
culture of Pericles; with slavery; and with the dark myths of
Aeschylus" (II 40).

He was not very specific about what appealed to him in Nietzsche's
reading of antiquity; at the very least, it was Nietzsche's protest against
the tendency toward moral complacency in German hellenism. In another context, Benjamin called German classicism a "symptom of reaction": whereas Kant had "torn open the abyss between the senses and

[30] Benjamin remained acutely aware of these differences even with those Germans
with whom he felt the closest intellectual kinship, as in his relationship with Florens
Christian Rang; see Bernd Witte, *Walter Benjamin*, 52–53.

reason" in order to demonstrate the autonomy of the ethical will, "what did classicism do? It reunited *Geist* and nature . . . and created the unity that can only be a unity of the moment, of ecstasy, of the great seer. . . . It cannot become the basis of life but only its aesthetic climax" (II 32). The attempt to embody absolute values in stabilized, harmonious forms must end by compromising the inviolable autonomy of the ethical will. But what lay at the root of this autonomy? Benjamin never invoked the Nietzschean doctrine of will in so many words, but at times he came very close indeed. In a cryptic piece titled "The Religious Position of the New Youth" (1914), he declared the hallmark of the new youth to be its religious urge toward "the decisive either/or," "the holy decision":

> *A generation wants once again to stand at the parting of the ways, but nowhere is there a crossroads.* Youth has always had to choose, but the objects of its choice were determined for it. The new youth stands before the chaos in which the objects of its choice (the holy objects) are vanishing. . . . it desires nothing more urgently than the choice, the possibility of choice, the holy decision as such. The choice creates its own objects—this is youth's most religious knowledge. . . . It trusts that what is holy and what is damned will reveal themselves in the moment when its common will to choice has tensed itself to the highest pitch. (II 73)

We know that Benjamin read Kierkegaard's *Either/Or* in these years (B 47), as the quasi-religious idiom here suggests; but the oracular tone he strives for points unmistakably to Nietzsche: the vision of the chaos of a world of devalued values; the notion that a will to decision can provide the Archimedean fulcrum for establishing new ethical values; and the pseudo-religious trust that unconditional standards—"the holy and the damned"—will reveal themselves in the moment of choice. It was not the biologistic popularization of Nietzsche but Nietzsche's own pathos of the urge for decision that attracted Benjamin.[31] "Nowhere is a Zarathustra-mood—it can be overstrained, as far as I'm concerned—more needed than in a mature and self-assured student," Benjamin noted in one of his letters to Strauß (II 841).

Benjamin propounded the rhetoric of a new religiosity with incomparably greater fervor than his mentor, Wyneken. In effect, Benjamin's notion of religiosity was a variation on his idea of youth: religiosity meant "to submit oneself to a principle, to permeate oneself with the idea" (II 76) in fervent expectation of the imminent irruption of a new

---

[31] Martin Greiffenhagen argues that decisionism was one of the hallmarks of German radical conservatism in *Das Dilemma des Konservatismus in Deutschland*, 249.

era. "Youth that professes itself to itself *means* religion, which as yet is not" (II 73). It was on the theme of the new religiosity that Benjamin's departures from the humanistic conception of *Bildung* were most dramatic. *Geist* did not serve to promote, amplify, and secure human autonomy; on the contrary, humanity was to serve the autonomy of *Geist*. In his "Dialogue on the Religiosity of the Present" (1912), Benjamin had his protagonist profess "a horror of the image of ethical autonomy" conjured up by his interlocutor. He equated humanism with pantheism as "incarnations of the aestheticist view of life" which are "incapable of determining the ethical life" (II 20–22). In a letter from 1913, he drove the point home with an arresting twist on the image of prostitution:

> "Either all are prostitutes or none are." . . . I say: we all are. Or we should be. We should be things and objects in the face of culture. Truly: if we wish to preserve some sort of private dignity of personality, then we will never understand the prostitute. But if we ourselves perceive all our humanity as an abandonment to *Geist* and tolerate no private disposition, no private will and spirit—then we will honor the prostitute. (B 67)

Here—and not for the last time—he employed the image of the prostitute as an allegory of objectification, inverting it to evoke the positive ideal of a dispersal of subjectivity.[32] Finally, for Benjamin, the new religiosity was also bound up with a specific mode of temporal awareness, a sense that the present is pregnant with the tasks of the future. "Only occasionally have individuals and peoples been struck by the illumination that they stand in the service of an unknown future, and it might well be plausible to characterize such illumination as historical sense. . . . We will never understand the past unless we will the future" (II 56, 59). Historical sense, he asserted, was not resignation to the inevitable course of things but the experience of crisis and a keen expectation of a historical caesura; and religious submission did not mean bowing to the present order but straining the anticipation of future tasks "to the highest pitch."

Benjamin's oracular pathos of "the coming" cast him into an ideologically ambiguous company, where the tone was set by the prewar neoconservatives. It was no anomaly that a piece like "The Religious Position of the New Youth" was published in *Die Tat*, which was mak-

---

[32] Christine Buci-Glucksmann explores Benjamin's images of women as allegories of modernity in the "Arcades" project and the Baudelaire essays in "Catastrophic Utopia: The Feminine as Allegory of the Modern." A more critical view is proposed by Rey Chow, "Walter Benjamin's Love Affair with Death."

ing a name for itself as the organ for neoconservative ideologists of all stripes.[33] This is not to say that Benjamin was a neoconservative in any simple sense. But he shared many of their gestures; he might well have been taken for one; and, most important, he could not yet state with any clarity what distinguished him from them. Indeed, in "The Religious Position of the New Youth" he said as much: "The unfree will always be able to show us the canon of their laws. But we will not yet be able to name the law under which we stand" (II 60). This was a perilous concession, given his ardent assurances that, whatever the canon, its imperatives would be unconditional and would leave no room for reservations. It was this latent ideological ambiguity with which Benjamin's heritage from Wyneken was freighted—and the particular constellation of that ambiguity—that were to prove significant.

4. Growing Estrangement

Benjamin was forced into a painful awareness of these ambiguities by the shock of events when war was declared in August 1914. He did not hesitate long in deciding that the war fever sweeping across Europe had nothing to do with the triumph of *Geist* over calculated self-interest; unlike so many who spoke the language of German idealism, he proved to be immune to what were known at the time as the "ideas of 1914." His own account in his *Berlin Chronicle*, composed in 1932, portrays these events as if the war suddenly jolted him into a rude awakening from youthful illusions. Though he had joined in the "storm of volunteers" who sought to enlist in the first days of the war, he had done so "without a spark of war fever in my heart . . . but only to secure a place among friends in the inevitable conscription" (VI 481). Whatever his initial motives, he was soon forced to face the personal consequences of the war, even without going to the front: on August 8, two friends committed suicide in the meeting rooms of the Berlin *Sprechsaal*, in a helpless gesture of protest against the war. One of them, the young poet Fritz Heinle, had been Benjamin's most intimate friend; the other, Rika Seligson, was the youngest sister of Carla Seligson, to whom Benjamin had addressed his most moving, revealing letters on the youth movement during the previous two years. The extraordinary power of Benjamin's relationship to Heinle is difficult to

---

[33] It should be noted, however, that under Eugen Diedrichs *Die Tat* also remained open to other viewpoints until late in the 1920s; see Gary D. Stark, *Entrepreneurs of Ideology: Neoconservative Publishers in Germany, 1890–1933*, 15–19, 58–110.

explain.[34] But Heinle's suicide precipitated the end of Benjamin's engagement in the youth movement. The shock was quite literally traumatic: his mourning spread into an emotional blackout during which even his "closest relations, apart from my marriage, became shadows" (B 157). "Months followed, of which I no longer know anything" (II 623), in the wake of which he refused to discuss the people and events involved. This reserve took on the dimensions of a strict taboo. According to Scholem, who made his acquaintance during this time, Benjamin thereafter referred to Heinle only as "my friend," never by name, and severed contacts with former friends and associates with "a personal radicalism, indeed, personal ruthlessness," that injured many of them.[35] By 1918, he could assert that "they no longer exist for me" (B 200).

The traumatic experiences of 1914 undoubtedly had consequences for Benjamin's entire intellectual identity. But just what did he find himself forced to realize? Here too, the *Berlin Chronicle* offers a neat and simple account: the futility of Heinle's gesture had opened his eyes to the impotence of the youth movement and the narrow limits set to its protest; the implication was that after 1914 he had simply severed his ties to the past (VI 478–480). Yet, on closer inspection, the evidence suggests that Benjamin's response was considerably more complex and differentiated than he himself was later prepared to recognize.

The most telling clues to how he actually went about settling accounts with the experiences of the youth movement can be found in a dramatic letter to Wyneken of March 9, 1915, in which he formally severed his relationship to his mentor. Particularly painful to him in the first months of the war—although hardly surprising to us in retrospect—was the fact that Wyneken too had joined in the chorus of prowar jubilation. In his letter, Benjamin took great pains to stress that he now felt forced to disavow Wyneken in order to affirm his loyalty to what he thought Wyneken had once stood for. Wyneken, as "the bearer of an idea," had enabled him to experience how "*Geist*, entirely

---

[34] Benjamin's references to Heinle in his letters are somewhat opaque. Eloquent testimony to the significance of the relationship for Benjamin lies in his composition of seventy-three sonnets to his dead friend (VII 27–64). These were important enough to him that when he was forced to flee Paris in 1940 he entrusted them, along with the manuscripts for the "Arcades" project, to Bataille for safekeeping in the Bibliothèque Nationale (VII 525–526, 568–569). On the sonnets, see Bernhild Boie, "Dichtung als Ritual der Erlösung: Zu den wiedergefundenen Sonetten von Walter Benjamin."

[35] Scholem, *Walter Benjamin*, 19; Scholem, "Walter Benjamin" in Adorno et al., *Über Walter Benjamin*, 134. See also the bitter reminiscences of Herbert Belmore, one of the rejected friends, in Herbert W. Belmore, "Walter Benjamin." Belmore and Carla Seligson married soon thereafter; she too seems to have been cut off by Benjamin.

alone and unconditionally, can be binding for living human beings"; as one of "an elect in these times," he had been "allowed to experience what leadership is." But now Wyneken had sacrificed his own best principles. Benjamin singled out two offenses he found particularly galling. He reminded Wyneken of his own words on coeducation, according to which the memory of a common experience of *Geist* in youth would provide "the strongest counterweight to the social struggle of the sexes" in adult life; but in sanctioning the war, Wyneken had committed the "dreadful, vile betrayal of the women who love your pupils." And he pointed out the beneficiary of this betrayal, the state. Wyneken himself had suffered at the hands of the state, having been forced to leave his experimental school at Wickersdorf when deprived of his license to teach. Thus, the bitterest irony was that in betraying youth he was quite literally betraying himself: "You have ended by sacrificing youth to the state, which has taken everything from you" (B 121–122). Had Benjamin really somehow managed to overlook the implications of Wyneken's ode to objective *Geist*, which foresaw and even sanctified the sacrifice of youth to the state? In any case, he took the position of having to profess his loyalty to Wyneken's idea by defying him. In closing, he underlined this point by laying claim to the legacy of the idea of youth: "Youth belongs only to the seers who love it, and in it the idea above all. It has fallen from your erring hands and will go on suffering unspeakably. To live with it is the legacy I wrest from you" (B 122). As these lines make clear, Benjamin responded as one who had been not deceived, but betrayed.

This stance gave him the rhetorical weapon with which to deliver an especially cutting rebuke. It enabled him to assign responsibility for the break to Wyneken himself, accusing him not only of treason but of self-betrayal as well. Yet it would certainly be wrong to regard this letter as only a verbal gesture, or as an attempt to save face when confronted with the collapse of his personal and intellectual commitments. For behind these formulations was a genuine insight with far-reaching consequences. The wave of idealistic war fever forced Benjamin to realize that Wyneken's call for a renewal of *Geist*, and the intellectual identity he himself had built on it, was burdened with fatal ambiguities. The rhetoric of German idealism, he discovered, lent itself all too easily to the sophistry of the "ideas of 1914"; as long as he went on speaking it so uncritically, he would be prevented from articulating what distinguished his intentions from those of the war enthusiasts. Yet he responded by posing as the lone defender of betrayed ideals, not by renouncing the substance of his former loyalties. He chose not to repudiate his idealism but to vindicate it. This was the narrow ground he set out to defend in the autumn and winter of 1914.

In fact, it was a choice that had long been in the making. The grounds for Benjamin's break with the youth movement and his renunciation of Wyneken had been prepared much more gradually than events at the beginning of the war might suggest. The war certainly precipitated the break, but the underlying causes of his estrangement went farther back. After all, his identification with Wyneken had placed him in an idiosyncratic, isolated position within the youth movement from the very beginning; he had long since grown used to defending isolated outposts. By 1914, he had begun to doubt the integrity of Wyneken's formulations as well, but he was still grasping to specify the sources of his discomfort. In retrospect, we can make out a series of developments that had made Benjamin's position within the youth movement increasingly untenable.

First of all, in the spring and summer of 1914 he was becoming increasingly disillusioned about the possibility of working within any of the established organizations of the youth movement. The radicals had been expelled from the Freideutsche Jugend, and Benjamin, in turn, found himself increasingly isolated from the radicals. Personal animosities, along with the vehemence of his rejection of social engagement, led to a series of unruly disputes and schisms in the Berlin *Sprechsaal*. In July 1914 he announced that he would no longer contribute to *Der Anfang* and spoke of the "Berlin chaos" as a "great swamp out of which . . . nothing living blooms any more" (B 112, 117). The only organization he still hoped to convert to his cause was the Freie Studentenschaft in Berlin, which had just elected him as its president. But here too his sense of isolation was growing rapidly, and it is not hard to see why. In his inaugural address, which he later adapted into the published text of "The Life of Students," he made a characteristically idealist attempt to stake out a position above the conventional conflict of parties, in this case between responsible, engaged progressives and debauched Corps students. But the peremptory tone in which he leveled the provocative charge that the independents had usurped the claim to autonomy was hardly calculated to win him supporters. It is not surprising that, according to his own report, the lectures he organized drew few listeners, of whom few were students (B 108). Having exhausted the possibility of working within the available forums, one after another, he had good reason to complain that he found himself "apart from the stabilized course of the youth movement" (B 113). Quite clearly, the tensions between Benjamin and the youth movement had already been strained to the breaking point by the outbreak of war.

These tensions found expression in a new tone that was beginning to surface in his writings. His letters to Carla Seligson in particular show a melancholy preoccupation with the idea of solitude as the true form of a "new youthfulness." Wyneken had placed great emphasis on the idea that the individual personality was a fetish to be overcome in a new form of community. Though Benjamin was (and remained) equally dubious of individualism, he now began to deny that community could be an end in itself; instead, he spoke of a "new solitude" in the face of the idea, which was to be expected as the true fruit of even "a perfect community." The goal of the youth movement could not be to obliterate solitude but to "deepen" it (B 86–88). "I am thinking (not socialistically, but in some other sense) of the multitude of the excluded and of *Geist*, which is in league with the sleeping" (B 95). He found it difficult to assign such sentiments a definite content and at one point even apologized for "responding to a simple question with metaphysics." In the context of events, however, these statements reflect an attempt to come to terms with the sense of isolation produced by an awareness that he would not sacrifice his conscience for the sake of strengthening his impact on the movement. The overstrained rhetoric of "The Religious Position of the New Youth," his last publication before the war, must also be read in this light. The "distress" of youth, with its desperate cry for "decision" in the face of "chaos," is exacerbated by the unavailability of dependable objects of choice. Youth "trusts that what is holy and what is damned will reveal themselves in the moment when its common will to choice has tensed itself to the highest pitch. . . . And yet: it may not give itself entirely to anyone, must never find what is within it entirely in the hero it honors or the woman it loves. For the relationship of the hero and the beloved to what is ultimate, essential—to what is holy—is dark and uncertain" (II 73–74). The pathos of these lines expresses Benjamin's own increasingly painful, almost desperate sense of isolation. He was even beginning to be plagued by a sense that his own words spun out of his control whenever he attempted to intervene in the public debates of the youth movement. "Chaotic" discussions in "unappreciative and unprepared circles" were becoming ever more burdensome to him; the issues were becoming "muddled, as does everything that gets caught up in the dreadful public discourse these days" (B 110). The only adequate response he could find was to withdraw from such discourse: "My silence is the only thing by which my friends recognize me," he reported in a letter of July 17, 1914 (B 117).

Equally important, if far less conspicuous, was a mounting disillusionment with Wyneken. The cooling had several sources. In the debates of the youth movement, Benjamin was repeatedly forced to answer the charge that his partisanship for Wyneken's ideas was precisely the kind of partial interest he was constantly at pains to deplore. He

regarded this accusation as a misunderstanding, but it was nevertheless irksome because it undercut one of his favorite "idealistic" rhetorical maneuvers—to place himself above "the embittered struggle of all
against all . . . each decorated with a party flag" (II 14); instead, he
found himself tarred with his own brush. In many ways, however, it
was Wyneken himself and not just Benjamin's style of advocacy that let
him in for such treatment. Wyneken's ambition of setting himself up as
a leader of the youth movement was arousing suspicion; Wyneken too,
and not just Benjamin's opponents, "misunderstood" his idea as a
movement. Partly as a result, Benjamin was growing increasingly reluctant to commit himself to any particular specification of *Geist:* "We
must not bind ourselves to a fixed idea; precisely for us, the idea of
youth culture should be only the illumination that draws the most
distant spirit into the shining light. But for many, Wyneken too, along
with the *Sprechsaal*, will be a 'movement'; they will have bound themselves and will no longer see *Geist* where it appears yet freer, more
abstract" (B 93). Not even the idea of youth culture was sacrosanct to
Benjamin if it showed signs of hardening into a fetter on the "steady,
pulsating feeling for the abstractness of pure *Geist*." To be sure, the
tendency to shed off past incarnations of his ideals went along naturally with the fact that Benjamin was, quite simply, continuing to grow
up. In a letter written to Carla Seligson a week before his twenty-first
birthday, he began a reflection on the theme of solitude with the question, "How are we to save *ourselves* from the experience of our twenties?" (B 71). Clearly, the limits of his own youth were beginning to
dawn on him. His inaugural address before the Berlin Freie Studentenschaft, delivered in the following spring, showed the kind of consequences he had begun to draw. No longer did the idea of youth as such
stand at the center of his program. Instead, he translated it into the
idea of the university as a "community of the knowing" divorced from
utilitarian pursuits; youth, as represented by the student, now func-
tioned as the "transformer" that was to infuse learning with *Geist*. *Geist*
now appeared "freer, more abstract" to him in the ideal form of the
university, and this was bound to confirm his sense of Wyneken's
limits.

But the trouble went beyond Wyneken's limitations. There was also
a great deal about his version of the doctrine of objective *Geist* that was
beginning to arouse Benjamin's suspicion, although his criticisms were
veiled and indirect at first. One of the central problems was the role the
state might play in a renewal of idealism. Wyneken equivocated on this
point: although in principle the state, like everything else, was "only a
tool" for the self-realization of *Geist*, in fact it might often turn out to be
the best incarnation of the objective ethical will. Such slippages were

no idiosyncrasy of Wyneken's; they had been characteristic of the German idealist tradition since its origins. Benjamin, however, steadfastly refused to play with such equivocations. On the contrary: when castigating the university's compromises with practicality and vocational training, he took particularly careful aim at the state:[36]

> So little does a profession follow from learning [*Wissenschaft*] that learning can even exclude one. For it is in the nature of learning to tolerate no detachment from itself; it never obligates the researcher, who in a certain sense is always a teacher, to the state's forms of profession as doctor, lawyer, or university instructor. . . . Those to whom the present-day state is the given, for whom everything is included in its line of development, must reject this; but let them not dare to demand the protection and support of "learning" from the state. For it is not the understanding between the institution of the university and the state—an understanding quite compatible with an upright barbarism—which bespeaks depravity, but rather the guarantee and the doctrine of the freedom of learning which is then after all expected, with a brutal matter-of-factness, to lead its disciples toward social individuality and service to the state. (II 76–77)

This impassioned, almost unworldly defense of the pure idea of learning against any form of service to the state whatsoever makes sense only if we heed its willfully anachronistic tone. The German *Bildungsbürgertum* had made a long series of compromises with the Prussian state and its system of bureaucratic absolutism since the turn of the nineteenth century; in effect, Benjamin was calling for nothing less than a revocation of these compromises. In its original formulations, the German neohumanists' and idealists' plea for the ennobling influence of self-cultivation had a decidedly emancipatory and universalistic cast. But this utopian potential was then increasingly compromised in the course of the nineteenth century, as the conception of *Bildung* degenerated into an ideological defense of the privileges and interests of the *Bildungsbürgertum*, acquiring a strong statist bias in the process.[37] Benjamin's immunity to this ideological drift need not be mystified, however. He acquired his critical leverage by taking idealism at its word, in an appeal to the tradition's own latent utopian re-

---

[36] In these years, Benjamin always contrasted the sheer impracticality and disinterestedness of pure learning with the state, and never with capitalism or commercialism. Here too he differed from the orthodox mandarin idealists. But this also means that to characterize his idea of youth as a form of romantic anticapitalism would be misleading.

[37] On the historical background of this drift from utopia to ideology, see Ringer, *Decline of the German Mandarins*, 15–25, 102–127.

sources—in his own words, to the idea of learning "as it lay in the spirit of the founders" of the University of Berlin (II 81).[38] His keen awareness of the tendencies that had hollowed out the idealist tradition from within served to intensify the shock when Wyneken too caved in to them at the outbreak of the war. Hence the understated bitterness with which he accused Wyneken of selling out youth to the state: where Wyneken had equivocated—with fatal consequences—Benjamin was most uncompromising.

The statist drift in German idealism was not all that bothered Benjamin; in fact, he seems to have overlooked Wyneken's entanglement in it until it was too late. What preoccupied him all the more were the ominous overtones he began to hear in Wyneken's elitism and his talk of serving *Geist*. As we have seen, much of the *unorthodox*, neoconservative element in Wyneken's program involved his portrayal of the youth movement as the proving ground for a *new* elite of leaders and bearers of culture. Once again, Benjamin's gnawing doubts found an outlet in his correspondence with Carla Seligson. His letter of September 15, 1913, in particular is replete with veiled, perhaps unconscious allusions to Wyneken's formulations. Here Benjamin traced the dismaying factionalism and partisanship in the youth movement to the presumption that *Geist* would realize itself in particular, readily identifiable forms. The surest antidote to this presumptuousness, he now proposed, was a radical reversal of such notions: *Geist* may manifest itself "in every person and in the most remote thoughts. . . . every person, every soul that is born can bring the new actuality." Such observations made an emphatic appeal to the spirit of pietistic utopianism that had fed the idealist tradition in its formative stage. And in accord with this spirit, he attempted to redefine the proper attitude toward *Geist:* "Being young means not so much to serve *Geist* as to expect it" (B 92–93). If one could never be sure of where and how *Geist* would irrupt into the given order of things, then there could be nothing to serve; consequently, the only permissible attitude was that of fervent expectation and attentiveness to the signs of its approach. He now referred to this as a "messianic" sense.[39] He did not say so ex-

[38] In particular, Benjamin reports having read Fichte's "Deducierter Plan einer in Berlin zu errichtenden höhern Lehranstalt"—"his bold meditation on the founding of the University of Berlin"—as well as Nietzsche's "On the Future of Our Educational Institutions" in preparation for the address (B 107).

[39] This seems to be the first context in which the term "messianic" appears in Benjamin's writings. The explicit reference is to a tract by the left-wing expressionist intellectual Victor Hueber, *Organisierung der Intelligenz*. Hueber was associated with the circle around Franz Pfemfert, publisher of *Der Anfang*.

plicitly, but "service" was among Wyneken's catchwords—"the fundamental axiom of all human action should be: serve *Geist*," as he had put it. The impression that Benjamin was at least subconsciously aware of this usage seems confirmed by the further twist on Wyneken's terminology that immediately followed. Whereas Wyneken had proposed the free school community as the "geometric locus" where *Geist* realized itself, Benjamin deplored even the slightest hint of an institutional fixation: "Almost all forget that *they themselves* are the locus where *Geist* realizes itself. . . . they make themselves rigid, into pillars of a building instead of vessels, hulls that can receive and hold an ever purer content" (B 93). It was in this context that Benjamin proposed his definition of youth as a "steady, pulsating feeling for the abstractness of pure *Geist*" in an attempt to fight off false, premature fixations of the idea which exalt means into ends. One must distinguish carefully among the variety of registers in Benjamin's rhetoric of a new religiosity: though it sometimes rings with the ominous intolerance of the demand for a "holy decision," at others it modulates into a fervent, expectant, and inclusive universalism. In the former mode, Benjamin was prone to lapse into uncritical mimicry of Wyneken's pseudo-prophetic posing; in the latter, however, there were the nascent elements of a perceptive critique of Wyneken and, by implication, of the perilous ambiguities of the decaying idealistic tradition behind him.

We are now in a better position to see what Benjamin meant in laying claim to the legacy he accused Wyneken of having sold out. He had come to realize that he could vindicate and sustain his own idealist commitments only by recasting that idealism so as to make such equivocations and slippages impossible. This process had begun before August 1914, and from *within* the idealist stance. As late as July 1914 he was still trying to temporize by explaining away Wyneken's shortcomings. "The years of pedagogical inactivity have damaged him extraordinarily," he wrote to Ernst Schoen; "I recognized it by how little he is up to the strain of the forms the movement is taking on in Berlin." At most, Benjamin managed to bring himself to suggest that, although Wyneken "was—perhaps still is—a great educator," nevertheless "his theory falls far short of his vision." He found that not only the reasoning was askew in Wyneken's doctrine of objective *Geist* but something more as well—only he could not yet say just what (B 110). Benjamin had not yet reached the point of coming out openly against Wyneken, not even to himself, but he was unmistakably headed in that direction. The outbreak of the war was indeed a rupture in Benjamin's development, but only in the sense that it abruptly culminated a process that was already under way.

5. The Break with the Youth Movement

Benjamin's reflections on the collapse of the movement to which he had committed his youth crystallized in the remarkable preamble he added to "The Life of Students" for its publication during the war. The very fact that he had the address published as the body of the text—not just once, but twice—is significant in itself: by reiterating his idealist conceptions of learning and the university, he affirmed his claim to the legacy he had sworn to wrest from Wyneken and asserted the continuity of his intentions.[40] But the preamble now embeds this idealism within a new framework. It sets a cautionary signal at the opening of the text: the following remarks are to be understood "only as a likeness, an image of a highest, metaphysical state of history"; youth culture, the life of students, the idea of learning, the university as a "community of the knowing"—these are not to be taken for the chosen agencies of objective *Geist*. To prevent such slippages, he heightens and radicalizes the idealist distinction between the given and the absolute. The idiom of objective *Geist* vanishes from his work, never to return; in its place he sets the notion of a "final state [*Endzustand*] of history, the messianic realm. The elements of this final state, he cautions, do not lie in the conspicuous, stabilized, and exalted phenomena of any given era

> but rather are deeply embedded in every present as the most endangered, most defamed and derided creations and thoughts. To form the immanent state of perfection into one utterly absolute, to make it visible and dominant in the present is the historical task. But this state of things is not to be circumscribed by a pragmatic depiction of particulars (institutions, customs, and so on); on the contrary, it eludes such portrayal. It can be caught hold of only in its metaphysical structure, as in the messianic realm or the French idea of revolution. (II 75)

The task of uncovering and realizing the immanent state of perfection, which is endangered and lies deeply embedded in the present state of things, is no longer assigned to a movement but to critique. Critique gathers historical forces and concentrates their energies in a focal point (*Brennpunkt*), a utopian image, in order to ignite "the crisis . . . that leads to a decision." It also receives a temporal inflection: its task is "in recognizing the coming, to free it from its distorted form in what is present [*das Künftige aus seiner verbildeten Form im Gegenwärtigen erken-*

---

[40] In 1915, "The Life of Students" appeared in *Der Neue Merkur;* in 1916, it was reprinted in slightly revised form in Kurt Hiller's *Das Ziel: Aufrufe zu tätigem Geist* (II 917).

nend zu befreien]." Ultimately, he asserts, the metaphysical structure of particulars, which relates them to the absolute state of perfection, can be established only through the dignity of a philosophical system; critique is strictly provisional. But in the interim, since "various preconditions of this system are not given"—a crucial qualification about which, surprisingly, he says no more—critique must stand in. At the end of the text, he then closes the bracket opened by the new preamble by reiterating his formula for the temporal inflection of critique.

Benjamin's new language carried over the essential bearings of his earlier idealism, with its concern for immanent, metaphysical structures and its fervent sense of "the coming." At the same time, he emphatically confirmed the reservations that had begun to surface, integrating them and according them equal weight. Claims to incarnate the absolute in stable form were suspect in principle; Benjamin instead declared his solidarity with the creaturely, suffering element of human existence, with "the multitude of the excluded," the "defamed and derided" of history. Now couched in terms of a messianic conception of history, these reservations took on a new, programmatic role: to immunize *his* idealism, at least, against the pervasive ideological abuses. There were remarkable continuities in the polemical bearings of this new strategy as well. Most notably, the progressives continued to serve as the foil against which he developed his own principles. The preamble opens with an attack on the same progressive conception of social and political engagement that had been his target in the body of the address. He now denounced the historical complacency that undercut the critical thrust of their program:

> There is a conception of history which, trusting in the endlessness of time, distinguishes only between the tempos at which men and epochs roll, rapidly or slowly, down the course of progress. To this corresponds the unconnectedness, the lack of precision and rigor of the demands they make on the present. The following reflection, however, is directed at a definite state, in which history is gathered and suspended in a focal point, as from time immemorial in the utopian images of the thinkers. The elements of the final state do not manifest themselves in a formless tendency to progress but rather are deeply embedded in every present as the most endangered, most defamed and derided creations and thoughts. (II 75)

The war had confirmed his worst suspicions about the impotence of the progressives' ethos, dealing a crushing blow to what he saw as their naive faith in progress and political activism. At the decisive moment, all their proclamations and manifestos, calls to political action intended to give history a push forward, had proved futile. Remarkably enough, Benjamin regarded the progressives' misconception of history as merely the obverse of that held by the vitalists. Both were implicated in an "empty" conception of historical time: whereas the progressives placed their faith in a homogeneous continuum of progress, which knows only quantitative distinctions, the vitalists adulated timeless natural forces. His inclination to identify these opponents with a common error also went back to the youth movement: by denying the autonomy of *Geist*, both courted the revenge of those "unmastered natural forces" he would soon designate as mythic. Their complementary, inauthentic annihilations of historical time yielded an "intoxication purchased at a high price": to be "punished by all the spiritual and natural powers" and, most devastating of all, by the war (II 85). Only an adequate conception of history could enable one to make demands on the present with "precision and rigor." As he put it soon thereafter, "the ultimate metaphysical dignity of a philosophical conception that claims to be truly canonical will show itself most clearly in its way of confronting history" (B 151).

But if Benjamin's invocation of a messianic conception of history initiated a radical, immanent critique of idealism, it also signaled a new role for Jewish and theological motifs in his work. For instance, during the war he went on to spell out his conception of historical time in the brief "*Trauerspiel* and Tragedy" (1916). Here he contrasted mechanical with truly historical time: mechanical time, in an image popularized by Henri Bergson, was a mere empty form measured by movements in space; historical time, on the other hand, was defined by the possibility of fulfillment. But such fulfillment could not be realized in any empirical event; fulfilled time was rather an "idea," designated in the Bible as the "divinely fulfilled time" of "the messianic age" (II 134). In this text messianic and idealist languages balance and shade into one another; in other texts dating from the war years, particularly "On Language as Such and on Human Language" (1916), the new theological topoi clearly predominate. The new prominence of theological motifs has usually led Benjamin's readers to assume that the distinctive conceptions of history and language he now began to unfold are directly attributable to sources in the Jewish mystical and messianic traditions, above all those of the Kabbalah.[41] The problem with this ap-

---

[41] The most emphatic version of this reading derives from Scholem. Intent on refuting what he called "the myth of the German-Jewish dialogue," he had particular reasons for trying to ensure that Benjamin's work be assigned to the correct tradition; see Scholem, "Against the Myth of the German-Jewish Dialogue" in *On Jews and Judaism in Crisis*, 61–64. The controversy over the so-called dialogue is an important one, and there is much to be said for Scholem's position on it in general. But it may not give us the most faithful picture of Benjamin's dealings with the German tradition. See Scholem's own elabora-

proach is that it rests on an anachronism. Our knowledge and appreciation of the Jewish mystical tradition owe their origins to Scholem, who went on to create the twentieth-century discipline of Kabbalah studies almost single-handedly.[42] But Scholem's own appreciation of this tradition was still only dawning in the years before he left Germany for Palestine in 1923.[43] Concepts that he later recovered cannot be invoked ex post facto as if they were Benjamin's sources. The direction of influence between Benjamin and Scholem more likely runs in the reverse direction: Scholem's own appreciation of the submerged traditions of Judaism owed a decisive impetus to Benjamin.[44] Later, Benjamin was always remarkably chaste about flirting with allusions to Jewish mysticism when addressing Scholem, who, as virtually the only scholarly authority at the time, could easily have called any bluff; in fact, in his letters to Scholem Benjamin sometimes candidly deplored his own ignorance in these matters.

But this is not to say that Jewish motifs were not decisive in shaping Benjamin's work, only that the mode of influence was less direct and more complex. As we have seen, before the war he already had a pronounced sense of cultural difference, and surely this awareness of a distinctively Jewish identity was among the causes that predisposed him to keep his distance from the slippages of orthodox idealism. But after the break with the youth movement, the terms of his balance between Jewish identity and work on German traditions shifted: he did not abandon his idealist commitments, but he began to mobilize his Jewish identity in the process of recasting them. This identity must be understood in terms of a specifically German-Jewish cohort within the generation of 1914, as Anson Rabinbach argues. Its members represented a new Jewish sensibility whose social and psychological roots

tion of his case in "Once More: the German-Jewish Dialogue," in *On Jews and Judaism in Crisis*, 65–70.

[42] Biale, *Gershom Scholem*, especially 1.

[43] A similar argument is made by Michael Jennings, *Dialectical Images: Walter Benjamin's Theory of Literary Criticism*, 94–96. Benjamin's most direct knowledge of the Kabbalah would have been through works of the nineteenth-century *Wissenschaft des Judentums*, such as Molitor's *Philosophie der Geschichte oder über die Tradition*, which denigrated or domesticated Jewish mysticism. See Biale, *Gershom Scholem*, 28–34. Benjamin had a second source as well in the tradition of references to the Kabbalah in non-Jewish philosophy since the Renaissance. Winfried Menninghaus draws a useful distinction between what he calls the first Kabbalah, the genuine Jewish tradition, and a second, "phantom" Kabbalah that was the speculative construct of non-Jewish thinkers and argues that Benjamin's contact was above all through the romantic version of this tradition of the "second" Kabbalah; see Menninghaus, *Walter Benjamins Theorie der Sprachmagie*, 188–226. On the history of the "Christian Cabala," see Frances Yates, *Giordano Bruno and the Hermetic Tradition*, and *The Occult Philosophy in the Elizabethan Age*.

[44] The view is confirmed by Biale, *Gershom Scholem*, 134.

lay partly in a vehement rejection of their parents' assimiliationist illusions. Their apocalyptic inclination to a total rejection of the existing order may have been shared by non-Jewish figures in the youth movement, expressionism, and the war generation; what distinguished the Jews was their way of combining this vision with an "esoteric intellectualism," "a certain kind of intellectuality as politics."[45] I would argue that it was this sensibility, rather than any apocryphal encounter with the Kabbalah, that generated the recourse to theological motifs in Benjamin's work. The important thing was the role these motifs played in his intellectual economy: messianic language provided him with a resistant and resilient idiom rather than an inventory of fixed concepts. In forging a new orientation he had no coherent body of specific doctrines to draw on; he was not simply shifting his allegiances to an alternative, given tradition. Instead, the messianic idiom became one of the germs of what we might call an intellectual project or strategy—a radical but immanent critique of German idealism whose essential coordinates were already latent in his involvement in the youth movement.[46]

By recasting his idealism within a new conception of history, Benjamin took a decisive step toward freeing it from many of its ambiguities, but others persisted with undiminished force. In the preamble to "The Life of Students," the most prominent of these residual ambiguities could already be seen in a trait he shared with the radical conservatives: faced with the question of how to realize the final state of history, he resorted once more to an exhortation to resolve the crisis of values by decision. He cautioned that his "likeness" or "image" of this final state was not to be mistaken for the manifesto of a movement; the final state was not to be reached by moving farther, or more rapidly, "along the course of progress." But he was obviously uncomfortable about presenting it as *only* an image, an unattainable ideal, for that would have quietistic implications; the "historical task," after all, was

[45] Rabinbach, "Between Enlightenment and Apocalypse," 80, 82. Although he focuses on Benjamin and Bloch as ideal types, Rabinbach argues that this was a generational phenomenon not limited to the left (82–83); his argument thus generalizes the case made by Michael Löwy in "Jewish Messianism and Libertarian Utopia in Central Europe (1900–1933)."

[46] The attribution of Jewish mystical influences can too easily serve as a kind of deus ex machina, seeming to explain the uniqueness of his project by invoking an outside source. This is a second problem with attributing Benjamin's distinctive conceptions to borrowings from Jewish mystical sources: such arguments tacitly assume a naive version of the influence model of intellectual history. They not only distract attention from the formative role played by Benjamin's critical reworking of sources within the German tradition, above all the *Frühromantik*, but they neglect the way that "outside" influences were bound to be refracted through a framework which, as I have argued, was carried across the divide of 1914.

to make "the immanent state of perfection" not only visible but also dominant (*herrschend*) in the present. Faced with this dilemma, which ultimately concerned the possibilities of political action, he asserted that his intention was to "point out the crisis which, resting in the nature of things, leads to the decision to which the cowardly succumb and the courageous subordinate themselves" (II 75). The controlled, deliberate intensity of the preamble as a whole speaks against discounting this as an empty phrase, a lapse in rhetorical force. On closer inspection, the idiom betrays its source: it was a reprise of "The Religious Position of the New Youth"; now, as before, "the courageous" remained those who "subordinate themselves" to absolutes somehow revealed by a "holy decision."

In its new context, this decisionism was far more than a vestigial holdover from an earlier way of thinking. For in a sense Benjamin was now forced to resort to it more than ever. The crux of his new strategy, after all, was to guard against idealist equivocations by driving a deep wedge between any given state of affairs and the absolute, final state of history. But the danger was that they would drift apart entirely. Just how was the "immanent state of perfection" latent "in every present" to be fashioned "purely into the absolute"? For Benjamin, the actualization of the absolute, messianic realm could not be instrumentalized as the goal of an organized movement. There could be no question of a direct connection between the two realms, no smooth road from one to the other; it was more like the other end of the rainbow than a palace at the end of a road up the hill. What one could do toward attaining it, he suggested, was to make it "visible" by gathering and concentrating the elements of a utopian image "in a focal point"—"in recognizing the coming, to free it." But what did this really mean? On the one hand, critique alone might well be considered a form of noninstrumental action, but in what sense was it a way of bringing about the final, metaphysical state of history? The contemplative alternative was bound to end in quietism and resignation. On the other hand, by the logic of his own argument, real action taken to realize the final state could not be judged by the kind of criteria derived from mediate goals within the course of progress. Its only criteria could be those given by the absolute, final state outside the course of history, which the decision itself would create. But the result of this alternative was that "anything goes," provided only that it was carried out radically and unconditionally—that is, "absolutely."[47] Although he proclaimed the

---

[47] Gershom Scholem, in *The Messianic Idea in Judaism and Other Essays on Jewish Spirituality,* identifies this odd ambivalence as a pervasive tendency throughout the Jewish messianic tradition, leading to an unstable oscillation between pessimistic resignation in horror at the course of worldly events and frenetic, amoral outbursts of violence in

absolute to be a metaphysical structure, in the end it turned out to look suspiciously like an act of will. His stance thus verged on nihilism, not only in the apocalyptic sense (which Benjamin frankly professed) that the present order must perish catastrophically for the new order to emerge, but in the risk that the choice of alternatives is ultimately arbitrary. Both alternatives, contemplation as well as decision, led to problematic, indeed unacceptable consequences. Benjamin's new strategy thus had its hidden price: by radicalizing the idealist distinction between the given and the absolute, it carried over and even intensified the decisionistic ambiguities already built into the neoconservative stance. The hyperidealist solution was to prove productive but by no means stable; it incurred the need for an ongoing series of clarifications and immunizations. Supplying these became a further element in the implicit dynamic that governed the subsequent development of his project—not only in his early work but until the very end.

To summarize all this, somewhat schematically, in terms of an orientation in the intellectual field, Benjamin emerged from his engagement in the youth movement by attempting to demarcate his position along three fronts. The first of these was established by his declared intention to vindicate the true legacy of the cause of youth. He thereby reaffirmed his commitment to a certain kind of idealism in which youth, as a "steady, pulsating feeling for the abstractness of pure *Geist*," was envisioned as the harbinger of a new historical era. The specific form of his identifications, the ideas of youth and university, no longer seemed viable; what now took their place was a solidarity with all that was "most endangered, most defamed and derided." Nevertheless, he meant to sustain the idealism he had somehow intended, which called for a thoroughgoing reformulation of idealism from within. This was by far the most complex task Benjamin had set himself, especially in light of the remaining pitfalls in his new conception of history. At the same time, this idealism had already guided his unrelenting criticism of what he saw as false forms of opposition within the youth and student movements, generating a second set of fronts. One was constituted by what he occasionally referred to as the demonic side of the youth movement: the vitalism of the Wandervogel, with their glorification of irrationality, and the cult of charismatic leadership and genius to which Wyneken himself had fallen prey. These demonic elements had

---

attempts to actualize the immanent messianic realm. For a forceful statement of this argument as a critique of the politics of the German Jewish generation of 1914, see Rabinbach, "Between Enlightenment and Apocalypse," 121-124. I find that this ambivalence arose primarily from the immanent tensions of Benjamin's participation in the idealistic youth movement and his attempt to free himself from certain of its pitfalls.

prominent counterparts in the adult culture of the time—in neoromanticism and *Lebensphilosophie*—and that, too, was to help sustain the continuity and resonance of his project. Finally, Benjamin was just as opposed to the small but important alternative represented by the advocates of social and political engagement gathered around *Der Anfang*. Their approach, he felt, was undermined by an unacknowledged complicity with the adult world: the instrumentalizing of thought and action into mere means to an end unconsciously reproduced the degraded, mechanized life of adult society. Benjamin castigated these tendencies within the youth movement no less caustically than he criticized the adult world in the name of youth culture; this had helped to make his isolation within the youth movement so severe. In laying claim to the legacy of the idea of youth, he carried this ideological force field into his mature work as well. During the war years, as his imprecise advocacy of the idea began to take on more concrete form and substance, the constellation under which he emerged from the youth movement would continue to provide the coordinates for his work.

Chapter Two

The Immanent Critique
of Romanticism

1. A "Harder, Purer, Less Visible Radicalism"

As the war began, Benjamin found himself faced with an enormous task of stocktaking and self-reflection. He vowed to remain faithful to the idea he had meant to stand for, but he was forced to recognize that his previous attempts to specify it had collapsed irretrievably. To Ernst Schoen, the recipient of his most telling comments on this period, he wrote of "the swamp which is the university today" and of how the "visible" youth movement had "perished so completely and with such heart-wrenching violence" (B 119, 140). The order of the day, as he saw it, was to submit oneself to a chastening process. Their radicalism had not been wrong; it had only been "too much a gesture." It was now to be refined to a crystalline clarity: "harder, purer," and yet "less visible," nurtured in seclusion and solitude. In pursuit of this goal, certain other "gestures" he had already cultivated were to prove of use: the gestures of withdrawing from the sordid fray of struggling parties, of retreating into esoteric inwardness, of apodictic proclamations of truth.

There were striking continuities between the debates among the isolated circles of war opponents with whom Benjamin maintained contact and the lines of conflict that had divided the radical wing of the youth movement before the war. During the winter of 1914/15 Benjamin remained in Berlin, where he took part in the evening discussions organized by Kurt Hiller. The tone in Hiller's circle was set by the same range of politically radical, expressionist intellectuals associated with *Die Aktion* and its editor, Franz Pfemfert, who had cosponsored *Der Anfang.* The content of the debates likewise reproduced the positions represented in *Der Anfang:* partisans of social and political activism, who were in the majority, faced off against isolated advocates of a pure renewal of *Geist*. Benjamin had his "Life of Students" published in Hiller's *Das Ziel* (1916); its new preamble seems to have been formulated in the course of debates on the idea of history in these circles. "Progressive" social and political activism thus continued to provide the foil against which he developed his own views.[1] His unbending opposition to engagement of any conventional stripe made him an outsider in these groups as well, a situation he alluded to in a disparaging remark about the futility of manifestos in the face of the war (II 75). This was a direct affront to the loudly proclaimed program of *Das Ziel*; privately, he deplored the fact that it was the least suitable forum for the piece. More to the point, however, he was clearly beginning to feel trapped by this increasingly sterile reproduction of old exchanges.

Benjamin responded to the war, and to the frustration engendered by such debates, by continuing along the path of inner emigration he had already set out on. Scholem reported that it was extraordinarily difficult to maintain contact with him at the time. Several unspoken rules had to be scrupulously observed, including both sharing his unconditional condemnation of the war and refraining from discussing the day-to-day developments of the conflict.[2] In part, this silence was surely due to the depression and hopelessness unleashed by Heinle's suicide, but beyond that it also expressed a profound, lasting suspicion of all quotidian politics, from which he always kept his distance.[3] His letters often expressed the sense of relief he found in the refuge afforded by geographic removals as well. On arriving in Munich to continue his studies in the winter semester of 1915, he thought he had "finally found the position—outside my home city—which I have needed" (B 123). Continuing to fend off the military draft on medical grounds, in 1917 he was able to move to Switzerland, where his sense of relief was palpable: "I find myself saved here in many senses: not in the leisure, security, and maturity of life, but escaped from the demonic nightmarish influences that hold sway wherever we turn, and escaped from the raw anarchy, the lawlessness of suffering" (B 140). The move had the particular advantage of freeing him from the immediate threat of military conscription. Geographic migration would come to play a central role in the economy of Benjamin's life. Berlin's intellectual circles never really provided him with positive impulses; even

---

[1] There were exceptions, however; Scholem reports Benjamin's respect for the position taken by *Die Internationale*, an illegal publication by left-wing Social Democrats, edited by Rosa Luxemburg and August Thalheimer (*Walter Benjamin*, 22). Both Scholem and Benjamin had older brothers associated with the left of the Social Democratic party.

[2] Scholem, *Walter Benjamin*, 34–35.

[3] In this it was distinct from the aristocratic and essentially aesthetic disdain that characterized Stefan George's opposition to the war.

when he rediscovered the city ten years later, it was not Berlin's intellectual culture but its cityscapes that fascinated him. He was always to be tempted by the solitude afforded by travel, until his exile in 1933 finally left him no alternative. But it was in the virtual space of willfully esoteric intellectual excursions that he sought the Archimedean fulcrum that would provide the leverage he needed.

Decisive impulses came from the period of his studies in Munich between 1915 and 1917.[4] As always, he was demonstratively contemptuous of the regular academic offerings. The courses offered by the luminaries of the day in philosophy, literature, and art history, whose subject matter concerned him most closely, disappointed him thoroughly. One of the few "fruitful" lecture courses, he complained, was on "the history of Old Catholic penance," where he took his place in a virtually empty hall "at the back of the monks."[5] Truly productive, on the other hand, was the private seminar given by Walter Lehmann, an authority on pre-Columbian ethnology and comparative mythology.[6] Held in Lehmann's "very elegant private apartment," amid his personal collection of "the most magnificent ancient American art objects," and attended by a peculiar circle including the poet Rilke and "an astronomer from Göttingen," it certainly provided the arcane atmosphere Benjamin seems to have been seeking. Exotic trappings aside, Lehmann's seminar had two substantial assets that provide important clues to the new directions emerging in Benjamin's thinking.[7]

The first of these was Lehmann's subject itself, comparative mythology. Lehmann's personal qualities impressed Benjamin profoundly; his "astonishing" breadth of knowledge and the "not inconsiderable demands" he made on the intellectual capacity of his students were absolute prerequisites for gaining Benjamin's intellectual respect. More important, there were substantive reasons for his fascination. Lehmann's field held out the prospect of a theory of mythological cultural forms that might provide Benjamin with part of the "comprehensive context" he sought to orient his thinking. He actually had little interest in the scholarly field of ethnology as such, and he never pur-

---

[4] On this period, see Scholem, "Walter Benjamin und Felix Noeggerath."

[5] Letter from Benjamin to Fritz Radt, November 21, 1915, cited in Scholem, "Benjamin und Noeggerath," 137.

[6] On Lehmann and comparative mythology, the citations are from Benjamin's letters to Fritz Radt of November 21 and December 4, 1915, in Scholem, "Benjamin und Noeggerath," 137–138, 140–141.

[7] Lehmann and Noeggerath were not so much influences on Benjamin as catalysts who helped crystallize his formulation of an intellectual agenda. The question of Benjamin's influences in general is difficult to sort out; the temptations are to refer to too many sources (drawing, for instance, on the profusion of figures named in Scholem's *Walter Benjamin*) or too few (by locating *the* single source for a given motif).

sued it with any persistence. It was rather the *philosophical* consequences of a doctrine of mythos that captivated him. The theme became a cardinal point of reference in his work from this time on.[8]

These philosophical consequences, in turn, were the primary concern of the second asset Benjamin found in Lehmann's seminar—Felix Noeggerath, to whom he referred at the time as "the universal genius" or, more simply, "the genius."[9] Like Lehmann, Noeggerath possessed the breadth of learning, the personal bearing, and that penchant for immersing himself in arcana that so impressed Benjamin. Moreover, Noeggerath's philosophical intentions at the time overlapped Benjamin's at many points. Noeggerath's interest in comparative mythology was already well developed. In part, this interest had personal grounds: his family had connections to various members of the circle of "Cosmics" associated with Stefan George, including Karl Wolfskehl, Ludwig Klages, and Alfred Schuler. Noeggerath himself, however, had begun to take a dim view of the Cosmics' infatuation with irrationalism and their dreams of fulfilling the romantic project of a new mythology. He therefore turned his attention to the systematic foundations of German philosophy, as they were being reconstructed by the "critical" Marburg neo-Kantians. When Benjamin met him, he was in the process of writing a doctoral dissertation titled "Synthesis and the Concept of System in Philosophy: A Contribution to the Critique of Antirationalism."[10] Noeggerath's general aim was to broaden the range of Kant's theory of experience; if that could be done, there would be no need to resort to irrationalism to account for various forms of "primitive" or precognitive experience. The explicit target of his analysis was the variety of philosophical vitalism expounded by Bergson, but one suspects that Noeggerath ultimately had the Cosmics in mind. Only by consolidating and expanding Kant's systematic intentions, Noeggerath argued, could the irrationalist consequences of "skeptical" vitalism be averted.[11]

[8] The importance of Benjamin's preoccupation with myth has often been noted; both Adorno and Scholem stressed it. All the more surprising, then, is the lack of any sustained and rigorous treatment of the issue. Winfried Menninghaus provides a suggestive starting point in *Schwellenkunde: Walter Benjamins Passage des Mythos*.

[9] The information about Noeggerath summarized in the following necessarily depends heavily on Scholem's portrait of him in "Benjamin und Noeggerath." Scholem's remarks must, however, be used with some care; see n. 13.

[10] Felix Noeggerath, "Synthesis und Systembegriff in der Philosophie: Ein Beitrag zur Kritik des Antirationalismus" (doctoral dissertation submitted to the department of philosophy, Erlangen). There is some confusion about the date: the dissertation itself notes that the oral examination took place on December 19, 1916, but in the official list of doctoral dissertations it appears under the year 1930. Moreover, it seems that no copy was sent to the archives in Berlin, contrary to the usual practice at the time.

[11] Noeggerath, "Synthesis und Systembegriff," 75–76. In general, however, Noeggerath's dissertation lacks the clarity of expression that Benjamin's enthusiasm would lead one to expect.

Benjamin was unusually generous in acknowledging his intellectual debt to Noeggerath. He was impressed enough to report that "the pure theoretical spirit has become so vivid for me" in discussions with Noeggerath "that I am obtaining certainty about my tasks and contributions."[12] On many points, as he put it to Scholem somewhat preciously, "I know myself to be one with the Genius" (B 150). Yet, in the same letter, he went on to hedge his identification with a serious reservation: despite the "deep-reaching identity of the images of truth which two men [he and Noeggerath] bear in themselves," a certain "inner affinity" was necessarily lacking since, as "German and Jew," their "intuitions" and "working methods" differed fundamentally.[13] Benjamin's intellectual debt to Noeggerath was real, but it should not be exaggerated. The point is that their relationship was emblematic of a constellation of concerns that was beginning to emerge in his thinking; he was slowly feeling his way forward on several paths at once. We can distinguish five problem complexes, which intersected at various points like five overlapping circles.[14]

The first was the need for a *systematic* philosophical framework, or at least a provisional, programmatic sketch of one. In the preamble to "The Life of Students," he had asserted that the only way to identify the latent "metaphysical structure" of particulars is "the system" (II 75). Now, in his 1917 study "On the Program of the Coming Philosophy," Benjamin identified the starting point for a comprehensive philosophical system in Kant. Neo-Kantianism was still the reigning philosophical school in the German universities. Benjamin was unimpressed by its leading lights, apart from Hermann Cohen,[15] yet at the time he still felt that the way ahead led through Kant rather than around him. On this point more than any other, he may have taken his cue from Noeggerath. "I firmly believe," he wrote while working on the piece, "that . . . there can be no question of shaking the Kantian system, but only of giving it granite foundations and extending it universally"; "the letter of his thought" was for Benjamin "a *tradendum,* something to be handed down (however much one may have to reshape it later)" (B 150). The greatest limitation of Kant's system as it stood—on this Benjamin and Noeg-

---

[12] Letter from Benjamin to Fritz Radt, December 4, 1915, in Scholem, "Benjamin and Noeggerath," 140–141.

[13] He also reassured Scholem about "how much I promise myself from *our* togetherness in this sense" (B 151). But Benjamin was playing both sides of this fence: in a letter to Ernst Schoen a year later, he stressed the limits to his collaboration with Scholem—precisely because Scholem was "occupied with Hebraic matters" (B 202).

[14] Detailed discussions of the individual works from this period can be found in Jennings, *Dialectical Images;* Witte, *Walter Benjamin: Der Intellektuelle als Kritiker;* Menninghaus, *Walter Benjamins Theorie der Sprachmagie;* and Wolin, *Walter Benjamin.*

[15] Benjamin and Scholem together studied Cohen's *Kant's Theory of Experience* while Benjamin was working on "On the Program of the Coming Philosophy" (Scholem, *Walter Benjamin,* 76).

gerath agreed with Cohen—was its tendency to conceive of knowledge as a relation between the entities of subject and object, which abridged the range of its theory of experience.[16] Unlike Noeggerath, however, Benjamin was interested in linking a comprehensive philosophical system to a critique of *particular* cultural formations.

The second circle of concerns revolved around the idea of mythic forms of experience. Benjamin had always been inclined to describe the irrational in terms of demonic and mythic forces, and now, like Noeggerath, he saw the starting point for a phenomenology of mythic forms in the borderline discipline of comparative mythology. This interest was also linked to the revision of Kant. Neo-Kantian philosophy, particularly as represented by Cohen's philosophy of religion, had operated with a strict antithesis between reason and myth: philosophy and, for Cohen, Judaism as a "religion of reason" represented a qualitative overcoming of mythic experience.[17] Benjamin employed a similar counterposition of theological and mythic motifs, replacing Cohen's stress on reason with a paradisiacal, "naming" language.[18] But he was interested in going beyond the antithesis to a philosophical *comprehension* of myth as well. His interest in systematically extending Kant's theory of experience aimed not only at overcoming Kant's exclusive orientation of epistemology toward the mathematical natural sciences but also—perhaps even more so—at recapturing the full range of experience from the monopoly being surrendered by default to the vitalist right.[19] Benjamin began to elaborate such a phenomenology of mythic forms in the early 1920s.[20] During this incubation period, he was primarily interested in the *category* of myth.

The category of myth was in turn an element of his third locus of concerns, the philosophy of history. For the time being, the term "myth" served as a placeholder, an abstract counter to a conception of "true," "fulfilled" historical experience. The category of history, in turn, had become for him the acid test of "the ultimate metaphysical

---

[16] As Ernst Cassirer points out, Cohen himself had long since begun reformulating Kant's epistemology so as to divest it of hypostatized categories; see Cassirer, "Hermann Cohen, 1842–1918."

[17] For instance, see Cohen, "Religion und Sittlichkeit," especially 126–134.

[18] See "On Language as Such and on Human Language" and the commentaries cited in n. 14.

[19] In fact, this was also among the cardinal interests of the most eminent neo-Kantian philosopher of his generation, Ernst Cassirer. See Cassirer's *Language and Myth* and his *Philosophy of Symbolic Forms*; on the role of myth in Cassirer's philosophy, see Crois, *Cassirer: Symbolic Forms and History*, 88–102. Readings of Benjamin's essay on Kant have been almost unanimously one-sided and have neglected developments within neo-Kantianism parallel to Benjamin's approach.

[20] He first did so in "Goethe's *Elective Affinities*" and then in the early notes for the "Arcades" project. By then, however, he had rejected the idea of a philosophical system.

dignity of a philosophical conception that claims to be truly canonical"
(B 151). Among Benjamin's most striking attempts to formulate his
own conception of history was an image of tradition developed in a
1917 letter to Scholem. Education, he argued, as a channel of cultural
transmission, must not be understood as a means to some other end; it
is an end in itself. The teacher's own learning passes over impercepti-
bly into teaching, because the goal of instruction is not to convey any
particular content but to draw the learner into the process of transmission itself. The epitome of this conception is the idea of tradition as a
medium: "Tradition is the medium in which the learner changes continually into the teacher. . . . in tradition all are educators and to be
educated." So understood, learning could be "the sole point at which a
free joining of the older with the younger generation takes place" (B
145–146). But far from conceiving of this continuity in complacent,
conservative tones, Benjamin stressed its climactic and culminating
aspect:

> Doctrine [*Die Lehre*] is like a surging sea, but for the wave (if we take it as
> the image of the human being) everything depends on giving oneself over
> to its motion in such a way that it crests and overturns, foaming. The
> tremendous freedom of this overturning is education. . . . [it is] tradition
> becoming visible and *free*. (B 146)

The process of tradition includes the "tremendous freedom of overturning [*die ungeheure Freiheit des Übersturzes*]," an overturning "out of
living fullness" (B 146). This, too, was a model of the fulfilled or messianic (II 134), which he counterposed to both the empty continuum of
mechanical time and the mythic time-form of eternal recurrence alike.

The fourth and fifth of these intersecting circles crystallized in the
course of an exchange with Buber in the summer of 1916: Benjamin
envisioned the prospect of a noninstrumental concept of language,
and for him this idea was closely bound up with defining a noninstrumental conception of political action as well. Benjamin wrote Buber to
reject his solicitation of a contribution to his new journal, *Der Jude*. He
held Buber's vitalism responsible for his disastrous misperception of
the war as a source of renewal for Jews and Germans alike. But the
grounds he cited for declining elaborated instead on the distaste for
activism and instrumental action he had developed in the youth movement. Repugnant as he found the enthusiasm for the war expressed by
the journal's contributors, Benjamin pointed to a deeper problem in the
idea of "politically effective writing" as such (B 125–126). He sharply
criticized the manipulative use of language and literature as means to
an end that lies outside them. Buber, he argued, fell prey to the com-

monplace assumption that language was merely a means of "preparing the motives" of the person addressed; deeds, in this conception, resulted from a more or less carefully examined "process of calculation." Language was thereby "degraded" into "a mechanism for the realization of the correct absolute." Not only language suffered; the result was "a wretched, feeble deed" as well. Benjamin was arguing that the exalted rhetoric of the activists' exhortations unwittingly parodied the dominant culture they were so noisily trying to denounce. In effect, the alternative of a noninstrumental conception of language now took up a place at the center of his thinking formerly held by the ideas of youth and the university.

Against this negative foil, Benjamin evoked a positive, "intensive" conception of language whose efficacy would be "salutary" and "genuine" (B 126–127). The key lay in ceasing to regard language as a vehicle for "conveying contents" and treating it, in some sense, as an end in itself; only this approach could bring "the purest disclosure of its dignity and essence." Cryptically, and somewhat awkwardly, he referred to the "secret (of the word, of language)" and to its "magic." But, paradoxically, he stressed that "the matter-of-fact, sober way of writing [*sachliche, nüchterne Schreibweise*]" was the quintessence of magical "immediacy." Sobriety demanded "the crystal-pure elimination of the ineffable in language," and it was the only linguistic mode indicated for their times. That was what disturbed him most about Buber's journal: the linguistic modes of poetry, prophecy, song, psalm, and imperative were all legitimate in their own right, but for a journal they were "out of the question." "Only the matter-of-fact way of writing" was admissible. Yet Benjamin equivocated between two visions of what would result from a purified use of language. One was quietistic: "I do not believe that the word is somehow more distant from the divine than 'real' action is." Because the status of linguistic utterance was at least equal to what was commonly considered action, it therefore need not be linked to any other deed. But a second formulation evoked a potent link between word and deed: "The elimination of the ineffable seems to me . . . to intimate the relationship between knowledge and deed within the magic of language . . . to lead toward what is denied to the word; only where this sphere of the wordless discloses itself in unspeakably pure power can the magic spark jump the gap between word and moving deed, where there is the unity of these two equally real moments" (B 127). Whichever he meant—and the ambiguity is clearly significant—he insisted that his intention was not to withdraw from politics but to formulate "an eminently political concept of style and writing." "True" language, "true" politics, a "true" conception of history: all would somehow hang together, if only one could get a fix on an adequate philosophical system; and all would provide crystal-pure alternatives to the ensnarement in myth, "the demonic night-marish influences that hold sway wherever we turn."

If one were looking to identify a single figure who provided a foil as Benjamin worked out this contellation of concerns, it would be the poet Stefan George.[21] George was a pervasive influence on many intel-lectuals—particularly Jewish intellectuals—of his generation.[22] Ben-jamin later paid moving tributes to George's poetry as the "asylum" and "song of solace" of his youth (III 398). The "decisive, shattering experience" wrought by George's work had been inextricably bound up with recitations of his poems at highly charged moments by those closest to him, and his words clearly link this experience to the memo-ry of his dead friend, the poet Heinle: "If youth is granted the privilege and the ineffable happiness of legitimating itself in verse, of appealing to verse in disputes and in love, then we thanked our experience of this" to George's poetry (II 622–623). The most conspicuous side of his relationship to George and his circle after the break with the youth movement was philosophical enmity: he saw them as the preeminent representatives of an aestheticism that had veered into the most per-nicious form of philosophical vitalism. George's "priestly doctrine of poetry" had hieratic pretensions and elitist implications he came to find intolerable. George and his circle stood for a revival of myth and a frankly pagan poetic ideal that "deifies the body and embodies the divine" (II 359).

But George was not simply Benjamin's antipode, nor was everything about his "cult of language" repugnant to Benjamin. Most important, George projected a vision of cultural crisis as rooted in an underlying corruption of language.[23] The remedy for this crisis was to renew and activate the purifying force of language through its springs in poetry. In the first decade of the century, George thus came to understand his adaptation of the symbolists' ideal of pure poetry, with its noninten-tional, noncommunicative language, as part of a larger cultural mis-

---

[21] Several of Benjamin's projects in these years were direct responses to George or members of his circle: his 1914/15 essay on Hölderlin was a response to Hellingrath's reading of him; Benjamin's translations of Baudelaire were alternatives to George's own; and his prospectus for a journal to be entitled *Angelus Novus* invokes George's concep-tion of a crisis of German language and poetry (II 243). See Michael Rumpf, "Faszination und Distanz: Zu Benjamins George-Rezeption," and Ansgar Hillach, "'Ästhetisierung des politischen Lebens': Benjamins faschismustheoretischer Ansatz—eine Rekonstruk-tion," 154–158.

[22] See the statements by contemporaries collected in Ralph-Rainer Wuthenow, ed., *Stefan George in seiner Zeit: Dokumente zur Wirkungsgeschichte*, vol. 1.

[23] See Claude David, *Stefan George: Sein dichtersiches Werk*. This topos had been widely invoked since the fin de siècle; for an introduction to some versions, see Allan Janik and Stephen Toulmin, *Wittgenstein's Vienna*.

sion. Benjamin's own proposal to "transfer the crisis into the heart of language" (B 131) and his evocation of the efficacy of a purified language testify to George's formative influence on his vision of the underlying causes of the cultural crisis. Less tangibly, George's signature can also be traced in many of Benjamin's gestures. Adorno noted strong ritualistic traits in details of Benjamin's private behavior and suggested that he had adopted the "schemata of ritual" from George.[24] But the most important of these gestures was his cultivation of an esoteric stance that went far beyond personal habits. What united Benjamin and George most deeply was the gesture of turning one's back on mere political or social efficacy in order to cultivate the hermetic resources of language. Benjamin had always rejected George's vitalism; he turned against his elitism in breaking with the youth movement; and the philosophy of language he went on to develop invoked Jewish and theological motifs to counter George's mythic and increasingly Germanic doctrine.[25] But beneath these antitheses an underlying faith in language and the esoteric stance associated with it became, if anything, more pronounced in response to the war. On many levels and issues, then, Benjamin's attempt to come to terms with George was crucial in shaping his particular constellation of concerns.

Given this complex of interlocking concerns, Benjamin might have hit on any number of topics to crystallize his interests. The series of private texts he wrote in 1916/17 can be read both as position papers and as sketches for far-reaching projects. Once in Bern, however, he began searching for a doctoral dissertation topic. For a while he thought of working on Kant's conception of history and his concept of the "infinite task." This would have joined two of his fundamental interests and forced him to reckon with the neo-Kantian philosophical orthodoxy of the time in a systematic and disciplined way. The plan lasted until the moment he actually picked up Kant's *Idea of a Universal History* and *Perpetual Peace* and read them. He described the result as "very unpleasant": "As the point of departure, or even the actual object for a self-sufficient treatise, I find Kant's ideas completely unsuitable" (B 161). The only mystery is how Benjamin took so long to realize that he would react this way.

He did not, however, remain stumped for long. His letters from 1916/17 abound with references to readings of the early romantics, particularly Friedrich Schlegel and Novalis, and his letter to Buber cited the *Athenäum* as the kind of cultural journal he had in mind. Ben-

---

[24] See Adorno's introduction to Benjamin's letters (B 15).

[25] As he put it in the essay on Kraus, he sought a conception of language in which it would serve as "the medium neither of 'vision' [*Seherschaft*] nor of domination" (II 359).

jamin's philosophical interests led him to think in terms of piecing together the early romantics' *"systematic* fundamental idea" (B 137). When it came to the dissertation, however, he focused somewhat differently: the philosophical foundations of romantic art criticism were to be his topic. This was a lucky stroke, probably luckier than he knew. In the same letter in which he announced the new theme to Schoen, Benjamin confessed to being "unable to complete a very important epistemological work"—the 1917 Kant study—"that has already been lying for months" (B 188). The new theme lifted the blockage, which may have consisted in no small part of the turgid academic philosophical literature of the time; Benjamin never did bring himself to return to it. Moreover, taking on the new topic did not mean putting aside the issues in the philosophy of history he had wanted to address. On the contrary,

> romanticism is the last movement which once again rescued and brought over the tradition. Its aim, premature in its time and sphere, was the madly orgiastic opening up of all the secret sources of the tradition, which were to pour out unswervingly over all of humanity. (B 138)

It was the early romantics who, in Benjamin's words, conceived of history as "tradition becoming visible and free," like a wave "crashing over out of living fullness." The dissertation turned out to be the most conventional, discursive treatment of a cluster of issues in his entire body of work. This discursiveness gives it a rather un-Benjaminian tone. Nevertheless, it rewards patient, painstaking unraveling.[26]

2. The Dynamics of Early Romanticism

Benjamin's decisive intellectual encounter during the war years was with the texts of the *Frühromantik,* the early German romantic move-

[26] Benjamin's dissertation long enjoyed stepchild status in the secondary literature; important exceptions are Jennings, "Mortification of the Text"; Chryssoula Kambas, "Walter Benjamins Verarbeitung der deutschen Frühromantik"; Winfried Menninghaus, "Walter Benjamins romantische Idee des Kunstwerks und seiner Kritik"; and Marcus Bullock, *Marxism and Romanticism: The Philosophical Development of Literary Theory and Literary History in Walter Benjamin and Friedrich Schlegel.* None of these, however, treats the full range of the dissertation's impact on Benjamin's thinking. In recent years the rereading of the *Frühromantik* through the lenses of poststructuralism and postmodernism has addressed itself to Benjamin as well. For three very different approaches, see Winfried Menninghaus, *Unendliche Verdoppelung: Die Frühromantische Grundlegung der Kunsttheorie im Begriff absoluter Selbstreflexion;* Philippe Lacoue-Labarthe and Jean-Luc Nancy, *The Literary Absolute: The Theory of Literature in German Romanticism;* and Karl-Heinz Bohrer, *Die Kritik der Romantik: Der Verdacht der Philosophie gegen die literarische Moderne.*

ment, and above all with the fragments published by Schlegel and Novalis in the *Athenäum*, the group's house organ during its origins between 1798 and 1800. In the *Frühromantik* he saw "the true nature of romanticism, utterly unknown in the literature," and "an infinite profundity and beauty in comparison with *all* late romanticism" (B 208, 138). It became his aim to identify, recover, and actualize the hidden, genuine core which he found in the origins of the movement, and which had been lost in the reception. The critical force of early romanticism could then be mobilized against the forms into which romanticism had collapsed after the turn of the nineteenth century—that is, the forms in which it had passed into the canon of the German tradition. For him, the genuine intention of the early romantics was to be found neither in the unbridled vitalism, subjectivism, and genius worship of the Storm and Stress school nor in the authoritarian mysticism of the Catholic restoration with which Schlegel had eventually thrown in his lot. It resided rather in their "radical mystical formalism" and their messianism (I 21, 12). These could be recovered only through the painstaking intellectual spadework of sorting and compiling the fragments with a view to their systematic implications, "an experiment to which I owe almost everything I understand of early romanticism up to now" (B 137–138). No school of interpretation was available to serve him as a base of operations; his concerns directed him toward a moment in the development of romanticism that set him athwart the entire previous reception.[27] This originality resulted in great part from the critical interests that guided his appropriation. Benjamin did not aim at establishing a new school of academic interpretation and, characteristically, found it difficult to press his results into the formal mold of a doctoral dissertation (although the result was certainly the most accessible of his major works). Instead, he mobilized the early romantics' philosophy of language, art, and criticism, of history and tradition, in order to work through his own unresolved dissatisfactions with the youth movement. Thus, the "harmony" of Schlegel's and Novalis's fragments that he prepared laid the groundwork not only for his dissertation but for many of his writings through 1925.

In fact, Benjamin's recovery and critique of early romanticism set the coordinates for all his subsequent work. In a sense, his identification was so complete that he can be said to have refought the early romantics' battles, working immanently. He cited Novalis's famous dictum that "the true reader must be the extended author," thinking the author's work further (I 68). But this also meant fighting against what he saw as the falsification and ideological abuse of these genuine inten-

---

[27] I consider the history of the reception of romanticism in Section 6.

tions in the subsequent development and reception of romanticism, abuses to which the early romantics themselves had contributed. In other words, these battles often had to be fought against the romantics themselves. His encounter with early romanticism therefore took the form of an immanent critique, an engagement with the movement and an intervention in its reception by advocating one of its moments against its own decay products. It was the contact between these two historical constellations—Benjamin's and that of early romanticism—that gave his interpretation its acuity and incisiveness.

Before examining Benjamin's actualization and immanent critique of romanticism, therefore, it is helpful to call to mind the dynamics of the German romantic movement at its origins. Early romanticism in all its varieties began as a rebellion against neoclassical culture; the romantics denied that the norms of an authentically modern culture—its ethical, aesthetic, and educational ideals—could be supplied by imitating or emulating models from classical antiquity. In challenging the predominance of neoclassicism, they were taking aim at far more than an isolated doctrine of aesthetics or style. Neoclassicism, as the cultural canon of the Enlightenment, was becoming a focal point of identification for the emerging German *Bildungsbürgertum,* the educated upper-middle class, to an extent that was eventually to take on the character of a "tyranny of Greece over Germany."[28] Neoclassicism itself had been spelled out in a variety of ways since the classical revival of the Italian Renaissance; for the young romantics, the relevant versions were those propounded in the eighteenth-century French and German Enlightenment.[29]

The predominant, orthodox variety at mid-century was the rationalist poetics expounded by Johann Christoph Gottsched, which in Germany was often regarded as French neoclassicism. Gottsched prescribed the observance of timeless, logically deduced rules of genre which alone, he asserted, could lead to a harmonious, beautiful, and morally instructive art. In practice, the exemplars to be imitated were invariably classical and Gottsched's rules were more or less faithfully derived from Aristotle's *Poetics,* the most famous case being the unities of time, place, and action in classical tragedy. In Germany this rule-bound, dogmatic neoclassicism was gradually supplanted by the idealist neoclassicism of Johann Winckelmann beginning in the last third of the century. Winckelmann's aesthetics was just as prescriptive as

---

[28] See E. M. Butler, *The Tyranny of Greece over Germany,* and W. H. Bruford, *Germany in the Eighteenth Century: The Social Background of the Literary Revival.*

[29] Good surveys of German aesthetics in the eighteenth century can be found in Ernst Cassirer, *The Philosophy of the Enlightenment,* 275–360, and Nicolao Merker, *Die Aufklärung in Deutschland,* 107–166.

Gottsched's and equally committed to the absolute preeminence of classical models. His orientation, however, was not Aristotelian but Platonic and idealist. He prescribed emulation rather than imitation: beauty was to be attained by recapturing the ideal, inner spirit of Greek wholeness and perfection rather than by slavishly and mechanically reproducing its merely external semblance. When translated into broader terms, Winckelmann's version of neoclassicism was eventually to supply one of the cornerstones of the characteristically German conception of *Bildung*, or cultivation, as the shaping of the individual through a direct, totally engaged encounter with classical models. Idealist neoclassicism was thus at the core of the *Bildungsbürgertum*'s ambitions at the turn of the nineteenth century—to claim a place for merit and the ennobling power of acquired cultivation in a society in which power and social status were distributed according to the criteria of birth and service to the state.[30]

Friedrich Schlegel, who was to become the moving spirit of the *Athenäum* circle, was himself deeply implicated in this German classicist revival. As an adolescent, he had chafed at his father's insistence that he train for a commercial or legal profession; only by plunging himself into the study of classical languages and literature was he able to free himself from the crippling psychological conflict that resulted. In his first major work, "On the Study of Greek Poetry" (written in 1795), he argued fanatically for the superiority of antiquity over modernity—so fanatically that it earned him the reputation of aspiring to become "the Winckelmann of Greek literature." The import of Schlegel's early classicism becomes more apparent if we consider both its social and psychological resonances. His passionate embrace of neoclassicism, which enabled him to reject a mundane, "merely useful" profession, also exemplified the strivings of the *Bildungsbürgertum* in general. By extension, his rebellion against neoclassicism in the name of romantic literature and culture—a change of course that began even before the essay was published—takes on a new dimension. For Schlegel himself, it meant rebelling against the very ideas that he had just so successfully begun to make the foundations of adult identity; in psychological terms, this already made it a precarious undertaking. Its social significance moved him into an equally exposed position: it represented a long step beyond the *Bildungs*-utopia of the educated upper-middle class which, far from being established, had only just begun to assert its claims against the existing social order.

---

[30] On the relationship between philosophical idealism and the rise of the *Bildungsbürgertum*, see Hajo Holborn, "Der deutsche Idealismus in sozialgeschichtlicher Beleuchtung," and Ringer, *Decline of the German Mandarins*.

As rebels against the predominant neoclassicism, the early romantics faced the problem of coming up with standards of orientation to replace the classical models they rejected. Such alternative standards might be located in the givens of an existing tradition—in the Catholic church, for instance, or in the roots of a national folk culture, choices that were often made later. But it was particularly characteristic of the early romantics, bent on rejecting dogmatism in any guise, to think in terms of *generating* such standards. Seen from this angle, their problem was by no means a peculiarity of the eighteenth century. In fact, the romantics were among the first to face one of the central dilemmas that has defined modernity ever since, that "modernity can and will no longer borrow its standards of orientation from the models of another period; *it must create its normativity out of itself.*"[31] Where and how was one to find cultural standards if not in classical models? The varieties of romanticism can be distinguished according to their answers to this question.

Among the first answers was the vitalism and radical subjectivism espoused by the Storm and Stress movement if the 1770s: the impassioned inwardness of Johann Georg Hamann's pietism, or the glorification of creative genius whose originality transcends all rules and models, as propagated by Johann Gottfried Herder at that time. The early romantics of the *Athenäum* circle in the 1790s adopted and carried on this vitalist, subjectivist revolt. But they also found a predecessor in Kant's critical philosophy, which provided an utterly different argument for human autonomy. Kant had described his philosophical achievement as a Copernican revolution: like Copernicus, he demonstrated that perception and knowledge are decisively shaped by the position of the observer or, in epistemological terms, by the subject's active role in cognition. But his critique of pure reason had nothing to do with psychological subjectivism; for Kant, the subject's contribution to cognition consisted of a logical framework of universal, synthetic a priori judgments. Accordingly, criticism meant objective reflection on the universal characteristics of the cognizing subject, not license to pass arbitrary judgments from an unexamined standpoint. Criticism did begin, however, by placing all inherited standards of orientation in question, rejecting any dogmatic prescription of givens and absolutes

[31] Jürgen Habermas, *Der philosophische Diskurs der Moderne,* 16. Habermas draws on the works of Hans-Robert Jauß in observing that the problem of modernity so defined first became an issue in the field of aesthetics (16–17); but he does not explicitly take up the early romantics' role in this process. On Schlegel's confrontation with Schiller over this issue, see, however, H. R. Jauß, "Schlegels und Schillers Replik auf die 'Querelle des Anciens et des Modernes'," which is included along with "Literarische Tradition und gegenwärtiges Bewußtsein der Modernität" in the collection of Jauß's essays titled *Literaturgeschichte als Provocation.*

whatsoever. Kant's "Answer to the Question: What is Enlightenment?" was uncompromising: "*Sapere aude*. Dare to know! Have the courage to make use of your own reason." In this sense, it too supplied the epistemological basis for an assault on neoclassicism, on the grounds that neoclassical aesthetics was a vestige of dogmatism incompatible with the critical philosophy. Thus, the early romantic program developed by Schlegel, Novalis, and the *Athenäum* circle after 1795 must be understood as syncretic. It attempted to synthesize diverse, often wildly divergent sources, from the subjectivism and vitalism of Storm and Stress to the critical rationalism of Kant's philosophy, a range that makes sense only in terms of their shared opposition to dogmatic neoclassicism. The resulting contradictions ran like geological fissures through the work of the early romantics.

The early romantics' rejection of the classical cultural canon and of the dogmatic assumptions behind it had historical and political implications as well. What lent the problem of standards its urgency was their sense of standing on the threshold of a new age inaugurated by the French Revolution. This urgency injected a messianic strain into their early ideas. As Schlegel put it, "I see the grandest birth of the new age already emerging into the light of day, modest as early Christianity, of which one could not tell that it was soon to devour the Roman Empire—just as the great catastrophe, in its broader circles, will swallow up the French Revolution, whose most solid value consists, perhaps, in having incited it."[32] These words capture the inseparability of the cultural and political dimensions of the revolution in the early romantics' vision. They regarded the French Revolution as only the prelude—nonetheless real and concrete—to a catastrophe that would bring an all-engulfing cultural transformation. This expectation made them unable to accept any given, already perfected canon of orientation. Their insistence on situating the political upheaval within an epochal cultural revolution also found expression in the often-cited, persistently misunderstood *Athenäum* fragment 216, which placed Fichte's *Wissenschaftslehre* and Goethe's *Wilhelm Meister* alongside the French Revolution as "the greatest tendencies of the age." This was not merely German cultural myopia or an attempt to spiritualize the revolution out of existence. By referring to Fichte and Goethe as tendencies the romantics stressed that they by no means offered perfected ideals but only pointers to the imperative of creating new forms and values. Weimar classicism, with its harmonizing ideals, seemed to them too

---

[32] Benjamin cites this passage from a letter of Schlegel's in a footnote to the introduction of the dissertation (I 12–13).

affirmative, too ready to transform only culture while reconciling itself with social and political realities. Critique, for the early romantics, was the indispensible counterpart to real historical change, not an alternative to it.

It must always be kept in mind, however, that the romantics rebelled in a spirit of metaphysical absolutism. They were not seeking to carve out a niche for an alternative culture, nor did they advocate skeptical tolerance of a fragmented, pluralistic culture in a relativistic spirit. Instead, they saw themselves as the harbingers of culture reunified under absolute, metaphysical principles, an orgiastic confluence and fulfillment of once-divergent strivings. Benjamin underscored this metaphysical absolutism by citing a fragment from the *Athenäum* that equates true modernity with the messianic sensibility: "The revolutionary desire to realize the kingdom of God is the elastic point of progressive development and the beginning of modern history. Whatever stands in no relation to God's kingdom is immaterial to it."[33] Novalis sometimes used the term "romantic" as a verb: to romanticize was to extrapolate from a particular, finite form until its absolute, metaphysical structure revealed itself. For all their opposition to dogmatic, socially confirmative cultural standards, therefore, the young romantics' philosophy of culture had a pronounced restorative bent as well. They felt afflicted, in Novalis's famous words, by a profound "metaphysical homesickness." Kant's critiques, they were sure, had banished the hated specter of dogmatic metaphysics, and that made "critique" into a kind of conjuring word for them. But Kant's achievement came at a high price: reason and feeling, the finite and the infinite had been torn asunder. The romantics, wracked by a longing for the lost security provided by metaphysical absolutes, reconciled their ambivalence toward Kant by taking his "Prolegomena to Any Future Metaphysics" at its word: Kant's strictures against metaphysics applied only to its speculative, dogmatic form; after all, he would never have written a *prologue* if the path to metaphysics was really to be closed off for good. What mattered to them was what they considered to be the historical achievement of Kant's critique, not his own restrictive use of the term (I 52). Critique was not primarily negative, as they conceived of it; critique was a positive, metaphysically productive method. Benjamin understood this perfectly well; indeed, this was precisely his own attitude toward Kant during these years, at a time when he still hoped that a systematic metaphysics might be possible (II 164). The early romantics' "cult of the infinite" (I 25) was bound to be of the most

---

[33] *Athenäum* fragment 222 (I 12).

passionate interest to him—precisely because they managed, for a short time, to hold the precarious balance between metaphysical absolutism and a resolutely antidogmatic stance.

From the foregoing, it is not difficult to see what was likely to happen as the early romantics retreated from the exposed position of their attack on classical standards. Since they had not proposed simply replacing the neoclassical canon with a definite, positive canon of their own, they were likely to lose their nerve when faced with the dizzying prospect of nihilism conjured up by their own *devaluation* of all values—particularly given their metaphysical homesickness. The paths of retreat from their original project led to the varieties of romanticism most commonly associated with the term. One branch of escape led to romantic subjectivism—a one-sided emphasis on the arbitrary generation of norms by the individual subject, in effect a reversion to the radical subjectivism of Storm and Stress. Nietzsche, who both decried and celebrated the unavoidable emergence of nihilism, was to state the decisionistic consequences of romantic subjectivism most forcefully; less drastically, the many varieties of aestheticism likewise posited the creative artist's limitless freedom and the absolute autonomy of art. The alternative to such subjectivism was to *locate* and *affirm* a given or "objective" canon of value. A broad spectrum of such solutions emerged: Schlegel himself and the political romantics later associated with him eventually opted for the firm hand of the Catholic Restoration; romantic mythologists, from Creuzer and Bachofen in the nineteenth century to Jung and Schuler in the twentieth, looked to primordial, mythological forces; in a similar vein, romantic vitalists such as Bergson and Klages proclaimed the primacy of life over mechanical civilization. Whereas the early romantics' critique of neoclassicism can be understood in many essential respects as a "self-critique of enlightenment,"[34] the decay products of romanticism, both subjectivist and affirmative, tended to develop into an ideology of counterenlightenment. And it was in the latter forms that romanticism survived into Benjamin's times, the early twentieth century.

Benjamin had no interest in sorting the varieties of romanticism into proenlightenment and antienlightenment pigeonholes. But neither did his appropriation of romanticism aim at "overcoming" the Enlightenment in some simple sense.[35] Rather, he sought to recover what he saw

---

[34] This formulation is used by Silvio Vietta, "Frühromantik und Aufklärung," 13. The view of early romanticism it suggests summarizes a broader trend toward recognizing essential continuities between the Enlightenment and early romanticism, especially the early romantics' poetology.

[35] It has become common practice to portray Benjamin as having sought to overcome the "shallow" Enlightenment, a practice that itself rests on a shallow notion of the

as the original, critical potential of romanticism in order to innoculate it against the decay products of which his break with the youth movement had made him so painfully aware. The early romantics had attempted to propose alternatives to dogmatic rationalism and vitalism alike; theirs too was a youth movement that had collapsed. In a telling slip of the pen, Benjamin referred to the ideas that embodied the early romantics' genuine intention as their *Jugendideen,* which suggests both the ideas of their youthful years and their "ideas of youth." The task he set for his doctoral dissertation, "The Concept of Art Criticism in German Romanticism," as its preface declares, was to reach "a precise determination of the romantic youth ideas as a positive achievement" (I 17).

3. Immanent Critique

Benjamin argues in "The Concept of Art Criticism in German Romanticism" that the early romantics' response to the dilemma of criticism lay in their conception of "immanent critique." Immanent critique, he finds, was their decisive methodological innovation, a genuine, fruitful alternative to both dogmatic rationalism and the cult of genial creativity; even more, he considers it the "cardinal principle" of criticism ever since, the distortion and neglect of which has vitiated criticism into his own times (I 71–72). The term itself is supplied by Benjamin, who frankly states his purpose to be philosophical: he aims not to compile a philological catalogue of the romantics' views but to analyze their concept of criticism "according to its most fundamental philosophical intentions" (I 80). "Romanticism," he insists, "*must* be (judiciously) interpreted" (B 138). The term "immanent" works so well because it bundles together the full range of features he sees as central to their concept of criticism. In some contexts, Benjamin uses "immanent" in the sense of intrinsic or inherent: immanent criticism heeds the primacy of the aesthetic object's own characteristics and properties. The work's immanent structure provides the "corrective of all subjec-

---

Enlightenment and of Benjamin's complex, ambivalent relation to it. Most often cited to support this view is the passage from "On the Program of the Coming Philosophy" (1917) in which Benjamin characterizes Kant's conception of experience as impoverished and "reduced to a minimum of significance" (II 159). Benjamin did indeed find crippling deficits in the Enlightenment's conception of experience. Less often noted, however, is his conviction that a grounding in Kant's system was indispensible; in this, Benjamin shared the early romantics' attitude toward Kant. The use of the Enlightenment as a philosophical straw man has never been overly productive, and it is certainly not helpful in sorting out what was at stake for Benjamin. I discuss his relationship to the traditions of the Enlightenment in the Conclusion.

tivity"; it refracts and reforms all extrinsic forces that pass through it. Thus, it is never simply an expression of the creator's personality, a "mere by-product of subjectivity," nor does it just provide malleable material for the critic to project a personal response. Schlegel "cast the laws of *Geist* into the work of art itself" (I 71), with the result that "the appraisal is immanent to the material investigation and knowledge of the work" (I 80).

In a second, equally essential range of meanings, "immanent" signifies indwelling *tendencies*—not just generalized properties but individual, self-activating propensities. When evoking these dimensions, Benjamin repeatedly uses the term "unfolding" (*Entfaltung*):

> The critique of a work is . . . its reflection, which of course can only bring about the unfolding, the germination of its immanent core. (I 78)

Though the metaphor of unfolding is organic, as employed here it does not depict the work as a self-contained, harmonious whole. Rather, it underscores the work's inner dynamic and the production of new stages from within it. Immanent criticism regards the work as essentially incomplete; it unfolds the work by making its potential qualities actual, its implicit features explicit. The result is to "reflect" the work, in the sense that criticism raises its object to a higher level of clarity and explicitness. In unfolding the work's own implicit reflection, therefore, criticism changes the work, goes beyond it—in a sense, even completes it. Benjamin's richest metaphor for such an immanent, reflexive critique adopts the romantic idiom of "awakening":

> Criticism is, so to speak, an experiment on the work of art, through which its reflection is awakened and it is brought to consciousness and knowledge of itself. (I 65)

Whereas unfolding suggests an open-ended process of drawing forth ever-new meanings from the object, "awakening" and "consciousness" introduce a new, more emphatic note. They imply that the process of unfolding has an ultimate terminus: criticism lifts *all* restriction from the object, absolutizes it—"romanticizes" it, as the early romantics themselves put it. In either case, immanent critique, attentive to the intrinsic dynamic of its objects, provides both the catalyst and the medium through which their latent, slumbering potential is activated. The method of immanent critique became one of the animating centers of Benjamin's own critical activity, so its implications themselves bear careful unfolding.

To begin with, Benjamin insists on the immanence of criticism in order to guarantee its objectivity: "The objective foundation of the concept of art criticism Friedrich Schlegel provides has to do only with the objective structure of art—as an idea, and in its works" (I 13). Benjamin repeatedly stresses "the force of objective intentions in early romanticism" and, in particular, the "objective lawfulness" of art in its concept of criticism (I 81, 83). More than anything else, this marks his interpretation as a challenge to the predominant view of the early romantics as advocates of willful, unbridled subjectivity. He admits that they themselves invited this misunderstanding by using an ambiguous terminology whose subjectivist implications cannot easily be explained away. In the pivotal *Athenäum* fragment 116, for instance, Schlegel declared the "first commandment" of romantic poetry to be "that the willfulness of the poet can suffer no law above itself." Similarly, two of his key concepts—reflection and irony—normally imply the free play of subjective, psychological self-consciousness. At one point in the argument, Benjamin tips his hand far enough to concede that "it may partly be quite impossible to unite these heterogeneous [subjective and objective] elements in a concept without contradictions" (I 81). Yet that is just what the dissertation attempts to do. Benjamin solves the problem by tracing the early romantics' inconsistent usage to the "methodological grid" (I 40) underlying their theories, the idealist principle of the "medium of reflection."

Reflection—"self-consciousness," the "thinking of thought," "knowledge about knowledge"—was the central epistemological category of German idealist philosophy, from Fichte's *Science of Knowledge* to Hegel's *Phenomenology of Spirit*. The early romantics made their own, distinctive contribution to the development of German idealism. Their direct philosophical inspiration came from Fichte, whose *Science of Knowledge* was described in the *Athenäum* fragments as one of the "greatest tendencies of the age." Fichte conceived of the apparently objective world as the product and projection of a transcendental subject. This cosmic ruse had a hidden purpose, however: the subject's attainment of self-consciousness. The resistance of objectifications to the subject's strivings, he reasoned, enabled it to discover its limitations and in the process to become aware of itself. Thus the course of history, in Fichte's view, was the fulfillment of a metaphysical task: the subject's rising to self-consciousness by progressively recognizing and reappropriating its own objectifications. Benjamin takes great pains to demonstrate that Schlegel and Novalis adopted this idealist philosophy of reflection with a single but decisive modification: rejecting Fichte's hypostatization of the transcendental subject as an absolute self, an entity on which the entire system pivots, they placed the process of reflection itself at the center of their nascent philosophical system.[36] Whereas Fichte regarded reflection as "the thinking of the ego" (*das Denken des Ich*), the early romantics considered "the thinking of thought" (*das Denken des Denkens*) to be the canonical form of reflection (I 54), its *Urschema* (I 40). In Benjamin's formula, the hallmark of early romantic idealism was its insistence that "reflection constitutes the absolute, and it constitutes it as a medium" (I 37). By contrast, the subjective and objective poles of the medium were demoted to the status of merely "relative centers of reflection." The subjective self-consciousness of the Fichtean ego may indeed constitute a "self," but "for Schlegel and Novalis [it] represents only a lower form of the infinitely many forms of self" (I 55). The medium and the process of reflection take precedence, whatever the matter at hand; in aesthetics, for instance, "the center of reflection is art, not the ego" (I 39). Measured against these epistemological foundations, the notion of subjective romanticism turns out to be a misinterpretation—indeed, a frequent *self*-misunderstanding on the part of the early romantics themselves.

Strictly speaking, the terms "subject" and "object" lose much of their sense in such a philosophy. They cease to denote anything like ontologically substantial entities; instead, they signify merely relative determinations of the medium of reflection, moments of a process. Benjamin says as much,[37] yet he continues—following the romantics' own usage—to employ the terminology of subject and object: "For the romantics there is, seen from the standpoint of the absolute, no non-ego, no nature in the sense of an entity that does not become self"; he even sums up their metaphysical creed in the concise formula "all that is real thinks" (I 55). Difficult though it may be to avoid, by continuing

[36] Benjamin also refers to the difference between Fichte and the romantics on the infinity of the process of reflection: "Fichte endeavors everywhere to exclude the infinity of the action of the ego from the realm of theoretical philosophy and to consign it to the practical realm, whereas the romantics seek to make it constitutive precisely of the theoretical, and thereby of philosophy as such" (I 22). These are actually two sides of the same coin, since the finitude of positing and reflection had to be assumed, in Fichte's view, to guarantee the unity of the ego. The early romantics rejected both the hypostatization of the limited subject and the finitude of reflection. Their program was based on the lifting of such restrictions, for which Novalis also used the verb "to romanticize" (*romantisieren*).

[37] For Benjamin, the romantic philosophy of reflection was thus an answer to the epistemological problem he had placed at the core of his "Program of the Coming Philosophy," written in 1917: "It is the task of the coming epistemology to find for knowledge the sphere of total neutrality with respect to the concepts of subject and object; in other words, to determine the autonomous sphere originally proper to knowledge, in which this concept no longer in any way designates a relationship between two metaphysical entities" (II 163).

to use this terminology he reproduced many of the ambiguities and misleading peculiarities of the romantic idiom. Moreover, Benjamin himself sometimes adopted this idiom not only for exegetical purposes, as in the dissertation, but in his own subsequent work. This usage can create the odd impression of a kind of animism. The most striking case is Benjamin's account of the aura, in which he speaks of regarding an object in such a way that it returns one's gaze. If Benjamin's concept of criticism adopts and modifies important elements of Novalis's theory of observation, then his later theory of aura seems to do something similar for Novalis's theory of perception. Indeed, such statements often *are* misleading; but, strictly speaking, the rejection of the traditional subject-object problematic rules out their animistic overtones. In light of the epistemological principle of reflection, romantic "subjectivity" means a self-activating, logical process of unfolding rather than psychological consciousness. For instance, in stating that "the subject of reflection is the work of art itself," Benjamin appears to be attributing psychological consciousness to objects (I 65). But he explains what he means by calling the work of art the subject of reflection: criticism "does not consist of reflection *on* a work, which could not . . . alter the work essentially . . . but in the unfolding of the reflection . . . *in* a work" (I 55–56); that is, criticism unfolds the work's implicit meanings. As is only fitting, he complements this apparent attribution of subjectivity to objects with its contrary, attributing objecthood to subjects. The unfolding of the work of art's reflection, he points out, "can, in this sense, be carried out by a variety of successive critics only if they are personified stages of reflection rather than empirical intellects" (I 68). In other words, the critic's task is to become the medium for the work's unfolding, not to project a unique personality. The point of such reversals of the conventional subject-object terminology is clear: they dramatize the fact that the medium of reflection represents the indifference point (*Indifferenzpunkt*) between subject and object in the romantics' conception of critique. The ascription of "objective" intentions to early romanticism serves his polemical point: the term provides a handy, effective counter to the widespread notion of romantic subjectivism.

The concept of reflection provided the epistemological foundation, Benjamin's argument continues, for the early romantics' conception of the entire range of possible objects of knowledge. Nature, art, history, religion: all these and more were to be reconceived as media of reflection. The methodology appropriate to any particular category of object, therefore, was really only a translation of the universal principle of reflection into a specific medium. In the two chapters at the core of the dissertation Benjamin attempts to demonstrate this interpretation by examining the homology between early romantic theories of nature and art, those objects for which Novalis and Schlegel, respectively, felt a special affinity: he elucidates Schlegel's theory of the work of art and its criticism on the model of Novalis's romantic philosophy of nature. In both cases, knowledge is a process of stimulating the object's self-knowledge.

Novalis's conception of a philosophy of nature can be derived, in effect, from this systematic presupposition (I 53). He spoke of the observation of nature as an experiment, by which he understood a process of activating the object through observation: "The experiment consists in evoking self-consciousness and self-knowledge in that which is observed. To observe something means only to stir it to self-knowledge" (I 60). Observation "awakens" the reflection, the latent self-unfolding tendency slumbering in the object. Varying Novalis's own characterization of his philosophy as "magic idealism," Benjamin terms this "magic observation." Magic observation is also an interactive process: "Whether the experiment succeeds depends on the extent to which the experimenter is able, through raising his own consciousness—through magic observation, one may say—to approach the object and finally to incorporate it into himself. In this sense Novalis says of the true experimenter: nature 'reveals itself more perfectly through him, the more harmonious his constitution is with it'" (I 60). The observer, too, is activated by observing. The harmony Novalis refers to, in Benjamin's view, has nothing to do with any personal, psychological affinity; quite the contrary: it depends on a certain *depersonalization*—on the observer's ability to become a "personified stage of reflection." The process of observation is thus reciprocally productive: in his capacity as medium the observer incorporates the object into himself; conversely, the object also changes by virtue of being intensified. The result, in Novalis's own words, "is simply the extension, division, multiplication, amplification of the object" (I 55)—"the intensification of the reflection" already immanent in it (I 52). The idea of magic observation, Benjamin notes, was "a central tenet of the natural philosophy of the times" (I 54). It exemplified the romantics' protest against what they saw as a mechanistic, instrumental conception of nature and natural science associated with the Enlightenment. Schlegel and Novalis found clear evidence of such instrumentalism in Fichte's idealism as well, in which the transcendental ego was conceived of as "using" nature, the non-ego, as a mere means to the end of attaining its own self-consciousness.[38] But in Novalis's transforma-

---

[38] Fichte would thus have been a prototype of the German idealist philosopher who

tion of Fichtean idealism, nature too "awakens" and "comes to it-self."[39]

Benjamin then presents Schlegel's theory of the work of art and its criticism as a translation of Novalis's philosophy of nature into the medium of aesthetics: "With respect to the work of art, criticism is the same as observation with respect to the natural object; the same laws show themselves in different objects" (I 65). The homology between them arises from the implicit "epistemological grid" they share in the romantics' conception of reflection. Yet the dissertation shows that Benjamin is uneasy about the relative adequacy of these two media. Although certain implications of the principle of reflection "emerge with particular clarity" in the philosophy of nature, only the concepts of art and history are legitimate fulfillments of the early romantics' systematic intentions (I 44). The reason for Benjamin's uneasiness on this point becomes clear if we recall the radical dualism of *Geist* and unmastered natural forces in his youthful writings. On the one hand, the program of his dissertation is to seek out the outlines of a unified philosophical system implicit in the early romantics' fragmentary work. This program is an attempt to fulfill his own hope, as formulated in the course of his break with the youth movement, of establishing a metaphysical groundwork for a form of critique that would be able, by "recognizing the coming, to free it from its distorted form in what is present" (II 75). Nevertheless, the very unity guaranteed by the principle of reflection admits of no fundamental distinction between the realms of art (or of history) and nature within its own bounds. Benjamin's discomfort is therefore significant: the romantics' inability to make this distinction marks the limit of his own appropriation of romanticism. The requirements of a doctoral dissertation afforded no opportunity to treat the "metaphysical" issues involved (I 62). His provisional solution is hinted at in an afterword he appended only after submitting it: the "paradoxical" possibility "that only in art, but not in the nature of the world, does the image of the true, intuitable, *ur*-phenomenal nature become visible" (I 113).[40]

---

mixes idealism and instrumentalism in a manipulative attempt to conceive "a mechanism for the realization of the correct absolute" (B 126). This was how Benjamin saw Hegel, whose spiritual physiognomy revealed "an intellectual thug [*Gewaltmensch*], a mystic of violence, the worst sort there is" (B 171).

[39] Benjamin's relationship to the romantic philosophy of nature was ambivalent. At times he spoke of it in relational terms that echo Novalis's magic idealism, as in "To the Planetarium" (IV 146–148). But at others he stressed the baroque vision of nature as transience and ruin, as in his discussion of allegory in the *Trauerspiel* study. On the Jewish motif of the lament of nature, which Benjamin interwove with the romantic idiom, see Irving Wohlfarth, "On Some Jewish Motifs in Benjamin," 167–177.

[40] A similar argument is made by Jennings, *Dialectical Images*, 133–135. Benjamin went

The principle of reflection proved its mettle in aesthetic theory, Benjamin finds, by providing a positive alternative to heteronomous critical standards: the immanent criterion of the work of art lies in its *form* (I 71–72). The romantics were the first to place the term "work" of art at the heart of their aesthetic theory; in doing so, they stressed the irreducible individuality of the object of criticism. Any work capable of being criticized was, for them, a complex sui generis, not a mere exemplar of a genre. The theory of reflection furnished the grounds for this view: the individual work's autonomy results from its being a "center of reflection," that is, "a particular modification of the self-limitation of reflection" (I 76). The "material expression" of reflection within the work is found in its form. The form of a work—its "immanent construction" (I 71) or "structure"—is not simply "the means of presenting its contents," a neutral vehicle for putting across a message (I 76). Rather, it is the first reflection of the contents of the work—a mute, inexplicit stage of reflection, however, which criticism must raise to consciousness by explicitly calling attention to it. In other words, criticism operates by evaluating the work on its own terms; by virtue of its form, each work is a law unto itself. Benjamin's insistence that romantic criticism is immanent, formal criticism has since been further corroborated by two fragments from Schlegel's *Literary Notebooks,* unavailable to him because they first came to light after World War II: "Criticism is not to judge works by a general ideal but to search out the individual idea of each work"; "Criticism compares a work with its own ideal."[41] The romantic concept imposes a strict discipline on the critic—the discipline of the individual form, the task of specifying the particularity of the work as revealed in its formal features. Yet the obverse of such strict attention to individual form is that romantic criticism must contend with a limitless plurality of forms. To Benjamin's way of thinking, this is precisely one of its cardinal virtues. Whereas neoclassical formalism prescribed a limited range of genres governed by general rules of harmony and beauty, the early romantics

---

on to clarify this point through his analysis of Goethe's conception of the *Urphänomen*, which, as he put it in a note to the *Trauerspiel* study, had to be transferred "out of the pagan, natural context into the Judaic nexus of history" for its truth to emerge, as he tried to do with his concept of *Ursprung* (I 953–954). Still later, in the "Arcades" notes, he adapted this idea in his conception of an *Urgeschichte* of the nineteenth century (V 577). But Benjamin's dualism would also be lifted in the redeemed nature he evoked in "To the Planetarium," a point that became clearer in the anthropological materialism he elaborated after 1925; see Chapter 4, Sections 2 and 3.

41 Fragments 1733, 1135, in the *Literary Notebooks,* as cited in Hans Eichner, *Friedrich Schlegel,* 36. Eichner, the editor of the notebooks, argues that these statements do not represent Schlegel's definitive opinion during the *Athenäum* period.

envisaged "an undogmatic, or free formalism, a liberal formalism" (I 77).

Romantic formalism is also free in the crucial sense that the form of the work is not only individual but necessarily incomplete. "Every work is . . . necessarily incomplete . . . with respect to its own absolute idea" (I 69–70). This, too, follows from conceiving of the form as the work's immanent reflection. As the "strict self-restriction of reflection," the work bears a moment of contingency, or arbitrariness; its unity is "only relative." The task of critique is not to stabilize the work by demonstrating its self-enclosed harmony but to place the relative center of reflection into the continuity of the medium, thereby "lifting all restriction" (I 73). The form of the work might better be described as a constellation of formal moments than as a rigid structure. The use of the term "moment" in this sense is characteristic of German idealist logic: a concept from mechanics referring to the tendency to produce motion ("momentum"), it signifies the dynamic features of a point in logical development. In an important turn of phrase, Benjamin underscores this dynamism by calling the immanent form of the work its "immanent tendency" (I 77). He also characterizes these dynamic tendencies in biological terms as embryonic, germinating cells (*Keimzellen*) within the work: "Critique . . . can only bring about the unfolding, the germination of the work's immanent core" (I 78). And since the work is folded up—incomplete—immanent critique unfolds the work and thereby completes it. "It is clear: for the romantics, criticism is much less the judging of a work than the method of completing it" (I 69).

Immanent critique is therefore "completing critique [*vollendende Kritik*]." This too distinguishes it from the neoclassical conception. Whereas neoclassical critics took it on themselves to pass dogmatic value judgments based on fixed, "rational" rules, the romantics sought an utterly different, nonjudgmental procedure. Schlegel described it as his goal "not to evaluate judgmentally but to understand [*verstehen*] and to explain" (I 78). The overtones of historicist past-mindedness are unmistakable: criticism seeks to understand rather than to judge. Indeed, the romantic concept of criticism did help lay the basis for the cardinal principle of philology propagated by the historical school, which sought to understand the past "as it really was." But the decisive moment in the romantic conception which was lost in the historicists' first commandment of abstinence is just what Benjamin insists on most firmly: the past work is incomplete and criticism, in completing the work, goes beyond it. In fact, because the work always points beyond itself, criticism can be faithful to the work *only* by doing so.

As in the "magic observation" of natural objects, then, the early romantics understood the relationship between criticism and the work of art as an interactive process. But the interactive character of criticism is consistent with its objectivity. By virtue of its form, the work of art is subject to a kind of "objective lawfulness" (I 77), yet this does not fix it irrevocably; rather, its potential must be developed—that is, its self-development must be catalyzed—by criticism.[42] Like a catalyst in a chemical solution, criticism only crystallizes a potential already latent in the solution. Yet critical reflection, like a chemical catalyst, alters the work essentially (I 65). Novalis conceived of the critic as the "true reader": "the true reader must be the extended author," provided that both are understood as "personified stages of reflection" rather than "empirical intellects." In fact, the personal terms can help illuminate the interactive implications. The critic must collaborate with the work's implicit, immanent tendencies; he must "discover the secret predisposition [*Anlage*] of the work itself, carry out its hidden intentions" (I 69). Recast into a psychoanalytic idiom, we might say that the critic must gain access to the work's unconscious and preconscious intentions. Benjamin actually fleetingly refers to what is "not yet conscious" in the work (I 70, n. 178). And just like any rigorous, genuine analysis, criticism involves countertransference; the analyst, too, is activated and must self-reflect. In the process, the critic changes as well. As in Novalis's philosophy of nature, the success of the critical experiment "depends on the extent to which the experimenter is prepared, by intensifying his own consciousness . . . to approach the object and finally to incorporate it into himself" (I 60).

Benjamin finds this interactive conception epitomized in the early romantics' demand for "poetic criticism" in which "the difference between critique and poetry is overcome [*aufgehoben*]" (I 69). Criticism is not derivative of art or parasitic on it, not mere commentary or an aid to art appreciation. Instead, it is the essential complement of the work, an intensification of it, literature to the second power—*Potenzierung*, as the early romantics often called it, the mathematical operation of exponentially expanding a symbol. The demand for poetic criticism is among the most frequently misunderstood romantic principles, because it invites a subjectivistic interpretation by appearing to license an emotional, rhapsodic, and above all private response to the work. For

[42] The notion of cultural images developing in the (photo)chemical sense finds a remarkable echo in a citation Benjamin later collected for use in the "Arcades" project: "Only the future has developers at its disposal that are strong enough to bring out the image in full detail" (I 1238, V 603). This citation combines the notion of chemical development with the temporal perspective that became so crucial for Benjamin by the 1930s, fusing his critical concepts with a philosophy of history. In the notes to the "Arcades" project we can see the shape this might have taken; see Chapter 5, Section 5, and Chapter 7.

Benjamin, this interpretation is ruled out by the immanence of critique, whose discipline of form guarantees sobriety. Criticism is more like psychoanalytic abstinence than the surrealist dialogue in which the words of the other are simply springboards for inspiration. The interactive moment in criticism is always governed by the immanence of reflection.

4. Destruction and Completion of the Work: The Antinomies of Critique

In summarizing the methodological features of the early romantic concept of criticism, Benjamin reached a seemingly paradoxical conclusion. Immanent critique changes the work in apparently contradictory ways. It completes it in a strong sense of the term, not merely by raising its indwelling level of consciousness by degrees, but by "making it absolute," discovering "its own absolute idea" (I 69–70). Criticism consists in "assimilating the limited work to the absolute" (I 85), "reconciling the conditional with the unconditional" (I 114). At the same time, since the romantics conceived of the absolute as a medium of reflection, "this means that the individual work is to be *dissolved* into the medium of art" (I 68, emphasis added). Benjamin takes the idea of a critical "dissolution [*Auflösung*] of the work" (I 98) so seriously as to call it "the destructive moment [*das Zerstörende*] in criticism" (I 85). The line of argument thus seems to lead in contrary directions, yet Benjamin insists that they in fact converge:

> In its central intention criticism is not judgment but rather on the one hand completing, complementing, systematizing the work, on the other hand dissolving it into the absolute. Both processes ultimately coincide, as will be shown. (I 78)

The thrust of the argument is clear: immanent critique, which simultaneously completes and destroys the work, has an antinomial structure. Or, since the romantics considered critique to be the work's *self*-unfolding, one might also say that the work's own structure is antinomial; that is, it harbors self-completing and self-destructing tendencies. Benjamin calls this "the problem of immanent critique" (I 78). The work achieves completion only "at the price of its ruin" (I 85). It releases its meaning "with increasing clarity" in the course of its decay. This antinomy is the seed of a figure of thought pervasive in Benjamin's work from this time on. When interpreted in terms of the historical process, it would take the form of what I call the antinomies of tradition.

Of the two moments in this conception of critique—completion and destruction—the destructive aspect remained underdeveloped in the dissertation, primarily because of the aims of the early romantics themselves, as Benjamin noted. Bent as they were on revealing the current of reflection flowing through all transitory appearances, "a necessary moment in all judgment, the negative," was "thoroughly atrophied" in their conception of criticism. "The moment of self-destruction, the possible negation in reflection carries no weight against the thoroughly positive element of the raising of consciousness in that which reflects" (I 66–67). The romantic philosophy of reflection suffered from an imbalance, in Benjamin's view—an imbalance he came to consider fatal. In fact, the remarkable thing is that he accorded a central position to the negative, destructive moment in the romantic philosophy of criticism at all. While conceding that the negative moment may have been atrophied and underdeveloped, he insisted that it was by no means absent. Benjamin's systematic reconstruction thus prepared the way for his own revision and appropriation of the romantic concept of criticism.

To begin from the negative side, Benjamin speaks of criticism as the dissolution or destruction of the work in two senses. The first is a relatively weak sense of the term: criticism "dissolves" the work by extricating its pure, formal structure from the mass of incidental detail in which it is embedded. The business of criticism is not to demonstrate the harmonious, self-enclosed necessity of the work in all its accidental and idiosyncratic features. As an individual center of reflection, the work necessarily "remains burdened by a moment of contingency"; criticism "purifies" the work by stripping away these contingencies. The unity of the individual work is "only relative" (I 72–73). Its true individuality consists in its unique place within the spectrum of all other works. Of course, not every work will bear such scrutiny; but for this problem, Benjamin notes, the romantics had an elegant solution: works that will not support such treatment are beneath criticism—that is, they are not true works. "Criticism . . . produces a selection among the works" (I 80).

In a far stronger sense of the term, however, Benjamin asserts that romantic criticism demolishes the "illusion" created by the work, its "appearance"—and, most particularly, its beautiful appearance. He illustrates how criticism undercuts the work's illusionary effect by analogy with the way formal irony operates within the work itself. Classical comedy provides the simplest illustration of formal irony. At times, the comic character steps out of his or her role within the action and comes forward on the stage to address the audience with a brief, wry comment on the action. Such asides create a second level of significance:

over and above the comic plot, the play delivers a commentary on itself. As a result, the frame of the work is deliberately violated, breaking the illusion of a self-contained structure. Yet the violation of the form calls attention to it, makes it visible by "reflecting" it. Oddly enough, the destruction of the illusion has a positive result; formal irony "represents the paradoxical attempt to build even in demolishing the work of art" (I 87).

Formal criticism, Benjamin points out, aims at something analogous to formal irony, but its effects must go much farther. In the early romantic conception, criticism was a form of knowledge, not an aid to art appreciation. Beauty, therefore, was at best an ephemeral effect produced by the work, something utterly inessential—"an object of 'amusement', of delight, of taste," not an attribute of its indestructible, absolute form. As such, it would simply be irrelevant to criticism, a frivolous distraction. But this was not all. Appealing to Hölderlin's poetology, Benjamin goes on to attribute a genetic theory of beauty to the romantics according to which beauty is a remnant of something older and more potent—an expression of "ecstasy," of "unmediated, inspired excitement," a trace of the Dionysian element in art. Beauty is the refuge of the cultic origins of art. Criticism may not simply ignore the beautiful appearance of the work: it must take aim at it and demolish it. Benjamin draws the iconoclastic conclusion that for the romantics "the form is no longer the expression of the beauty" of art; "in the final analysis," therefore, "the concept of beauty must give way from the romantic philosophy of art" (I 106–107). As he cites approvingly, "these romantics wanted to keep clear of precisely the 'romantic', as understood then and now"—clear, that is, of "romantic" cults of rapturous beauty. The antidote, he suggests, can be found in their stress on literary technique, the craftsmanlike (*Handwerksmäßige*), mechanical, and even calculating element in art: "The work is constituted soberly . . . by mechanical reason." The sobering liquidation of cultic remnants was to be the task of the destructive moment in romantic critique.

The completion of the work, on the other hand, involves the relationship to be established between the individual work and the "absolute idea" of art. If the idea of the individual work consists in its form, then the idea of art as such is that of a *continuum* of forms. Just as the individual work, by virtue of its form, is reflexive and self-unfolding, so too is the medium of reflection. In Benjamin's formulation of this principle, "all forms of representation hang together continuously, pass into one another, and unite themselves into the absolute form of art, which is identical with the idea of art. The romantic idea of the unity of art thus lies in the idea of a continuum of forms" (I 87). Considered as a medium of reflection, art is a coherent continuum of forms that progressively unfolds itself. This unfolding enacts an organizing motion toward ever greater articulation and clarity, and thus toward unity. As a result, the continuum of forms "fulfills" the individual work. This fulfillment is teleological: the continuum of forms unfolds out of the work as from a germinating cell; yet, once it has unfolded, the continuum reveals the sense of the process that produced it. This absorption of the individual work into the absolute medium of forms is the innermost center of the romantic concept of critique, Benjamin argues. What he called their "liberal formalism" at the level of the individual work looks quite different from the perspective of the absolute. Their apparent liberality reveals itself as a "radical mystical formalism" (I 21), the vision of a metaphysical continuum in which all forms hang together.

"The romantic idea of the unity of art lies in the idea of a continuum of forms"; that is, the idea of art is not something separate from the individual works, external to them or above them, but rather their virtual unity. Benjamin introduces a metaphor for such articulated diversity, for which he once again looks more to Hölderlin than to Schlegel or Novalis (I 104). He likens it to the optical spectrum produced when white light is refracted ("broken," in German) by a prism into a continuum of colors. The unity of the continuum of forms is that of white light to the spectrum of colors. This prismatic metaphor has an impressively broad resonance in early romantic thought. It was important in romantic philosophies of nature, which attempted to overcome the mechanical cast of Newtonian science; the best-known was Goethe's critique of Newtonian optics in his *Farbenlehre*. In literary studies, Schlegel's "Study of Greek Poetry" portrayed the progression of genres in classical Greek literature—from the Homeric epic, through Pindar's lyric poetry, to the tragedies of Sophocles—as a differentiated but unified spectrum. Finally, the optical metaphor has an underlying epistemological reference: the image of the medium of reflection itself is optical.[43] Benjamin himself notes that "light occasionally occurs as the symbol of the medium of reflection" in the writings of the early romantics (I 37, 104). Thus, the prismatic conception of the continuum of forms was deeply rooted in romantic conceptions. Benjamin's use of it, moreover, was a productive extension of the tradition. Its strategic importance, though unobtrusive, was decisive: it enabled him to appropriate romantic figures of thought without invoking the vitalist implications he was determined to exclude.

The unity of the continuum of forms, as Benjamin's formulation

---

[43] Wohlfarth points this out in "Politics of Prose," 136.

makes clear, develops progressively. This sense of progress is, however, by no means commonplace. The reflexive self-unfolding of the medium generates new forms, which "pass into one another"; yet the result is not a homogeneous stream but an ever-greater articulation of the continuum, its "progressively more precise suffusion and ordering" (I 92). The proliferation of forms does not disperse energies; it heightens the unity of the continuum. The prismatic metaphor captures this phenomenon as well: as the spectrum is refracted, more and more of its colors and shadings appear; yet, when blended together—reflected into one another—they produce the white light that constitutes the unity of the spectrum. Benjamin is careful to speak of the unity of art in the romantic sense as something "in a state of becoming": *die werdende Einheit der Poesie* (I 91). Schlegel declared the actualizing of the potential unity of forms to be the defining characteristic of romantic poetry and criticism. As "progressive universal poetry," the task of romantic literature is "to reunite all separate genres of poetry. . . . it encompasses all that is poetic, from the grandest systems of art, which in turn contain several systems within themselves, on to the sigh, the kiss breathed by the poetizing child in artless song. . . . Other types of poetry are finished and can now be dissected. The romantic type of poetry is still in a state of becoming; indeed, that is its true essence—forever to become, never to be complete."[44]

"The romantic type of poetry" actualizes potential unity by spanning form together with form—the lowest with the highest, genre with genre. As a progressively universalizing process, it must be more than just one more form alongside all others. The task of romantic poetry is to *culminate* the unfolding continuum of forms by activating the immanent unity of all that has come before. This gives it a temporal aspect: "It is not a matter of advancing into empty space, of a vague ever-better-poetizing, but rather of a continually more encompassing unfolding and intensification of the poetic forms" (I 92). Unity "in a state of becoming" is not an unfolding through homogeneous time but a process of steadily mounting intensification. In this sense, the concept of progressive universal poetry intimates the romantics' messianic philosophy of history within their concept of criticism.

The romantics conceived of the emerging unity of the continuum of forms as a kind of "invisible work," a virtual unity. They had many designations for this emerging unity and its visible signs. For Schlegel, it was best exemplified by the form after which he named his ideal of romantic literature—the novel, or *Roman*.[45] This notion makes sense

[44] *Athenäum* fragment 116.
[45] Schlegel's choice of the term "romantic" to signify his ideal has been controversial. In its eighteenth-century usage, it involved a rich and complex field of meanings. Ben-

only if we keep in mind what Schlegel, still on the threshold of the nineteenth century, understood by the term. By comparison with classical genres, the novel was characterized by "an outward disorderliness and lack of restraint" (I 98). If one thinks of a work like Sterne's *Tristram Shandy*, for instance, it seems that a novel could break any and all rules and yet still remain a novel; novels could be lyrical, dramatic, epic, satirical, and polemical by turns. Schlegel considered these offenses against the dictates of classical form to be the novel's cardinal virtue. The nature of the novel consisted in its ability to "reflect on itself at will, to mirror back any given stage of consciousness, in ever new reflections, from a higher position." The novel was thus the reflexive literary form par excellence. It was not "one genre among others" but quite literally the genre to end all genres, an idea in the romantic sense—*the* idea of art. In its ability to encompass all genres within itself, in its potential for reflection on ever-higher levels, the novel could enact the historical culmination of all previous forms and become the "tangible appearance of the continuum of forms" (I 98–100).

Benjamin, however, places quite a different capstone at the summit of the romantic edifice: not the novel, he claims, but the medium of prose is the ultimate terminus of their implicit system, the "actual sense" and the "deepest intention" of their theory of the novel (I 101–102). At this point in the dissertation his painstaking philological scruples appear suddenly to break down. As he admits, the theory of prose was to be gleaned only indirectly from Novalis's texts and scarcely at all from those of Schlegel; Benjamin's source was outside the *Athenäum* circle in the works of Hölderlin.[46] The philological strain gives a kind of signal: by placing the concept of prose at the summit of the romantic system, Benjamin was supplying a corrective to romanticism for pur-

---

jamin explicitly endorsed Rudolf Haym's judgment: "Surely Schlegel gladly took into account the ambiguity that lies in the designation 'romantic', if he did not indeed seek it out. As is well known, in the linguistic usage of the times 'romantic' means 'courtly', 'medieval', and behind this meaning Schlegel hid his true opinion, as he loved to do, which must be read out of the etymology of the word. One therefore must definitely understand the expression 'romantic', as Haym does, in its essential significance as 'novel-like' . . . [as the] sum of all that is poetic" (I 99). Behind this playful argument about Schlegel's elusiveness, the basis for Benjamin's claim was his underlying argument that the category of reflection provides the "methodological grid" underlying Schlegel's thought. In later romanticism, the medieval and chivalrous connotations of the term came to the foreground.

[46] Michael Jennings explores the full range of Benjamin's debts to Hölderlin in "Benjamin as a Reader of Hölderlin: The Origins of Benjamin's Theory of Literary Criticism." He argues persuasively that it was an encounter with Hölderlin's work that led Benjamin from his systematic interest in Kantian philosophy to literature and the *Frühromantik* (549).

poses of his own appropriation—a corrective whose consequences were to shape all his work from this point on.

Three grounds for placing the idea of prose at the culmination of the system can be distinguished in Benjamin's brief, highly compressed discussion.[47] First, there is the unifying function of prose to which Novalis had testified: prose represents the "balancing and reconciliation" of the multiplicity of limited poetic forms, the merging of their rhythms; "in prose, all bound rhythms blend together and combine into a new, prosaic unity, which Novalis calls the 'romantic rhythm'." In the terminology of reflection, prose is the "creative ground [Boden] of all poetic forms, which are mediated and dissolved in it as in their canonical creative ground [Schöpfungsgrund]" (I 102)—the originary medium from which they emerge and to which they return. Second— and here Benjamin turns exclusively to Hölderlin—"the prosaic" is "a metaphorical designation of sobriety." As such, only prose can fittingly culminate the movement of reflection "as a thinking, composed attitude." Prosaic sobriety is "the opposite of ecstasy, of Plato's mania" (I 103–104). In Benjamin's version, the ascending continuum of forms thus ends with a decisive reversal, an unromantic break in continuity. In a sudden twist, the culmination of the poetic turns out to be not an ecstatic climax but sober, prosaic presence of mind. With this reversal Benjamin fulfills his pledge to show that the completion of the work, its placement into the absolute continuum of forms, arrives at the same result as its destruction—that is, the purging of its cultic vestiges.

Finally, the idea of prose forms the culmination of Benjamin's version of the romantics' system because it provides the ultimate "legitimation of critique" (I 108–109). At earlier stages of the argument, during the painstaking construction of the philosophy of reflection, the legitimation of critique is based on its "methodical structure." Now, at the very end—"for the sake of which the inquiry had to proceed via apparent detours" (I 100)—it receives its "final, substantial determination" in a brief formula: "Critique is the representation of the prosaic core in every work" (I 109). The object of critique is thus "the eternal, sober durability of the work," and critique "represents" this object— produces it, "in the chemical sense"—in a sober, colorless "form of expression," the transparent, "unbound" rhythms of prose. "Critique,

---

[47] He returned to the notion of prose as the creative ground of unfolding forms in his notes for works in the 1930s. Particularly in his notes for "On the Concept of History," he equated it with "the messianic idea of universal history" (I 1235). The persistence of this motif, despite its overt disappearance in his published works, testifies to the significance of his encounter with the romantics. Wohlfarth's "Politics of Prose" provides a suggestive, associative treatment of these themes. The regulative idea of sobriety was to play a leading role in Benjamin's encounter with surrealism, which in many respects resumed his confrontation with the early romantics on a new level; see Chapter 5.

as a process and as a product, is a necessary function of the classical work" (I 109).

5. Romantic Messianism: The Antinomies of Tradition

As has already become clear, these early romantic concepts of reflection, art, and criticism imply a latent philosophy of history. Benjamin considered history to be the other legitimate fulfillment, alongside art, of Schlegel's conception of the absolute medium of reflection (I 44). In fact, he often suggested that the romantics' concept of history was the more fundamental of the two. Their idea of art supplied the "materials, but not the point of view," for determining their authentic intentions; "this point of view is to be sought in romantic messianism" (I 12). Messianism was "the center of romanticism" (B 208), "the central metaphysical principle of their worldview" (I 62). Yet the dissertation kept it on the horizon, pointing toward it with no more than a series of glancing comments. Considering the cardinal importance he himself assigned to the philosophy of history, Benjamin played a peculiar game of hide-and-seek on the topic, as if reluctant to commit himself to a definite, explicit position. It would be convenient to explain this peculiar behavior by pointing to the constraints of an academic dissertation; he did complain about the "complicated and conventional scholarly attitude expected [of me], which I distinguish from the genuine one" (B 208). Yet his private, "esoteric" texts, which employ figures of thought that suggest both Jewish and romantic messianism, are similarly elusive.[48] It is almost as if he felt compelled to indirection on just those subjects that were most important for him. "One does not always proclaim aloud the most important thing one has to say," he once observed (II 314). Benjamin often seems to have been unwilling, or unable, to entrust it even to himself.

Yet, as the dissertation proceeded, he became guardedly optimistic about the results. During the writing, he ventured to suggest that "what I am learning through it, namely, insight into the relationship of a truth to history, will of course least of all be made explicit, but hopefully noticeable for clever readers" (B 202–203). On completion of the

---

[48] None of the three texts that address these questions most directly was ever intended for publication: "*Trauerspiel* and Tragedy" (1916), "Theological-Political Fragment" (probably 1920 or 1921), and "On the Concept of History" (1940). Ironically, the latter has become one of Benjamin's best-known and most-discussed texts (the title "Theses on the Philosophy of History" was not Benjamin's; it was assigned by the editors of the 1955 *Schriften*). "Nothing is further from me than the thought of publishing these notes (not to mention in the form in which you know them)," he wrote to Gretel Adorno; "this would throw the door wide open to enthusiastic misunderstandings" (I 1227).

rough draft, he confirmed the fulfillment of these hopes: "It has become what it was supposed to be: a pointer to the true nature of romanticism, which is utterly unknown in the literature"; most important, the essentials of the romantics' messianic concept of history "could be read from between the lines" (B 208). Before submitting the work, he even felt confident enough to append what he called "an esoteric afterword, written for those to whom I meant to address it as *my* work" (B 210). The key to reading the early romantics' concept of history "from between the lines" of the dissertation is to recognize the centrality of the principle of reflection. The philosophy of history is not a separate compartment of their system, with its own principles; rather, it is another determination of the medium of reflection—in a sense, a translation or permutation of their concepts of nature and art. The term "philosophy of history" can therefore be misleading. In the early romantic sense, it does not mean artificial speculation about the course of historical events. Instead, it is more a sense of time and of the rhythms in which the forms unfold.

The temporal dimensions of reflection are contained in one of Benjamin's summaries from the epistemological chapters of the dissertation: "Schlegel sees . . . all that is real, in its full content, unfolding with rising distinctness through to the highest clarity in the absolute" (I 32). The process of reflection so described has three closely interwoven yet distinct aspects. First, the unfolding of forms is a *continuous* progression; latent in the idea of the medium of reflection is that of a differentiated, articulated, and unified continuum. Second, the progress of reflection enacts a motion onto ever *higher* levels: forms unfold "with rising distinctness" (I 32) and, in the process, the distinctness and unity of the stages are both increased and intensified. Finally, the progressive unfolding and intensification of reflection has an indwelling goal—"highest clarity," or universality. The fully unfolded continuum would fully articulate the medium, thus producing unity. Benjamin characterizes this fulfillment as the *"absolute* reflection," which contains all previous, lower stages within itself. This absolute is not, however, some hypothetical, finite point at the end of the continuum. Rather, as Benjamin repeatedly stresses, their concept of the absolute was inseparable from its infinity.

In the dissertation, Benjamin comes closest to indicating where the messianic element in this conception lies when explicating the romantics' idea of art as progressive universal poetry. He sets particular emphasis on refuting the "modernizing misunderstanding" that easily arises from conflating this idea with the modern "ideology of progress" (I 91–93). This ideology, he points out, is likewise built around the ideas of continuum, progress, and infinity, but it employs them in a sense utterly contrary to that of the romantics. In the modern idea of progress time is a homogeneous continuum, like the flow of mechanical clock time. Benjamin calls this homogeneity "empty," "an advance into empty space." Progress in such an empty continuum can be conceived of only as quantitative, measurable in terms of "a certain, only relative relation of the stages of culture to one another." The infinity (*Unendlichkeit*) of progress, finally, is seen simply as an endless (*unendlich*) movement into the future, as if along a time line with no end.[49] The romantic concept of history, Benjamin insists, differs decisively on all these points. Time is not a homogeneous, empty space; rather, it is structured by the "progressively more precise suffusion and ordering" of the continuum of forms. Progress is not quantitative, or additive, but qualitative and intensifying: "It is not a matter of some vague ever-better-poetizing but of a continually more encompassing unfolding and intensification" of forms. Finally, the infinity of progress as conceived by the romantics lies not in the fact that it goes on and on but that it culminates and fulfills what has come before: progress, "like the entire life of humanity, is an infinite process of fulfillment, not of mere becoming." The core of the romantics' messianic idea, therefore, lies in fulfillment. Benjamin had alluded to this in his letter on tradition, with the image of tradition as a wave at its crest, crashing over "out of living fullness" (B 146).

For Benjamin the concept of fulfilled time was at the center of the romantics' elusive concept of history. Once the romantic bearings of this messianism have been recognized, we can read a wealth of metaphors for messianic fulfillment from between the lines of the dissertation. What is most striking is that in many of these images messianic fulfillment *breaks* the continuity the romantic concept of history seems at first sight to postulate.[50] One of the most potent—it was later to play a central role in Benjamin's own conception of history—is the image of awakening. Observation, it will be remembered, awakens the reflection slumbering in the object. Awakening (*wachrufen*), however, implies much more than unfolding (*entfalten*) or even intensifying (*steigern*), two other frequently used images of reflection. Awakening is not continuous with slumber but breaks with it. It enacts a qualitative, not a quantitative, transformation. In the fulfillment of the reflection, the continuity of its unfolding is broken. Discontinuity is likewise im-

[49] These formulations suggest that the implicit target of these comments was Kant's conception of history and his idea of the infinite task. Criticism of the "bad infinity" of such conceptions was a stock-in-trade of romantic and idealist philosophers; the Hegelian version of the argument is the best known.

[50] In stressing that Benjamin finds these moments of discontinuity within the *Frühromantik*, my emphasis differs from that of Menninghaus, *Unendliche Verdoppelung*, 220–222.

plicit in the idea of prose as the culmination of the continuum of poetic forms.[51] Prose turns out to be the creative ground of the poetry: whereas the poetic always bears traces of ecstasy, the prosaic is by its nature sober. Thus, prosaic sobriety culminates the rising continuum of poetic ecstasy by breaking with it as well. Most generally, messianic fulfillment is the standstill that interrupts the course of progress, an idea Benjamin cites from Schlegel's *Lucinde*: "What good is unconditional striving and progressing without standstill and a center? Can this storm and stress of the infinite plant of humanity, which in tranquility grows of itself and develops itself, provide nourishing sap or form? This empty, restless busyness—it is nothing but northern rudeness" (I 93). Benjamin seizes on this passing use of the term "standstill" in Schlegel's works as his "fundamental position on the ideology of progress."[52] Awakening, sobriety, standstill: all involve a discontinuity in the course of development scarcely to be reconciled with the "radical mystical formalism" of the romantics' metaphysical credo of reality as a seamless medium. Benjamin tacitly acknowledges this difficulty in the same breath, with the cryptic comment that "romantic messianism does not exercise its full force" in Schlegel's theory of art. Continuity and discontinuity, continuum and standstill coexist uneasily in Benjamin's "pointer" toward the romantic concept of history in his dissertation. The antinomy of criticism—as completion and destruction of the work—reappears in the philosophy of history in the form of an antinomy of tradition.

In this conception of history, there is yet another potential for discontinuity—not the "progressive" messianic interruptions of fulfillment and sobriety but the ever-present danger of a sudden historical relapse. The beautiful appearance of the work of art, Benjamin argues, is a remnant of cultic ecstasy. Although this remnant is supposed to fall away with the fulfillment of art in prosaic sobriety, nothing guarantees that a modern cult of unspoiled experience—"unmediated, inspired excitement"—will not gain the upper hand.

The threatening presence of latent, archaic impulses was only a marginal theme in the dissertation. It predominated, however, in the

[51] Wohlfarth demonstrates many of the linkages between Benjamin's conception of prose and his messianic conception of history in "Politics of Prose." He sees an essentially triadic structure in the messianic concept, likening it to a generalized German idealist pattern of thinking, but this pattern seems to me more characteristic of Hegel than of the early romantics as Benjamin read them.

[52] This may have been Benjamin's first use of the term "standstill" to designate the interruption of historical continuity; it later became part of the concept of "dialectics at a standstill," first formulated in the early "Arcades" notes and applied to Brecht's theater and then to the philosophy of history in the later "Arcades" project and in "On the Concept of History." The passage cited from Schlegel would not seem to warrant Benjamin's reading here.

three major works of the period that followed: "Fate and Character" (1919), "On the Critique of Violence" (1921), and "Goethe's *Elective Affinities*" (1922). In all these works, Benjamin referred to it as the mythic force lingering over human history. The romantics' appreciation of cultic and mythic forms of culture was precisely the moment of their work that fascinated the proponents of *Lebensphilosophie*. Benjamin's account of mythos as the contrary of messianic fulfillment was thus a further pursuit of his immanent critique of romanticism. The results, as we see in Chapter 3, had a decisive impact on the reformulated aesthetic theory presented in the preface to *The Origin of German Trauerspiel* (1924/25).

Finally, it should be noted that the duality of Benjamin's conception of the aura was already clearly visible in the dissertation. The atavistic moments in his later accounts clearly have at least part of their ancestry in Novalis's idea of magic observation and in the conception of beauty as the refuge of cultic ecstasy. Yet Benjamin's more positive account of the aura as harboring the object's historical authenticity can also be traced to romantic motifs. The intensifying potentiation of reflection in an object as it is mediated with ever more centers of reflection produces, as he put it at one point, a kind of radiation: "The thing radiates to the extent that it heightens the reflection in itself" (I 57). Novalis's theory of natural observation would have to be translated into historical terms for its valid intentions to emerge. Benjamin did not, however, regard the early romantics' philosophy of nature as a misconception, a mere intellectual error. Rather, he saw their inability to distinguish between the realms of nature and history as evidence that they were prey to mythic forces that were very real indeed.

6. The Politics and Strategy of Interpretation

Although in the dissertation he seldom referred to the secondary literature on early romanticism, Benjamin showed an acute awareness of the politics of interpretation.[53] To a great extent, the bearings of his interpretive strategy were set by his position in the prewar youth and student movements and his final break with them at the beginning of the war. In effect, the dissertation represented Benjamin's first major step toward coming to grips with the traumatic events of 1914. The sources of his identification are clear: the early romantics had also attempted a generational rebellion in the name of an idea; Benjamin characterized them as partisans of a cult of the infinite, much as he

---

[53] Menninghaus reviews the academic secondary literature cited by Benjamin and shows that it was not the reception in this narrow sense that provides his orientation (*Unendliche Verdoppelung*, 230–236).

himself had once defined youth as a "steady, pulsating feeling for the abstractness of pure *Geist.*" They had found support for their convictions in their sense of standing at a watershed in history, on the threshold of a new age; this temperament was shared by the Benjamin of the youth movement, and its resonance was then sustained, and even amplified, by his apocalyptic sense of the war. Nevertheless, his involvement in the youth movement had also sensitized him to both the affirmative and the vitalist misuses of romanticism. This sensitivity generated a mistrust that assured that his reception and appropriation of romanticism would be critical. The first means of innoculating romanticism against its own decay products lay in his focus on the *Frühromantik* as a distinct moment in the early development of the movement—"its infinite profundity and beauty in comparison with *all* late romanticism." He carried this through by carefully situating the early romantics' epistemological, aesthetic, and critical principles at an equal distance from "dogmatic rationalism" and the "boundless belief in the rights of genius" (I 53). As we have seen, he was at pains to delineate romantic doctrines against organicism, subjectivism, and charismatic genius—in short, against all attempts to place the romantic tradition at the service of vitalism and *Lebensphilosophie.* Benjamin thus found a vindication of his own youthful idealism in the early romantics' radical mystical formalism and their messianic philosophy of history. This success, in turn, provided a productive point of departure for his further work.

Although such observations go a long way toward explaining the inner dynamics and development of Benjamin's work, they do not yet capture the full import of his critique of romanticism. The dissertation was undoubtedly a creative resolution of his earlier problems, but it did not simply ransack the cultural tradition for arguments to settle scores with his own past. Rather, the ideological fronts guiding his interpretation coupled his argument with fundamental, underlying conflicts in German intellectual culture. To appreciate this, we must consider his arguments as part of the larger reception of romantic traditions in Germany.

It can be argued that the reception of romanticism has been more politicized than that of any other literary tendency in German cultural history.[54] As a result, the shifting conceptions of romanticism provide a

---

[54] Klaus Peter, "Einleitung" to Peter, ed., *Romantikforschung seit 1945*, 5. Peter places the development of literary scholarship on romanticism in Germany into a long-term, sociopolitical perspective. See also his more specific comments on Schlegel scholarship in his *Friedrich Schlegel*, 86–90. Silvio Vietta, "Frühromantik und Aufklärung," covers similar ground. A newer, iconoclastic rereading of the reception is argued by Bohrer, *Kritik der Romantik.*

textbook case of the politics of interpretation. In the post-Napoleonic era, romanticism was equated by its liberal opponents with the reaction per se. The best known example is Heinrich Heine's polemic *Die romantische Schule* (1836). Whereas the advocates of the Enlightenment had fought for liberty, rational science, and progress, romanticism—identified with its late, Catholic phase of development—became the emblem of the authoritarian, irrationalist, medievally oriented forces in this liberal view.[55] But by 1870, with the impending unification of the German states under the empire and the reconciliation of large parts of the liberal opposition which followed in its wake, the rigid juxtaposition between liberal enlightenment and reactionary romanticism began to ease. Liberal scholars began to attempt a rapprochement with romanticism in the name of historical objectivity. Rudolf Haym's study, likewise entitled *Die romantische Schule* (1870), showed the way, likening the conflicts of Heine's era to "a dream we have shaken off." The new liberal evenhandedness he espoused was facilitated by a chronological shift away from late romanticism toward the more complex, more contradictory tendencies of the *Frühromantik*.

A second study that appeared in the same year, Wilhelm Dilthey's *Leben Schleiermachers*, was to have more far-reaching consequences. Dilthey shared Haym's liberal perspective on the romantics in many ways; he too found their best impulses in their early works and explicitly condemned the wave of conversions to Catholicism in their later years as a surrender of their best forces.[56] But Dilthey's real interests lay not in literary history but in hermeneutics. He wanted to correct what he saw as the positivistic self-misunderstanding of the Historical School by placing the romantic categories of experience (*Erlebnis*) and expression (*Ausdruck*) at the center of a comprehensive theory of the cultural sciences. Criticism, for Dilthey, was essentially an understanding (*Verstehen*) of expressions. In other words, he wanted to recover and actualize certain basic romantic principles—as he interpreted them—in order to give cultural scholarship a new identity. This "critique of historical reason," as he termed it, would clarify the distinction between hermeneutics and the mathematical, mechanistic positivism of the natural sciences. Only on this basis could the *Geisteswissenschaften* do justice to the totality of human experience or life. Quite apart from the substance or the possible validity of Dilthey's arguments, his conception of the *Geisteswissenschaften* became a crystallizing point for the increasingly ideological tendencies of German aca-

---

[55] Bohrer argues that among nineteenth-century intellectuals not romanticism but the critique of (a selectively defined) romanticism was the orthodoxy (*Kritik der Romantik*, especially 11).

[56] Cited by Peter in *Friedrich Schlegel*, 86.

demic culture in the late nineteenth century.[57] Posing as guardians of the totality or wholeness of life and *Geist*, mandarin academics saw the *Geisteswissenschaften* as a protest against the increasing mechanization and rationalization of life. While most preferred the idealistic overtones of *Geist*, their position could easily be exploited as a *Lebensphilosophie* with vitalistic overtones as well.[58] But ultimately—and this was important for the subsequent reception—Haym's and Dilthey's studies helped to modernize and generalize the appeal of romantic doctrines by freeing them from a narrow identification with medievalism and Catholicism.

The new romanticism, with its vitalist and idealist emphases played up, was thus in a position to flourish by the turn of the century. The title of Ricarda Huch's *Blüthezeit der Romantik* (1899/1901) evokes a blossoming of romanticism in both the age it portrays and the age for which it was written, a revival she intended to promote. Within orthodox academic culture, the romantic revival took its place alongside a revival of German idealism as a bulwark against the specter of modernity. This trend culminated in statements like those of Julius Petersen, an eminent professor of German literature, whose *Wesensbestimmung der deutschen Romantik* became a standard work of literary history in the Weimar Republic: "The man of today may hardly be characterized as romantic. But now more than ever, perhaps, in his antiintellectualism, in his religious and metaphysical urge for eternal values, and in his striving to see things from within, he senses an elective affinity that drives him toward old romanticism."[59]

The religious and metaphysical urge for eternal values eulogized by an orthodox academic like Petersen was even more striking in the nonacademic literary and popular movements of the time. Neoromanticism unfolded in an immense array of forms and varieties. The romantic revival in "high" literature associated with George, Hofmannsthal, and Rilke was complemented by popularizations of the romantic

---

[57] For a detailed account of these trends, see Ringer, *Decline of the German Mandarins*.

[58] The issue of whether Dilthey understood hermeneutics as a psychological reexperiencing of the author's intentions remains controversial. See Hans-Georg Gadamer's critique in *Truth and Method*, 218–242, as well as Rudolf Makreel, *Dilthey: Philosopher of the Human Sciences*, 247–253, and Michael Ermarth, *Wilhelm Dilthey: The Critique of Historical Reason*. A related issue concerns the relationship of what Dilthey called *Lebensphilosophie* to positions such as those of Bergson or Klages. On the latter issue, Benjamin later decided that Dilthey was indeed a precursor of Klages (I 608).

[59] Julius Petersen, *Die Wesensbestimmung der deutschen Romantik*, 3, cited by Klaus Peter, "Einleitung," 8. Petersen's reference to "old romanticism" (*alte Romantik*) is significant: the 1920s saw a rehabilitation of the authoritarian Catholicism of Schlegel's later years in the specialist literature. Benjamin wrote in a letter from 1918, while working on the dissertation, of "the neo-Catholic currents at present, which have even especially seized hold of intelligent Jews" (B 180–181), but it is not clear just whom he was referring to.

literary tradition like Huch's.[60] *Jugendstil* sought to restore organic forms and ornamentation to the decorative arts. The popular cultural criticism of Paul de Lagarde and Julius Langbehn fueled the vogue of vitalistic and charismatic romanticism, and via this channel it suffused the symbolism of the German youth movement. In its most extreme formulations, the romantic revival became a straightforward appeal to irrationality and a glorification of primal forces. It was no accident that the revival of interest in the works of Bachofen, the nineteenth-century scholar of mythology, was spearheaded by members of the George circle.

Against this background, the full dimensions of Benjamin's interpretative strategy begin to become clear. His image of early romanticism recovers a core of authentically romantic doctrines and secures it against attempts to place romanticism exclusively at the service of either *Lebensphilosophie* or orthodox idealism. In other words, the dissertation can also be read as a critical intervention in the reception of romanticism. With it Benjamin attacked what he called "the entirely false modernization of romantic doctrines . . . which is so widespread" (I 83). What is impressive is the concentration with which he addressed a whole range of targets—ideologies both academic and nonacademic, elite and popular. Beneath the restraint imposed by the academic form he chose, he delivered a critique of the rhetoric of *Leben* and *Erlebnis*, life and living experience, in all its forms. As an alternative, he activated a critical potential latent in the *Frühromantik*, stressing its valorization of technique rather than inspiration, sobriety rather than ecstasy. At the same time, Benjamin's *Frühromantik* checked the affirmative temptations of idealism by underscoring the destructive moment in critique and the messianic interruption of historical continuity. He would go on to radicalize his immanent critique of romanticism on both fronts.

---

[60] Bohrer characterizes Huch's study as the true programmatic manifesto of neoromanticism and points out its favorable reception among academic literary historians as well (*Kritik der Romantik*, 276–280).

Chapter Three

Allegorical Destruction

During the first half of the 1920s, Benjamin completed two major studies: one was an extended essay on a single work, Goethe's novel *Elective Affinities;* the other, *The Origin of German Trauerspiel,* was a more formal, scholarly treatise in literary history and philosophical aesthetics, built on an entire genre. In methodological terms, both were exemplary romantic critiques in the sense defined in Benjamin's dissertation. Proceeding from intrinsic, formal properties, he sought to unfold the immanent idea latent in their objects.[1] In the first project he explicated a single work of art from within; in the second, by identifying the content and formal principles uniquely characteristic of *Trauerspiel,* or German baroque tragic drama, he dispelled classicist prejudices and set a modern genre in its rights.[2] At the same time, however, Benjamin was continuing to pursue his own immanent critique of romanticism itself. In each work, he proceeded against a danger latent in early romanticism, dangers that had emerged from the romantic movement as its decay products: whereas the Goethe study attacked the vitalist cult of symbolic expression and myth, the *Trauerspiel* study turned its fire against the aesthetics of affirmative idealism. The implicit coordinates of Benjamin's project, in other words, were still set by the constellation that had guided his break with the youth movement. Behind the immanent criticism of the works themselves stood an immanent

[1] Benjamin now referred to the idea in this sense as the philosophical truth content of a work, for reasons examined below; above all, he wished to avoid the implications of the idealist conception of the symbol as the appearance of an idea in a work of art.

[2] In keeping with common practice, I retain the German term *Trauerspiel* as a reminder of the distinction. The alternative is "tragic drama," but that invites confusion with "tragedy." In the published English translation, oddly enough, while *Trauerspiel* is used throughout the text, the title is rendered *The Origin of German Tragic Drama.*

ideological critique that can only be understood in terms of the dynamics of the intellectual field.

In the process, Benjamin's own theory and practice of criticism outgrew the confines of early romanticism. Most important, the destructive moment in critique—a moment present but insufficiently defined in the dissertation—was given a sharper profile in both studies. The motif of destruction could be played out against the glorification of unified, living expression and the harmonizing totalities of idealism alike. Yet the generative tension between destruction and completion of the work, between critical dissolution and absolutization, was not resolved but heightened. The antinomial structure of his conceptions emerged more clearly than ever. One crucial result was an enormous enrichment of his sense of historical processes: his working conception of history acquired a complex, layered quality that his own pronouncements on the philosophy of history never fully captured. Above all, it is the difference between the two studies that is important. The *Elective Affinities* essay is immersed in the novel's world of appearances, its rich overgrowth of mythic phantasmagoria, in a search for the moments that struggle to break the hold of mythic compulsion from within. The *Trauerspiel* study, on the other hand, decodes the allegorical form's vision of history as a permanent catastrophe, a "petrified, primordial landscape." *Immersion in* symbolic complexity and a liberating *destruction of* it: the difference in the approaches of these two works adumbrates the antinomy of tradition as it was to develop later. But as Benjamin moved from the one to the other, a certain flattening out of his implicit conception of history took place. That too would recur in his later work.

Finally, we see elements emerge that were to lead Benjamin farther, beyond the framework of his philosophical critique of the German tradition as such and into his engagement with modernist and avantgarde culture. Baroque *Trauerspiel* had long been regarded as part of the culture of an age of decay, a decadent by-product of the breakdown of Renaissance classicism. Yet Benjamin discovered that so-called eras of decay have a coherence all their own, confirming his suspicions about the lament over the decay of a classicist culture in his own times. Moreover, it provided him with concrete insights into modernist culture. Baroque allegory's ultimate corrective to classicism—its liquidation of the aesthetic sphere itself—provided an important clue to affinities between particular modernist currents and Benjamin's own critique of vitalism and affirmative idealism. In exploring what he sometimes referred to as the allegorical way of seeing, Benjamin developed an implicitly modernist aesthetic of his own. His intensive exploration of baroque allegory gave him an eye for forms he would later discover in nineteenth-century modernity. In his work after 1925, therefore, he neither broke with his earlier project nor simply translated a preestablished stock of concepts and images into a new idiom. Rather, he continued to pursue his earlier intentions. This continuity with his earlier work was ultimately grounded in the presence of the intellectual field that provided his guiding constellation.

1. "Goethe's *Elective Affinities*"

Benjamin's next major project after the dissertation was an extended essay on Goethe's novel *Elective Affinities* (1921/22). Little is known about the immediate circumstances under which he chose the topic and worked it into a full-length study.[3] It clearly did not fit into any sort of plans for an academic career: unlike the dissertation, it was not designed to observe the philological rules required of an academic work, and not until two years later did Benjamin decide to submit it as a *Habilitationsschrift*—and then without success. Its polished, cultivated, and ever-so-slightly inaccessible form of presentation signals the full-dress debut of a private literary scholar. The little we know about its concrete origins is more than compensated, however, by its manifold significance for the pursuit of his long-term intellectual project.

The first continuity is quite simple: in the *Elective Affinities* essay, Benjamin sought to give a practical demonstration of the romantic theory of immanent criticism he had constructed in the dissertation.[4] "The idea of illuminating a work entirely from within," as he himself later put it, was his methodological guide (VI 216, 218). In fact, he was never again to devote such sustained critical attention to an individual work. The choice of a novel by Goethe as his object likewise represented continuity with the romantics: Schlegel's own exemplary essay in literary criticism had taken Goethe's *Wilhelm Meister* as its object. The German title of Schlegel's essay was built on a pun: "Über Goethes Meister" signaled that Schlegel intended not only to write on Goethe's *Meister* but to rise above and thus surpass both the novel and Goethe,

---

[3] See the editors' commentary in the *Gesammelte Schriften* (I 810–811). Scholem calls attention to the fact that the essay was "written by Benjamin in a human situation that corresponded uncannily to that of the novel" ("Walter Benjamin and His Angel," in *On Jews and Judaism in Crisis*, 202). On the disintegration of Benjamin's own marriage at the time, his relationship to Jula Cohn, and the correspondences between Cohn and the figure of Ottilie as Benjamin portrayed her, see Witte, *Walter Benjamin: Der Intellektuelle als Kritiker*, 61–63, 201, n. 165.

[4] An effective account of the essay from this angle alone is provided by Menninghaus, "Walter Benjamins romantische Idee," 428–439. But Benjamin's study also entails decisive modifications of the romantic concept of criticism, as I argue here.

the master (*Meister*) himself. By repeating this romantic gesture in the pursuit of his own goals, Benjamin underscored his relation to the *Frühromantik*.

Benjamin had also described immanent criticism as discovering the hidden reserves and carrying out the secret intentions of the work of art. Goethe's novel, which portrays the deadly consequences that follow from the decay of a relationship, had always been read as an object lesson on the ethical sanctity of marriage and the disastrous consequences of unfaithfulness. Benjamin flatly denies this reading. The fateful, compulsive unfolding of the action results not from the partners' violation of the marriage bond, he insists, but from their attempt to cling to the legal institution after the substance of their relationship has evaporated. In doing so, they entangle themselves in a network of compulsions whose source remains invisible to them. These compulsions, the fate they call down on themselves, are the true object of the novel. Benjamin calls them mythic forces. "The inescapably dreadful element in the proceedings lies solely in the disaster that is roused. . . . The object of *Elective Affinities* is not the marriage. Its ethical forces are nowhere to be found in the novel. They are vanishing from the beginning, like the beach under water at floodtide. . . . In its dissolution, all that is human becomes mere appearance and the mythic alone remains as the essence" (I 130–131). Appearances to the contrary, then, Goethe's novel delivers a potent condemnation of the bourgeois world it seems to be defending:

> What the author conceals a hundred times over can be seen quite simply from the course of things as a whole: that according to ethical laws passion loses all its rights and its happiness when it seeks a pact with the bourgeois, the abundant, the secure life. . . . In the mute entanglement that encloses these people in the circumference of human, nay bourgeois mores, hoping to save the life of passion for themselves there, lies the dark transgression, which demands its dark expiation. (I 185)

Not to be overheard in these words is Benjamin's allusion to his own attempt to keep faith with the idea of youth by refusing any "pact with the bourgeois, the abundant, the secure life." In his critique, therefore, the novel indeed does pivot on "the fable about abnegation" (I 143), but the trick is to see through this fable. Goethe's *Elective Affinities* is not the parable about the virtues of self-denial it so noisily pretends to be but an exposure of the bourgeois fable that self-denial is the royal road to happiness.

Proceeding from the postulate that "the mythic is the material content of this book" (I 140), Benjamin can use his critique to address another of the desiderata established by his break with the youth movement: to set out the categories of a phenomenology of mythic forms. The novel presents a virtual world permeated through and through by mythic compulsions. Benjamin calls the mythic force that governs this world fate. Unrecognized by the characters who are hopelessly ensnared in it, fate rules over the greatest and the least of their actions and perceptions. It therefore appears in a variety of guises: in the sense of guilt that hangs over the characters, in their anxious reading of portents, and in the blindness and delusion of their choices. Above all, fatality shows itself in the "bleak ritualistic tendency" (I 142) of their actions, through which they unwittingly attempt to expiate their guilt for violating the statutes of marriage by sacrifice. These futile efforts end in the sacrificial suicide of an innocent, the maiden Ottilie, as a gesture of atonement. "The death of an innocent," Benjamin observes, is the "mythic archetype [*Urform*] of sacrifice" (I 139). But he finds the crucial sign of mythic fatality in the work in the way it saturates even "the entire landscape—whether in the literal or the extended sense" (I 132). The natural world itself is permeated by a death symbolism (I 135). And the characters themselves cannot help but give expression to natural forces. "An obscure power manifests itself" in their existence: "Humans themselves must manifest the force of nature. For nowhere have they outgrown it. . . . the figures of the novel . . . [are] completely bound by nature. . . . At the height of cultivation, they are subject to those forces that cultivation passes off as having been mastered" (I 133–134). Thus, a particularly powerful sign of fate is the compelling force of objects: "Once one has sunk to this stage, even the life of apparently dead things acquires power. Gundolf has quite rightly pointed out the significance of the thing-like in the proceedings" (I 139). Mythic fate permeates the novel's entire world of appearances, human and natural, animate and inanimate.

The mythic substrate of the novel in turn occasioned the fourth of Benjamin's concerns in the *Elective Affinities* essay, a polemic against the glorification of myth promoted by the George circle, in this case as represented by Friedrich Gundolf's *Goethe* (1916). Gundolf's biography was an apotheosis of the Goethe cult, deliberately mythologizing Goethe's life as the fate of a creative genius struggling to shape his age and his works as the vital expression of his essential nature. It therefore provided a natural target for Benjamin, a first opportunity to bring his latent polemic against vitalist cults of all sorts, in the youth movement as in romanticism, into the open.[5] Since Benjamin himself insisted so

[5] Benjamin referred to the essay as "an attack on the ideology of the circle around George" and hoped that its place of publication—Hofmannsthal's *Neue Deutsche Beiträge*—would make it impossible to ignore (B 341). He was mistaken, although it did

firmly on the mythic content of the book, it was incumbent on him to explain just what separated his view from Gundolf's. The heart of Gundolf's delusion, he found, lies in the mystifying assumption of a unity of essence, work, and life in Goethe. Such unity may indeed be a primary characteristic of "the realm of myth" (I 157), but belief in it is a fatal stumbling block to critical insight. Benjamin's crucial claim is that Gundolf's fascination with Goethe as a mythic figure blinded him to the signs of a struggle to get free of mythic ensnarement in Goethe's life and work—and particularly in *Elective Affinities:*

> [Its] testimonial force concerns not only—and not most deeply—the mythic world in Goethe's existence. There is a struggling for release from its embrace and this struggle, no less than the essence of that world, finds testimony in Goethe's novel. . . . If the constantly renewed . . . effort of the years of his manhood was to submit himself to those mythic orders wherever they still rule, indeed to do his part to secure their rule . . . with *Elective Affinities* he began to register a protest, which grew steadily more powerful in his later work, against the world with which he had made a pact in his manhood. *Elective Affinities* is a turning point in this body of work. (I 164–165)

The point on which *Elective Affinities* itself turns, according to Benjamin, is in the novella Goethe inserted within it. The freedom with which the young lovers find their way to one another in "The Marvelous Neighbor Children" holds up an inverted mirror to the proceedings of the novel: "To the mythic motifs of the novel correspond those of the novella as motifs of salvation. Thus, if the mythic in the novel can be regarded as the thesis, then the antithesis can be seen in the novella" (I 171). The core of the novel, constituted by the tension between the two, is a struggle for release *from within* ensnarement in myth. Gundolf's error lay not in recognizing the prevalence of the mythic in Goethe's life and work but in erecting a monument to their unity. He had been taken in—far more than Goethe—by the lures of myth.

Finally, however, and most important for our purposes, Benjamin's analysis of the mythic substrate of the book entailed a decisive recasting of his concept of critique. The *Elective Affinities* essay is far more than a practical application of an existing theory, for it translates and extends the romantic concept of immanent critique. The most striking departure is a new theory of appearances (*Schein*) and of beauty. Romantic criticism, in Benjamin's rendering of it, had no place for these

---

win him Hofmannsthal's esteem and support; see Witte, *Walter Benjamin: Der Intellektuelle als Kritiker,* 99–106.

categories, since immanent critique penetrates beneath the surface to the inner form of the work. But this rigorism had its limitations. To decipher the mythic content of the novel and penetrate to the secret locked up in it—"the struggling for release" from mythic fatality—one had to *account* for its world of appearances rather than simply dismiss it as inessential. In the aesthetic realm, appearances take the form of beauty.[6] Benjamin therefore emphasizes a proper understanding of the sense in which beauty is an appearance: "The essential law of beauty thereby shows itself to be that beauty appears as such only in what is veiled. Beauty itself, therefore, is not mere appearance, as philosophical banalities teach. . . . Not mere appearance, not a veil for something else is beauty. . . . For neither the veil nor the object that is veiled is the beautiful, but rather the object in its veil" (I 194–195). Accordingly, critique cannot seize the artwork's beautiful appearance directly, nor should it strive to "expose" the secret of the work by stripping away appearances to get at the truth they conceal. "The task of art criticism is not to lift the veil but rather, through the most precise knowledge of it as a veil, to raise itself to the true conception of the beautiful . . . to the conception of the beautiful as that which is secret" (I 195). And since "all mythic meaning seeks secrecy" (I 146), criticism thereby recognizes the beautiful appearance itself as a mythic phenomenon.

This is not to say that critique places itself at the service of the work's own mythic constitution. On the contrary, it seeks out what Benjamin calls the truth of the work or, in the idiom of the dissertation, the work's immanent idea. But it must first give itself over to the artwork's mythic world of appearances in order to find that which is striving to free itself from this ensnarement from within. Abandoning the romantic terminology of form, Benjamin now formulates this duality of criticism as a distinction between the "material content [*Sachgehalt*]" and "truth content [*Wahrheitsgehalt*]" of the work (I 125).[7] His investigation aims at a kind of "exhaustiveness" in illuminating "the significance of the realia in the work," and this requires a certain amount of "commentary" on the material content before the question of the truth content can be addressed. But such commentary is not a mere antiquarian exercise in explaining obscure details, which have since "become extinct in the world," before getting down to the real business of critique. For the *significance* of the realia was hidden "from the author as from

---

[6] Benjamin discusses the question of the "beautiful appearance" (*schöner Schein*) above all with reference to the figure of Ottilie. To spell this out would require a longer excursion into the novel itself than is possible here. The best treatment of Benjamin's conception of beauty is still Rolf Tiedemann, *Studien zur Philosophie Walter Benjamins*, 71–76.

[7] Benjamin does, however, *use* the category of form in interpreting the novel. Menninghaus, "Benjamins romantische Idee," shows how in some detail.

the public of his time." Commentary must establish what the material content actually is in the first place. The passage of time is not an obstacle to this labor but a crucial ally: by estranging the appearances from later readers, draining them of deceptive familiarity, it forces a harder look at them. So it is that Benjamin asserts the material content of the novel to be not the sanctity of marriage but the forces that proceed from the decay of the relationship. "In this sense, the history of works prepares their critique" (I 125). Only once the true material content has been discovered can one even begin to address the properly critical question of the secret of the work, a secret once so bound up with the material content as to be invisible—"the more significant, the more inconspicuously and intimately." It is precisely the decay of the apparent unity between material content and truth content that opens access to critical insight.

The extended concept of criticism developed in "Goethe's *Elective Affinities*" has several advantages over the concept of immanent critique expounded in the dissertation. In many senses, it is simply a fuller theory. It addresses both the surface of the work, its world of appearances, and the necessity of penetrating to what Benjamin now calls the work's inner secret. The romantic concept of form did not so much deny that this was possible as bypass the problem completely. The new terminology of material content and truth content also lends sharper contours to many of Benjamin's earlier concerns. By insisting on the dissolution of the original unity of material and truth content, he fills out his earlier notion that the work unfolds in time and clarifies how it is that critique can complete the work only at the price of destroying its unity (I 181). And in so doing, he focuses attention on the way the individual work—not only the genre or the continuum of reflection—changes in the process.

The new concept also establishes linkages to the content of critique. Broadly speaking, Benjamin set up a force field whose poles could be called ensnarement in myth, on the one hand, and a struggle for release from mythic compulsion, on the other. He saw the relationship between the two as the fundamental issue of the philosophy of history (I 196). There is a great temptation to schematize this philosophy of history, drawing on the many hints scattered throughout the text. Benjamin himself avoided this temptation, and there are good reasons to follow his lead on this point. Such schematization creates the false impression that Benjamin worked according to an implicit blueprint drawn from a preexistent source, distracting attention from the process of his own ongoing development of these concepts. It also suggests that there ultimately *was* a single blueprint. In fact, Benjamin's conception of history developed on many levels that were not always coordinated or even consciously theorized. Because it was not a rigid scheme, various facets came to the fore and were developed successively in his encounters with various objects.[8]

What Benjamin was really aiming at is better illuminated in terms of his break with the youth movement. Read against this background, the *Elective Affinities* essay delivers a scathing critique of the bourgeois forms of life with which Benjamin had refused any pact as a world permeated with mythic compulsions. The burden of the argument is a critique of the aestheticizing, vitalistic glorification of myth of the kind promoted by the George circle. But with a slight twist in the formulations, the same critique could also be turned against affirmative idealism in all its guises. These critiques of *Lebensphilosophie* and idealism converge in the category of "the symbolic." The symbolic, as he defines it almost in passing, "is that in which the indissoluble and necessary bonding of truth content to material content appears" (I 152). In mythic perception, for instance, the phenomenal world is saturated with archetypal significance. In this, however, it resembles the idealist insistence "that the most essential contents of existence are capable of imprinting themselves on the world of things—indeed, that without such imprinting they are incapable of fulfilling themselves" (I 126). Both generate "the false, errant totality—the absolute totality" (I 181). And both lead to the same fatal result: "The person petrifies in the chaos of symbols and loses his freedom" (I 154).[9] In tracing affirmative idealism and the mythic consciousness alike to the common form of the symbolic, Benjamin was able to join two of the essential branches of his critique, to unite two of the ideological fronts.[10] It was to the symbolic

[8] Menninghaus, *Schwellenkunde*, 109, makes an analogous point about the various elements in Benjamin's conception of myth.

[9] Thus, when Benjamin characterizes Kant's work as having sketched "the guide through the barren forest [*Wald*] of reality," he is praising, not disparaging, Kant's achievement. Gundolf's work, by contrast, is a "jungle [*Urwald*] where the words, as chattering apes, swing from branch to branch, bombast to bombast, so as not to have to touch the ground that would betray that they cannot stand—the ground of logos, where they should stand and account for themselves" (I 163). In a note for the "Arcades" project, he described it as his own intention to "forge ahead with the whetted axe of reason, looking neither left nor right so as not to fall prey to the horror that beckons from the depths of the primeval forest [*Urwald*]. All ground must sometime be made arable by reason, cleared of the tangled undergrowth of delusion and myth" (V 570–571). At the same time, however, he was cultivating the art of "losing himself" in the "forest" of symbols of a modern mythology (IV 237). The *Elective Affinities* essay, in which he attempts both to immerse himself in the "false, errant totality" of mythic appearances and to cut through it, was really his first *open* confrontation with this ambivalence. See the further discussion in Chapter 5, Section 5, and Chapter 7, Section 3.

[10] As this example shows, Benjamin forged alliances not only among his allies but between his adversaries as well: thus, Buber was guilty of both vitalism and instrumentalism; Fichte combined idealism with instrumentalism; capitalism reactivated and intensified the forces of myth; and so on.

itself, and to affirmative idealism, that he next turned his critical attention.

2. The Locus of the *Trauerspiel* Study

In the preface to *The Origin of German Trauerspiel*, Benjamin unabashedly proclaimed the task of philosophical criticism to be "the representation of ideas." He left no room for doubt that the term "idea" was to be understood, at least generally, in a metaphysical sense. Ideas were the "objective interpretation of phenomena," "eternal constellations," metaphysical "Being," or "the essential content of beauty." Such language was not without its risks, as Benjamin's own bitter experience had shown him. And in evoking it now, he mounted a simultaneous assault on the affirmative biases of idealist aesthetics and worked out an alternative way of seeing—the allegorical "intention"—whose yield he then incorporated into his own philosophy of criticism. Benjamin's *Trauerspiel* study moves between these two poles. The points of reference that define its locus, in other words, are ultimately to be found in his long-term intellectual strategy.

The immediate circumstances under which the *Trauerspiel* study was composed were marked by a tangle of academic politics and a crisis in Benjamin's relationship to his parents. In 1922, on concluding the *Elective Affinities* essay, he decided to attempt to acquire the *venia legendi* (a lecturer's accreditation) through a *Habilitation* at a German university. His motives, however, did not include any acceptance of the inevitability of making his peace with academia. If anything, his distaste for the German university world had increased since the disillusionments of 1914. He spoke of further signs of decay in the universities and foresaw that a lectureship would only distract him from his "tasks" (B 302, 311). At a point in the proceedings when the chances looked good, he professed "a horror of almost all that would go along with a successful outcome" of his application (B 373). He could not even count on acquiring a secure income from the university: since *Privatdozenten* were unpaid, it was only through subsequent promotion to an associate professorship (*Extraordinariat*) that he might reach a salaried position. The income he hoped for was supposed to come from his parents. As he candidly explained, he sought the *Habilitation* as a "certificate of public recognition, which will call them to order" and persuade them to continue their financial support or even pay out his inheritance in advance (B 293). The pressure of this conflict was increased by the fact that at the time the thirty-year-old Benjamin, his wife, and their son were living with his parents at their home in Berlin. His ambivalence about embarking on an academic career was thus even more highly charged by personal pressures.

The choice of a suitable university was a complicated affair in itself. The unwritten rules of anti-Semitism set limits on the number of Jews likely to be accepted as members of any given faculty. After deciding that the newly founded university in Frankfurt offered the best chances of success, Benjamin mobilized his connections and established contact with Franz Schultz, a full professor (*Ordinarius*) in the department of German language and literature. Schultz, whose support of Benjamin was circumspect and at best tepid throughout the *Habilitation* proceedings, soon deflated his hopes of submitting the Goethe essay as a *Habilitationsschrift*. Instead, he proposed a new work on the German *Trauerspiel* of the baroque period. The choice of topic testified to Schultz's shrewd sense of academic politics: the literature of the baroque, long neglected in German literary studies, was showing the first signs of an oncoming boom in scholarly interest; it was therefore a promising topic for an aspiring academic and for his prospective patron as well. Benjamin's own feelings were quite different. He was understandably disappointed at having to embark on a major new project for mercenary reasons. Even worse, he found the proposed topic "refractory" at first, and the work "forced" (B 302). Nothing could have been better calculated to confirm his fears about losing the independence he enjoyed as a *Privatgelehrter*. "This work is a conclusion for me—by no means a beginning," he insisted on its completion (B 373). On this point he proved to be wrong. He may have been through with the universities, but for the rest of his life economic necessity would force him to accept assignments and topics dictated by circumstances. What is more, he became a master at the art of turning them to his own purposes—just as he did, for the first time, in the *Trauerspiel* study.

In its overall construction, *The Origin of German Trauerspiel* is a strikingly pure exercise in early romantic criticism. The first of its two major divisions, *"Trauerspiel* and Tragedy," sets out to establish the autonomy and legitimacy of a modern genre against the tyranny of classical models. Ancient Greek tragedy, Benjamin insists, is not a transhistorical aesthetic genre; rather, it corresponds to a specific historical moment— humanity's struggle for freedom from ensnarement in prehistoric forces. Its content is the struggle against mythos enacted in the conflict of a tragic hero, who asserts his or her ethical autonomy, with the dark forces of fate called forth by the violation of unwritten statutes. Baroque *Trauerspiel*, in contrast, has an entirely different object: "Its content is historical life, as that epoch [the Catholic Counter-Reformation] conceived of it" (I 242–243). Its particular concern is "the elementary force of nature in the historical course of events" as revealed by the inescapable transience of all worldly things (I 308). What animates it is not the tragic conflict but the play of mourning, of sorrow. When judged by the standards of classical tragedy, it can only appear as an inept, derivative form. But "the world of *Trauerspiel* is a particular world, which asserts its greatness and equality of birth against tragedy as well" (II 140). In this respect, Benjamin did for *Trauerspiel* what the early romantics had done for the novel, which also lacks the "unity" and "purity" of the classical genres. Yet in vindicating it he had to counteract a whole host of romantic prejudices as well. As the product of an educated officialdom, *Trauerspiel* was not Germanic and folkloristic enough for later romantic philologists, nor had its German version found a "sovereign genius" equal in stature to Shakespeare or Calderon (I 229–230). The romantics themselves had helped to build the closed cultural canon Benjamin was trying to break open.

The second major division of the study is titled "Allegory and *Trauerspiel*." In it Benjamin works with the romantic theory that the immanent idea of a work of art lies in its form. The form proper to baroque *Trauerspiel* is allegory—not allegory in general but the historically specific baroque version of allegory, which Benjamin explicitly refers to as a borderline form (I 366, 390). If the specificity of *Trauerspiel* can be seen from its content, its coherence as an aesthetic form in its own right emerges only in the relationship between form and content. In the language of the dissertation, the allegorical form would be described as the work's immanent reflection of its content: "The presentation may, indeed must, linger so insistently over the allegorical structure of this form because it is only thanks to this structure that the *Trauerspiel* can assimilate, as its content, the materials provided to it by contemporary conditions" (I 390). Now, however, Benjamin recasts the form-content relationship as one between material content and truth content, using the terms introduced in the *Elective Affinities* essay. "The object of philosophical critique"—his own procedure—"is to show that the function of the aesthetic form is precisely this: to make historical, material contents, which provide the basis of every significant work of art, into philosophical truth contents" (I 358). And by philosophical truth content he explicitly understands the "concretely conceived metaphysics" represented in a work of art (I 228). Aesthetic form, in other words, is the key to "metaphysical content" (I 233).

As in the case of the Goethe essay, however, such intentions took Benjamin beyond any mere application of the early romantic concept of criticism to his immanent critique of romanticism itself. The romantic idealists were sure they knew what form absolute ideas appear in: they appear in the guise of the aesthetic symbol. Symbolic works of art— harmonious incarnations of the true, the good, and the beautiful—

were understood as stabilized incarnations of a world of absolute and eternal values. Moreover, this preference for the world of beautiful appearances had an implicitly polemical bent as well: aesthetic images that did not provide such visions of wholeness were denied the status of true, genuine images. Aspects of experience not susceptible to such expression, facets of the world not visible to the symbolic way of seeing, were filtered out of the aesthetic realm in advance. Enormous portions of the cultural canon challenged by the early romantics' genre theory thus reappeared in the romantic idealists' doctrines of aesthetic form—through the back door, as it were. Moreover, they had reappeared in a particularly affirmative fashion, since the possibility of aesthetically transcending the flawed world of experience tends to devalue the experience of its brokenness. Such false aesthetic transcendence was just what baroque *Trauerspiel* denied. In order to gain access to its allegorical form, therefore, Benjamin would have to demolish the affirmative biases built up around the romantic conception of the aesthetic symbol. Yet his own theory of allegory would have to be more than a theory of a literary trope. It would have to demonstrate the broader coherence of what he referred to as the allegorical way of seeing, the allegorical intention.

This, in turn, led Benjamin to a new departure in his cultural criticism from within his previous frame of reference. By discovering unsuspected coherence in a "broken" age, an age to which wholeness of experience and harmony of expression had been denied, the *Trauerspiel* study mounted a challenge to the notion of eras of decay (*Verfallszeiten*). A scholarly rehabilitation of baroque culture was already under way in academic cultural history at the time. It had been long enough in coming: well into the twentieth century, despite the historicist dictum of past-mindedness, the baroque continued to be treated as a twilight zone between the glories of Renaissance and neoclassical culture.[11] To Benjamin's mind, this belated arrival of historicist evenhandedness fell far short of what was needed. It might produce apologetic appreciations of the baroque, but as long as it remained ensnared

[11] The landmarks in the history of the visual arts were Heinrich Wölfflin's *Renaissance und Barock* (1888) and *Kunstgeschichtliche Grundbegriffe* (1915). Benjamin attended Wölfflin's lectures while studying in Munich during the war. He had hoped to find a teacher in him but came away bitterly disappointed (see the letters to Fritz Radt cited in Scholem, "Benjamin und Noeggerath"). The two brief studies that later formed the core of the *Trauerspiel* study, "*Trauerspiel* and Tragedy" and "The Significance of Language in *Trauerspiel* and Tragedy," were written shortly afterward. Benjamin's occupation with baroque *Trauerspiel*, therefore, was not simply dictated to him by Schultz. It is also significant that his attention was drawn to it during this incubation period in his development—just when he was beginning his studies of the *Frühromantik*.

in the system of classicist poetics it did nothing to promote insight into the allegorical way of seeing (I 233). At best, it could correct "the valuation, but not the understanding," of allegory (I 345).

Benjamin found his own model for dealing with "eras of decay" outside the field of baroque literary history in the exemplary *Late Roman Art Industry* by the Viennese art historian Alois Riegl.[12] The object of Riegl's study was a very different era of "decadence," the decline of the Roman empire and the tribal migrations at the twilight of classical antiquity. The inward and outward "strife [*Zerrissenheit*]" of the times left its mark on artistic production, in which "a well-formed expression of genuine content can hardly be wrested from the conflict of the forces that have been unleashed" (I 236). But Riegl did not equate the failure to achieve classical harmony of form with incoherence or a relapse into barbarism. His close examination of intricate, ornamental detail in the decorative arts of the period revealed an astonishing new repertory of figure-ground relationships. The formal principles that were beginning to emerge testified, as Benjamin put it, to a "new feeling for space" (III 170). By delving into such intricate detail, Riegl had been able to glimpse the emergence of a new "organization of perception" undergirding the new world of aesthetic forms (I 478). When Benjamin referred to the coherence of the allegorical way of seeing, therefore, his own vision had been schooled by Riegl. He was adopting what he took to be Riegl's decisive achievement for his own purposes: to establish "the contemporary relevance of the baroque after the breakdown of German classicist culture" (I 235).

As this suggests, Benjamin's ultimate point of reference was not the baroque but the accelerating breakdown of German classicist culture during his own time. The term "decay" plays a telling role in his reflections on the state of affairs in postwar Germany, particularly with respect to the monetary inflation and its cultural consequences. In fact, he conceived and began the *Trauerspiel* study just as the postwar inflation was spinning out of control. A 1923 manuscript that exists in various versions (under such titles as "A Descriptive Analysis of the Germany Decay" and "Imperial Panorama: A Tour of the German Inflation") testifies to his attempt to come to terms with the treacherous ambiguities of diagnosing cultural decay.[13] Benjamin was in fact quite

---

[12] Benjamin acknowledged his debt to Riegl on several occasions, including the "Epistemo-Critical Prologue" to the *Trauerspiel* study; his curriculum vitae; the review "Books that Remain Alive" (III 169–171), in which he juxtaposed it to Alfred Gotthold Meyer's study on iron construction in nineteenth-century architecture; and "The Work of Art in the Age of Its Mechanical Reproducibility." On Riegl and Benjamin, see the extended account by Jennings, *Dialectical Images*, 151–163.

[13] The fate of two of these uncannily exemplifies the directions in which he felt himself pulled. The "Descriptive Analysis" version was supposed to appear in the journal *Red*

susceptible to the kind of rhetoric typically involved by reactionary idealists and radical conservative vitalists. Precisely where the perception of decay was at issue, he was by no means immune to the ideological ambiguities that had bedeviled the youth movement. In deploring an "uncertainty, indeed perversion of vital instincts, the impotence and decay of the intellect," for instance, he blundered his way into company he was otherwise careful to avoid (IV 98, 929). He even indulged himself in the pseudo-diagnosis of a corruption of "essences." "All things," he warned, "are being deprived of their essential expression [*Wesensausdruck*] in a relentless process of mingling and contamination [*Verunreinigung*], and ambiguity takes the place of authenticity" (IV 100, 927). He called attention to the very real poverty and suffering that were spreading all around him but was repeatedly distracted by the lament over an invasion of the realm of intellectual privilege: "The freedom of conversation is being lost. The topic of the conditions of life, of money, intrudes itself sooner or later in every sociable exchange" (IV 917).[14] Another phrase, one that does not appear in the version Benjamin had published, shows where this jargon of decay could lead him: the "mob" (*Pöbel*)—a particularly brutal term—"has been seized by a frenetic hatred for intellectual life" (IV 920).

Yet his susceptibility to such rhetoric must be balanced against a thorough immunity to other strains of the lament over decay. In a climate overheated by nationalist agitation, for instance, he was quite clear about where he placed the blame for Germany's troubles: "The obduracy with which this people outdoes itself in prolonging its stay in the prison of solitary confinement" (he was referring to German isolation from the rest of Europe during the 1923 Ruhr crisis) was beginning "if not to bury its cultural assets then at least to make them rusty, heavy to wield and to move" (B 311). Almost in passing, Benjamin used two extremely unorthodox terms for dealing with the cultural tradition: to "wield" (*handhaben*) and to "move" it. Culture was not a store of essences and ideals that could only be contaminated by the "intrusions" of the "conditions of life," a realm accessible only to the contemplative gaze of seers; it was deeply implicated in the present state

---

Guard in Moscow—but never did; another version, untitled, was given to Scholem in the form of a rolled manuscript on his emigration to Palestine in September 1923. The "Imperial Panorama" version was finally published in *One-Way Street* (IV 94–101). All parts of the extant manuscripts have now been reprinted in the *Gesammelte Schriften* (IV 916–935).

[14] One might make this out as a dawning awareness of the pervasiveness of commodity fetishism, but the rhetoric of "essences" and "vital instincts" is more characteristic of right-wing anticapitalism.

of things and susceptible of being mobilized.[15] An awareness that a general melting down of the inherited culture was unavoidable was beginning to dawn on him. There was no use lamenting that "it can't go on like this." He was beginning to see through the rhetoric of decay and his own implication in it:

> The helpless fixation on notions of security and property deriving from the past decades prevents the average person from perceiving the most remarkable stabilities of an entirely new kind underlying the present situation. Since the relative stabilization of the prewar years favored him, he believes he must regard any state of affairs that dispossesses him as unstable. But stable conditions need by no means be pleasant conditions, and already before the war there were strata for whom stabilized conditions meant stabilized misery. (I 94)

There was indeed a relationship between decay and critique, but not what the conservative lament would make it out to be. Periods of alleged decay, particularly the decay of classicist cultures—whether the baroque or his own—had a coherence of their own and offered chances for insight and knowledge. Benjamin's insight into the coherence of the baroque allegorical way of seeing, in which "remarkable stabilities of an entirely new kind" had emerged, in turn helped train his eye for the new stabilities of his own time. In both cases, the presupposition was to own up to the "poverty of experience."

3. Symbol and Allegory

What, then, was at stake for Benjamin in his exploration of baroque allegory? As the study neared completion, he called its conception of allegorical form "the essence whose recovery was my concern" (B 366). His long-term intellectual strategy set the negative coordinates for this recovery, for access to the genuine form of allegorical expression could be opened only by overthrowing "the domination of a usurper who came to power in the turmoil of romanticism"—the idealist concept of the aesthetic symbol (I 336–337). This "usurper," though aided and abetted by "the romantic aestheticians' wooing of a resplendent . . . knowledge of an absolute," had its origins in the idealist neoclassicism the early romantics themselves had sought to unthrone.

---

[15] Benjamin's language here anticipates the Brechtian idiom of "using" culture, the instrumental implications of which Adorno found so troubling. There is a tension between this language and the noninstrumental evocation of ideas suggested in the *Trauerspiel* preface.

By exposing the affirmative biases that ultimately overtook them, therefore, Benjamin took his immanent critique of romanticism a decisive step farther. In the process, he found a new, positive point of orientation for his own concept of criticism. In its allegorical form, he asserted, "baroque proves to be the sovereign opponent of classicism, as which only romanticism has been acknowledged until now . . . . And it can scarcely be denied that the baroque, that contrasting prelude to classicism, offers a more concrete, authoritative, and lasting version of this correction" (I 352).

Benjamin's salvage operation begins by clearing away ideological misconceptions. To gain access to the true, lost nature of the allegorical, one first has to strip away the encrustations of a contrast that has dominated German idealist aesthetics since its origins—the opposition of symbol and allegory. Reduced to its simplest terms, the orthodox conception of the aesthetic symbol defined it as "the 'appearance' of an 'idea' in the work of art" (I 336). The term "idea" carried the idealist sense of a transcendent, absolute, and timeless value rather than the artist's subjective notion; "appearance" (*Erscheinung*) implied that the idea does not merely occur in a work of art, which serves as an incidental vehicle, but shines forth in and through the work, lending it beauty and totality. Benjamin quickly sketches out the implications of this basic conception. The idealist symbol posited a seamless continuity between the aesthetic and ethical realms, an "unrestricted immanence of the moral world in the world of beauty." This metaphysical construction went back to the German neoclassicists' "apotheosis of existence in the . . . perfected individual," that embodiment of the true, the good, and the beautiful in a harmonious, well-balanced unity. Winckelmann's veneration of Greek sculpture had supplied the prototype for this "plastic" vision of the well-formed individual, just as neohumanism enthroned "the human" as the highest "fullness of being" (I 340–341). The key to this whole complex, named by Benjamin almost in passing, is in the ideal of *Bildung:* "The radius of cultivation [*Bildungsradius*] of the perfected, beautiful individual describes the circle of the 'symbolic' " (I 337). For him, the salient features of the symbolic are therefore a certain "noncontradictory inwardness" and a "will to symbolic totality" (I 362), whether in the work of art or the individual. The "theosophical aesthetics of the romantics" has simply "placed this perfected individual into an . . . eschatological, indeed sacred progression of events" (I 337).

The "speculative counterpart" to the neoclassical symbol was a negative caricature of allegory. According to the "classicist prejudice," allegory was simply an inferior artistic technique. Goethe saw it as an artificial technique of seeking out particulars to fit a preconceived, general scheme, whereas true artistry meant "grasping the particular in all its vitality," reaching the general only in and through the particular.[16] This contrast reinforced a self-serving view of the baroque as a clumsy prelude to the higher stage of artistic development that was blossoming in German neoclassicism. Schopenhauer addressed the philosophical dimensions of the contrast more explicitly. Allegory was merely the "expression of a concept [*Begriff*]," whereas the symbolic work of art was the "expression of an idea [*Idee*]." The clincher in his line of argument was to equate allegory with script, for script was seen as "a conventional relationship between a signifying image and its meaning, . . . a mere mode of designation," or "a playful illustrative technique" at best (I 338–339). The "art of the symbol" versus the mere "technique of allegory": the enthroning of this contrast was a constitutive act in legitimating the reign of neoclassical and idealist aesthetics. Insight into allegory, therefore, had not simply been lost in the shuffle of historical change. Its genuine intentions had been removed from view by being defined out of existence. This process of repression "tended all the more to take place in silence as it was unconceptualized, profound, and bitter" (I 337).

Allegory, Benjamin insists, is a "form of expression," an intention or way of seeing in its own right. But he does not simply accept the polarity of symbol and allegory at face value and then reverse the orthodox valuation.[17] Instead, his object is to redefine the relationship through what he calls a "historical and philosophical penetration" of the allegorical form (I 345). Recovering its authentic nature requires a complex series of steps. His procedure—as far as can be reconstructed from the text—can be broken down into two phases.[18] The first is to glean hints at the true state of affairs by reading the theories of romantic cultural philosophers against the grain; the second is to identify the peculiarly baroque version of allegory—an extreme, historically specific, "borderline form" of allegory (I 390)—by drawing on the historical iconology of the Vienna school of art history.

Having begun by demonstrating the romantics' ensnarement in clas-

---

[16] In the dissertation, Benjamin noted the counterpart to this aesthetic doctrine in Goethe's theory of the observation of nature, with which he stood close to the romantics: "There is a tender empiricism that makes itself so inwardly identical with the object that it thereby becomes true theory" (I 60). Benjamin sometimes claimed that his own ideal of (re)presentation was one in which "the factual [is] already theory" (B 442–443).

[17] This important point is well made by Bainard Cowan, "Walter Benjamin's Theory of Allegory," 111. Cowan, however, focuses on the redefinition of allegory and does not deal with Benjamin's chastened, redefined concept of the symbol as *momentary* totality.

[18] It cannot be assumed that the text simply reports how Benjamin actually went about making this discovery. For one thing, essential features of the theory of language involved can already be found in the 1916 reflections "On Language as Such and on Human Language." The compelling argument he presents in the *Trauerspiel* book does, however, rest on the logic reconstructed here.

sicist prejudices, Benjamin then sets out to disentangle their valid insights. For, ironically enough, "with the romantics, allegory began to come to itself" despite their intentions (I 360).[19] His first line of approach is an immanent, philosophical critique of romantic theories of mythology and language. Here he looks not to the early romantics but to Friedrich Creuzer's *Symbolik und Mythologie der alten Völker* for the telling clues. Creuzer had drawn an emphatic contrast between the Greeks' "symbol of the gods, which wonderfully unites beauty of form with the highest fullness of essence" and the "mystical symbol," or allegory, in which "the ineffable, in seeking expression, ultimately bursts the too-fragile vessel of earthly form by the infinite power of its being" (I 341). This characterization was meant as a denigration of allegory, but to Benjamin's eye it unwittingly goes straight to the heart of the matter. Allegory is indeed like script: it "immerses itself in the abyss between pictorial being and meaning" by probing the inevitable discrepancy between arbitrary signs and absolute, stabilized significance. Schopenhauer, too, had been closer than he knew to the truth about script. The *failure* of human language and signification to capture and stabilize that which they intend supplies the baroque form of allegorical expression with its generative tension. This shows itself clearly in the decisive category of time. The symbol embodies "momentary totality," "self-contained, concentrated, steadfastly remaining itself," whereas allegory has the discontinuous structure of a series of moments, of transitory, failed attempts to capture meaning.[20]

This semiotic insight into the nature of allegory has to be complemented, however, by historical analysis. Here Benjamin leans heavily on the findings of the Viennese iconologist Karl Giehlow, who was the first to demonstrate just how baroque allegory differs from its medieval predecessor.[21] The ground for modern allegory, Giehlow found, had

[19] His own words are *die Allegorie kam zum Anfang einer Selbstbesinnung*—a straightforward use of the romantic idiom of self-reflection. He later speaks openly of the "virtual romantic theory of allegory" as "an unmistakable monument to the affinity between the baroque and romanticism" (I 388). The idea that an appreciation of the baroque allegorical vision makes a true history of authentically romantic intentions possible constitutes an important subtheme of the *Trauerspiel* study. The connection reinforces the case for reading the study as a continuation, not an abandonment, of his engagement with early romanticism. It also suggests the complex historical sensibility Benjamin was developing, constructing a prehistory and posthistory of a submerged moment of early romanticism; see the discussion of his later theory of reception in Chapter 7, Section 3.

[20] Actually Benjamin introduces his own formulation of the distinction by philological proxy, citing a letter written by Görres to Creuzer. The move reinforces the sense that Benjamin's critique of the romantic theories is truly immanent, but it does not lend particular clarity to his exposition.

[21] The reference is to Giehlow's *Die Hieroglyphenkunde des Humanismus in der Allegorie der Renaissance, besonders der Ehrenpforte Kaisers Maximilian I* (1915). Benjamin manages to repeat three times within the space of a page that "only since Giehlow" has it become possible to grasp the specifically baroque form of allegory (I 344–345).

been laid by the humanist scholars of the Renaissance. In their efforts to decipher ancient Egyptian hieroglyphs, they came upon esoteric theories to the effect that the pictorial writing of the Egyptians preserves traces of a lost, mystical philosophy of nature. Such "hierograms" had been seen as a kind of "sacral instruction"—an allegorical key to the book of nature, closer to divine revelation than was the degenerate, phonetic form of script. Obsessed as they were with unriddling the wisdom of the ancients, the humanists themselves began to compile and develop their own pictorial codes, "writing with thing-images [*Dingbilder*] (*rebus*) instead of letters." The Renaissance was dominated by a classicizing, neo-Platonic theory of art, and so these pictorial inscriptions were restricted to decorative purposes. In the baroque, however, "hieratic ostentation" gained the upper hand and the "hieroglyphic," emblematic form emerged as a central stylistic principle of baroque art. With its passionate Christian emphasis on the fallenness of nature and humanity, the baroque rejected the Renaissance emphasis on harmony and serenity of form. But whereas medieval Christian allegory had served didactic purposes, as in the morality play, baroque allegory preserved the esoteric and hieratic intentions of its humanist predecessor. In historical terms, baroque allegory was a unique fusion of medieval and Renaissance elements.

From the mid-sixteenth to the mid-eighteenth century, a flood of literary and graphic "emblem books" poured across Europe.[22] These collections were veritable lexica of allegory, catalogues of picture puzzles— compendia of the allegorical way of seeing. Allegory gradually "worked its way into all realms of spiritual activity . . . from theology, the study of nature, and morality, down to heraldry, occasional poetry, and the language of love" (I 349). Yet this very proliferation unexpectedly turned into a liability: "The further the development of emblematics branched out, the more inscrutable this form of expression became." A chaos of codes developed as Christian, Greek, and even Egyptian traditions were mixed together indiscriminately. Thrown back on their own ingenuity, the allegorists added more and more objects to their stock of requisites and even began to "dissect" objects by allegorizing each of their parts and properties individually. "The most astonishing," Benjamin reports, was "a complete hieroglyphics of color" built on all possible permutations of two hues. Eventually, every inspiration might call forth "an eruption of images . . . a chaotic heap of metaphors." In the end, therefore, the profusion of attempts to read the book

---

[22] A vast compendium of baroque emblematics has been compiled by Arthur Henkel and Albrecht Schöne, *Emblemata: Handbuch zur Sinnbildkunst des XVI. und XVII. Jahrhunderts.* Schöne's *Emblematik und Drama im Zeitalter des Barock* confirms Benjamin's insistence on the importance of emblematics in both the text and the staging of *Trauerspiel.*

of nature allegorically defeated its own hieratic ambitions. In Giehlow's words, "one and the same thing could just as well signify a virtue as a vice, and in the end anything at all" (I 350).

The combination of these philosophical and historical insights provided the basis for Benjamin's own theory of allegory. In its semiotic dimension, baroque allegory reveals "the abyss between pictorial being and meaning." But it does not rest there in "contemplative calm" (I 342), the serene composure of neoclassicism's "noncontradictory inwardness." Rather, "it enacts a reversal between extremes," an "eccentric and dialectical motion" between the poles of the sign and the signified, the emblem and the hidden wisdom to be deciphered in visible nature, flights of hope and plunges of despair. "The haughty ostentation with which the banal object seems to rise up from the depths of allegory soon gives way to its dreary, everyday countenance . . . [to] disappointed abandonment of the emptied emblem" (I 361). In enacting this failure to stabilize meaning, allegory provides what Benjamin calls "an ur-history[23] of signifying or of intention" (I 341–342).

Once this desperate oscillation has been appreciated, however, the content expressed by the allegorical form becomes visible. Allegory acts out "an extraordinary crossing of nature and history" (I 344) to which Benjamin gives the awkward name "nature-history" (*Naturgeschichte*). Allegory captures an experience of nature that was necessarily inaccessible to classicist symbolism: the "lack of freedom, the imperfection, the brokenness of the sensuous, beautiful physical world" (I 352–353). Nature remained the school or art for the baroque, as it had been for Renaissance classicism, but with a decisive difference: to the allegorist, nature "appears not in bud and bloom but in the overripeness and decay of its creations . . . as eternal transience" (I 355). The baroque vision of history—the "philosophy of history" inherent in its version of the allegorical form—results from assimilating the conception of human history to this experience of nature. History is "subject to nature [*naturverfallen*]," meaning that it is "a process not of eternal life but rather of irresistible decay [*Verfall*]" (I 354) and "subjection to death [*Todesverfallenheit*]":

> In allegory the *facies hippocratica*[24] of history lies before the eyes of the observer as a petrified, primordial landscape. Everything about history which, from the very beginning, has been untimely, sorrowful, unsuc-

---

[23] The term *Urgeschichte* as used here might also be rendered "originary history." In the 1930s, as Benjamin worked out his theory of modernity in the notes for the "Arcades" project, it took on new dimensions; see Chapter 5, Section 5, and Chapter 7.
[24] = "death's head."

cessful expresses itself in a countenance—no, in a death's head. . . . in this, the figure of man's most extreme subjection to nature, is pronounced the enigmatic question not only of the nature of human existence as such but of the biographical historicity of the individual. This is the core of the allegorical way of seeing, of the baroque, secular account of history as the Passion [*Leidensgeschichte*] of the world, a world that is meaningful only in the stations of its decay. The greater the significance, the greater the subjection to death, because death digs most deeply the jagged line of demarcation between physical being and significance. (I 343)

As in the case of nature, the allegorical form captures a facet of historical experience inaccessible to the classicist symbol: the experience of all that is untimely, sorrowful, and unsuccessful. It does justice to the creaturely, suffering element of human existence and to its lack of fulfillment. The allegorical emblem for history itself, therefore, is not an expressive countenance—as Benjamin realizes in catching himself—but a grinning skull, the macabre negation of all living expression; a death's head expresses nothing but grim mockery of human intentions. "Seen from the perspective of death, life is the production of corpses" (I 392) and history the building of ruins. "Significance and death come to fruition together in historical development" as enacted in the allegorical form of baroque nature-history (I 343).

Idealist and romantic aesthetics, by enthroning a usurper—the concept of the aesthetic symbol—had obscured the genuine allegorical intention. But the burden of Benjamin's argument is not only to rehabilitate the allegorical way of seeing. For allegory, he insists, does not simply capture another facet of things; it is no mere complement to the aesthetic symbol. The critical point is ultimately that the classicist symbol itself—not only the idealist and romantic aesthetic theories built on it—actually falsifies human, historical experience. Symbolic images present themselves as stable, material embodiments of timeless, even transcendent, perfection. The hallmark of the symbol is a certain way of transfiguring appearances so as to lend them beauty, harmony, and totality.

The connotative richness of the German word for transfiguration, *Verklärung*, plays a crucial role at this juncture in Benjamin's argument. It suggests, first of all, a transformation in which an object takes on a certain radiance. The object glows; it beams, like a face transfigured by bliss, or shines, as does the beautiful appearance (*schöner Schein*) of the work of art. Transfiguration often involves an exaltation into the transcendent; in a religious apotheosis, for instance, the divine, spiritual essence shines forth through earthly appearances. But finally, *Verklärung* may also mean an idealization of something in the negative sense of distortion or even falsification; memory may transfigure the past by bathing things in a sentimental glow, making the good old days appear more beautiful than they actually were. The aesthetic symbol's transgression, in a word, is *Verklärung*, a falsifying transfiguration. By contrast, Benjamin underscores the lack of radiance (*Scheinlosigkeit*) of baroque allegory: things "bear the seal of the all-too-earthly on their mandate to signify allegorically. Never do they transfigure themselves from within" (I 356).[25] As opposed to the classicist symbol's image of harmonious totality, allegory offers a patchwork of amorphous fragments: "The false appearance of totality is extinguished" (I 352). Keeping faith with the transitory nature of things and with the historical experience of suffering and failure, "allegory declares itself to be beyond beauty" (I 353–354). "And although all 'symbolic' freedom of expression, all classical, harmonious proportion, all humanity . . . is lacking" in the allegorical image, "the nature of human existence as such" and "the biographical historicity of the individual" are done justice (I 343). Allegory is the most potent antitoxin to the aesthetic symbol's transfiguration of appearances.

To Benjamin, the orthodox doctrine of the aesthetic symbol is not only a tyrant but an impostor, an illegitimate claimant to the title of the symbolic, for there is a conception of the symbolic that does not falsify transience and suffering. Here too, the romantic mythologists had unwittingly pointed the way. The genuine symbol was what Creuzer had disparaged as the "mystical" symbol, that paradoxical "unity of a sensuous and a supersensuous object" (I 336) in which "the ineffable . . . bursts the too-fragile vessel of earthly form by the infinite power of its being" (I 341). Symbolic totality that does not falsify the radical transience of nature and human history can be had only at the price of its temporal duration. The point Benjamin extracts from a tortuous exegesis of Creuzer's theories is that

> the measure of time proper to the [genuine] experience of the symbol is the mystical instant [*Nu*]. . . . Under the decisive category of time, the introduction of which into this field of semiotics was the great romantic insight of these thinkers, the [true] relationship between symbol and allegory can be captured incisively and formulaically. Whereas in the symbol—the transfiguration [*Verklärung*] of destruction—the transfigured countenance of nature fleetingly reveals itself in the light of redemption, in allegory the *facies hippocratica* of history lies before the eyes of the observer as a petrified, primordial landscape. (I 342–343)

[25] Just as allegorical *Scheinlosigkeit* serves here as Benjamin's counter to the illegitimate radiance of the idealist conception of the symbolic, so in the *Elective Affinities* essay "the expressionless" (*das Ausdruckslose*) provided the counterpoint to the expressive, vitalist symbol (I 181).

The aesthetic symbol's affirmative bias thus lies in its pretense of incarnating a "plastic," *stabilized* totality. Symbolic totality of a sort is indeed possible, Benjamin asserts, but only—he adopts Creuzer's terms—if it is "startling," "sudden," with the "brevity" of a "lightning flash" (I 340). The light of redemption reveals the true countenance of things only fleetingly.[26] Instantaneously, the true symbol "draws the meaning into its hidden . . . interior."[27] This absorption of meaning "into" the symbol also distinguishes it from the resolute externality of allegory. The symbol provides a fleeting glimpse of totality, whereas the allegorical gaze reveals history and nature as a devastated landscape subject to irresistible decay. This, for Benjamin, is the genuine counterpoint of symbolic and allegorical forms.

The way Benjamin recasts this counterpoint is particularly important in light of his own interests. His definitions of symbol and allegory must also be read against the background of the formulations used in the preamble to "The Life of Students."[28] On the one hand, a theory of symbolism that avoids the pitfalls of affirmative idealism must be mindful of the fragility and fleetingness of the truly symbolic image. In 1915, wary of what happens when existing institutions and cultural forms are regarded as concrete embodiments of an absolute idea, he had cautioned that his own images of youth culture, the life of students, and the idea of learning were to be understood "only as a likeness" of a metaphysical absolute. On the other hand, true to the idealist intentions he had sworn to vindicate, his goal was nevertheless to lay bare the metaphysical structure of particular cultural formations. Since the exalted, would-be incarnations of the idea—the state, the university, youth—had discredited themselves, one had to learn to glimpse it in the "most endangered, most defamed and ridiculed creations and thoughts." Benjamin kept faith with the youth movement

[26] This is the origin of a persistent motif in Benjamin's works, culminating in the fifth thesis of "On the Concept of History": "The true image of the past *whisks* by. The past can be seized only as an image that flashes at the instant it can be recognized, never to be seen again" (I 695). Benjamin linked such momentary knowledge to the need for decisive action in a text from *One Way Street*: "Before . . . prophecy or warning has been mediated by word or image, its best strength has already ebbed away—the strength with which it strikes us at the core and compels us, though we scarcely know how, to act in accord with it. . . . The moment is the Caudine yoke, beneath which fate is to be bowed. To change a threatening future into a fulfilled 'now'—this . . . is the work of bodily presence of mind" (IV 141–142). See Irving Wohlfarth's commentary in "Walter Benjamin's Image of Interpretation," 91–96.

[27] The full text reads "hidden and, if one may put it so, wooded interior." He also speaks of "the naturally mountainlike and plantlike in the overgrowth of the symbol and Creuzer's emphasis on the momentary within it." Here Benjamin himself seems to be unable to check the metaphorical overgrowth. On the forest symbolism, which was important to him, see n. 9.

[28] See the discussion of this text in Chapter 1, Section 4.

by searching for an adequate form of solidarity with the untimely, sorrowful, unsuccessful experiences of creaturely lack of freedom, imperfection, and brokenness. In a sense, then, his own goals corresponded closely to the authentic allegorical and symbolic intentions as he now constructed them. The desire to unmask the official monuments to progress, the stabilized totalities and transfigured appearances of the dominant culture, by casting them in the light of the petrified, primordial landscape created on the battlefields of the war—that gave Benjamin his eye for the coherence of the allegorical way of seeing. And nevertheless to catch a fleeting glimpse of the immanent state of perfection that lies deeply embedded in every present by collecting images in a momentary focal point, a flash point: that compelled him to swear loyalty to metaphysical absolutism all the same.

4. An Aesthetic of Destruction? The World of Baroque Allegorical Forms

Benjamin's interest in the allegorical way of seeing went beyond vindicating it as a form in its own right. His argument in philosophical aesthetics also cleared the way for a rich, material exposition of the profusion of allegorical forms. It is easy to overlook this level of his study, in part because of his own stress on deciphering *the* allegorical form itself—as if there were essentially just one such form—as a vision of the petrified, primordial landscape of history. In fact, his exploration of "the baroque type of form-giving impulse" (I 358) uncovers a layer that lies between this single, ultimate philosophical core of baroque allegory, on the one hand, and the vast mass of baroque emblematic images, on the other. Along with his theory of baroque allegory, Benjamin explicated an ensemble of allegorical figures, patterns, and rhythms that constitute what we might call an allegorical aesthetic of destruction.

Many of the figures of this allegorical aesthetic would later recur in Benjamin's encounters with modernist and avant-garde culture. In a sense, the *Trauerspiel* study deploys an *implicitly* modernist aesthetic. Part of the explanation for this resonance between the worlds of baroque and modernist forms derives from his own intellectual development. His intimate knowledge of baroque forms sharpened his eye for particular aspects of the world of forms in which he was later to immerse himself. Yet it would be wrong to place too much stress on the idiosyncratic basis for this resonance, reducing it to a personal vision of baroque and modernist culture. There were genuine, structural correspondences between baroque and modernist forms: Benjamin's point of access to the baroque was his immanent critique of the *Frühromantik*, and romanticism, in turn, provided the seedbed of much modernist culture. The corrective to the affirmative temptations of romanticism Benjamin found in baroque allegory would later prove incisive, therefore, when turned on the culture of modernism.

The fundamental law governing the baroque allegorical mode of expression is to be found in what Benjamin calls "the antinomies of the allegorical" (I 350). He repeatedly contrasts the dialectical rhythm of allegory with the balanced, harmonious inwardness of classical forms. But his invocation of the much-abused term "dialectical" has nothing in common with its more familiar and comfortable usage in Hegelian traditions. Rather, he understands dialectics as an "eccentric" motion that "enacts a reversal between extremes" (I 337). The antinomies of allegory involve a radical, despairing alternation between unbridgeable antipodes; the comforting prospect of a harmonious synthesis is denied. Such drastic reversals recur at all levels of Benjamin's analysis. On the substantive level, the extremes result from the emblematists' search for significant constellations of objects. Employed as "requisites of signification," pointers to a hidden wisdom, objects suddenly seem to rise above their banal, everyday existence. But as the codes of signification proliferate to the point that "any person, any object whatsoever, any relationship can mean anything else at all," this exaltation suddenly yields to its opposite: objects are cheapened and degraded. "This possibility pronounces a devastating yet just verdict on the profane world," understood, as in the baroque, under the sign of transience. "It is characterized as a world in which the details are not so terribly important. . . . Thus the profane world, considered allegorically, is both elevated and devalued" (I 350–351).

This dialectic of content has a whole series of formal, stylistic correlates. All allegory—not only its baroque variant—leans heavily on convention, on a tacit framework of codes and values behind the appearances that its very artificiality allows to show through. Yet baroque allegory is also a powerful expression of despair over the creaturely element of human existence. The conventionality and expressivity of allegory are thus constantly at odds: the more skillfully conventional references are employed, producing a seamless web of appearances, the less allegory expresses—and vice versa. With respect to its fecundity in the production of images, moreover, allegory seems "cold" and "facile," calculated and controlled. Yet, here too, the further the codes of signification multiply, the greater the tendency for every idea to unleash "a veritable eruption of images" (I 349). And ultimately the very coherence of baroque literary works is torn between two poles in an analogous fashion. "Things"—emblematic references—are collected and assembled fervently "in the unremitting expectation of a miracle," a hieratic revelation (I 354). But the result is chaotic disorder, a heaping of elements rather than an orderly, organic whole. The "law" that governs such works is therefore an alternation between "scatteredness" and "collectedness":[29] "Things are assembled according to their significance; indifference to their existence scatters them again. . . . In the dialectic of this form of expression, the fanaticism of collecting is balanced against the slackness of the arrangement" (I 364). The antinomial rhythms of baroque allegory, in form as in content, have a wild extremity that resists domestication.

The single most important allegorical figure in Benjamin's construction is that of the fragment. Baroque *Trauerspiel* is replete with images of the fragmentary, and Benjamin's theory of allegory helps to explain why. Fragments serve as emblems of decay and destruction. The "false appearance of totality is extinguished" wherever the fragment comes into its own (I 352). The architectural ruin, for instance, exemplifies the destructive effect wreaked by nature on history: "In decay, and in decay alone, the course of historical events shrivels up and is absorbed into the setting" (I 355).[30] The apparent flow of temporal progression is frozen and "petrified," "captured" in a spatial image. And in the process the human social order is unmasked as "a natural phenomenon of the highest order" (I 271–272). The baroque fascination with the corpse— the ruins of the human body—has the same sense. The corpse is "the epitome of all emblematic props" on the baroque stage. *Trauerspiel's* indulgence in gruesome torments is not capricious, however; its inner logic dictates that "the human body could be no exception to the commandment decreeing the destruction of the organic, so that the true meaning, as it was written and ordained, might be gleaned[31] from its fragments. . . . The characters of the *Trauerspiel* die because only so, as corpses, can they enter the allegorical homeland. Not for the sake of immortality do they meet their end, but for the sake of the corpse" (I 390–392). Death "prepares" the body for allegorical dismemberment, for an emblematic "distribution" of its parts "to the manifold regions of significance." The baroque obsession with rubble, both architectural and human, thus expresses "the primacy of the thinglike over the personal, of the fragmentary over the total" in the conception of "nature-history" (I 362). On the stage, in *Trauerspiel*, the props take over the show—as they ultimately do on the world stage as well. And since

---

[29] The terms he uses—*Zerstreuung* and *Sammlung*—both play key roles in his explorations of modernist culture.

[30] He reiterates this formulation in other contexts in the *Trauerspiel* study, with slight variations (I 271, 353).

[31] Benjamin uses the word *auflesen:* literally, "read up."

allegories themselves are fragments of meaning, shreds of a lost whole, ruins are allegories of allegory: "Allegories are, in the realm of thoughts, what ruins are in the realm of things" (I 354). Fragments and ruins are therefore the allegorical emblems par excellence.

The danger lurking in such an aesthetic of the fragmentary is that a beautiful appearance can be won even from decay and destruction. The prime example is the effect of picturesque delapidation later popularized by romanticism and art photography. Far more sinister are Ernst Jünger's "storms of steel," with which he aestheticized the brutality of trench warfare in World War I, and Emilio Marinetti's futurist aesthetics of warfare. Allegory attempts to "declare itself to be beyond beauty"; therein lies its critical force, the philosophical truth content Benjamin is seeking to distill. Yet, ironically, the allegorical way of seeing may end by opening new realms for aesthetic perception, new harmonies and false totalities. Benjamin thus finds himself forced to emphasize elements that forestall any such reaestheticization of decay and destruction. One of these is to stress that the destructive effects of the passage of time release "significance" and "knowledge." The danger is clear to him: philosophical criticism of the kind he intends "may not attempt to deny that it reawakens the beauty of works"; but "without at least an intuitive grasp of the life of the detail through the structure, all affection for beauty remains mere dreaming" (I 357–358).[32] The penetration of past forms of experience carries with it the risk of falling prey to the spell cast by their reawakened beauty. But the knowledge they yield can be had at no other price.

This critical maxim is supplemented by a stress on the unabashedly constructed quality of baroque allegorical works of art. Instead of offering works that bloom forth as organic wholes, the artists of the baroque built their works as ruins from the very beginning. Allegorists heaped together building stones culled from the quarries of classical, medieval, Renaissance, and contemporary emblematics without attempting to disguise their technique. On the contrary, technique was ostentatiously flaunted. Genius lay neither in "creation" nor in the faculty of imagination later exalted by the romantics but in "manipulating models with a sovereign skill." "The writer must not conceal the fact that he arranges and combines, since it was not the mere whole but rather its obviously constructed quality that was the center of the intended ef-

---

[32] The entwinement of decay with the release of significance was to become a pervasive motif in Benjamin's reading of modernist culture. It recurs in his exposition of the surrealists' discovery of the "revolutionary energies that appear in the 'antiquated'" (II 299); in his portrayal of Proust's involuntary memory as the "rejuvenating force" that provides "a match for the relentless process of aging" (II 320); and in the "new beauty" that appears in the vanishing art of storytelling (II 442).

fect. Hence the display of workmanship, which . . . breaks through like the masonry of a wall in a building whose stucco is crumbling away" (I 355). Benjamin thus once again upgrades craftsmanship and technique in the "work" of art, as he did in his study of the *Frühromantik*. Although they can only detract from the dazzling façade of beautiful appearances, with the passage of time they are bound to break through the surface for later readers. And, ironically, the constructed quality of baroque allegorical works keeps faith with the destructive forces of time and nature in a fashion denied to the pretense of organic creation. Baroque allegory's ultimate corrective to transfiguration is therefore its corrective "to art itself" (I 352). For Benjamin, it is not so much a counteraesthetic as a counter *to* aesthetics. After 1925, this principle would become the key to his affinity for radical versions of the avant-garde project.

The antinomies of the allegorical also generate an eruption of images typical of the baroque type of form-giving impulse: "With each idea, the moment of expression coincides with a veritable eruption of images, whose precipitate is a chaotically scattered heap of metaphors. This is how the sublime presents itself in this style" (I 349). The "rank metaphorical overgrowth" (I 374) of baroque literature had long been held up as telling proof of its artistic inferiority. Its extravagance was disparaged as a squandering of means, by contrast with the austere, "natural" economy of expression embodied by classical models (I 352–353). For Benjamin such sumptuous, even wasteful profusion is neither a flaw nor an incidental by-product but part of the generative core of the allegorical form of expression. An "endlessly preparatory, digressive, voluptuously hesitant manner" and even an "awkward ponderousness" are essential to it (I 358, 363). Here, too, baroque allegorists took lessons in the school of nature: what fascinated them, however, was not the economical precision of Newtonian mechanics but the rank, squanderous proliferation of natural history; not harmonious, stabilized beauty but decay and decomposition.

This proliferation of images had its historical roots in the philologists' pursuit of ever-new pictorial codes. In a sense, it was a pursuit of novelty. As Giehlow had put it, allegorists found themselves impelled "to exploit ever more remote characteristics of the signifying object as emblems, in order to outdo even the Egyptians with new subtleties" (I 350). The eruptive flood of images drove the mill of a "fashionable business" in the seventeenth century—the vogue for emblem books. But the effectiveness of emblems is inseparable from their "startling quality." The power with which banal objects point beyond themselves is a form of provocation, and the allegorist must supply fresh infusions of ingenuity as the shock effect wears off through habituation. "Allegories become dated" (I 359). The rhythm of these waves of fashion strikes back at the allegorist:

> The overbearing ostentation with which the banal object seems to rise from the depths of allegory may soon give way to its dismal, everyday countenance; the absorbed engagement of the sick man in the isolated and trivial may be followed by disillusioned abandonment of the emptied emblem. A speculatively inclined observer might find this rhythm tellingly repeated in the behavior of apes. But amorphous details, which can only be taken allegorically, keep imposing themselves. (I 361)

The allegorist becomes ensnared in a compulsion to repeat. Disillusioned by repeated disappointments of the childish hopes invested in objects, he nevertheless remains insatiable and thus condemned to find his hopes flaring up once more when some fresh detail of the banal world catches his eye. The pursuit of novelty turns manic and becomes the tyranny of fashion. The eruption of images thus enacts a melancholy, compulsive dialectic to which Benjamin would later see the moderns condemned—above all, in the unprecedented dominance of fashion in nineteenth-century Paris.

The world of baroque allegorical forms is also marked by a peculiar kind of linguistic dissociation. Benjamin characterizes it as an "antithetics of sound and meaning," of the spoken word and script (I 383). Here is where emblematics come into full play. The baroque conception of script is essentially pictorial: nature itself is understood as a kind of script, a source of divine instruction to the fallen, creaturely world; and emblematic images, as constellations of signifying objects, are part of a search for the lost key to reading the book of nature. The meaningful image, therefore, is the concrete written image—not alphabetic script but a rune or hieroglyph. The hieratic ostentation of baroque allegory can be satisfied only by writing in picture puzzles. The most general term for such "thing-images," rebus, had been coined by Renaissance philologists (I 346). Yet the importance of the rebus form lies not only in the speculative pretensions of baroque philology but in its role as a formative, stylistic principle in baroque culture. The emblem books provide both the "stock of requisites" and the "schema" of *Trauerspiel* (I 404–405). A *Trauerspiel* is a "reading-drama" to be "brooded over" (I 361) or, in the words of an older study cited by Benjamin, "an allegorical painting executed with living figures and changes of scene" (I 371).[33] The rebus form is essential to the allegorical way of seeing as

---

[33] This view has since been confirmed by Schöne, *Emblematik und Drama im Zeitalter des Barock*, chap. 5, "Das Theater als emblematisches Schaugerüst."

incarnated by the baroque, in which "the written word tends toward the pictural image" (I 351).

The spoken word, by contrast, is left stranded. Since meaning is inseparably bound up with pictorial, emblematic script, sound is left "self-indulgently intent on unfolding its own impetus." The result is a "language heavy with material pomp. Never has poetry been less winged" (I 376). In extreme cases, a kind of "phonetic savagery" breaks through the logical façade of the verse form (I 380). Benjamin deciphers this "dismemberment of language," once again, in terms of the baroque intuition of the necessary failure of incarnating absolute meaning in stabilized form.[34] "This poetry was in fact incapable of releasing the profound meaning captured by pictorial script into inspired sound. . . . For its script does not transfigure itself in sound." Instead, the yawning "gulf that is torn open" between sound and script "forces . . . the gaze into the depths of language" (I 376). The reference to transfiguration is the key to Benjamin's argument: the dissociated language of *Trauerspiel* refuses to breathe organic life and harmonious immanence of meaning into verbal expression. On the contrary, since "meaning has its home in script, . . . the sounded word is afflicted by it as if by some inescapable disease; it breaks off in the midst of resounding and the damming up of the feeling that was ready to pour forth arouses sorrow [*Trauer*]" (I 383). The bombastic excesses of *Trauerspiel* are not an aesthetic flaw, therefore, but a "methodical, constructive linguistic gesture." The dissociation of language is a constitutive form of expression of the allegorical intention.

The final allegorical form to be considered here might be called the degradation of objects. Throughout the section "Allegory and *Trauerspiel*," Benjamin builds steadily on the implications of allegory's arbitrariness. Reduced to simplest terms, allegory means using something to say something else—not only employing the object but exploiting it. "The object . . . lies before the allegorist, surrendered to his mercy or displeasure. That means: from now on it is quite incapable of emanating[35] a meaning, a sense of its own; whatever significance it has is lent it by the allegorist. He puts it into it and reaches beneath it. That is not psychologically but ontologically the case here. In his hands the thing becomes something different" (I 359). Exposed to the pitiless gaze of allegory, objects must submit to its purposes, surrendering any

---

[34] He finds traces of a similar sense of language among the surrealists: "Language only seemed itself where sound and image, image and sound interpenetrated with automatic precision and such felicity that no chink was left for the penny-in-the-slot called 'meaning'. Image and language take precedence" (II 296).

[35] The word used is *ausstrahlen* and could also be rendered "to radiate." Benjamin often used it in contexts that relate directly or indirectly to the concept of aura.

claims of their own. They become means to ends that lie outside them. The arbitrariness of allegory is a "drastic manifestation of the power of knowledge" that is "not in accord with the authority of nature." Its objects are "exposed," "made soulless," "drained of life," and even "dismembered" (I 360–361). Pursued to its logical extreme, the kind of "knowledge" embodied by allegory proclaims "the triumph of subjectivity and the onset of an arbitrary rule over things" (I 407).

As such formulations accumulate, the tenor of Benjamin's account changes radically. Having profiled allegory as a demystifying alternative to the pretensions of the classicist symbol, he then begins to play out the hopeless delusions that result, in turn, from the antinomies of baroque allegory. Most pointed, he likens allegory to sadism. Both "betray and devalue" their objects, violating them "in unspeakable fashion": "Significance rules voluptuously, like a sinister sultan in the harem of objects. . . . Indeed, it is characteristic of the sadist to degrade his object and then—or thereby—to satisfy it. And this is what the allegorist does in this age drunk with atrocities both imagined and experienced. . . . The function of baroque pictural script is not so much to unveil objects as to strip them naked" (I 360). But the sadist, like the allegorist, remains trapped in a compulsive repetition, alternating between fascinated absorption and "disillusioned abandonment of the emptied emblem." In principle, no limits are set to this unrelenting drive to violate the dignity of objects. The "emblematic fury" thus leads to vertigo: "As those who are falling turn somersaults as they plunge, so would the allegorical intention fall, from emblem to emblem, into the dizziness of its own bottomless depths" (I 405). Allegory's subjection of the world of objects to its own purposes ends in a "frenzy of destruction [*Vernichtungsrausch*] in which all earthly things collapse into a heap of rubble."

At this point, however, the world of allegorical forms culminates in a figure we encountered in Benjamin's reading of the early romantics—in a reversal. Allegory ends by turning on itself. The very destruction of those requisites of signification on which allegory depends leaves it "empty-handed" and reveals its own hieratic ostentations to have been "self-deception," "abysmal profundity" (I 404–406). But this is what finally releases it from its frenzy:

> It would be a complete misunderstanding of allegory to distinguish between the store of images in which the reversal into salvation and redemption takes place and that grim store of images that signify death and hell. . . . The desolate confusion of the charnel house, which can be read out of thousands of engravings and descriptions from the period as the schema of allegorical figures, is not only an emblem of the desolation of all

human existence. In it, transience is not so much signified, or allegorically represented, as, in its own significance, offered as an allegory. As the allegory of resurrection. (I 405–406)

With this stunning reversal at the height of the argument, transience itself suddenly appears as only an allegory, the final, ultimate riddle of the allegorical way of seeing. The metaphors Benjamin uses to comment on this reversal are striking. One, that of awakening, follows from the baroque's own religious idiom of resurrection as a rising from the sleep of death: "Yea, when the Highest comes to reap the churchyard's harvest / So will I, a death's head, become an angelic countenance." The other points to the sudden contraction of time: the "seven years" of allegory's confinement in the charnel house "are only a day." Whereas the image of awakening from the sleep of death prefigures Benjamin's treatment of surrealist dream images as phantasmagoria, the sudden contraction of time in the light of remembrance adumbrates the redemptive power of memory, whose key he would find in Proust.[36]

Yet the status of this reversal remains unclear. Benjamin is avowedly following the immanent movement of the baroque allegorical form-giving impulse. Yet it is equally clear that he ascribes a vitally important critical role to the allegorical way of seeing. That makes it incumbent on him to explain what distinguishes the redeeming destruction into which allegory reverses from the destructive frenzy that precedes the reversal. The implications of endorsing the allegorical vision would otherwise be dangerously nihilistic. Benjamin himself seems to sense this in the words with which he concludes his prologue to the study. Under the heading "Pro Domo" he cautions that "the danger of allowing oneself to plunge . . . into the abysmal depths of the baroque state of mind is not negligible. The characteristic feeling of dizziness induced by the spectacle of the epoch gyrating in its spiritual contradictions" is known to him (I 237). Only from a "secure position," he asserts, can one maintain the "sovereign attitude" needed "to take in the whole panorama and yet remain in control of oneself." Did Benjamin himself succeed? That is the question to which we now turn.

5. Allegory and Critique

Enough has been said to suggest the ambiguity of the relationship between Benjamin's theory of baroque allegory and his own critical

[36] See Chapter 5, Section 5, and Chapter 6, Section 2.

theory and practice. His appreciation of the allegorical way of seeing undoubtedly rested on its affinity with his own philosophical intentions. As a corrective to aesthetic transfiguration, baroque allegory offered "a more concrete, more authoritative, more lasting" alternative than romanticism. The true, "sovereign opponent of classicism," allegory resolutely extinguishes the "false appearance of totality." And Benjamin explicitly extended this authority to the realm of criticism as well: "Criticism is the mortification of the work . . . not therefore—in the romantic sense—awakening consciousness in living works but settling knowledge in those that have died off" (I 357). Yet such formulations must not be understood as an unequivocal embrace of the allegorical vision. For allegory ultimately loses itself in "the abyss of bottomless profundity. Its data are incapable of entering into philosophical constellations." Having enacted the "triumph of subjectivity and the onset of an arbitrary rule over things," in the end "allegory goes away empty-handed" (I 404–407). He warned against "the danger of allowing oneself to plunge from the heights of knowledge," yet he would scarcely have felt such vertigo—nor would the study have been so productive—had its resonance with his own intentions not been so deep (I 237). How did he in fact maintain the "sovereign attitude" he felt was called for? How, in particular, did he go about integrating baroque allegorical correctives into his own theory of criticism?

Benjamin prefaced the *Trauerspiel* study with an "Epistemo-Critical Prologue" that echoes the language of his preamble to "The Life of Students" ten years earlier and is governed by the same basic tension. Critique, as Benjamin understands it, must declare its loyalty to an unabridged, indeed extreme form of philosophical idealism. It must reveal the metaphysical structure of cultural particulars (II 75) in order to pursue what he now openly declares to be "the original task of philosophy, the representation of ideas" (I 214). It must penetrate to "the immanent state of perfection" that is "deeply embedded in every present" and latent in even "the most endangered, discredited, and ridiculed creations and thoughts" (II 75) or, as he now puts it, "the clumsiest and most helpless experiments as well as the overripe developments of a decadent age" (I 227). And critique must free such phenomena from their "disfigured form in the present order of things" (II 75) or, in unabashedly idealist terms, "rescue" and "redeem" the phenomena (I 214). Yet it must do all this without falling prey to the spell of transfiguration cast by the affirmative variety of idealist aesthetics. Only once *this* danger has been recognized does the tortuous labyrinth of Benjamin's argument in the prologue begin to make sense. His primary problem was not to rehabilitate metaphysics and secure access to the realm of ideas. On the contrary, that was the commonplace, utterly orthodox goal of a tradition of idealist aesthetics that was being renewed in his times—a renewal for which Benjamin found scathing words.[37] The real difficulty lay in getting to ideas without forfeiting what he saw as the genuine, critical intentions of idealism—above all, a solidarity with the creaturely element of human existence and the promise of a radical break with the existing order of things. That meant cutting off the conventional routes of access to the idea while ultimately holding out for an extreme, idiosyncratic idealism after all. The key to understanding the prologue lies in recognizing the wealth of strategies of indirection it deploys. In such strategies one senses the virtual but compelling presence of the intellectual field in Benjamin's argument.[38]

"This introduction is an outrageous chutzpah," as he flirted in a letter to Scholem, "namely no more and no less than a prolegomenon to a theory of knowledge . . . dressed up as a doctrine of ideas" (B 372).[39] Presenting his theory in Platonic guise did little to help make his intentions transparent, but his ostentation had a point. The idealist credo he now openly professed was a hyperidealism—an idealism so extreme and uncompromising as to foreclose the possibility of its being subsumed under any of the dominant traditions of German academic philosophy since Kant. The point of departure for Benjamin's argument is a radical disjunction between the goal of philosophy in its "complete, finished form," which would possess the "authority of doctrine [Lehre]," and the results attainable by "the power of mere thinking" (I 207). While positing the existence of an absolute and authoritative standard, therefore, he seemingly places it beyond reach. He spells out this disjunction in two ways, in a distinction between truth and knowledge and in a discussion of the relationship between ideas and phenomena.

Benjamin's disjunction between truth (Wahrheit) and knowledge (Erkenntnis) does not provide a rigorous, positive account of what he means by "truth"; instead, he evokes it negatively, as that which knowledge is not and cannot be. Knowledge is defined in the Kantian

---

[37] I discuss his critique of academic idealist literary scholarship in Chapter 4, Section 2.

[38] Or, to change metaphors, Benjamin's strategies aim at immunizing idealism against misuse. I have found two other approaches to the prologue helpful, both of which differ from mine: Fred Lönker, in "Benjamins Darstellungstheorie: Zur Erkenntniskritische Vorrede zum Ursprung des deutschen Trauerspiels," points to analogous problems in the history of philosophical idealism—particularly in Plato and Leibniz, to whom Benjamin explicitly refers. Lönker's point is not so much to identify influences, however, as to call attention to systematic conundrums that seem to be built into philosophical idealism. The other is Menninghaus's Walter Benjamins Theorie der Sprachmagie, which traces Benjamin's "epistemocritical" reflections back to his early philosophy of language. Menninghaus stresses Benjamin's attachment to romantic traditions in which "idea" is understood as "linguistic form" (79–95).

[39] Benjamin's own words are als Ideenlehre frisiert.

sense, as inherently conceptual: it does not create its objects, but it does constitute them *as* objects. Knowledge is therefore both "relational" and "intentional" (I 928).[40] Truth, by negative definition, is that which somehow lies beyond the grasp of conceptual knowledge: "Truth never enters into relations, and particularly not intentional ones. The object of knowledge, as something determined in the intention inherent in concepts, is not truth. Truth is intentionless being [*Sein*] made up of ideas. The conduct appropriate to it, therefore, is not the intending involved in knowing but an entering into it and disappearing. Truth is the death of intention" (I 216).

Benjamin then employs the same negative procedure for the second, explicitly ontological disjunction, which invokes the Platonic distinction between ideas and phenomena. Following Plato, Benjamin affirms that ideas are somehow present in phenomena as their being. Ideas are "the force that shapes the essence of the empirical realm" (I 216). But the manner in which phenomena participate in ideas is problematic, just as it had been for Plato. Ideas are not simply given in the phenomenal world, and phenomena are neither incorporated nor contained in ideas (I 214). "As being," therefore, "truth and the idea acquire that supreme metaphysical significance emphatically attributed to them in the Platonic system" (I 210). But "the being of truth, as something ideal, differs from the mode of being of appearances"; in fact, strictly speaking, being is "beyond all phenomenality" (I 216). As in baroque allegory, the emphasis is on the unavailability of absolute meaning in the phenomenal world. A danger thus seems to arise: if ideas, as intentionless being, elude any intentional access whatsoever, can they be reached at all?

Benjamin's argument hinges on opening this gap. Ideas *cannot* be "reached"; at best, their presence can be evoked. His theory of ideas ultimately concerns the varieties of indirection that make this possible. The task of philosophical critique is "the representation of ideas"; about that there can be no doubt for him. The entire prologue therefore hangs on the easily misunderstood term "representation" (*Darstellung*).[41] *Darstellung als Umweg*—"representation as a detour" or, better, "as indirection"—there lies the crux of the problem for Benjamin (I 212). What does he mean by equating representation with indirection?

In the first place, representation must not be misconstrued as mere

---

[40] Passages cited here from I 925–948 refer to an earlier draft of the prologue found in the notes to the *Gesammelte Schriften*.

[41] Lönker, "Benjamins Darstellungstheorie," stresses this point. Though the problem may indeed be inherent in the logic of philosophical idealism, I want to show that the particular way Benjamin was forced to face it resulted from the logic of his intellectual project.

portrayal. Critical representation is not a neutral, depictive procedure but an active intervention that changes the object. Benjamin had already used the term in the dissertation to characterize the romantic concept of criticism: "Criticism is the representation [*Darstellung*] of the prosaic core in every work. Here the concept of 'representation' is understood in the chemical sense, as the production of a substance through a particular process to which others are submitted" (I 109). *Darstellung* in the chemical sense means to produce a substance by disengaging it from an existing compound; it captures the duality of the romantic concept of criticism as the completion and the destruction of the work. Benjamin does not explicitly invoke the chemical metaphor in his discussion of representation in the *Trauerspiel* prologue. But the image and, along with it, the romantic conception of criticism remains alive in his argument. Criticism extricates the idea or "philosophical truth content" of the work of art—what in the dissertation is called its "prosaic core"—only by dissociating it into its elements.

The new departure is that with the benefit of what he learned from the *Trauerspiel* study Benjamin now speaks more emphatically of the destructive moment in criticism.[42] Several passages in the prologue suggest a direct adoption of the allegorical vision to explain the relation of phenomena to ideas. "Phenomena do not enter into the realm of ideas integrally, in their raw, empirical state, adulterated by appearances," he insists, "but only in their elements. . . . They are divested of their false unity so that they may partake, in dispersal, of the true unity of truth" (I 213). The concrete implications of such statements are illustrated by the *Trauerspiel* study itself. Benjamin does not even attempt to provide a descriptive account of *Trauerspiel* as a "phenomenon" in its "raw, empirical state." He does not catalogue the content of individual allegories, nor does he offer reconstructions of individual works. The constitutive tension he finds in *Trauerspiel* is in the span between its "material content"—human history as such—and its form, the antinomies of allegory. The philosophical truth content that arises from this tension, the vision of nature-history, is the idea of *Trauerspiel*. But this idea will be found neither in any single image nor in the "appearance" of any individual work. It can be distilled only by dissociating the compounds of the works and dispersing their elements into new complexes, such as the concepts of ruins, eruptions of images, or linguistic dissociation.

The destructive moment also shows itself in a sharper sense of the function of time in the dissociation of the work. The apparent unity of the work of art, its immediate appearance of totality, decays with the

---

[42] The prologue was written after the rest of the study had been completed.

passage of time. The seamless illusion it weaves loses its self-evident, natural quality for later readers, who stumble over antiquated realia and the awkward conventionality of extinct forms of expression. The *Elective Affinities* essay had already pointed out how this affects the reception history of symbolic works. But *Trauerspiele*, in a sense, had been built as ruins to begin with: "Critique lies unfolded with rare clarity in their further duration. From the very beginning they are set up for that critical dissociation wreaked on them by the course of time" (I 357). Baroque allegorical works make no attempt to disguise the fact that they contain the seeds of their own destruction. Works may turn out to contain immanent, absolute ideas, but never in the way they purport to. That, for Benjamin, is the critical yield of the allegorical way of seeing. The task of criticism is not to conjure up the appearance of the work "as it really was," restoring a false totality to it, but to collaborate with the corrosive effects of the passage of time. Decay is an indispensible ally of the indirection necessary to a philosophical criticism that seeks to avoid transfiguration.

But if the passage of time makes it possible for the idea represented by the work to break through the surface of its false totality, then the effects of time are not only corrosive. And in stressing this, Benjamin's theory of criticism parts ways with the allegorical way of seeing. This brings us around to the second, positive sense in which he employs the term "representation" in the prologue. Ideas are not only to be represented by criticism; they "represent themselves"—we might say "deploy themselves"—in the phenomenal world in a series of incarnations. Benjamin thus historicizes the theory of ideas, but in an utterly unorthodox fashion. He proposes to link ideas to history through a conception of the work as an "origin" (*Ursprung*):

> Origin, although a thoroughly historical category, has nothing to do with genesis [*Entstehung*]. . . . The origin stands, like a vortex, in the stream of becoming and pulls the material involved in a genesis into its rhythm. That which is originary never shows itself in the naked, manifest existence of the factual. . . . In every originary phenomenon [*Ursprungsphänomen*] is determined the figure in which an idea confronts the historical world again and again, until it lies perfected in the totality of its history. The origin does not rise above the actual findings, therefore, but concerns their prehistory and their posthistory (*Vor- und Nachgeschichte*]. (I 226)

On the one hand, Benjamin proposes an almost rabid form of philosophical idealism: metaphysically self-subsistent ideas confront the historical world and pull historical material into themselves. Ideas "take on a series of historical formulations" (I 227). Yet the point of this historicization is to stress that ideas are *never* fully present in any particular incarnation, but only in their historical deployment. Works are originary in a dual sense: their creation crystallizes a prehistory of precedents and adumbrations that had only been latent before;[43] but since works are not stable totalities, their creation also initiates a posthistory, a conception Benjamin had previously designated with the romantic metaphors of the unfolding or "afterlife" (*Nachleben*) of works. Only in the full configuration of this prehistory and posthistory—and even then only virtually—would their idea be present.[44] Insight into any particular embodiment depends, therefore, on recognizing the dual rhythm inherent in any originary phenomenon: the particular "must be recognized on the one hand as a restoration, a reestablishing, yet precisely in this as something incomplete and unfinished, on the other" (I 226).

The conception of the idea as an origin neatly dispenses with the facile gesture of seeing works as incarnations of eternal values, but its romantic underpinnings are unmistakable.[45] The early romantics, after all, had also seen the reflective potentiation of the work of art as generated by its posthistory. Benjamin's antidote to any affirmative temptations this may imply is yet another dose of indirection: he stresses the necessarily *discontinuous* structure of representation. This discontinuity pertains, first of all, to the representation of ideas by philosophical criticism. Unity and totality cannot be attained by the "unbroken chain of deduction" characteristic of philosophical systems (I 213). Instead, they can be evoked only by foregoing this sort of rigor. Philosophical criticism involves "the art of interruption" (I 212); as in the production of a mosaic, the "micrological craftsmanship" devoted to the individual pieces and the configuration of the whole determine its success (I 208). On the other hand, Benjamin insists that what he calls the "structure of the world of ideas" itself is also discontinuous (I 213). The self-representation of ideas as originary phenomena, their historical self-deployment, is not a process of steadily unfolding on ever-higher levels in a continuous approach to ultimate, ideal perfection. Rather, to use one of the most-often invoked terms from the prologue, it takes the form of an astronomical constellation—an image that springs forth

[43] In the same spirit Jorge Luis Borges describes how Kafka, like "every writer," retroactively "creates his own precursors" in the sense that "his work modifies our conception of the past, as it will modify the future" ("Kafka and His Precursors," in *Labyrinths*, 201).

[44] In his theory of reception in the late 1930s, Benjamin extended the concept of posthistory to mean a history of effects and receptions and spoke not of an idea but of a "force field"; see Chapter 7, Section 3.

[45] Benjamin's model is Goethe's conception of the *Urphänomen*. Benjamin's *Ursprung* transposes this principle from Goethe's philosophy of nature into the realm of history (I 953–954); see Chapter 2, n. 40.

from a configuration of discrete, otherwise discontinuous points (I 214–215). The measure of time proper to an ideal constellation is not continuity but virtual simultaneity.

These complex strategies of indirection were Benjamin's provisional answer to the transfiguring, affirmative tendencies of idealist aesthetics he was attempting to resist. As the following chapters show, he found himself forced to radicalize them still further, producing a line of development that leads from the theory of ideas in the prologue to the concept of dialectical images at the heart of the "Arcades" project. Before turning to those issues, however, we might pause to ask how Benjamin's theory of critique measures up to his own critical practice. Does the prologue really explain how the *Trauerspiel* study works? Or, to be more precise, does it explain why it works when it actually does?

If one focuses on Benjamin's conception of the linguistic form of the work of art as its immanent idea, which is an eminently romantic notion, then the answer is yes. Baroque allegory is the formal reflection of its material content: the preoccupation with the brokenness of the physical world, the ineluctable transience of human history, and the absence of a stabilized fullness of meaning. But in other respects that are particularly important for his long-term intellectual strategy, the answer has to be no. For one thing, the theory of works as originary phenomena and ideas as constellations still puts the emphasis in the wrong place. It stresses the fact that ideas are eternal constellations after all, whereas the concepts of pre- and posthistory suggest that it would be equally plausible to construe them as constellations of past and present. And that, in fact, would capture what had already become an essential part of Benjamin's actual working method. He learned from Riegl's work to seek out signs of coherence in periods when classicist cultures break down, so-called eras of decay. His theory of baroque allegory did just that; as we have seen, one crucial impetus for it stemmed from a growing mistrust of the antimodernist rhetoric of decadence in his own times. There was a hidden constellation, he now sensed, between the true intentions of baroque allegory, the missed chance of the *Frühromantik,* and the slender hopes remaining for an uncorrupted idealism in his own times. Nor is this simply a projection of what he already knew about modernity back onto the baroque. On the contrary, the relationship is thoroughly reciprocal. His own philosophical intentions had alerted him to an unrecognized potential in the world of baroque allegorical forms, and this in turn helped sharpen his eye for modernity. In all this one begins to sense a complex conception of history and tradition informed but scarcely captured by his idealist theory.

Benjamin's theory of ideas also obscures a second crucial feature of his working method, the procedure of immanent ideological critique. His deciphering of allegory, for instance, shows how his ability to disentangle the romantics' valid insights from their mystifications was an essential part of his schooling in the baroque allegorical way of seeing. When explaining his procedure, however, Benjamin completely passed over this stage of his work. Instead, he spoke only of the need for micrological study, "immersion in the most minute details of the subject matter" (I 208). Such demands for concretion will be a welcome relief to anyone familiar with the kind of orthodox cultural history common at the time, in which the spirit of the age is constantly called down from above like a deus ex machina.[46] But they are prone to weave their own mystique of immediate, intuitive insight, a mystique that Benjamin himself was often at pains to expose. As he later put it, it is not enough to do justice to the concrete situation of the object in its own historical context. Critique must also reflect the concrete, historical circumstances of its *own interest* in the object (V 494, 1026). Though his critical practice was already tacitly informed by this principle, he had yet to begin to make good the deficit in his theory.

[46] Benjamin himself made this case in his review "Rigorous Study of Art" (III 363–374).

Chapter Four

Owning up to the Poverty of Experience: Benjamin and Weimar Modernism

In 1933, following his flight from Germany in the face of the Nazis' rise to power, Benjamin composed a short statement titled "Experience and Poverty." With it he refused the conventional gesture of claiming to have brought the heritage of the "good Germany" with him into exile as part of his cultural baggage. "For who can seriously assume that humanity will ever get across the narrow pass that lies before it if burdened with the baggage of a collector or an antique dealer?" (II 961–962). Instead, he called for owning up to the impoverishment of experience—and even more radically, professing it—in order to "begin from the beginning, make a fresh start, make do with little" (II 215). He spoke not of surviving the destruction of a culture threatened by a fascist opponent but, more radically, of surviving culture itself. Those he cited as exemplars of this sensibility—Brecht, Loos, Le Corbusier, Scheerbart, and Klee—had all, he asserted, taken leave of "the traditional image of humanity—ceremonious, noble, decked out with all the sacrificial offerings of the past" (II 216). The appropriate response to the poverty of experience was not to long for any renewal of experience or attempt to rejoin oneself to the great traditions of humanism and idealism: no, "people have 'gorged' themselves on all that, on 'culture' and 'man', and become glutted and tired" (II 218). The order of the day was rather to collaborate in the work of destruction. Anticipating the charge that this would amount to collaborating with barbarism, Benjamin embraced the term frankly and defiantly: "Barbarism? Yes indeed. We say it to introduce a new, positive concept of barbarism" (II 215). This "new, positive" barbarism—"the good kind"—was justified as the only match for the barbaric powers of fascism.[1] Culture is dead,

[1] In "On the Concept of History," Benjamin would take the even more radical position that "there is no document of culture that is not at the same time a document of

[156]

Benjamin declared, and bid it good riddance, calling for "total disillusionment about the age and nevertheless an unreserved profession of loyalty to it" (II 216). Here the radical antihumanism of his earlier work found its purest expression, as he seemed to move beyond recovering neglected forces within the tradition to call for the liquidation of traditional culture itself.

Benjamin gave this new, positive concept of barbarism little content in "Experience and Poverty." In fact, its protagonist—whom he had once also called "the destructive character"—disavowed responsibility for what he would leave in his wake. In a characteristically iconoclastic reversal of the fetish of "creativity," Benjamin praised his modus operandi as the way to cope with dead-end situations:

> The destructive character's only watchword is: make room; his only activity: clearing out. . . . The destructive character envisions nothing. Where others come up against walls or mountains, there too he sees a way. But because he sees ways everywhere, he also has to clear the way. Not always with brute force, sometimes with its refinement. . . . He reduces the existing to rubble, not for the sake of the rubble but of the path that leads through it. (IV 396–398)

Benjamin had many reasons for absolving the destructive character and the new barbarism of responsibility for envisioning what would follow. Among them, certainly, is that the concerted rhetorical force of "Experience and Poverty" gives voice to the recent exile's angry defiance. But these texts cannot be so easily reduced to their biographical occasions; as programmatic statements, they represent an abiding liquidationist moment in Benjamin's thinking. Nor are they simply projections of Benjamin's personal idiosyncrasies; read strategically, they attempt to steal the idea of the decline of experience from cultural conservatives, the energies of barbarism from the fascists, and to reverse the conventional valuations of creativity and destruction.

Yet the very strategies that help make sense of Benjamin's gesture do not resolve questions about the destructive character's responsibility but only sharpen them. For what separates positive barbarism from fascist violence? Just how, if at all, does Benjamin's "Apollonian version of the destroyer" (IV 397), at work for the sake of the path that leads through the rubble, differ from the nihilistic aestheticism of a fascination with destruction for its own sake? These were by now old questions for Benjamin, who, from the time of the youth movement to

---

barbarism," for all past cultural achievements owe an unacknowledged debt to the "anonymous toil" of contemporaries (I 696). This left only a choice of barbarisms, but no alternative to it.

his work on allegory, constantly faced the issue of distinguishing himself from the wrong kind of nihilism. After 1925, such questions would take on a new urgency as Benjamin moved into the role of a politically engaged cultural critic, addressing political considerations more explicitly, and in more public forums.

In fact, whereas Benjamin may have absolved the destructive character of responsibility for envisioning what would follow from his work, he was less sparing of himself. Here as always, we should avoid conflating his position too simply with that of any one of his literary personas. For in the latter half of the 1920s he was indeed beginning to develop models for what was (or might be) to come, by working out a new theory of technology. Benjamin looked to a thoroughgoing transformation of humanity's relationship to nature which was at least potentially progressive, and he read signs of it in the changing conditions of aesthetic perception. He did in fact have models for what might emerge from a salutary liquidation of traditional culture, which he found in the works of the constructivist avant-gardes, in aesthetic theorists like Valéry and utopian visionaries like Scheerbart. The liquidation of culture may have been a dangerous leap—to which society was in any case being driven—but it need not be a leap in the dark.

I begin, then, by considering why Benjamin shifted his attention to modernist and avant-garde culture and what he understood by his turn to politics. The intellectual field relevant to his work expanded significantly to embrace the broader cultural politics of the Weimar Republic, and while holding fast to his earlier nihilism he now found himself compelled to clarify his ambivalent relationship to the aestheticism and nihilism advocated by Weimar's radical conservatives. Benjamin's "real humanism" was one response to this constellation, as was his belated alliance with the obvious heterodoxy in the German field, Marxist materialism; but I argue that his effort to articulate a vision of technology, as part of a distinctive philosophical anthropology, was also a response to the pull of this larger field. It was only through his encounter with Brecht and his work, after 1929, that this vision became concrete enough to offer a convincing response. Finally, however, we see that even in these most radical statements of the liquidationist and constructivist impulses in his work there were connections to a purified concept of tradition and even, quite unexpectedly, to certain traditions of the radical Enlightenment. This dialectical reversal was embodied, for Benjamin, in the work of Brecht, and ironically enough Benjamin's encounter with him would lead to important statements of what a genuine and legitimate recourse to tradition would involve.

1. Developing Strategies: Modernism, Politics, and Nihilism

The years 1924/25 undoubtedly marked a transition in Benjamin's life and work.[2] In completing the *Trauerspiel* study, he closed out the period of his works on traditional German literature, and the failure of his attempted *Habilitation* at the University of Frankfurt put an end to his ambivalent hopes of securing an academic position (B 455).[3] The main focus of his critical attention now shifted from *Germanistik* to recent and contemporary literature. These years also brought his first direct acquaintance with contemporary Marxist works, most importantly Lukács' *History and Class Consciousness,* and personal relations with active communists, including the Latvian activist Asja Lacis, his sometime lover. Meanwhile, his relationships to his wife and parents continued to deteriorate, while his financial dependence on them further undermined his increasingly slender prospects of personal security. Finally, in response to all this, he was beginning to negotiate a crucial shift in his social role, making the transition from *Privatgelehrter* to cultural journalist and publicist. Benjamin himself favored the term "politics" to mark the transformation as he understood it: "As long as I do not reach the stance appropriate to me, that of a textual commentator," he declared in a 1924 letter to Scholem, "I will spin a 'politics' out of myself" (B 368). All these changes involved a mixture, characteristic for Benjamin, of choice and external compulsion, sometimes laced—as in the failed *Habilitation*—with a moment of self-sabotage. Taken together, they form the pivot on which periodizations of his work have turned.

Without minimizing the importance of these shifts, we can also see important underlying continuities in his work. To be sure, Benjamin's primary critical attention turned to modernist and avant-garde culture, and his approach to criticism now became explicitly strategic and political. But neither of these elements was entirely new to him. Understanding the relationship between his earlier and later writings there-

[2] For a more detailed account of the changes summarized here, see Witte, *Walter Benjamin,* chap. 5, and *Walter Benjamin: Der Intellektuelle als Kritiker,* 137–144; Momme Brodersen, *Spinne im eigenen Netz: Walter Benjamin, Leben und Werk,* 146–155; and Werner Fuld, *Walter Benjamin: Zwischen den Stühlen, eine Biographie,* 179–195.

[3] For details, see the account assembled by the editors of the *Gesammelte Schriften* (I 868–902, VI 771–773) and, above all, the material uncovered by Burkhardt Lindner in the University's archives, "Habilitationsakte Benjamin: Über ein 'akademisches Trauerspiel' und über ein Vorkapitel der 'Frankfurter Schule' (Horkheimer, Adorno)." It turns out that the final blow to Benjamin's application was dealt by an assessment of the *Trauerspiel* study provided by Hans Cornelius's graduate assistant, the young Max Horkheimer. On Benjamin's response to the rejection, see Irving Wohlfarth, "Resentment Begins at Home: Nietzsche, Benjamin, and the University."

fore depends on a careful assessment of the changing role they played in his work. The underlying continuities of his long-term intellectual strategy remained decisive, yet as Benjamin expanded his terrain of operations to a larger intellectual field his strategy itself developed further. Only against this background does the specific increment of his modernist and political criticism come into focus.

Beginning in the second half of the 1920s, Benjamin began the series of essays on the works of modernist culture and the avant-garde that he continued to the end of his life; in fact, he may be said to have opened this series with an important modernist work of his own, *One Way Street* (1926). But modernist literature had already been a presence in his early work. In 1923 he published a translation of Baudelaire's "Tableaux parisiens," parts of which dated back to 1914, and he credited Mallarmé's theory of poetry as a source of his own philosophy of language. Indeed, Charles Rosen argues that not only Benjamin's theory but even his actual practice of indirect critical representation, as set out in the *Trauerspiel* book, was inspired by the methods of symbolist poetry.[4] And, as we have seen in the previous chapter, he assembled a collection of baroque allegorical forms whose implicitly modernist aesthetic strikingly anticipates his later, direct explorations of modernist and avant-garde works. It might thus be argued that there was no need for a turn to modernism since it had guided his work all along.[5]

But if modernism did help teach Benjamin how to "see" the romantic and the baroque, surely the reciprocal influence was even more telling. In his studies of the *Frühromantik* and of baroque allegory, he opposed the pernicious pretensions of artworks to symbolic totality and was becoming increasingly dubious of the transfiguring qualities of the aesthetic sphere itself. But neither of these critical lessons was to be learned from symbolist poetry, the most important modernist influence on his earlier work. Rather, on these points it was his early critiques that sharpened his eye for certain features of modernist culture. Benjamin himself did not use this term; his theory of the modern, and his criterion for selecting significant modernist works, remained implicit: he found the important art of his time to be that which involved a radical transformation in the nature of art itself. What he called the "melting down of literary forms" (II 687) comprised two distinct phenomena. In its most radical form, it meant "the end of art" as pursued in the avant-garde project of undermining the autonomy of the aesthetic sphere itself, especially its constructivist and surrealist versions. But it was not only such harbingers of a "nonauratic" art that fascinated

---

[4] Rosen, "The Origins of Walter Benjamin."
[5] For example, see Peter Bürger, *Theory of the Avant-Garde*, 68.

him.[6] Equally important was art that transformed genres from within by pushing them to their limits, an idea that goes back to the early romantic conception of prose; important cases included the novels of Proust and Döblin, the dramas of Brecht, and Baudelaire's lyric poetry.[7] The exploration of modernism thus provided not so much a new departure in Benjamin's work as a new medium in which to pursue his abiding concerns to more radical conclusions.

Something analogous is true of Benjamin's turn to politics. As we have seen, Benjamin's early work was already guided by a resolutely strategic sense that his apodictic tone tended to obscure. Thus, when Benjamin now declared, in *One Way Street*, that "the critic is a strategist in the literary struggle" (IV 108), he was not just making a statement about the social and political function of criticism in his time or affecting a new, provocatively militant idiom.[8] He was also, for the first time, making an implicit dimension of his own practice more explicit. But now, Benjamin's changing circumstances led him to develop the strategic moment of his work in new ways, as he found himself forced to sharpen his strategic and tactical skills on many fronts at once. He cobbled together a livelihood, however precarious, as a contributor to several publications. *Die Literarische Welt*, the closest thing to a "broad church" organ of Weimar's cultural politics in the late 1920s, was his mainstay until political complications forced him to shift his focus toward the feuilleton of the *Frankfurter Zeitung*, where, however, his standing was less secure. In 1930/31 he placed a series of his most forceful pieces on the politics of German writers and intellectuals with *Die Gesellschaft*, an important Social Democratic journal, and throughout these years he wrote reviews and occasional pieces for a host of other publications. Often he was unable to choose the subjects of his reviews. But if he found the adjustments forced on him to be painful,

[6] Bürger's argument, with its focus on the issue of the autonomy of the aesthetic sphere, construes Benjamin's conception of modernism too narrowly; Benjamin's theory of the modern encompasses more than his theory of the avant-garde. See Bürger, *Theory of the Avant-Garde*, 47–54, and my further discussion in Chapter 5, Section 3.

[7] In 1929–31 Benjamin formulated a series of notes on the theory of criticism in which he worked on translating the early romantic conception of criticism, together with the allegorical correctives he had meanwhile incorporated into it, into political terms (VI 161–180). These notes clearly demonstrate a continuing allegiance to key tenets of the romantic conception as he understood it, reintroducing motifs such as the "afterlife [*Fortleben*] of works" (VI 170, 174) and even "magic criticism" (VI 173–174); see the suggestive summary on VI 179. What is more, he was still willing to own up to this allegiance publicly: in "Against a Masterpiece," an important 1930 review of Max Kommerell's work, he invoked the Schlegels' conception of the role of criticism in the "growth" of works (III 259). Later in the 1930s he developed some of these ideas into a theory of reception based on the notion of the afterlife of works; see Chapter 7, Section 3.

[8] The ninth of his "Thirteen Theses on the Technique of the Critic" ventures that "a genuine polemic takes up a book as lovingly as a cannibal preparing an infant" (IV 108).

he also learned how to turn them to his advantage: his dozens of book reviews show how adroit he became at using occasional pieces to develop ideas and formulations that furthered his own agenda; his vision seemed to broaden as he was forced to disperse small parts of his larger projects into the most disparate materials. And, while navigating these currents, he continued to tack amid persistent ambivalences about his new role. So, for instance, he wrote to Scholem in 1930 declaring his ambition "to be considered the premiere critic of German literature"; the letter, however, was in French (B 505). For our concerns, in any case, the most important aspect of his new focus on strategy involves what he understood by politics and how his conception of critique developed accordingly.

By setting the word "politics" in inverted commas in his 1924 letter to Scholem, Benjamin signaled his distance from the conventional sense of the term. Certainly he was not declaring any intention to engage in Weimar's quotidian party politics; his writings and letters shun virtually all reference to contemporary political events in this period, as they had during the war.[9] His closest approach to politics in this sense was to consider joining the Communist party, a step he left dependent on "a final push from chance" that apparently never materialized (B 382, 425, 530). Rather, for him politics meant, first of all, what he called the "politicization of the intelligentsia" (III 225). On the face of it, this was hardly a novel proposition; the politicization and polarization of culture were virtual hallmarks of the Weimar Republic. What Benjamin was proposing, however, was not the espousal of pronounced political opinions but a sociological conception adapted from the Marxist analysis of class polarization (VI 619).[10] He assumed that "independent" intellectuals, like the petit bourgeoisie with whom they shared a great deal, were doomed to disappearance by the deepening contradictions of capitalism (III 227). The bourgeoisie, finding itself increasingly hard pressed, could no longer afford the luxury of an apparently classless intelligentsia and would increasingly seek to discipline them in the interests of the class (III 174–175). The appropriate response would be for intellectuals to work at clarifying their own position and liquidating their previous class role. But how? Here Benjamin gave the Marxist

[9] See the discussion in Chapter 2, Section 1. This is not to say that Benjamin did not respond to political developments in his work; see, for instance, Philippe Ivernel, "Paris, Hauptstadt der Volksfront oder das postume Leben des 19. Jahrhunderts," and Chryssoula Kambas, *Walter Benjamin im Exil: Zum Verhältnis von Literaturpolitik und Ästhetik.*

[10] The following account draws on several Benjamin texts: his review of Pierre Mac-Orlan's novels (III 174–176); "Surrealism" (II 295–310); his two reviews of Siegfried Kraucauer's *Die Angestellten* (III 219–228); the "Memorandum for the Journal *Krisis und Kritik*" (VI 619–621); and "The Author as Producer" (II 683–701).

analysis his distinctive stamp.[11] He insisted on a realistic appraisal of the limits social class placed on the identity and the audience of bourgeois intellectuals. The problem was that "even the proletarianization of an intellectual," which he was experiencing at first hand, "almost never creates a proletarian" (III 224). He thought it a delusion that "artists of bourgeois origin" could remake themselves as "masters of 'proletarian art'" (II 309); they could not hope to deny their identities and pose as proletarians or even pretend to address the working class directly. As for himself, "Where do my production facilities lie? They lie—about this, too, I harbor not the slightest illusion—in Berlin West-West-West, if you wish. The most highly developed civilization and the 'most modern' culture do not only make for my private comfort; they are, in part, the very means of my production. That means: it does not lie in my power to move my production facilities to Berlin East or North" (B 531). The intellectuals' task, therefore, was to mobilize the culture with which their bourgeois origins had endowed them in order to address and politicize their own subclass, their fellow intellectuals: "An author who teaches writers nothing teaches no one" (II 696). This meant fostering an awareness of their class position and social function, including the social function of literature. It also meant working to ensure that the inexorable liquidation of bourgeois culture took place in the right fashion (IV 122). In 1930/31, Benjamin collaborated with Brecht on plans for a journal to be called *Krisis und Kritik* which, they hoped, would provide a forum for this project.[12]

The ultimate goal of this process, in a transformed society, would be a total recasting of cultural production—*Umfunktionierung*, as Brecht called it—through which cultural consumers would be transformed into producers, "readers or spectators into collaborators," until the mutual exclusivity of the roles vanishes (II 696). Thus, when Benjamin called for intellectuals to work toward their own dissolution as a subclass, he envisioned a transformation of their identity from independent arbiters of *Geist* into facilitators of a broadly participatory culture. He sometimes referred to the Soviet writer Sergei Tretjakov as a model for such an "operating" writer (II 686). Yet this example showed that the new role would really only become available under thoroughly transformed social conditions.[13] Whereas this Brechtian vision held the

---

[11] Benjamin's position on these issues can be inserted into Marxist debates of the times, aligning him with Brecht against both the League of Proletarian-Revolutionary Writers and Lukács. But, although he was undoubtedly aware of such debates, he did not participate in or refer to them directly; see Helga Gallas, *Marxistische Literaturtheorie: Kontroversen im Bund proletarisch-revolutionärer Schriftsteller*.

[12] The journal was never published; see Witte, *Walter Benjamin: Der Intellektuelle als Kritiker*, 170–172.

[13] Kambas makes this point in *Walter Benjamin im Exil*, 45.

promise of an unprecedented opening of intellectual life, Benjamin proposed rather different political tasks for intellectuals who, this side of the threshold of bourgeois society, would meanwhile continue to find themselves addressing one another. The first of these tasks was unabashed polemical criticism, aimed at exposing and sharpening contradictions. "The devastating critique," he proposed, "must reconquer its good conscience" and place itself at the service of clarifying the objective situation rather than express the critic's subjective tastes (VI 161, 177).[14] But there was also another field of operations available to the intellectuals, one even less immediately political: deploying themselves at "important locations in the sphere of images" (II 309), they were to discover, decipher, and mobilize the images deposited by society in its popular and material culture. Such images were to be found not only in literature and art but also—literally—in the street; one had to pursue them "wherever they may dwell" (III 196). And likening these images to dream images—one of the central conceptions of the "Arcades" project—Benjamin proposed for the intellectual the role of "political dream interpreter" (III 227).[15] If his own effectiveness in the first of these political roles all but ended with the demise of the Weimar Republic, he turned his energies to the second in his years of exile.

This conception of the politicization of intellectuals dramatically enriched and expanded Benjamin's project. His attitude toward intellectuals was not the result of having his head turned by a conversion to Marxism; as we have seen, among the crucial motives for his break with the youth movement was his repudiation of the notion, once so central to his own identity, that *Geist* can legitimately be represented by an elite. Yet in the early work his position had rested on a purely moral imperative. Without abandoning this emphatically moral tone, he now saw his view confirmed by the development of an objective social crisis as well: the intelligentsia's claim was not only pernicious, it was doomed by the inexorable logic of social development. In this new departure, Benjamin rested his claims on Marxist class analysis and proposed an innovative sociology of literary reception to elaborate it. One finds a similar balance between continuities and new departures

[14] In "Thirteen Theses on the Technique of the Critic," published in *One Way Street* (IV 108–109), he stresses this polemical element but misleadingly omits the constructive context of polemics emphasized in the 1929–31 notes on the theory of criticism (see n. 7). His insistence on the critic's "objective" tasks extends his argument about the early romantics' conception of criticism as a medium and the critic as a personified stage of reflection (see Chapter 2, Section 3).

[15] Benjamin's models were the surrealists and Siegfried Kracauer's *Die Angestellten*. The addressee of such analyses remained unclear, however. According to his own theory, the audience should be fellow intellectuals, but the Kracauer review also implies a link between intellectuals and other endangered, intermediate strata such as the petit bourgeoisie.

in his emphasis on polemics; for instance, he broached the idea that polemics be understood as an extension of the destructive moment of critique that he had earlier called the "mortification" of works (VI 170, 179). And there were striking resonances in yet another characteristic element of his account, which registered in his tone: whenever politics is at issue, Benjamin's language modulates into a militantly decisionist timbre. Regarding what he called the two ways of leaving the "purely theoretical sphere"—in "religious or political observance"—he asserted:

> I will not concede any quintessential difference between these observances. But just as little any mediation. I am speaking here of their identity, which shows itself solely in the paradoxical reversal of the one into the other (in whichever direction) and only under the indispensible precondition that each mode of action proceeds ruthlessly enough, and radically in its own sense. The task is therefore to decide, not once and for all, but at every moment. But to *decide*. To proceed always radically, never consistently in the most important things—that would also be my attitude, if one day I were to join the Communist party. (B 425)

This was Benjamin's own most forceful assertion that nothing essential had changed with his turn to politics.[16] But indirectly he was also making a statement about what he understood politics to be, defining it not in terms of its substance but as a mode of action that is "radical" and single-mindedly disdainful of consistency and consequences. What matters above all is to decide. This insistence on decision echoes the pathos of his 1914 piece "The Religious Position of the New Youth," with its urgent longing for decisive choice, "the holy decision as such," the choice that "creates its own objects" (II 73).[17]

These passages in fact point to the second basic sense of politics in Benjamin's work of this period. Along with the politicization of the intelligentsia, politics meant unconditional, decisive action.[18] The task of the "true politician," whom he evoked in *One Way Street*, was to find the crucial moment at which to strike and interrupt the course of history: "Before the spark reaches the dynamite, the burning fuse must be cut" (IV 122). In the politics of culture, it was the surrealists who embodied this awareness; their political virtue, for Benjamin, consisted

[16] For an incisive reading of Benjamin's messianic politics that takes this claim at its word, see Irving Wohlfarth, "'Immer radikal, niemals konsequent . . .': Zur theologisch-politischen Standortsbestimmung Walter Benjamins."

[17] See Chapter 1, Section 3.

[18] This is argued, on various grounds, by Sandor Radnoti, "Benjamin's Politics"; Jürgen Habermas, "Consciousness-Raising or Redemptive Criticism," 55–56; and Rolf Tiedemann, "Historischer Materialismus oder Politischer Messianismus? Politische Gehalte in der Geschichtsphilosophie Walter Benjamins."

not least in their proclamation of an absolute state of emergency; "They exchange, to a man, the play of their human features for the face of an alarm clock that rings every minute for sixty seconds" (II 310). Benjamin was most explicit about this sense of politics in discussing his early approach to communism with Scholem in 1926. At that time, he could not take communist goals (which he did not name) seriously, disparaging them as nonsense and even nonexistent. In fact, he asserted that the very notion of political goals was meaningless to him. What drew him to communism was rather its form of action, by which he seemed to mean its disciplined militance (B 426). Benjamin had long been committed to this sort of position by his radical antiinstrumentalism, which dated back to his break with the youth movement.[19] He consistently advocated a politics of pure action uncontaminated by the calculation of worldly effects, frankly subscribing to a position that he himself had described as nihilism (II 204). Though his interest in Marxism would eventually change, becoming more substantive, his stress on decisive political action remained a constant. In fact, Benjamin had foreseen this outcome of his encounter with communism from the time he first seriously considered it. Writing to Scholem in 1924, he predicted—perhaps, at the time, hoping to mollify Scholem as well—that in the process of political reflection the "fundaments" of his nihilism would inevitably come to the fore (B 355).

The danger of this position was that if the mode of political action is what ultimately counts, then the choice of goals is essentially arbitrary. Aesthetic criteria will do as well as any others, and the best values may simply be those that are most emphatic. Benjamin frankly admired the political theory of Carl Schmitt, which centered on the idea that sovereignty inheres in whoever can master the state of emergency.[20] But this result, and the affinity with Schmitt, were extremely problematic for Benjamin, since they would collapse his position into the decisionism of the radical conservatives. Why prefer the nihilism of Benjamin's new barbarism to that of Ernst Jünger's warrior figures if politics comes down to a contest over which of them most decisively liquidates bourgeois culture? Until the mid-1920s, Benjamin lacked an effective response to this dilemma. Precisely here lay the decisive importance of the new, sociological turn of his work. If he could convincingly show that the emerging, participatory culture had an objective basis, then his justification would no longer simply rest on the force or decisiveness of the assertion. Benjamin's way of showing this was to

[19] See Chapter 2, Section 1.

[20] Benjamin invoked Schmitt's theory of sovereignty in the *Trauerspiel* study and sent him a copy in 1930, along with a letter explaining that he saw a confirmation of his aesthetic theory in Schmitt's political philosophy (I 887).

develop a theory of *Technik* as the basis for this fundamental transformation of culture. His sociological turn and his exploration of the technology would therefore be crucial in the balance of his intellectual economy. More than just new interests, they were essential to the consolidation of his position, a point brought home to him by what he called the "question of neighborhoods" (B 531) and the uncomfortable proximity of radical conservatives. To put it another way, Benjamin's nihilism may be read as an enduring part of his temperament or, less psychologically, as a part of a set of persistent metaphorical preferences; undoubtedly it was both. But it must also be seen in terms of its changing, dynamic role in the logic of his larger argument about culture, particularly as he began to confront a broader intellectual field with explicitly strategic and polemical goals.

2. The Question of Neighborhoods: Mapping the Politics of Weimar Culture

The intellectual field Benjamin entered as a politicized cultural critic after 1925 was broader and more complex than the one that had shaped his work since the youth movement. In part, this was because he was stepping beyond the boundaries of a field largely defined by academic institutions, but it also had to do with the complexity of "Weimar culture" itself. The notion of a relatively unified Weimar culture is a fiction that has not stood up to close scrutiny. The problem is not only that prewar outsiders did not really become the insiders of the republic's cultural establishment; more important, the image of the "golden twenties," with its emphasis on the formal innovations of bourgeois modernist culture, registers only one band in the spectrum of an extraordinary cultural profusion.[21] The culture of the first German republic was in fact a diverse force field of competing positions. Its institutionalization was diffuse, ranging from the circles of critics and litterateurs gathered around small-circulation journals to mass market publishing and the press, from party-affiliated cultural policy to marginal *Privatgelehrter*. As yet, we lack the historical literary sociology needed for a rigorous, empirical reconstruction of this larger field.[22]

[21] Peter Gay, *Weimar Culture: The Outsider as Insider;* Walter Laqueur, *Weimar: A Cultural History, 1918–1933;* Jost Hermand and Frank Trommler, *Die Kultur der Weimarer Republik;* John Willett, *Art and Politics in the Weimar Period: The New Sobriety, 1917–1933;* Wolfgang Schivelbusch, *Intellektuellendämmerung: Zur Lage der Frankfurter Intelligenz in den zwanziger Jahren.*

[22] For a promising approach based on Habermas's conception of the transformation of the public sphere, see Peter Uwe Hohendahl, ed., *A History of German Literacy Criticism, 1730–1980.*

Nevertheless, some of its broad features seem clear. The first concerns the role of idealism, which served as an institutionalized orthodoxy in the culture of the German mandarins. In literary culture at large, idealism was less dominant than in the universities, but it was significant nevertheless. This was largely due to the commanding position it had assumed in the axial period of the late eighteenth and early nineteenth centuries, the decisive era in establishing the terms of distinctive national discourses on culture in western and central Europe. By comparison with France and England, German academic culture at that time was more influential in shaping the terms of debate in the public sphere at large; and, once established, these discourses became relatively autonomous. Evidence of the persistent influence of this idealist discourse can be seen in German intellectuals' preoccupation with the dilemma of *Geist* and *Macht*, culture or intellect and power, well into the twentieth century. Moreover, in the late nineteenth and early twentieth centuries literary intellectuals were facing anxieties analogous to those plaguing the German mandarins: the explosive commercialization of the press and of publishing led to dislocations in the status and self-image of writers and critics, who felt themselves being displaced from their secure role as representatives of an educated public. They often responded, as did the mandarins, by *heightening* their claims for the power of literature and ideas in order to compensate for this perceived loss of influence.[23] The salience of idealism therefore represented an important element of continuity in the fields that governed Benjamin's work before and after 1925.

The most striking difference in the larger field was a far greater range of heterodox options, which became especially pronounced with the politicization of culture under the republic. Outside the universities there was a vigorous socialist left with its own tradition of theoretical and cultural debates. The materialism the mandarins dreaded had its bulwark in the "orthodox" Marxism of the Social Democratic subculture, which constituted a field within a field. Under the republic, this materialist left split and was fiercely divided against itself; the division spawned competing cultural models that ranged from assimilation to the culture of the *Bildungsbürger* through agit-prop to the modernist experiments of Piscator and Brecht. There was also a non-materialist left of independent socialists and radical democrats whose philosophical orientation can be described as humanistic idealism; they would be a favored target of Benjamin's polemics. To the right stretched an array of conservative options that lay beyond the pale of

---

[23] See Russell Berman, "Literary Criticism from Empire to Dictatorship, 1870–1933," in Hohendahl, ed., *History of German Literacy Criticism*, 328–336.

the mandarin habitus; conservatism outside the universities was shaped not only by mandarin idealism but also by the many inflections of vitalism, from traditionalist, *völkisch* doctrines to a radical conservatism infused with Nietzschean elements. The final elements of the broader intellectual field important for Benjamin's project were the currents of literary modernism and aestheticism. These were not located in any single camp but cut across them; politically, their identity was ambiguous and volatile. Aestheticism could be appropriated by the right, as in the cases of George and Jünger, or by the left, where it became an important element in the avant-garde project.[24] Exposing the dangers of aestheticism while harnessing its energies for the left would become central concerns for Benjamin in the late 1920s.

How did these multiple polarities affect Benjamin's work? Since the time of the youth movement, his long-term strategy had been governed by the triangular constellation of orthodox idealism, vitalism, and instrumentalism; as we have seen, he sought to keep his distance on all three fronts at once while rescuing the critical force of idealism. This older constellation remained in force, not least because all its elements were present, though at different magnitudes, in the larger field. But now, broadly speaking, three important changes in his strategy emerged. First, many of his important texts sat at the intersection of several contexts, addressing them simultaneously. As a result, his discourse became increasingly layered and complex: speaking the languages of several fields at once and often seeking to reshape them in the process, he performed a kind of glossolalia in these works.[25] Second, Benjamin now identified himself with the materialist heterodoxy he had resisted at the time of his break with the youth movement, though it had been an obvious alternative to idealism. In doing so, he was not adopting the materialist conception of history in any conventional sense but bringing what he called a materialist "posture" to the complex conception of history developed in his encounter with romantic criticism and the baroque allegorical vision (B 525). And finally, through reflections on technology and on dream and memory images, he now began to develop a philosophical anthropology of his own. His polemical target *and* dialogical partner for this project was not idealism but *Lebensphilosophie*. Benjamin's relationship to the vitalist right might best be described as a kind of intimate enmity: the intimacy resulted from his appreciation for the vitalist right's sensitivity to the textures of

[24] Bürger, *Theory of the Avant-Garde*, 32.
[25] As J. G. A. Pocock points out, "a speech act may innovate in and on a context consisting of several languages in interaction—or, more brutally . . . it may innovate in several languages at once"; see his "Introduction: The State of the Art," in *Virtue, Commerce, and History*, 16.

mythic forms of experience and from the ambiguous implications of his own nihilism; the enmity was political and unambiguous.

If in his early work Benjamin conducted a sustained, immanent critique of idealist aesthetics, after 1925 he addressed it directly only on occasion. At least in part, this was because idealism in this formal sense held a less commanding position in the broader field of literary politics. From now on he treated it primarily in book reviews of academic works, lowering his sights from the classic formulations of the idealist tradition to the neoidealist model of cultural studies (*Geisteswissenschaften*) that claimed descent from it. Benjamin was frankly contemptuous of mainstream academic literary scholarship, at one point venturing that "the strongest imaginable propaganda for the materialist approach has reached me not in the form of communist pamphlets but in the 'representative' works of my discipline—literary history and criticism—that have appeared from the bourgeois side over the past twenty years" (B 522). His distaste produced reviews that bristle with some of his sharpest invective. In "Literary History and Literary Studies" (1931), for instance, he heaped scorn on the "false universalism" of the orthodox *Geisteswissenschaften*. Their practitioners' attempt to proclaim values, he found, was based on the misguided notion of an unmediated relation between *Geist* and human culture (III 320), and he castigated their presumptions to knowledge of the totality as a "lecherous urge for the big picture" (III 286). Their hermeneutic principles were a monstrosity bred of idealist and vitalist concepts: "In this swamp, the hydra of academic aesthetics with its seven heads—creativity, empathy, timelessness, re-creation, reexperiencing, illusion, and art appreciation—is at home." Benjamin invoked his own theological idiom to lampoon their hieratic pretensions, which were turning research into the "lay practice of a cult . . . in which the 'eternal values' are celebrated according to a syncretic ritual" (III 286). The ultimate goal, as he saw it, was to "exorcize" critical and historical knowledge of literature by installing it in "sacred groves sheltering the temples of timeless writers" (III 289). The whole enterprise had degenerated into little more than an "idolatry of *Geist*" (III 320).

These polemics against the method of the *Geisteswissenschaften*, like the theological idiom in which he couched them, were largely an extension of his earlier critique of symbolism. But now he added a new line of attack, taking aim at their social functions as well. Corresponding to the bloated rhetoric of vulgar idealism was a broader "crisis of *Bildung*" in which literary history was implicated (III 287–288). Literary culture no longer served the aims to which it had once aspired; it was now a status marker and an object of consumption, and the function of literary history was to provide "certain strata" with "the illusion of participating in the cultural assets of high literature." In effect, the hieratic pretensions of the neoidealist *Geisteswissenschaften* were a form of un-witting, hysterical overcompensation, meant to disguise the hollowing out of the social and political substance of *Bildung*. Yet beyond this compensatory function Benjamin glimpsed something more sinister, an arrogance he called "privileged thinking." In the grand schemes of orthodox *Kulturgeschichte*, he noted, the term *Geist* was embedded in a narrative of the rise of "Western man" that served to justify his domi-nation over other peoples and races. This was the "equivalent in real-politik" of an "'idea of man' . . . characterized by an interweaving of exploitation and mission" (III 319–320).[26] In this case the neoidealist rhetoric of the cultural sciences mystified, not by compensating for a loss of real substance, but by dissembling the exercise of domination. It disguised "the barbaric conditions . . . to which any contemporary hu-manism is bound" (III 321).

Benjamin therefore remained adamant that the idealist tradition of humanism, and the classical ideal of humanity itself, were thoroughly compromised. Not the preservation of these traditions but only a pu-rifying liquidation could hope to save what had once animated them. Attempts to preserve them intact could now only lead to the sort of mendacity that had justified the bloodshed in the trenches of the war as a defense of the ideals of *Kultur*. In the acerbic words of Karl Kraus, "humanity, cultivation, and freedom are precious goods, for which blood, reason, and human dignity are not too dear a price" (II 355).[27] In his 1931 essay on Kraus, which he himself considered one of his pivotal works,[28] Benjamin made his most forceful statement of his attitude toward humanism. He identified profoundly with the image of Kraus as *Unmensch* and *Menschenfresser*, a man-eating satirist who chewed his way through not only his opponents but the classical ideal of humanity itself in order to clear the way for a "more real humanism" (II 366).[29]

---

[26] In 1939, Benjamin would denounce this imperial arrogance as a betrayal of the original promise of the Enlightenment, referring to "the peoples and race that had appeared to the age of Enlightenment in their paradisiacal dispersion" (III 565). On Benjamin's attitude toward the Enlightenment, see the Conclusion to this book.

[27] The English translation of Benjamin's Kraus essay in *Reflections* misleadingly trans-lates the phrase *realer Humanismus* throughout (except once, in the penultimate para-graph) as "materialist humanism."

[28] See B 524 and the letter cited in Scholem, *Walter Benjamin*, 206.

[29] "The satirist is the figure in whom the cannibal *[Menschenfresser]* was received into civilization," he noted, recalling his own likening of polemical technique to devouring an object (see n. 8). In fact, Benjamin equivocated on the issue of Kraus's radicalism. In another passage, he criticized him for idealizing "the convergence of manorial noblesse and cosmopolitan rectitude . . . in which Weimar humanism was at home." In fact, Benjamin's full position is that classical and real humanism were the two poles of Kraus's cultural world (II 363). Bernd Witte, combing the manuscript variants published in the *Gesammelte Schriften*, points out that in the published version of the essay Benjamin toned down more critical phrases found at crucial junctures in an earlier version (*Walter Ben-jamin*, 93).

This "real humanism" meant, for Benjamin, adopting the standpoint of "the impoverished, reduced human being of our days." And if this poverty was to be understood metaphorically, as the cultural poverty of the private individual—which was in fact the "most stunted form" of poverty—then this, too, only on the model of the "private life of the poor," "that sort of private life which, in opposition to the bourgeois . . . is dismantling itself, is shaping itself openly" (II 341–342). To oppose the barbaric conditions in which orthodox, "classical" humanism was implicated was to profess the "more real humanism" of a "humanity . . . that proves itself in destruction" (II 367).

The "real humanism" of the Kraus essay was thus a variant of the "new barbarism" of "Experience and Poverty." Formulated in conscious opposition to the dominant form of humanism, it was one of the few positive designations of his own position that Benjamin ever allowed himself. Together with his advocacy of the radical modernist project, it established a clear position from which to operate on the terrain of Weimar's cultural politics. It was thus all the more significant that he identified this real humanism with materialism. Citing Marx among its proponents, he now declared that there could be "no idealistic but only a materialist deliverance from myth" (II 365). But as he explained in his essay on surrealism, the materialism he had in mind was not the "metaphysical materialism of communist theory." Rather, it was an "anthropological materialism," rooted in the latent existence of a "bodily collectivity" rather than "abstract matter" (II 1040–1041). The presence of this embodied collective could be traced in two spheres: a sphere of images (*Bildraum*), whose outcroppings had been sighted by the surrealists and by Proust, among others; and a bodily sphere (*Leibraum*), which was beginning to come into its own through recent developments in technology (II 309).[30] These terms mark the outlines of a distinctive philosophical anthropology peculiar to Benjamin.[31] Though he saw many possible affinities between his anthropological materialism and Marxist materialism, the two were not identical. From the mid-1920s onward, he constructed an experimental alliance between them, adapting discrete elements of Marxism: an explanation for the misuse of technology; an analysis of the class position of intellectuals; the notion of false consciousness; and, finally, the idea

[30] The latter is explored in the next section, the former in Chapters 5 and 6.

[31] Benjamin never developed a single, extended account of this philosophical anthropology, but he evoked it in images and arguments dispersed throughout his writings. Apart from the closing passages of the "Surrealism" essay cited here, important texts included his "Schemata on the Psychophysical Problem" (VI 78–87), the "Doctrine of the Similar," and "On the Mimetic Ability" (II 204–213). A full account would involve reconstructing his theory of experience, which goes beyond the scope of my concerns here.

of commodity fetishism.[32] But it was a Marxism divested not only of "metaphysical materialism" but also of any traces of instrumental reason or the domination of nature. When Benjamin characterized his position as materialist, therefore, he meant this anthropological materialism and "real humanism," for which the avant-garde project gave a signal he likened to "the sharp tip of an iceberg" (II 1035).

Benjamin's avowal of the "materialist deliverance from myth" has often been read as a formal repudiation of his own earlier idealism.[33] His early work had pushed the immanent critique of idealism as far as it was possible to go, culminating in the hyperidealism of the *Trauerspiel* preface; now, he was finally making a delayed move to the more obvious form of heterodoxy, a move he had resisted at the time of his break with the youth movement. Yet Benjamin himself refused to acknowledge that by invoking materialism he was repudiating his earlier positions, in part because of his frankly strategic aim of creating an alliance of heterodoxies. In a 1931 letter to Max Rychner, he protested that his allegiance to materialism was not the profession of a worldview but a determination to focus on "those objects in which truth appears most concentrated at the time. And today those are not 'eternal ideas' or 'timeless values'" (B 523–524). His distaste for the "smug complacency of bourgeois scholarship" and "the profoundest circumlocutions of the realm of ideas emerging from Heidegger's school these days" was strong enough to create a feeling of kinship with "the crude, rough-hewn analyses of a Franz Mehring." But Benjamin had substantive reasons for refusing the alternative as well. He saw grounds for "a mediation, however tense and problematic," between the conventional alternatives of materialism and idealism. In his philosophical anthropology, *Bildraum* and *Leibraum* served as *alternate* designations of the messianic realm, "the world of all-sided and integral actuality." The two must be brought into a fusion in which "body and image so interpenetrate that all revolutionary tension becomes bodily collective innervation, and all bodily innervations of the collective become revolutionary discharge" (II 309–310). The Dionysian overtones of this vision were not fortuitous; Benjamin cited Nietzsche and Rimbaud among its progenitors. Yet he could not have wished for the ritual, ecstatic element of Nietzsche's account, for the messianic world's "festive performance" would be "cleansed of all ceremony," and its language would not be a bacchanalian chant but "liberated prose that has burst the

---

[32] Along with Lukács's *History and Class Consciousness*, we know from his list of readings that he was also familiar with Marx's *Class Struggles in France* and Korsch's *Marxism and Philosophy* (VII 460, 463). In the early 1930s he met Korsch through Brecht.

[33] For Witte, the statement represented self-criticism (*Walter Benjamin*, 93); Scholem saw it as self-betrayal (B 525).

fetters of writing" (I 1235). The danger lurking in *this* neighborhood, then, was not affirmative idealism but *Lebensphilosophie;* distinguishing his philosophical anthropology from that of the right became a running concern in Benjamin's work from this time on.

When Benjamin scrutinized the Weimar literary scene's independent left, he found neither a consequential alternative to the corrupted humanism of the academy nor a viable political conception. Though familiar with the profusion of styles, political tendencies, and circles on the left—to the point of deploring the "incredibly vehement and rapid proliferation of sectarianism" (VI 162)—he saw expressionism, activism, and Neue Sachlichkeit as cut from the same cloth (III 280).[34] In all of them he found the idealism not of the professors but of the independent litterateurs, a delusional belief in the efficacy of intellectuals and of moral appeals for progressive causes. Its clearest form was Kurt Hiller's call for a "logocracy," or rule by an elite of *Geist*, which he had been promulgating since his attempt, amid the councils movement in the 1918 revolution, to create a "council of intellectual workers." Hiller was well connected in left-wing expressionist circles; in fact, both Wyneken and Benjamin had been associated with him during the war years, so Benjamin's attack on "the error of activism" (III 350–352) amounted to a public settling of an old account.[35] He granted that Hiller's active commitment to a host of worthwhile goals, ranging from the antiwar movement to reform of the penal codes on sexuality, entitled him to a certain amount of sympathy. The tone of his polemic was more condescending than withering; Hiller's failing was not arrogance but impotence. His call for intellectuals themselves to play leading political roles pitifully demonstrated "how even the déclassé bourgeoisie cannot take leave of certain ideals from its glory days" (III 351). Benjamin saw a corresponding delusion about the efficacy of humanistic moral appeals in the writers loosely identified with Neue Sachlichkeit, such as Erich Kästner, Kurt Tucholsky, Walter Mehring, and Hermann Kesten, whose views were representative of the left-wing circles gathered around such journals as *Die Weltbühne* and *Das Tage-Buch*.[36] Whether in the form of documentary reportage or impressionistic social satire, the artists associated with Neue Sachlichkeit attempted to elicit a direct, "unprejudiced" moral reaction in the viewer or reader. To Benjamin, this was a naive attempt to short-circuit the

---

[34] An exception was formed by those leftists he once included in a category of outsiders whom he respected despite reservations: Siegfried Kracauer, Werner Hegemann, and Alfred Döblin (VI 183).

[35] On Hiller, see Wurgaft, *The Activists*, and Mosse, "Left-Wing Intellectuals in the Weimar Republic," in *Germans and Jews*.

[36] An excellent account of this milieu is provided by Istvan Deak, *Weimar Germany's Left-Wing Intellectuals: A Political History of the Weltbühne and Its Circle*.

necessarily mediated and indirect effect of political writing posited by his own theory of intellectual politics. Such naiveté testified to either a grotesque overestimation of "the absolute political importance of left-wing writing" or an attempt to get by with the least personal investment (VI 178).

But Benjamin also had a sociological analysis of the independent left's illusions which, when played out, suggested that Neue Sachlichkeit was more pernicious than expressionism had been. The "humanistic anarchism" of the litterateurs was an expression of their precarious position between the classes, a position they had held with at least some success since the mid-nineteenth century (III 175). Now the crisis of capitalism was eliminating their niche. But instead of facing up to this fate soberly, these litterateurs were performing ever greater contortions in order to perpetuate the mirage of their free-floating status. In the worst cases, this mendacity could lead to a complete corruption of their emotional responses: in Kästner's poetry, Benjamin found a cheap irony about the grotesqueries of bourgeois society, an irony that had meanwhile become so routine that it deadened the ability to experience disgust at real indignities (III 280). His most damning charge was that Kästner, Tucholsky, and their like were converting misery and discontent into "objects of distraction and amusement, to be supplied for consumption" by a bourgeois audience. And here was the key to exposing the true political function of such left-wing literature, a function that undercut the progressive humanism inscribed on its banner:

> In short, this left-wing radicalism is precisely the stance to which no political action whatsoever any longer corresponds. It stands to the left not of this or that position, but left of anything possible, for from the beginning it intends nothing but to enjoy itself in negativistic repose. The transformation of the political struggle from a compulsion to decide [*Zwang zur Entscheidung*] into an object of enjoyment, from a means of production into an article of consumption—that is the latest hit of this literature. (III 281)

This was the irresponsible aestheticism he called "left-wing melancholy." "Never," he concluded, "has one settled more cozily into an uncomfortable situation."

These illusions seemed all the more dangerous to Benjamin because they revealed the cultural left's underestimation of their opponents on the radical right. Not only did Benjamin take them seriously, but his encounter with them prompted crucial new developments in his intellectual strategy. His view of Weimar's radical conservative scene was in fact selective; it bore the indelible imprint, dating back to the youth movement, of the figures of Stefan George and his circle.[37] His reckoning with the right was therefore bound to be doubly charged, and Benjamin denounced it in forceful and eloquent terms. Yet his relation to the George circle went beyond simple enmity, even with the political turn of his work; his dealings with them were marked by deep ambivalences. He was always careful to distinguish between George's poetry and his "teaching," that "priestly doctrine of poetry" which he found repellent (II 623). He also drew precise distinctions among the various members of the circle. George himself was spared direct criticism; Benjamin delegated his most damning and eloquent judgment to a higher power: "If ever God has struck down a prophet by fulfilling his prophecy, then that was the case with George" (B 578). But if he could not bring himself to raise his own hand against the poet of his youth, George's disciples were fair game. Most notably, he held Gundolf in contempt, pouring scorn on him in print.[38] Between these extremes, however, were others whom Benjamin regarded as worthy opponents, such as Max Kommerell and, most important, Ludwig Klages. In responding to their work, Benjamin was able to work through his ambivalence productively. His confrontation with them was sometimes explicit but just as often tacit; he responded not only with polemics but with dialogue, since their aestheticism and vitalism contained a kernel of truth which, however distorted, had to be redeemed.[39]

The distinctions Benjamin drew were important because aestheticism and vitalism could be played out in various ways. And just as the circle's doctrine changed, in the course of his life George developed a variety of channels for propagating his vision of spiritual regeneration. Among them was to recruit a generation of scholars who would carry his cultural theory into the universities.[40] These academics generated a potent alternative to the orthodox, idealist vision of the German literary tradition, replacing balance and harmony with heroic and martial virtues. The most distinguished of them, in Benjamin's eyes, was Kommerell, whose *Poet as Leader in German Classicism* he felt would have to

[37] On Benjamin's formative relation to George, see Chapter 2, Section 1. In the 1920s he had indirect personal links to the circle via Jula Radt and Franz Hessel, through whom he developed a fleeting acquaintance with Karl Wolfskehl; but otherwise, the relationship remained purely intellectual.

[38] See Chapter 3, Section 1.

[39] The dialogue culminated in Benjamin's work on Baudelaire, for George stood "at the end of a cultural movement that began with Baudelaire" (III 398).

[40] See Michael Winkler, *George-Kreis*; Hermann Lebovics, *Social Conservatism and the Middle Classes in Germany, 1914–1933*; and Hans Norbert Fügen, "Der George-Kreis in der 'dritten Generation'."

count as the magna charta of any self-respecting German conservatism (III 252). He respectfully titled his review of the work "Against a Masterpiece" and lavished praise on Kommerell's physiognomic gifts. But he also exposed the book's vitalist agenda, which, by mythologizing both Greece and German hellenism, portrayed the Germans as heirs to the mission of Greek heroes. In this "Germanic soteriology," Weimar classicism appeared as "the first canonical case of a German revolt" against modernity, led by its cultural elite (III 254–255). Politically, this was the sort of fable that made it possible to suggest "the compatibility of Weimar and Sedan," of culture and militarism (III 258). And Benjamin saw, allied to its troubling politics, a critical method inspired by philosophical vitalism, employing intuitive vision to evoke timeless, archetypal images. He responded to Kommerell's "flaming-flowery" invocation of "German fate" with a potent image of his own:

> We, however, must stand by the plain, ungainly truth, the laconism of the seed, of fruitfulness, and therewith by theory, which leaves the spell of the charmed circle cast by "vision." There may be timeless images, but there are certainly no timeless theories. . . . The genuine image may be old, but the genuine thought is new. It is of today. This today may be shabby, granted. But one must grasp it firmly by the horns in order to be able to consult the past. It is the bull whose blood must fill the pit if the spirits of the departed are to appear at its edge. (III 258–259)

As this inversion of a ritual image shows, what disturbed Benjamin in Kommerell's vision was not the martial moment per se. True critique also knows its sacrificial bulls, but its weapon is "the lethal thrust of thought." In place of mythic vision (*Schau*), then, Benjamin called for theory and knowledge; and in place of mythic timelessness he insisted on the dialectic of past and present moments. One must take a firm grasp of the present—straitened though it may be—to learn from the past. Yet this inversion of ritual knowledge also accepted its terms in one crucial respect: the task still involved summoning the "spirits of the departed" in the guise of "images." Benjamin was not proposing any simple, rationalist demystification; rather, he was implying that the vitalist right appreciated the presence of a dimension of experience that rationalism neglected at its peril. His response to this sort of radical conservative cultural doctrine, then, was to invoke a historically informed theory to illuminate allegedly timeless images and place historical knowledge at the service of the present. No less was necessary to preserve the present against "seers whose visions appear to them over corpses" (III 259).

But there was also another version of *Lebensphilosophie* that dated

farther back in George's own career, to before his distinctive appropriation of Weimar classicism and his mission to the universities. It had
emerged from an earlier incarnation of his circle around the turn of the
century known as the Cosmic Round; its members, including Klages
and Alfred Schuler, were not academics but *Privatgelehrter* and bohe-
mian outsiders who played significant roles in the conservative revival
of Bachofen's work. Unlike the literary scholars, their version of
George's aesthetic revolt against modernity aimed not to recast tradition but to cast it aside, liquidating all ties to history in order to regain
contact with a pure form of archaic consciousness. Klages's works laid
out a speculative philosophical anthropology that sought to revive the
cultural memory of a "natural mythology" buried under millennia of
forgetfulness (III 44).[41] He posited the existence of *Urbilder*, primary
cultural images accessible only via ecstatic states capable of circum-
venting the conceptual thought that had unhappily superseded them;
hence, as the title of his great synthetic work proposed, the mind was
the adversary of the soul—*Der Geist als Widersacher der Seele*.[42] Benjamin repeatedly expressed respect for Klages on the same grounds as
he did for Kommerell: calling him a great philosopher and an-
thropologist, he made a point of praising the learning and acuity that
distinguished him from the "official theoreticians of German fascism"
(II 230; see also II 44, B 515). Klages's belief in the surreptitious persistence of mythic elements precisely *in* modernity was bound to appeal to Benjamin as was, in some measure, his invitation to liquidate a
historical world that had been the scene of a single, ongoing catastrophe. Yet the violence of Klages's prophecies of decline blinded him to
the necessity, so vital to Benjamin, of unconditional loyalty to the present. And even more fundamentally, Benjamin objected that Klages's
rigidly polarized contrast between a vital and a mechanized world—a
"crude metaphysical dualism" (B 515)—committed him to a "hopeless
rejection" of everything technical. Benjamin developed two lines of
response to Klages, and both were at the center of his concerns in this

[41] Benjamin's first exposure to Klages dates back to the youth movement. Klages's
address "Mensch und Erde" (1913) was published in the festschrift for the Meißner
festival, and Benjamin invited him to speak to the Freie Studentenschaft in Berlin; he also
admired Klages's graphological talents. In fact Benjamin was hoping to find Klages in
Munich when he went there to study in 1915, but Klages had already moved to
Switzerland in a gesture of protest against the war. Scholem ("Benjamin and Noeggerath," 148) points out the irony that instead he met Noeggerath, the critic of vitalism.
The firmness with which Klages stayed aloof from the war certainly contributed to
Benjamin's respect for him. In "Mensch und Erde," Klages wrote that "'Civilization'
bears the traits of an unleashed lust for murder, and the fullness of the earth withers at
its poisonous breath" (20). In a preface to a later collection of essays under the same title,
he pointed to the atrocities of the European war as a grim fulfillment of his prophecy
("Vorwort zur ersten Auflage," 8).
[42] The argument had a clear anti-Semitic subtext, and Benjamin was well aware of
Klages's anti-Semitism.

period. One, as with Kommerell, was not to deny the existence or power of mythic images but to develop a theory capable of permeating them with historical knowledge; he began this task with the first version of the "Arcades" project.[43] A second response, however, was to articulate a positive theory of *Technik* that would transcend the crude dualism on which *Lebensphilosphie* was founded. Benjamin suggested several times that a detailed reckoning with Klages remained a desideratum. Though he never completed one in so many words, he redeemed the promise indirectly through his theory of *Technik*.[44] Of course, Klages was not the only target of this argument. If technology could be shown to have a telos that was ultimately noninstrumental, this would make a case against its misuse in the present as well.

Moreover, there were others on the radical right propounding a very different conception of myth and technology, in something of an inversion of Klages's scheme. Whereas *Lebensphilosophie* set them up as antitheses, Ernst Jünger, the Italian futurists, and others conjoined them: technology, particularly the unprecedentedly destructive technology of warfare, might provide aesthetic spectacles of undreamed-of intensity and even serve "the production of cult values" (I 506). Benjamin titled his 1930 review of a volume of war essays edited by Jünger "Theories of German Fascism"; in it he first formulated the basic principles of his analysis of fascism as what he would later call an "aestheticization of politics." Here, however, his emphasis was on the dangers of an aestheticization of *destruction.* In the romanticization of the front-fighter's experience Benjamin saw not only a "boyish rapture that ends in a cult and an apotheosis of war" but evidence of "an uninhibited transposition of the principles of art-for-art's-sake onto war" (III 240). In their misguided attempt to come to terms with the "lost war," these authors had reached the point where they were ready to portray "their own annihilation as an aesthetic pleasure of the first order" (I 508). Benjamin began by ridiculing their departe attempt to cling to a heroic conception of combat as a hopeless anachronism, outmoded by the technology of mass destruction. But this real point was rather different: in the more serious contributions to the volume he found a concerted attempt to pervert the new technology by placing it at the service of a revival of myth: "In the face of the landscape of total mobilization, the German feeling for nature has had an undreamed-of upsurge. . . . The metaphysical abstraction of war professed by the new nationalists is nothing but an attempt to solve the mystery of an idealistically perceived nature through a direct and mystical use of technology, rather

---

[43] On Klages's significance for the early version of the "Arcades" project, see Chapter 5, Sections 4–5.

[44] In 1937 he proposed writing a critique of Klages and Jung for the *Zeitschrift für Sozialforschung,* but Horkheimer vetoed the idea (V 1157–1161).

than using and illuminating the secrets of nature via the detour of the organization of human affairs" (III 247). The mordant humor of Benjamin's suggestion about Germans' immersion in the landscape had its entirely serious point: the unleashing of technology leads to unprecedented devastation because the "elemental forces of society" have not yet been mastered (III 238). The mysticism of war promulgated by Jünger and other "habitués of chthonic forces of terror" was therefore to be taken seriously. In them Benjamin recognized a distinctive form of the radical right's ideology, one with social consequences more potent than those to be feared from Klages. There is no evidence that he read Jünger as carefully as he did Klages—there was less to be learned from him—but certainly he took him seriously. To counter this attempt to aestheticize destruction, Benjamin would have to show that it was based on a perverted conception of technology, one that violated its true telos. "Deeply imbued with its own depravity, technology brought forth the apocalyptic countenance of nature and reduced nature to silence, though it was the force that could have given nature its voice" (III 247). In effect, Benjamin's response to Klages's and Jünger's very different notions of technology was to work out a theory of *Technik* of his own.

3. *Technik*

In the years after 1925, Benjamin both broadened his earlier conception of *Technik* and moved it to a central position among his concerns. *One Way Street* (1926), for instance, signaled this new emphasis with opening and closing pieces on technology. Now, *Technik* no longer primarily meant technique, as it had in his studies of early romanticism and baroque *Trauerspiel*, but what in English would be called technology; and his consideration of it expanded beyond the craft of the work of art to the full range of technology.[45] A simple affirmation of technology was not in itself enough to guarantee what Benjamin needed. In the latter half of the 1920s, such affirmations were commonplace across the ideological spectrum. Helmut Lethen describes how this "habitus of assent" to technology was created by the iconoclastic though paradoxically widespread gesture of rejecting the terms of antimodernist cultural pessimism.[46] The governing metaphors of

[45] The German word *Technik* encompasses both "technique" and "technology."

[46] Lethen, "Neue Sachlichkeit," 168, 172–173; see also his extended study *Neue Sachlichkeit (1924–1932)*. In a similar vein, Herbert Schnädelbach points out the dependence of *Lebensphilosophie* on such simple polarities; see his *Philosophy in Germany, 1832–1933*, 139.

antimodernism were based on a set of conventional polarities; one simply adopted these and reversed their signs, valuing mechanism instead of organism, urbanity rather than rootedness, coolness over warmth. This move produced more than just an atmosphere of *Sachlichkeit;* Lethen rightly stresses that such gestures created "peculiar alliances, clear across the lines of the entrenched political camps."[47] It also became more difficult to perceive and draw distinctions within the ideological camps. On the left, for instance, affirmations of technology could be treacherously ambiguous: if sometimes they amounted to little more than a fascination with machines, often they betrayed a naive faith in rationalization, efficiency, and progress. Via Taylorism and Fordism, many on the left unwittingly ended up espousing little more than functional adaptation to the changing demands of the capitalist economy.[48]

Benjamin's particular path to this culture of technology gave him an awareness of its ambiguities that many others lacked. He had espoused the technique of the work of art as a sobering antidote to mystifications of creativity; but his equally resolute antiinstrumentalism helped to preserve him against any uncritical affirmation of technology. Moreover, his critique of idealist aesthetics guided him to engage the debate over technology via the most radical versions of the avant-garde project, those that proposed a thorough transformation of the relationship between aesthetic form and life. In baroque *Trauerspiel* he had found not only an alternative to idealist aesthetics but a liquidation of the transfiguring aesthetic sphere itself; now he found portions of the contemporary avant-garde arguing that new technology could be channeled to produce such a transformation in the society at large.[49] Of course, these predispositions could not guarantee complete immunity to the prevalent ideologies of technology. To some extent, Benjamin undoubtedly did partake of Lethen's "habitus of assent"; one can find passages that display an uncritical fascination with the machine metaphor.[50] But he was driven to do more than simply reverse the terms of romantic antimodernism. He needed to distinguish himself from the

[47] Lethen, "Neue Sachlichkeit," 169. One of these alliances was found in what Jeffrey Herf calls the "paradox of reactionary modernism," a phenomenon first defined (though not so named) by Benjamin. See Herf, *Reactionary Modernism,* especially chap. 1.

[48] Charles Maier, "Between Taylorism and Technocracy: European Ideologies and the Vision of Industrial Productivity in the 1920's."

[49] Andreas Huyssen stresses this link, pointing out that "in Benjamin's work of the 1930s . . . the hidden dialectic between avant-garde art and the utopian hope for an emancipatory mass culture can be grasped alive for the last time" ("The Hidden Dialectic: Avantgarde—Technology—Mass Culture," in *After the Great Divide,* 14). Not all versions of the avant-garde project put technology at the center of this transformation; on surrealism's attempt to put an end to art by fusing it with life, see Chapter 5, Section 1.

[50] A good example is "Filling Station," the opening piece of *One Way Street* (IV 85).

reactionary modernists, but to do so without backing up into a simple faith in rationalization or progress. What he sought to develop might be called the paradox of an antiinstrumental affirmation of technology.

Where did Benjamin look for ways of understanding the potential hidden in technology? Although Germany and the Soviet Union were at the forefront of the avant-garde's encounter with technology, one of his key sources lay to the west, in the works of the French poet and critic Paul Valéry. Valéry's work provided Benjamin with an ideal bridge to constructivist views, because Valéry himself had once been associated with the aestheticism of the French symbolist poets. One of Benjamin's first reports as the Paris correspondent for *Die Literarische Welt* portrayed a talk given by Valéry at the Ecole Normale in 1926 (IV 479–480); in it, he first enunciated motifs crucial to his later views on technology and art. One of these was a telling extension of his stock of images for the creative process. Valéry introduced him to a reading of Mallarmé's work quite different from his own stress on the evocative plurality of imperfect languages in "The Task of the Translator"; here, the symbolist poets' attempt to emulate and compete with music was construed in terms of "building" and "construction." Valéry, himself a leading symbolist poet, was recasting symbolism's self-understanding by proposing a theory of the poetic process as a methodical, calculated procedure. In effect, Valéry was pursuing a French version of the demystification of creativity that Benjamin himself had traced within the German baroque and romantic traditions. Both were asserting that technique, not inspiration, provides the model for the production of artworks: Benjamin had used the German romantic image of the skilled craft; now, Valéry's Cartesian idiom of clean slates and construction would help him to take that critique a step farther. Moreover, Mallarmé's "Un coup de dés . . ." innovated not only sonorously but graphically, by manipulating script on the written page.[51] Strikingly, Benjamin likened the result—phrases dispersed across the page in varying type fonts and sizes—to the innovative graphic techniques of advertising. Mallarmé was no avant-garde transgressor of boundaries, seeking to violate separations between high and popular culture or art and everyday life; rather, his example showed how a radical, consequential pursuit of tensions *within* traditional literature and aestheticism could lead to an art that uncannily anticipated larger technical and social processes.[52] The point, which he stated laconically, was that

[51] Scholem reports that Benjamin owned a copy of this edition as early as 1919 (*Walter Benjamin*, 110).

[52] In the theses on reproduction, he illustrated the same point with the case of Dada and film and stated it as a general principle: "One of the foremost tasks of art has always been to produce a demand whose full satisfaction is not yet possible. The history of every artform includes critical periods when the form strives for effects that can be freely produced only with a changed technical standard, that is, in a new artform" (I 500–503).

"absolute poetry taken to its extreme reverses into its apparent opposite." The architectural metaphor, the potent yield of aestheticism, and the anticipation of tendencies at work in "mass" culture by "high" culture all became crucial topoi in Benjamin's work from this time on.

Benjamin later elaborated his views on Valéry by stressing the antihumanist, liquidationist elements in his makeup. The short essay "Paul Valéry" (1931) drew him into the company of those "destructive characters" Kraus and Brecht (II 386–390). Describing Valéry's character Monsieur Teste as "the negation of the 'human'," Benjamin explicitly compared him with Brecht's Herr Keuner, "the thinker"; he praised Teste's Cartesian disposition to mathematical calculation and his willingness to begin again from a tabula rasa.[53] In fact, his notes to the essay contain even stronger formulations than the published text, stressing Teste's "methodical parsimony and sobriety" and even his ruthlessness: Teste represented "a ruthless, relentless materialism" that Benjamin likened—once more, approvingly—to the radical materialism of the eighteenth-century French encyclopedists (II 1145). Yet in pivotal statements such as "Experience and Poverty" Valéry no longer figured as an exemplar. The omission is significant and is explained by the pointer to Valéry's limits in "The Social Position of the French Writer" (1934). Here, Benjamin reached the verdict that Valéry left his own best insights stranded halfway to their true destination: while enunciating the idea of "planned construction" for the work of art, he drew back before the crucial threshold of extending planning to "the human community" (II 794). His work thus remained inconsequential. Although willing to surrender the ideal of the harmoniously developed individual, he inconsistently tried to reconcile this surrender with the illegitimate preservation of "certain privileges." The "melancholy secret of Monsieur Teste" was that "the intellect remains private" (II 1146).[54]

But this was just where the new Soviet culture was going farther. It supplied the necessary complement to what Valéry provided—the social and political dimensions of what Benjamin took to be the emerging order. He traveled to Moscow in the winter of 1926/27 with a commission from Martin Buber's journal *Die Kreatur*. Ironically, he arrived at a time when the fortunes of the cultural avant-garde associated with the early, heroic phase of the revolution had already begun to wane. His diary of the trip and the reports he filed show that it was social and

---

[53] *Die Negation des 'Menschlichen'* might also be rendered "the negation of the 'humane'" since the German term *menschlich*, as used here, can suggest both "humane" and "human." He first likened Teste to Keuner in his 1930 radio talk "Bert Brecht" (II 663).

[54] Benjamin continued to draw on Valéry's insights into the poetic process; most prominent is his motto for the final version of the theses on reproduction (I 472). See the editors' list of Benjamin's later Valéry citations (II 1144).

political conditions, more than the technological visions of the constructivists or the theoretical reflections of Soviet filmmakers, that
made the most lasting impression on him there (B 444). The first of the
new conditions was what he termed "absolute publicity" (Öf-
fentlichkeit). For the writer and artist, this meant the surrender of privileges formerly associated with bourgeois status, the elimination of privacy, and a thoroughgoing politicization of one's work (II 743).
Underlying these changes in the status of the writer was a second
condition, a new set of social functions for art. The new culture would
face primarily didactic tasks. This didactic focus entailed a concern for
the conditions of aesthetic reception; he noted discussions on founding
an institute to conduct research into audience responses to film (II 750).
But he also observed, somewhat surprisingly, that the urgent questions
on which literary and cinematic debate focused all concerned subject
matter rather than aesthetic form. In the new Russian naturalist literature, this predominance of subject matter—"the crude heaping of
material, the unconditional presence of political details"—reminded
him of the collapse of form in the German baroque (II 744–745). He
made fewer references to LEF (the Left Front of Art) and other "formal
tendencies" than one would expect, and those were not always clearly
favorable. What Soviet culture provided, then, was the social context
for his conception of technology; what he adopted from it concerned
not so much the technology itself, or its aesthetic implications, as the
social needs it would meet. And as his reflections on Valéry showed,
Benjamin stressed the anticipatory moment of culture and technology:
he was inclined to see technological developments, much like modernist and avant-garde art, as anticipating social developments whose
character would only later become clear.

This theme was prominent in the central European avant-garde
movement in architecture, which was a third source for his thinking on
technology. Benjamin's reading of this movement was selective. While
his programmatic statements invoked Le Corbusier, the important impulses came from the works of Sigfried Giedion, Adolf Behne, and
Adolf Loos.[55] Benjamin's understanding of the modernist project in
architecture drew most heavily on Giedion's Building in France (1928), a
study of the origins of iron and glass construction. Giedion was a
classically trained art historian who took up the banner of the modern
movement in architecture.[56] "The task of the historian," as Giedion

[55] This pattern is shown by the early notes for the "Arcades" project as well as by his
list of his readings, which includes Behne's Neues Wohnen—neues Bauen and Eine Stunde
Architektur (VII 460–461).
[56] Giedion had been a student of Heinrich Wölfflin, the historian of baroque art; see
Sokratis Georgiadis, Sigfried Giedion, eine intellektuelle Biographie.

saw it, was "to lay bare those elements within the enormous complex of a past age that become the point of departure for the future," a view congenial to Benjamin's sense of the anticipatory element in technology; his study aimed to provide the proponents of the "new building" with a historical tradition.[57] Giedion found precedents for their work in the functional constructions pioneered by French engineers in the previous century. "As if out of fear," however, nineteenth-century architects had felt compelled to disguise their forward-looking constructions in "historicizing masks," ornamental embellishments drawn from the styles of past eras.[58] Giedion interpreted this fear as the reflex of a more general social process: the "collective apparatus of industry" had unleashed vast new productive forces, but the benefits had been diverted for the consumption of only a few. His reading of modern architectural history gave substance to Benjamin's intuitive sense that technology anticipated new collective needs, and his plea against the distortion of construction by historicist embellishment resonated with Benjamin's avowal of the parsimony demanded by the new poverty of experience. He found this fierce parsimony best incarnated in the figure of Loos, the inveterate enemy of ornament.[59] What Benjamin saw in the architectural avant-garde, then, was not a model of rationalization and efficiency but the constructive anticipation of a form of social practice that breaks with bourgeois society.[60] But if the motifs he prized in Giedion and Loos were undoubtedly central to the avant-garde movement, other elements were curiously absent. Perhaps the most striking omission was the movement for settlement architecture, or *Siedlungsbau,* which designed and built innovative modernist housing for low-income families on the fringes of major cities. Benjamin could hardly have overlooked this, since Frankfurt am Main was one of the most active centers for such work in the 1920s.[61]

This omission might be interpreted in many ways, but at the least it suggests that Benjamin was interested more in the visionary than the practical aspects of the new architecture. Through all his engagements with technology, his most lasting yet elusive affinity may have been with the works of the utopian visionary Paul Scheerbart.[62] Benjamin

---

[57] Giedion, *Bauen in Frankreich,* 1.

[58] This idea was at the heart of the original conception of the "Arcades" project; see Chapter 5, Section 4.

[59] Michael Müller shows that Loos the practitioner was not quite the inveterate enemy of ornament presented in his theory; see *Die Verdrängung des Ornaments,* 95–147.

[60] Michael Müller, "Architektur für das 'schlechte Neue'," 287–289.

[61] On "the new Frankfurt," see Christoph Mohr and Michael Müller, *Funktionalität und Moderne: Das neue Frankfurt und seine Bauten, 1925–1933.*

[62] Unfortunately, his most important statement on Scheerbart, a critique of *Lesabéndio* under the tantalizing title "The True Politician," is lost (II 1423).

had been devoted to his novels since the war years. Scheerbart's *Lesa-béndio* portrays the asteroid utopia of the planet Pallas, an anarchic society without property or institutions. Its inhabitants live in a thoroughly transformed relationship to nature: their natural needs are met through adapation to their environment, yet they continue to pursue technological projects meant to embellish rather than exploit the planet. Scheerbart's purpose, as Benjamin saw it, was to disabuse people of the "base and vulgar opinion that they are called on to 'exploit' the forces of nature" and to portray a world in which technology would liberate both humanity and, "fraternally," the rest of creation along with it (II 630–631). In Scheerbart's "utopia of the body . . . the earth and humanity together form a single body [*Leib*]" (VI 148). Benjamin also prized the resolute refusal of interiority and psychological complication in Scheerbart's characters (II 618). As he explained in "Experience and Poverty," this was what had led Scheerbart to champion the new glass architecture: the transparency of glass made it the enemy of secrecy and privacy and thus the antidote to the suffocating complications of the bourgeois interior. Whereas Jules Verne simply transported ordinary bourgeois characters into outer space, Scheerbart was interested in the deeper question of how technology would transform the very basis of human nature (II 216–218). His visions provided the utopian vanishing point of Benjamin's conception of technology.

Benjamin pursued his new concern with technology on three levels, which must be clearly distinguished if we are to grasp the full import of his emerging conception. The first, which he would explore most closely, involved changes in the media of cultural production, a transformation he linked to changing modes of perception and aesthetic reception. In widely dispersed pieces of the late 1920s Benjamin began to lay the foundation for the materialist aesthetic of "The Author as Producer" (1934) and "The Work of Art in the Age of Its Technical Reproducibility" (1935/36).[63] Yet he saw these aesthetic issues as but one aspect—if for his own work the salient one—of a larger conflict over the social control of all technology. Here he adopted a straightforwardly Marxist analysis, ascribing the misuse of technology's liberating potential to capitalism. Finally, he placed this social conflict within an even more encompassing framework: technology was ultimately to be understood as regulating the interchange between humankind and

---

[63] Remarkably enough, despite the widespread attention the theses on reproduction have attracted, the earlier development of the view of technology underlying them has never been thoroughly explored. The best treatment is still Müller, "Architektur für das 'schlechte Neue'," though it is limited to architecture and synthesizes a single, consistent theory drawing on all periods of Benjamin's work.

nature. During these years Benjamin was beginning to sketch out the rudiments of a philosophical anthropology that provides the underpinnings of his entire conception of *Technik*. The most striking formulation of these second and third aspects can be found in "To the Planetarium," the brief, visionary text placed at the conclusion of *One Way Street* (IV 146–148).

"To the Planetarium" is built on a contrast between ancient and modern modes of relating to nature or, as he calls it here, the cosmos. In antiquity, experience of the cosmos was collective and ecstatic (*rauschhaft*); by contrast, the modern experience of it is individual and detached, as exemplified by the exclusively optical relationship signaled in the rise of modern astronomy. But the ancient form of cosmic experience, though disdained by moderns as idle superstition, is by no means obsolete. On the contrary, "it comes due ever and again," and the modern disparagement of it is a "menacing aberration." Just how menacing this could be was shown, Benjamin asserts, by the recent war. The massive, technologized destruction on the battlefields of the Great War must ultimately be understood as an unwitting "attempt at a new and unprecedented wedding with the cosmos," fusing body and landscape in one of Jünger's "storms of steel"; at bottom, it was no less than a perverted attempt to reenact the ancient ecstasies of cosmic experience. The modern view, blind to the significance of the archaic, fails to appreciate what was ultimately at stake in the war. But what caused the perversion of this "great wooing"? Certainly not any inherent incompatibility between technology and cosmic experience; on this point, Benjamin parts company with antitechnological radical conservatives such as Klages. The problem is rather a *misuse* of technology. Benjamin actually gives two distinct grounds for this misuse. One is intrasocial: under capitalism, technology is deployed to serve "the lust for profit of the ruling class." The second, however, is found not so much within society as at the interface between humankind and nature: the ancient practice of giving oneself over to cosmic experience has been supplanted by an attempt to dominate nature. For both reasons, "technology has betrayed humankind and transformed the bridal bed into a bloodbath."

One one level, then, Benjamin's explanation for the perverting of technology is classically Marxist: technology's vast potential is fettered by the existing relations of production; in the age of imperialism, the consequence is war; and Benjamin identifies the agent who will put this right as the proletariat. But on another level, he locates the crux of the problem in something broader, and quite distinct from capitalism. He advances a critique of technology not as an intrasocial phenomenon but as a civilizational force, as the domination of nature. In accordance with this second explanation, one version of the theses on reproduction would later ascribe the attempt to dominate nature to technology's origins in ritual practices (VI 359). The two levels of his critique are captured in the dual formula he uses to characterize coming wars as at once "imperialist wars" and "slave revolts of technology" (III 238).[64] In either case, the problem is not technology itself—his thesis is not that technology is inherently bound up with domination—but rather "the misbegotten reception of technology" (II 475, III 576).[65] The images of an oppressed slave and a misbegotten reception in turn suggest a conception of a liberated technology. Benjamin's positive conception of technology might on first reading seem to be Marxist; the misreading is tempting, because his affirmation follows so closely on his invocation of the Marxist explanation for the technology's misbegotten deployment. But, like his critique, it leads somewhere rather different. "To the Planetarium" eloquently states what separated him from Marx's philosophical anthropology, which takes productive work as the fundamental form of human activity. The point of technology, Benjamin asserts, is not to master nature but to master the relation between humankind and nature. He makes this argument through an analogy with education, which, he points out, should aim to master not the children themselves but the relation between the generations. This discrete but unmistakable reference back to a theme of the youth movement lends his case an understated passion.

Benjamin then presented his own philosophical anthropology—his account of the proper relation between humanity, technology, and nature—through the figure of the body.[66] In this image, technology is not an ensemble of implements, of objects physically distinct from human bodies, but the extension of a collective, social body, "the bodily collectivity [*das leibliche Kollektivum*]" (II 1041).[67] With the new technology, he suggested, humanity is organizing itself a new *physis*, a "new body [*Leib*]" (II 319–310, IV 148).[68] The sphere of bourgeois indi-

---

[64] These terms are from "Theories of German Fascism" (1930).

[65] Via Benjamin's influence on Adorno, this shift in the scene of domination from society to nature was a precursor of Horkheimer and Adorno's *Dialektik der Aufklärung*. Later, in "On the Concept of History," Benjamin contrasted "progress in the mastering of nature" with "regression in society" (I 699). But Benjamin's differences with the *Dialektik der Aufklärung* should be noted as well: Benjamin never implied that technology was *inherently* an instrument of domination.

[66] The following account draws together passages from "To the Planetarium," "Surrealism" (and his notes to it), "Theories of German Fascism," and "Experience and Poverty."

[67] The terms *leiblich* and *leibhaft* suggest both "embodied" and "bodily"; that Benjamin intended the second, stronger of these senses seems clear from passages in his drafts of the surrealism essay, where he plainly stated that "the collective, too, has a body" (II 1041).

[68] *Physis*, the Greek term for "nature," can mean "physique" in German; in both German and English it denotes nature as the source of growth or change.

viduality and interiority would be dismantled or, rather, dismembered, until "no limb remains unrent," and then reconstituted.[69] In this extraordinary image, the war appears as an epileptic fit, the uncontrollable, shuddering trauma that follows an anticipatory glimpse of happiness; the postwar uprisings were then the first collective efforts to bring this new body under control. The war had shown that society was not yet "mature enough to make technology its organ" (III 238). Later, in "Experience and Poverty," Benjamin evoked this philosophical anthropology more playfully in a reading of early animated cartoons such as Mickey Mouse, in which he saw less traumatic glimpses of future happiness. In these early cartoons, he pointed out, the characters constantly and effortlessly improvise miraculous physical feats surpassing the capacities of present-day technology; and the most remarkable thing is that they do it all without a trace of machinery, out of the powers of their bodies alone (II 218). What might seem the mere escapist dreams of popular culture appeared instead as a confirmation of Benjamin's vision: technology had been incorporated into the (social) body to the point that it effortlessly merged with nature once again; "here nature and technology . . . have become perfectly one." In the terms of "To the Planetarium," the ancient experience of the cosmos could thus be restored on a higher level.

Benjamin's corporeal imagery is evocative rather than precise; it does not spell out a full-blown theory of technology. But it served several important purposes for him. Above all, "To the Planetarium" was a pivotal, programmatic statement: while confirming the antiinstrumentalist philosophical anthropology of his early theory of language, he was now declaring his intention to join it with Marxist social analysis and contemporary political polemics. The piece also gave expression to a historical sensibility with its roots in the youth movement: on this issue, too, humanity had arrived at a moment in which both great danger and the possibility of redemption were at hand. At a time when the cultural climate was shifting to sobriety and *Sachlichkeit*, Benjamin's view of technology held fast to the heady optimism of constructivist utopias.[70] Equally striking is his adamant warning that failure to come to terms with technology would result in war rather than, say, a regimented and administered society. The point is easily overlooked, given our retrospective knowledge of the war that was indeed to follow; his insistence testifies not only to foresight but also, once more, to the

[69] Rainer Nägele suggests that this dismembering of the old *Leibraum* recapitulates the allegorical dismemberment of the corpse in *Trauerspiel*; see *Theater, Theory, Speculation: Walter Benjamin and the Scenes of Modernity*, 154.

[70] The heady tone characteristic of this period, despite its awareness of dangers, contrasts with the later theses on reproduction which, even when couched in similar terms, were a defiant assertion of an increasingly isolated position.

decisive, formative impact the Great War had on his cultural criticism. But thus far, it was less clear what this liberated and liberating technology might look like. The answer was to be found in the aspect of technology that he did examine in a sustained way, the new conditions of aesthetic production and reception.

"Technical revolutions," so runs Benjamin's thesis, which he had already formulated by 1927, "are the sites of ruptures in the development of art," sites at which the deeper political trends implicit in the new art break into the open (II 752).[71] And at the interface where new technologies were transforming inherited aesthetic forms and creating new ones, the outlines of a new, progressive mode of perception were emerging. This complex view, distilled from his readings of Valéry, early Soviet culture, and avant-garde architecture, served as the guiding principle for his explorations of the relationship between technological change and aesthetic form. It was, then, a view he held well before his encounter with Brecht or his work, though Brecht's example and influence became crucial spurs to its development. Eventually it would become the core of "The Work of Art in the Age of Its Technical Reproducibility," which spells out six dimensions of a progressive mode of aesthetic reception being fostered by cinema.[72] This emerging mode of perception would involve, first of all, a critical, testing stance toward experience, an attitude fostered both by qualities of the works and by the participation of the audience. The works would employ the modernist techniques of montage and interruption to give the work a "ballistic" quality, a shock effect that would be met by heightened presence of mind (I 503). This almost tactile quality, by "bringing things close" (I 479), would disrupt their auratic spell, which requires an inviolable distance. From the audience's side, the attitude of the expert examiner would result from its "identifying with the technical equipment [*Einfühlung in den Apparat*]," meaning that the audience would

---

[71] In "The Author as Producer" (1934), he reformulated this idea into the thesis that the correct political tendency of a literary work is inseparable from its employment of a progressive technique; see Kambas, *Walter Benjamin im Exil*, 32–39.

[72] See also my discussion of the concept of the aura in the Introduction. I risk offering this highly compressed reading of "The Work of Art" as an orientation for the analysis in the remainder of this section and as an alternative to two kinds of reductive reading. First, I mean to stress the multiple dimensions of Benjamin's account, which is too often reduced to montage and shock effect or read simply as a translation of Brecht's alienation effect into cinematic terms. Second, I caution against too simple a reading of Benjamin's call for a politicization of art. What he meant was not a mirror image of the fascist "aestheticization of politics" (Wolin, *Walter Benjamin*, 184) or a propagandistic art but a conscious use of techniques of modernist art to tap the critical potential being prepared by this unconscious process of training. Of course, the sloganeering parallelism of Benjamin's own closing formulation—"This is the aestheticization of politics promoted by fascism. Communism responds to it by politicizing art" (I 508)—did much to encourage misreadings.

assume the camera's active and constructive position rather than one of contemplative passivity (I 488). Second, it would involve a more intensive exploration of the visual environment that leads to a "deepening of apperception" and reveals an "optical unconscious": "a different nature opens itself to the camera than to the naked eye" (I 498–500). Third, the new mode of reception would be collective and public rather than individual and private, as with the novel or oil painting (I 504). Fourth, despite the language of visual testing, this was not a rigoristic ideal; the new mode of perception would provide visual pleasure: "The masses expect the work of art to be something that will warm them," and rightly so (V 500); "in the cinema, the audience's critical and pleasurable attitudes coincide" (I 497). Fifth, and closely related, the development of critical habits of perception would not be a matter of deliberate effort but a process of training that, up to a point, could take place unconsciously, even in a state of "distraction," through the absorption of the qualities of the medium (I 504). Finally, the ultimate product of this transformation of the mode of perception would be a new bodily collective with a transformed relation to nature. "Identifying [Einfühlung] with the technical equipment" in fact had a double significance: it referred not only to taking up the attitude of critical examiner but to appropriating and absorbing technology into an expanded human sensorium. The audience "absorbs" not only the work of art but the medium itself (I 504). This schematic summary is not meant to imply that the theses on reproduction presented a closed, definitive theory; rather, they were Benjamin's attempt at a provisional summary of his previous work. The elements of this complex view had been assembled gradually over the course of the late 1920s and early 1930s.

In the late 1920s, Benjamin found his first evidence of this emerging mode of perception in two media: a distinctive mode of filmic perception, and a new organization and experience of space through modernist architecture. His first recorded reflections on film, which date to his trip to Moscow, show how early he began to see it as a medium with revolutionary qualities, in terms sometimes adopted almost word for word into the later theses on reproduction. In a polemic with a German critic of Eisenstein's Battleship Potemkin (1927), he argued for the first time that the important thing about early film was not its content or even its aesthetic form but rather the revolution in Technik it represented. To his way of seeing, this revolution was in the process of creating "a new region of consciousness" in which an emerging collective subject, the proletariat, would find itself at home (II 752–753). The expanded consciousness Benjamin discerned here was what he later called a deepening of apperception that would reveal the melancholy sites of everyday life to be full of unsuspected possibilities: "In and of themselves, these offices, furnished rooms, bars, city streets, railway stations, and factories are ugly, incomprehensible, hopelessly sad. Or rather: they were so and seemed so, until film came along. Film then exploded this entire dungeon-world with the dynamite of the tenth of a second, so that now, among its far-flung debris, we set out on long adventurous journeys."[73] In other words, the aspect of filmic perception that first caught Benjamin's attention was not what he would later call the critical, testing attitude but the disclosure of a new perceptual space. But what guaranteed the progressive character of this new optic? What distinguished this expanded consciousness from an escapist mirage? At this point, Benjamin's case rested not on the manner of seeing but on a political claim about the occupant of these spaces: "The proletariat is the hero of those spaces to whose adventures the bourgeois, his heart pounding, abandons himself in the cinema. . . . The proletariat, however, is a collectivity, just as these spaces are the collective's spaces" (II 753). Surprisingly, he delivered a resounding vindication of Eisenstein's film without relying on or even mentioning his theory of montage.[74]

Modern architecture was the second field in which Benjamin found signs of a new mode of perception. Here, too, what fascinated him was the interplay between a transformation of space and the emergence of a collective subject. The technical revolution in architecture proceeded not from the creation of a new medium, as with film, but from the introduction of new materials, glass and iron. The modernist architecture based on them served Benjamin as a potent source of images. Its austerity and purity struck him as the only dignified response to the new poverty of experience and a bracing antidote to the profusion of false riches typical of the overstuffed bourgeois interior (II 217–218). But he also saw it as the harbinger of a social transformation: glass and iron constructions held the promise of a new spatial transparency; by lifting the spatial distinction between street and interior they would promote the overcoming of social distinctions between private and public, isolated individual and mass. The technical revolution in building thus promised to generalize the abolition of private life Benjamin had observed in Moscow, where it was a matter of party policy and straitened living conditions (IV 327).[75] Living in glass houses would

---

[73] Compare "The Work of Art," section XIII (I 498–500).

[74] The role of montage in Benjamin's theory of film stems from Brecht; see the next section.

[75] He found a similar rearrangement of public and private spheres in Naples, where, with no sharp distinction between indoor and outdoor space, private life was "dispersed, porous, and commingled" (IV 314). On Asja Lacis and Benjamin's Naples–Moscow connection, see Buck-Morss, Dialectics of Seeing, 26–32.

become not just a "revolutionary virtue" (II 298) but a widespread form of life. The new architecture was already providing the emerging collectivity with a setting for the new regime of "absolute publicity" (II 743).

In fact, the way space is experienced through architecture—collectively, through a process of unconscious appropriation—would become Benjamin's model for other forms of aesthetic reception, including film.[76] Architecture provided the model form of reception because the built environment has a direct influence in organizing everyday experience; through it, "laws of technical construction . . . become laws of life itself" (III 170). But Benjamin was still not ready to pursue this reception model in detail. Rather, in a note for the first version of the "Arcades" project that is characteristic of his concerns in this period, he suggested that the new architecture was part of a reconstruction of the social body itself. In *Building in France,* Giedion had argued that the nineteenth century's glass and iron constructions, hidden beneath ornamental exteriors, played the role of a repressed unconscious. Benjamin proposed a reformulation: "Shouldn't one rather substitute [for the unconscious]: 'the role of the bodily processes', on which 'artistic' architecture would then lie like dreams supported by the scaffolding of physiological processes?" (V 1027). In this image, the new collective architecture of arcades and railway stations figures as more than just the "house of the dreaming collective" (V 1012).[77] It is literally an extension of the bodily collectivity, its physiological scaffolding or *physis.* In Michael Müller's apt description, it is "like a new sensory organ" in that it "opens up new realms of experience."[78] This image was more than a fanciful literary conceit. In it, Benjamin joined two levels of his view of *Technik,* using the emerging mode of aesthetic reception to present his larger philosophical anthropology. And once again, as a justification for the work of the architectural avant-garde, this was an argument in which efficiency and rationalization played no role.

Before his encounter with Brecht, then, Benjamin was developing a complex conception of *Technik* that balanced diverse and even conflicting elements. He sought to articulate a view that was at once pro-technology and antiinstrumental, and in pieces like "Experience and Poverty" his image of technology combined the disillusioned sobriety of reduced circumstances with a visionary quality reminiscent of Scheerbart's utopias. Indeed, the very complexity of the theory leaves many questions open. The burden of Benjamin's argument is that tech-

[76] Benjamin pointed to this in "The Work of Art" (I 504).

[77] On the decoding of these dream images in the "Arcades" project, see Chapter 5, Section 5, and Chapter 7, Sections 1–2.

[78] Müller, "Architektur für das 'schlechte Neue'," 124.

nology has a telos that ultimately is not instrumental. His observations on film and architecture can, of course, be judged on their own merits as hypotheses on aesthetic reception. But when seen in terms of his larger argument, they must yield more: they must provide concrete examples of what a liberating, noninstrumental technology might look like. This requirement helps explain why his early reflections on film and architecture return so insistently to the theme of his philosophical anthropology, the emergence of a bodily collective subject. They highlight the new technology's noninstrumental quality as a *medium* in which this emerging collectivity represents itself.[79] Even the didactic aspect of Soviet film, which would seem unabashedly instrumental, is ultimately understood in terms of this goal. Although this may be a plausible reading of culture, the logic of his argument means that culture must adumbrate the possibilities of *all* technology, not just the technology of cultural production. But it is not clear that cultural production and reception can do this, and Benjamin provided no explicit argument to demonstrate that they could. In one version of the reproduction theses, he did explicitly ascribe to art a "socially decisive function" as a medium in which "the interplay between nature and humanity" can be "practiced" or trained; this interplay, he argued, is the goal of a second *Technik* that will supersede a first *Technik*, with its origins in ritual, which aims at the domination of nature (VII 359). The idea of art as a sphere where the reconciliation of tensions can be practiced through play recalls Schiller's *On the Aesthetic Education of Humanity*. But Benjamin's suggestion does not resolve the problem, for it begs the question of whether the techniques involved in culture are really analogous to those of all technology.[80]

The complexity of Benjamin's conception also raises questions about its internal coherence. To this point in his work, the Marxist element was least well integrated. It provided a largely ad hoc explanation for the misuse of technology; beyond that, Benjamin often equated the "collectivity" of his own philosophical anthropology with the proletariat in such phrases as "the proletariat, however, is a collectivity" (II 753). But did the reverse hold? Did the collectivity as Benjamin understood it resemble the proletariat in any substantive sense? As yet, the answer would have to be no; Benjamin did not define his collectivity as the producing subject of social labor. Nor did he use

[79] Here the conception of *Technik* recapitulates the argument of his early theory of language, which downplayed its instrumental and communicative functions; see Menninghaus, *Benjamins Theorie der Sprachmagie*, 9–77.
[80] This has long been Habermas's argument against the conception of an alternative technology in Benjamin, Marcuse, and Adorno; see, for example, "Technology and Science as 'Ideology'," 87–89.

Marxist theory to establish the relative causal roles of the various strands of his account. In fact, when not making programmatic statements he tended to accord relative autonomy to technology, aesthetic form, and social needs.[81] But the point is not so much to judge the consistency of Benjamin's Marxism as to recognize that he had an original conception of technology whose beginnings owed little to Marx. Instead, it was rooted in the mystical collectivism of his own, distinctive anthropological materialism.

But finally, we should recall the strategic bearings of Benjamin's emerging conception of technology: his vision of a noninstrumental telos of technology had to provide an alternative to radical conservative conceptions. Prior to his encounter with Brecht, Benjamin's conception of technology did not really measure up to this task; in place of concrete theses on reception, it offered reiterations of his philosophical anthropology. His association with Brecht would result in a qualitative leap in his reception theory. And, in the process, he would also integrate Marxian positions more plausibly into his work.

4. Brecht

By any account, Bertolt Brecht must be counted among the elective affinities that were most decisive in shaping Benjamin's intellectual physiognomy. Yet even within this inner circle of figures the relationship was unique, for it was his only sustained collaboration with a major, working artist. This personal relation has been an object of speculation almost since the beginning of their acquaintance. If Brecht's influence led Benjamin to betray the sources of his inspiration, as some have believed, then it has often been tempting to explain this psychologically, as the result of Benjamin's fascination with Brecht's person. After all, Brecht was the only writer whose work Benjamin was willing to support "without (public) reservations" (B 534–535), and it has been observed, not without reason, that in his commentaries on Brecht he adopted the stance of an authorized exegete.[82] In terms of intellectual influence, certainly, the relationship was clearly asymmetrical; Benjamin learned from Brecht, but not vice versa. All this has been taken as evidence of a peculiar submissiveness on Benjamin's part, even a perverse vulnerability to suggestion. Benjamin was prey to

---

[81] This was the scheme Benjamin himself later proposed in the first version of "The Work of Art" (I 456–457); in the final version, the point was relegated to a footnote (I 500–501, n. 26).

[82] Rolf Tiedemann, " 'Die Kunst, in anderer Leute Köpfe zu denken': Brecht—kommentiert von Walter Benjamin," 181.

the attraction of opposites: Brecht, the *Kraftmensch* and gruff advocate of crude thinking, was irresistibly attractive to Benjamin, the sensitive, scrupulously tactful, exquisitely complex philosopher.[83] In responding to such charges, Benjamin usually sought to keep the issues on the terrain of the work, and in this he has generally been followed by those who find that the association was productive for him.[84] It is all the more interesting, then, that on one occasion when he did address the personal dimension, in a 1934 letter to Gretel Adorno, Benjamin himself did not categorically deny its significance. Such charges had been leveled at him before, he noted, even raising the ante by recalling his fateful relationship with Fritz Heinle (II 1369). Declining the opportunity to refute the accusations, he instead asserted that such dangerous liaisons were an essential part of his life as well as his work; the breadth of his thinking and "the freedom to move matters and ideas thought to be incompatible into proximity receive their face only through danger." It may be that the problem lies less with invoking the personal dimension as such than with the one-dimensional terms used to characterize it. In fact, it is not at all clear that the relationship between the two was animated by any simple attraction of opposites; for all their striking differences, they did share certain traits.[85] In their personal relations, both Benjamin and Brecht balanced ruthlessness with a courtesy bordering on inscrutability, and both relished public polemics. Nor, on closer look, was Brecht's work always as blunt as its reputation: though he strove for plain, concise language, he often used it wryly to generate the kind of unresolved ambiguities that would stimulate thought.[86]

Apart from their biographical interest, these considerations provide an important pointer to Brecht's many-faceted complexity, which one must appreciate to understand the full range of Benjamin's elective affinities for his work. It could almost be said that when their paths crossed Benjamin had just spent several years trying to invent him: in Brecht, he found a writer who seemed to step directly into the locus he himself had been working to define since 1925. Brecht joined left politics to the avant-garde project in an exemplary way; in geographic terms, he occupied a German middle ground between French modern-

---

[83] This line of argument was begun by Adorno and, especially, Scholem; see the discussion in the Introduction, Section 2. Richard Wolin takes this to the point of suggesting that "Benjamin's devotion to Brecht would seem to signify in no uncertain terms a death wish," *Walter Benjamin*, 140.

[84] This view is bolstered by Benjamin's own aversion to psychological explanation; see Wohlfarth, "No-Man's-Land," 50–51.

[85] Nägele suggests this in *Theater, Theory, Speculation*, 135.

[86] This is true, for instance, of the Keuner stories, which were important stimulants of Benjamin's interest in Brecht.

ism, which was breaking down the autonomous work of art from within bourgeois culture, and the new Soviet culture, which was breaking through (or so it seemed) to a new, nonautonomous art governed by straightforwardly didactic and political considerations. In Benjamin's polemical writings, the name Brecht could therefore come to serve as an all-purpose counter to the forms of literary practice he opposed.[87] Finally, Brecht and his circle became the main channel for Benjamin's assimilation of Marxism, guiding its development from a stance into a substantive, theoretical concern. Brecht's understanding of dialectics as *eingreifendes Denken,* thinking that intervenes in practice, was especially congenial to Benjamin's attempt to find a connection to politics.

But Brecht's own political stance cannot be reduced to the single dimension of communism, orthodox or otherwise. Even after his own turn to Marxism, it was still animated by his earlier anarchism, nihilism, and antimorality, and precisely these elements made Brecht the advocate of a Marxism Benjamin could seriously engage. In her essay on Brecht, Hannah Arendt argues that his entire sensibility rested on a historical sense engendered by the depredations of the war: he felt himself to be the occupant of "a world swept clean and fresh" by destruction both literal and cultural, a world in which everything was therefore allowed.[88] This sense of historical rupture produced by cataclysmic violence resonated deeply in Benjamin, who likewise saw a radical discontinuity in recent history. A break with the past was not so much a principle to be advocated as a pervasive, almost tangible fact that formed the point of departure for everything else. Both of them felt sure "that tomorrow may already bring destruction on such an enormous scale that we will find ourselves separated from yesterday's texts and productions as if by centuries"; but this was the kind of "knowledge from which the courage of despair can be drawn" (II 540). In Brecht this response to the war produced the same scorn for traditional humanism, combined with a defiant affirmation of the poverty of experience, as it did in Benjamin. "A fine saying of Brecht's gets us farther, much farther: 'Efface the traces!'" (II 217). Hence, too, the Brechtian maxim with which Benjamin closed the journal of his summer visit with Brecht in 1938: "Do not build on the good old days, but

[87] For example, see "Useful Poetry? But Not Like This!" (III 183), "Left-Wing Melancholy" (III 283), and "The Author as Producer" (II 696).

[88] Arendt, "Bertolt Brecht, 1898–1956," 229. Mary Gluck points to the generational specificity of this response to the war and shows how such generational differences played into the cultural debates of the interwar period; see "Toward a Historical Definition of Modernism: Georg Lukács and the Avant-Garde." She also notes (853, n. 32) that there were important exceptions to the pattern. Benjamin was six years older than Brecht.

on the bad new ones" (VI 539). In a sense, then, Brecht incarnated the liquidationist moment in Benjamin's own work and temperament. While listening to Brecht speak, he felt "a force acting on [him] that is a match for that of fascism . . . a force that springs from historical depths no less deep than those of fascism" (VI 539).[89]

A second, related affinity to Brecht was the cult of antibourgeois decadence celebrated in his works of the 1920s. Brecht's first response to the hypocrisies of postwar society drew on the traditions of Villon and Rimbaud rather than those of political or social radicalism. In fact, Benjamin's first published references to Brecht praised him not as the practitioner of epic theater but as a chansonnier and legitimate German heir to the "traditions of decadence" (III 183). Brecht's achievement, as Benjamin saw it, was to turn these traditions to new political purposes, linking decadence with revolution. Thus his early works portrayed not virtuous proletarians but self-centered, asocial hooligans as "virtual revolutionaries": "If Marx, one might say, posed the problem of how to produce the revolution out of its absolute opposite, capitalism, without calling on any ethos to do so, then Brecht transposes this problem into the human sphere: he seeks to develop the revolutionary . . . in the laboratory of baseness and vulgarity" (II 665). Benjamin argued that this antimorality became an integral part of epic theater. But Brecht's debts to the decadent tradition went beyond the themes of his work into reaches where one least expects them, including his very stance as a writer. Surprisingly, Benjamin's praise for Brecht's continuation of the traditions of decadence calls to mind that other German poet he praised as a "perfecter of decadence," Stefan George (III 399). Strange as this pairing may seem, the traditions of decadence created at least one subterranean affinity between them: like George, Brecht was concerned with cultivating a certain *Haltung*, a posture or bearing. George affected the aristocratic role of the secret emperor, but, as Hans-Thiess Lehmann notes, Brecht was not above self-stylization and assiduously tended his image as a "wise man, ascetic, or proletarian."[90] The dif-

---

[89] A brief, tantalizing note dated by the editors to late 1938 or 1939 suggests that later Benjamin was beginning to rethink the political implications of this force of Brecht's. In it he discusses and accepts Heinrich Blücher's judgment that the violence of "expropriating the expropriators," which Brecht approved of in a poem from his "Lesebuch für Städtebewohner," introduced a sadistic element into politics that corresponded to "the most unscrupulous element of National Socialism," its persecution of the Jews. Benjamin now rejected his own earlier commentary on the poem as a "pious falsification" and a cover-up of Brecht's complicity with the policies of Stalinism (VI 540). We have no evidence of whether Benjamin went on to reconsider his own espousal of a new barbarism. Ironically, in the *Gesammelte Schriften* this note now appears on the reverse side of the page with the passage from Benjamin's 1938 diary in which he speaks of Brecht's "force . . . that is a match for that of fascism [*eine Gewalt . . . die der des Faschismus gewachsen ist*]" (VI 539).

[90] Hans-Thiess Lehmann, "Portrait Bertolt Brechts," 274.

ference between Brecht and George was less their aestheticism as such than what they made of it. It has often been argued that Brecht's turn to Marxism meant the end of his "anarchistic cult of decay, putrefaction, and decline," which henceforth became metaphors for the inhumanity of capitalism; on this view, his aestheticism was absorbed without remainder.[91] But whether or not Brecht "overcame" his earlier aestheticism so neatly, Benjamin was bound to be fascinated by just this attempt to reroute the volatile energies of decadence from the right and harness them to revolutionary politics instead.

A third affinity between Benjamin and Brecht rested on yet another of Brecht's identities, that of *Aufklärer,* or "enlightener." At the time they met, in 1929, Brecht's own work was turning away from the celebration of decadence, a turn signaled by the *Versuche* and in particular the figure of Herr Keuner, "the thinker." Benjamin prized Brecht as an *Aufklärer* in several senses of the German word. In a literal sense, he saw Brecht as a demystifier, right down into the pores of his language; he once defended Brecht to Scholem as the creator of a sober literary language "cleansed of all magic."[92] Brecht also aspired to be an *Aufklärer* in the popular pedagogical tradition of *Kalendergeschichten* and Johann Peter Hebel, long one of Benjamin's favorite writers. But above all, Benjamin saw in Brecht the exemplary living instance of that "real humanism" he had invoked in his essay on Kraus. Brecht's plebeian radicalism, though partly a stylistic affectation, was also more than that. His avowal of the poverty of experience placed him in a line that led around the nineteenth-century tradition of the *Bildungsbürger* and back to the German Enlightenment, a tradition Benjamin movingly evoked in *Deutsche Menschen.* The virtue of this tradition, for him, was its appreciation that "a meagre, straitened existence and true humanity are dependent on one another" (IV 157). In fact, Benjamin's association with Brecht was the stimulus for a crucial extension of his own appreciation of the German tradition to include this element of the Enlightenment legacy.[93]

But the final affinity between the two, and the one most germane to our concerns here, was Brecht's epic theater, which proved to be the catalyst for Benjamin's theory of aesthetic reception. The complement to Brecht's liquidationist vision was a constructive practice that aimed, as far as literary practice could, to help the producers take things over for themselves; his notion of *Umfunktionierung,* functional transformation, provided a comprehensive theory that encompassed the form of the work as well as the social conditions of its production and reception (VI 182). This was an effective response not only to the right but to

---

[91] For example, see Lindner, "Brecht/Benjamin/Adorno," 15.
[92] Scholem, *Walter Benjamin,* 258–259.
[93] See the Conclusion.

the independent left as well: with Brecht, politics was not just the expression of a conviction but a changed form of social practice; citing Georg Christoph Lichtenberg, Benjamin asserted that "the important thing is not one's convictions. It is what those convictions make of him" (II 662). The interaction with Brecht and his work was decisive in lending Benjamin's theory of *Technik* the specificity it urgently needed.

Benjamin's encounter with Brecht contributed three new elements to his theory of aesthetic reception.[94] One was a sharp separation of modes of perception into progressive and regressive types, modeled on theater. There were two possible conceptions of theater at present. The first, that of "high bourgeois theater," remained imprisoned by the notions of symbol, totality, and the *Gesamtkunstwerk* (II 774). This was a form of theater whose illusionistic character was grounded in the orchestra pit, an "abyss that separates the players from the audience like the dead from the living," heightening the sublimity and rapture of the performance—all qualities that unmistakably betrayed the cultic, sacral origins of this theatrical mode. The other conception of theater— Brecht's epic theater—sought to liquidate these cultic elements and replace them with literary practices that transformed a "spellbound zone" (*Bannraum*) into an "exhibition space" by refashioning the relations between stage and audience, text and performance, director and actors (II 520–521). And the hallmark of this new, progressive mode of staging, performance, and reception was its sober confrontation with the technical advances of the new media and a thoughtful incorporation of them. By 1931/32, then, Benjamin had already formulated the basic contrast that would reappear as the dichotomy of auratic and nonauratic art in "The Work of Art in the Age of Its Technical Reproducibility." Variations on this polarity were the contrast between creative and constructive photography in the "Small History of Photography" and between progress and regression in literary technique in "The Author as Producer" (II 384, 686). In each case, Benjamin assimilated his description of the regressive mode to his own categories of myth. But what were the positive qualities of the progressive mode?

To begin with—and this was the second decisive impulse that came from Brecht—it entailed a thoroughgoing transformation of the relations between cultural producers and audiences. Benjamin had already noted this tendency in some currents of Soviet art during his trip to Moscow, but it was only after his engagement with Brecht that it be-

---

[94] The following account draws primarily on the radio talk "Bert Brecht" (II 660–667), the first version (1931) of "What Is Epic Theater?" (II 519–531), and "Theater and Radio" (II 773–776).

came central for him. The point of epic theater was to undo the "false, veiling totality 'audience' " by provoking it to engage in "debates, responsible decisions, and attempts to take up its own well-founded positions" and thus to become productive in its own right (II 527–528). As he put it in "The Author as Producer," not only theater but all cultural production should have an organizing function; organizing meant, not propagandizing, but empowering audiences of formerly passive recipients to take over the work and organize themselves. Progressive culture would "guide other producers to produce" and "place an improved apparatus at their disposal" (II 696). The case of Brecht's epic theater suggests that the realization of this organizing function depended entirely on the artist's deliberate effort, but Benjamin also saw cases in which the media themselves might involuntarily meet such intentions halfway. In "The Newspaper" (1931), he suggested that the apparent demise of the quality of writing at the hands of journalism could lead to unexpected results.[95] In the press, writing was being corrupted by the "consuming impatience" of the reading public with its insatiable demand for "facts"; journalism was degenerating into an indiscriminate flood of unarticulated information. And, as part of this process, newspapers had begun seeking to exploit their readers' appetites (and secure their loyalties) by creating columns in which they could write in to lodge their own questions, opinions, and protests. But this "indiscriminate assimilation of readers" by the press produced an unintended outcome: by lowering the barrier between readers and writers, "writing gains in breadth what it loses in depth" as the roles become more fluid. Benjamin also suggested that such readers were likely to register their protests as specialists and experts for their own concerns. The result, in a phrase from Brecht, would be a "literarization of the conditions of living." Through a kind of cunning of the media, then, a dialectical reversal would take place: "It is in the theater of the unbridled debasement of the word—the newspaper— that its redemption is under way" (II 629). In this elegant reversal of laments over vulgarization, the medium unwittingly defeats even the most cynical of intentions.

In the case of the newspaper, Benjamin did not really offer an argument as to why readers would be *entitled* to be considered experts, but he did for epic theater and film.[96] This was the third result of his collaboration with Brecht—a characterization of the progressive mode of reception as a critical, testing attitude. Benjamin was particularly

[95] Benjamin later incorporated this piece verbatim into "The Author as Producer." His model for this critique of journalism was Kraus's polemics in *Die Fackel*.

[96] He suggested that this qualification would follow from their "polytechnical training": "Work itself takes its turn to speak" (II 629).

alert to this aspect of Brecht's work because his path to Brecht's theater led by way of the *Versuche* and the character of Herr Keuner. All Brecht's disreputable characters know how to make the most of their vices, and the peculiar vice of Herr Keuner—"Mr. Nobody," in the Augsburg dialect of Brecht's youth—is to think "coldly and incorruptibly," to disarm and to dismantle assumptions until he produces "a certain unease" that provokes his readers into thinking for themselves (II 662–664). The project of epic theater, Benjamin suggested, could be seen as an attempt to shift Keuner's operations to the stage, and introducing this critical, appraising attitude into the theater would ultimately involve activating the audience. Benjamin approvingly cited Brecht's ideal of "a theater full of experts, just as one has sports arenas full of experts" (II 522–523).

Achieving this goal called for translating the principles of the new cultural technology, particularly film and radio, into a dramaturgical technique suited to the medium of the stage. Epic theater must strive to be "up to the level of development of technology" (II 524). The fundamental device used by epic theater was to interrupt the action, and the art of interruption, Benjamin noted, was "nothing but a transformation of the methods of montage, which are decisive for radio and film, from a technical process back into a human one." Such interruptions were meant to elicit a critical, questioning response through two related but distinct effects. The first was to estrange the audience from the naturalness of the proceedings before it: epic theater did not develop plots but expose circumstances by treating "the elements of reality as experimental arrangements"; in place of identification and catharsis, Brecht's non-Aristotelian dramaturgy distanced the audience from the proceedings and provoked it into an attitude of astonishment (II 521–522). The second effect was to isolate and focus on the actors' gestures, an element of epic theater by which Benjamin laid great store. These gestures served many functions: they were more reliable guides to the characters than their deceptive claims and devious actions; as a corporeal language, they were also a means against interiority and subjectivity, providing epic theater with a device that would rebuff the audience's "propensity for empathy" (II 538). Finally, gestures were "quotable" and therefore capable of being learned (II 521). Here lay the frankly pedagogical aim of epic theater, whose most important product was meant to be the inculcation of a new attitude (*Haltung*), a stance that could be trained and practiced (II 662).

The gestural element of epic theater was therefore crucial to its didactic purposes. This may seem at odds with Benjamin's (and Brecht's) claim that the point of epic theater was to activate the audience's own critical and self-organizing tendencies. For instance, when Benjamin linked the organizing function of progressive works to the writer's own "directing, instructing stance," such language might suggest manipulation, the inculcation of behavioral responses rather than a stimulus to autonomous action (II 696). This possibility becomes especially treacherous in the case of film, since it would hollow out the critical, testing attitude and collapse it into the manipulations of propaganda or the culture industry. But it must be remembered that the primary attitude epic theater sought to inculcate was that of indefatigable questioning. In fact, the reverse might be equally true: Brecht's love of paradox and conundrum might actually disable the formation of clear political convictions. Benjamin noted Brecht's tendency to "put everything back into question almost before it has been achieved" and attributed this to his destructive character (VI 538). This misunderstanding is related to a second frequent misreading of Benjamin's point: he was not claiming that technological progress itself would automatically produce a more progressive mode of reception, as his critics have often argued. If that were true, there would simply be no need for epic theater; progressive artists would do better simply to concentrate their efforts on film and radio. Epic theater represented not a mechanical adoption but a creative translation of the principle of cinematic montage, in an experimental attempt to distill its progressive potential. And this translation could in turn be translated back into cinematic language, as Benjamin himself went on to do in the theses on reproduction in order to sharpen the distinction between the progressive and regressive uses of film. Benjamin's argument was that the new media provided a potential that could be used or misused. He did not invoke any sort of technological determinism; in fact, he was not making an argument from causality at all but proposing that the new conditions of reception contained a latent, progressive *telos*.[97] Benjamin himself made this case, if indirectly, in "The Author as Producer." "A political tendency," he asserted, "is the necessary, never the sufficient condition of the organizing function of the work" (II 696). In the context, he was arguing that political tendency alone does not make a work progressive unless its literary technique is as well. But this also clearly implied the converse: a deliberate choice on the part of the artist was also necessary. There was, however, one consequence of technical change and pedagogical goals that Benjamin accepted unflinchingly— the end of "literature" in the traditional sense. The gestures and words of epic theater "have first a pedagogical, then a political, and only lastly a poetic effect"; with it, art becomes a "byproduct in a far-reaching process of changing the world" (II 662).

[97] The argument about film thus parallels the larger argument about technology originally put forward in "To the Planetarium."

What, then, were those differences with Brecht that Benjamin chose not to air publicly? The problem was not so much that Brecht's notions of liquidation and *Umfunktionierung* were wrong as that they were incomplete; he remained systematically blind to certain of the "depth" dimensions involved in liquidating the past. The issue of depth was a persistent sore point between the two. Brecht could not help seeing it as obscurantism and nonsense that "doesn't get you ahead" (VI 527–528).[98] In a journal entry, he scorned Benjamin's conception of the aura as "so much mysticism, coupled with an antimystical stance. . . . it is pretty awful."[99] But for Benjamin cultural images from the past contained experiences locked within them that could be decoded only at the risk of entering into their auratic depth dimension, and he was convinced that these contents would have to be redeemed precisely if the *present* were to be saved. Brecht's literary practice, with its insistently and, to Benjamin's mind, productively antimagical prose, nevertheless flattened out the deeply etched contours of what Benjamin called the *Bildraum*, the sphere of images. Before meeting Brecht, in his essays on the surrealists and Proust as well as in early work on the "Arcades" project, Benjamin had already begun to construct a "dialectical optic" that aimed to capture both "the everyday as the impenetrable and the impenetrable as the everyday" (II 307). For all his dialectical skill, Brecht's view of this optic was one-dimensional.

To put it another way, for Benjamin's purposes Brecht's stress on the "revolutionary use-value" (II 693) of culture was salutary but ultimately too narrowly conceived. The political events of the 1930s would conspire to place this limitation in a harsh light. Brecht was uninterested in speculation he regarded as unrelated to "what is socially practicable."[100] But what might "revolutionary use-value" mean when no revolutionary situation was in sight? The course of events in Germany and the Soviet Union constricted the range of socially practicable options, not least those of exiled intellectuals. In this context, Benjamin's concern with the sphere of images can be seen as extending the meaning of what is socially practicable: in such straitened circumstances, it might mean bearing witness to the unredeemed sufferings of the defeated in history. In fact, when he proposed this it earned him the accusation—leveled not by Brecht but by Max Horkheimer—of advocating an impermissibly idealistic theology: "Past injustice is done and over," Horkheimer insisted. "The dead are really dead." Benjamin granted that whereas this might hold for history conceived as a science

---

98 Benjamin responded that depth was "his way of going to the antipodes" (VI 528).
99 Brecht, *Arbeitsjournal. Erster Band, 1938 bis 1942*, 16.
100 Witte, *Walter Benjamin*, 90.

of determinate facts, when history is conceived as a form of re-membrance the past is never really completed (V 589). It continues to unfold in a virtual life, because it is always construed through the interests of a constantly changing present; that is, it unfolds in *tradition* understood as something alive and changeable. The conception of his-tory Benjamin invoked here was a translation of the early romantic notion of the continued growth of the work even after its apparent completion by the artist's own hand; Benjamin transferred that concep-tion from the medium of art to social life and cultural images.[101] When Benjamin responded to Horkheimer—much as he had to Brecht six years earlier—by defending the rights of theology as a supplement to materialist dialectic, part of what he meant by theology was this ex-tended sense of tradition.

But Benjamin was also well aware of the subtle, productive dealings with tradition involved in Brecht's own work.[102] He traced Brecht's "untragic heros," for instance, to an anticlassical tradition in the Ger-man stage that ran back to baroque and medieval drama. This tradition comprised not simply a formal device but a profound solidarity with the creaturely element of human existence. But in this relation to tradi-tion there was nothing of the "complacency of someone entitled to an inheritance" (III 525). Such traditions were not a broad, royal road to truth but a "hidden smuggler's path" along which subversive goods might be run (II 523). In a similar vein, Brecht was adept at the tech-nique of adopting and reworking traditional materials; employing "reason and cunning," he inserted "tricks" into them in order to outwit the forces of myth—a description Benjamin coined not for the work of Brecht but of his apparent opposite, Franz Kafka (II 415). The sort of relation to tradition Brecht exemplified, and Benjamin prized, had nothing to do with the "false riches" of a secure cultural inheritance: "For the cultural estate is at present no better secured than the mate-rial. And it is the business of thinkers and researchers . . . to counter the 'affirmative concept of culture' with a critical concept of culture. . . . [T]o pursue the technical conditions of cultural creation, its reception and its survival, makes way—at the expense of comfort-able agreement—for genuine tradition" (III 525). Brecht's work repre-sented one moment—and however crucial, it remained only one mo-ment—in Benjamin's account of what a legitimate, genuine recourse to tradition would involve.

---

[101]On Benjamin's use of the romantic conception of the afterlife (*Nachleben*) of works, see the discussion of his reception theory in Chapter 7, Section 3.

[102] For another account of Brecht's complex relation to tradition, see Hans Mayer, "Bertolt Brecht und die Tradition."

Chapter Five

Benjamin and Surrealism:
Awakening

1. An Immanent Critique of Surrealism

In 1928 Benjamin declared it his ambition to "take up *the legacy* of surrealism" (B 483). The surrealists had made an astonishing discovery, as he put it in the essay on surrealism he was writing at the time. They were "the first to hit on the revolutionary energies that appear in the 'outmoded'" (II 299). To reverse decadence into an explosive force: that could well serve as the formula for what Benjamin himself hoped to achieve in all his mature work, from the *Trauerspiel* study onward. But he suspected that the surrealists were not always equal to their own best insights. It might no longer be enough for sympathetic critics to admonish them for the "very disturbing symptoms of deficiency" cropping up in their activities, or even to expose the "pernicious romantic prejudices" they remained ensnared in (II 297, 307). In fact, even before the essay was published, Benjamin was ready to propose himself as their heir—not the curator of their literary estate, however, but one who steps in after a debacle. He pictured himself exercising "all the powers of command of a philosophical Fortinbras" in order to mobilize the legitimate energies of surrealism for his own work (B 483). Might we then think of Benjamin himself as an idiosyncratic, last-ditch surrealist, determined to defend surrealist positions even if the movement itself were to betray them?

There is indeed a great deal to be said for this view, and the changes have been rung on it with great success.[1] Benjamin's affinities with surrealism permeate his mature work; they extend beyond discrete

---

[1] See Ernst Bloch, "Revueform in der Philosophie," and Susan Sontag, "Under the Sign of Saturn."

ideas or influences and go deep into the form, imagery, and detail of his texts. A fascination with the search for the true face of the city— "and no other face is surrealistic in the same degree as the true face of a city" (II 300)—became a central motif in his work after the mid-1920s. The city figured as an image of the subject's lack of unity, its spatialization and dispersal into a multiplicity of places and crossings. For Benjamin it was a labyrinth where losing oneself was not a hazard but an art to be learned (IV 237). Susan Sontag writes eloquently of the analogy between the city's difficulties and obstacles—barricades, detours, dead ends—and those constantly thrown up by Benjamin's own labyrinthine temperament—stubbornness, blundering, slowness.[2] And the "autobiographical" texts he collected under the suitably impersonal title *Berlin Childhood around 1900* in fact disperse personal history into the discontinuous series of urban sites where the child's first, enigmatic encounters with the adult world took place. The form of adult experience that opened his eyes to the "childhood side" of the city, in turn, was that of the flaneur, that wandering idler, ostentatiously free of all purpose, whose first home was the streets of nineteenth-century Paris. Yet the flaneur whose twentieth-century comeback Benjamin hailed was no idle dandy but a successor who was learning to read the city's phantasmagoria by submitting himself to the intoxications of juxtaposition and superposition hidden in its landscape. This latter-day flaneur—in this respect like another of his ancestors, the ragpicker— also had an eye for junk, obsolete and decrepit objects full of that promise of meaning peculiar to the ephemeral, discredited, and neglected. The surrealists themselves tended a cult of found objects, artifacts deposited by the recent past yet already so obsolete that they seemed like relics from an extinct, prehistoric age. Benjamin went so far as to suggest that the true history of the nineteenth century could be read *only* in its "ruins" (V 59) and "refuse" (V 574–575). One might well say that Benjamin's unfinished project "Paris, Capital of the Nineteenth Century" was an attempt to make good an inspiration the surrealists themselves had defaulted on.

Further affinities could be adduced almost at will. Benjamin's encounter with surrealism was undoubtedly among his most fundamental, formative identifications; given his extraordinary ability to give himself over to his objects and absorb impulses from them, it was bound to have far-reaching implications. But what drew him to surrealism in the first place? What led him to see "those things at work" in the surrealist movement "that occupy me as well" (B 446)? Benjamin's discovery of kindred intentions can best be explained in terms of the

[2] Sontag, "Under the Sign of Saturn," 111–114.

implicit agenda we have traced through his earlier work. The surrealists were enacting, in an open and extreme form, many of the
conflicts he had found at the heart of the German *Frühromantik*.
Through his encounter with surrealism, therefore, Benjamin continued
to extend and radicalize his own immanent critique of romanticism.

To trace that process, we must first recognize the conflicting tendencies at work within surrealism itself. The surrealist movement was rent
by a clash between impulses that derived from extreme aestheticism,
on the one hand, and an attempt to break out of the confines of aestheticism through strategies of politicization, on the other. Among the
stimulators of surrealism, invoked by the surrealists themselves, were
the French symbolist and decadent poets from Baudelaire through
Rimbaud, Lautréamont, and Apollinaire. Aestheticism has often been
captured in the phrase "art-for-art's sake," but this meant many things.
To begin with, it was both an attitude toward life and a doctrine about
the function of art in bourgeois society—the idea that art serves no
purpose and is not to be subjected to the criteria of utility and morality
by which social phenomena are normally judged. In fact, aestheticism
radicalized a belief in the autonomy of the aesthetic sphere whose roots
go back to the eighteenth century. This radicalization also has implications for the construction of works of art. Aestheticism favors the creation of art about art by stressing the self-referential dimension of
aesthetic forms. The content of artworks yields to a growing fixation on
the medium itself. The discursive, representational, and communicative moments of language decline in importance; instead, the tex-
tuality of texts is stressed. Compartmentalized space and sequential
time are dissolved through the techniques of juxtaposition and simultaneity. Aestheticism thus departs from the romantic tradition of art as
self-expression as well. Instead, the self and the poetic voice are dissolved into the structures of language and form. Of course, when
driven to extremes the pursuit of a self-referential, utterly autonomous
art could lead to a retreat into solipsism. One way of responding to this
isolation was to posit that aesthetic experience, far from being an ethe-
real phantom, affords access to a substratum of original, archaic experience. This mythologizing tendency created an elective affinity between
aestheticism and *Lebensphilosophie*. It became increasingly pronounced
in modernist culture after the turn of the twentieth century; the development of Stefan George and his circle provides a particularly clear
example of this drift.[3]

The French surrealists acted out all these aestheticist impulses after

---

[3] On the instability of aestheticism when subjected to these pressures, see Carl
Schorske's account of Hofmannsthal's development in "The Transformation of the Garden," in *Fin-de-Siècle Vienna: Politics and Culture*.

their own fashion. Although they proclaimed the end of art and its fusion with life, in practice that often meant transforming everyday life by infusing it with experiences and forms previously limited to the aesthetic sphere. The surrealists thus presupposed standards set by the aesthetes' purity of experience.[4] Similarly, their works continued to draw on the repertoire of formal devices and associative techniques developed by aestheticism, pursuing them farther through automatic writing, the cultivation of trancelike states, and methods of juxtaposition. Like the symbolists, they rejected the notion of art as forceful, individual expression, a notion fostered by some schools of romanticism. Finally, the surrealists often made the same move from aestheticism to vitalism, claiming wider validity for their experiences by interpreting them as discoveries of unconscious or mythological forces latent in modern society.

But the surrealists parted ways with aestheticism by adopting new strategies for breaking out of the splendid isolation of withdrawal, strategies that involved a politicization of art in several senses. First and foremost, politicization meant a rebellion against the social function of art, its supposedly autonomous status.[5] This rejection of aestheticism grew out of the Dada revolt in the nihilistic climate of the last years of the war. The writers and artists at the nucleus of the fledgling surrealist group defiantly insisted that they were not out to create a new aesthetic style, the latest in a long series of "isms"; their products were not meant for the consumption of a cultivated elite. In other words, unlike earlier aesthetes, they concentrated their fire on the social institution of art, not only on the aesthetic medium itself. But this intention was in turn reflected in the construction of their works. The surrealists adopted many of the modernists' formal innovations, but they used them to disrupt the normal modes of contemplative reception essential to the social institutionalization of art. Finally, the politicization of art also had a very concrete meaning: Breton's group sought to associate itself with the French Communist party. The stormy history of that courtship unfolded in a series of crises over whether the

[4] This point is stressed by Peter Bürger, *Theorie der Avantgarde*, 67, although Bürger's interpretation of surrealism and other contemporary avant-garde movements emphasizes their break with earlier modernist tendencies.

[5] The analysis of autonomous art as a social institution and the definition of the avant-garde movements as an attack on that form of institutionalization stem from Bürger's *Theorie der Avantgarde*. Critical responses to Bürger can be found in W. Martin Lüdke, ed., *"Theorie der Avantgarde": Antworten auf Peter Bürgers Bestimmung von Kunst und bürgerlicher Gesellschaft*. The contrast between Bürger's theory and the overarching view of modernism that stresses the continuity between aestheticism and the avant-garde is worked out clearly by Jochen Schulte-Sasse, "Theory of Modernism versus Theory of the Avant-Garde." Leaving the question of periodization aside, it seems obvious that both tendencies were at work in surrealism.

surrealists' intentions were really aesthetic or political, the alternative being understood as an either/or choice. These conflicts touched a genuine sore point in the surrealists' venture—the danger of a relapse into aestheticism. Scandals, after all, had become an accepted form of provocation in French literary life, and their decreasing shock value made ever more sophisticated forms of provocation necessary. But this spiral only reinforced the self-referential quality of such rebellions, which could easily develop into a pseudo-political aestheticism of re-volt-for-revolt's-sake. Similarly, the fusion of art and life they preached might amount to little more than glorifying and extending a kind of experience artificially bred outside everyday life—an aestheticization of everyday life but not a real transformation of it.[6] In its most extreme form, surrealism would be tempted to glorify the irrational as such, simply because it falls outside the domain of purposive rationality.

The essential point is that the surrealist movement was driven by both of these impulses—the aesthetes' radicalization of the autonomy of art and the avant-garde's rebellion against the social institutionaliza-tion of that very autonomy. This creative tension defined the move-ment and drove it forward; when the tension collapsed and the sur-realists accepted the status of their works as art, the movement broke down. Benjamin had found an analogous set of tensions at work in the German *Frühromantik*. Schlegel's philosophy of reflection defined art as a formal medium, a self-referential process of unfolding. Benjamin, however, insisted that romantic messianism precluded the notion of a continuum of reflection that unfolds endlessly on itself. Instead, the process of reflection culminated with a reversal of cultic, poetic ecstasy into prosaic sobriety. His reconstruction of the early romantics' philos-ophy of reflection hinged on the claim that these two moments—the self-referential unfolding of aesthetic forms and the self-abrogation of that world of forms—were inextricably linked. Moreover, the sur-realists, like the symbolists before them, sought to dissolve the self into the structures of language and experience. Benjamin had also argued for a sharp distinction between the glorification of subjectivity and self-expression in Storm and Stress romanticism and the program of the

---

[6] In an essay on Roland Barthes, Susan Sontag makes an illuminating distinction between exclusive and inclusive varieties of aestheticism. Exclusive aestheticism, the older mode, is typified by the dandy. It restricts itself to the pleasure of a small number of things and remains "cool," understated, and often disdainful. Inclusive aestheticism, on the other hand, is its "modern, democratizing form": it involves a willingness to derive pleasure from the widest variety of things, including the vulgar and the banal. It tends to be enthusiastic, effusive, and ecstatic ("Writing Itself: On Roland Barthes," xxvi-xxvii). The surrealists were among the pioneers of this "open" aestheticist sensibility. But how much do the extension of scope and the shift in tonality really alter in the aestheticist outlook? An *illegitimate* extension of aestheticism to everyday experience was exactly what Benjamin came to fear.

Frühromantik. Schlegel and Novalis rejected Fichte's preoccupation with striving of the transcendental ego by shifting the emphasis to the "indifference point" between subject and object. Of course, Benjamin was well aware that the early romantics themselves had abdicated what he held to be their genuine intentions. To reinforce those intentions, he went on to recover part of their prehistory by reaching back to the tradition of baroque allegory. In his reconstruction, the allegorical way of seeing provided a more resilient corrective to the symbolic transfiguration of appearances than the romantics themselves had found. The surrealists, in turn, could be understood as part of the posthistory of these genuinely romantic intentions. Like the Benjamin of "Goethe's *Elective Affinities*," they were grappling with the problem of how to break out of the "false, errant totality" of transfiguring appearances from within.

Along with these tensions, the surrealists' discovery of a modern mythology provided a second affinity with their pursuits. A critique of the ensnarement of humanity in mythic forces had been a cardinal point on Benjamin's agenda since his break with the youth movement. The demonic influences that had undermined it, in his view—cults of nature, vitality, leadership, and genius—had also poisoned the thinking of those he had looked to as models, Wyneken and George. Mythic consciousness was not confined to a stage of history that had long been left behind. Its delusions and compulsions were still at work in bourgeois society and in those who seemingly stood at the height of cultivation. Nor was myth the exclusive preserve of those who advocated returning to the healthy irrationality of archaic experience. Benjamin's darker suspicion was that forms of instrumental, purposive-rational action—not only capitalism and the state but even most progressive political engagement—were also helplessly mired in delusions. How else could the inferno of the Great War have followed on a century of progress? Historical regression was not an abstract possibility but an immediate, threatening reality. Here the surrealists' explorations opened Benjamin's eyes: they believed they had stumbled on the traces of a specifically modern form of mythic consciousness. Under their willfully distracted gaze, artifacts of the nineteenth century's urban and industrial culture—allegedly products of conscious, rational activity—dissolved into an ensemble of dreamlike projections. In this respect, too, Benjamin's encounter with surrealism enabled him to rejoin issues that had long concerned him.

The new departure the surrealists made possible followed from their proclamation of the end of art, which shifted attention away from aesthetic forms to the forms of everyday perception and experience. In Benjamin's words, they had set out to pursue images "wherever they may dwell" (III 196). Before 1925, Benjamin had dealt above all with the category of myth as reflected in ideas (fate, character, and law), ideologies (Gundolf and the George circle), individual works of art (Goethe's *Elective Affinities*), or literary genres (tragedy and *Trauerspiel*). Now, however, he turned his attention to the forms of mythic consciousness themselves. "There is a history of perception that is ultimately the history of myth" (VI 67): this proposition now became a guiding principle of his work.[7] Mythic blindness is not primarily a question of ideology in the conventional sense; delusions do not first arise when things become the objects of mystifying theories. Rather, myth permeates the very texture of everyday experience. As he later put it, the most commonplace "products and forms of life" appear "sensually 'transfigured' [*verklärt*] in their immediate presence, not just in theoretical elaboration. They present themselves as phantasmagoria" (V 61, 1256).[8] The *Elective Affinities* essay had already aimed to illuminate the realia of the work in detail and to show how the characters' delusion itself was a hallmark of mythic consciousness. The micrological examination of everyday experience he now proposed, therefore, was not entirely new. Nor did Benjamin simply drop his immanent critique of ideology in order to get at perception and experience directly. But he did begin to explore works of art with an eye to their symptomatic value for detecting underlying changes in modes of perception and experience. Moving between cultural and social history, he turned his attention to artifacts and forms of experience deposited by the nineteenth century.

Taking up the surrealists' pointers toward the latent presence of archaic forms in modern experience was not without its dangers, however. The surrealists themselves were vulnerable to the mythologizing tendency that had characterized romanticism since its origins. They dethroned the aesthetes' cult of art only to replace it with a cult of ecstatic experience released from the confines of art, thereby edging themselves into the company of vitalism and *Lebensphilosophie*. The vision of a modern mythology could not be dispensed with lightly, for otherwise how was one to perceive the disguised threat of regressive forces? Surrealistic forms of experience extended the perceptual repertoire in a way that could help to make such forces visible. Yet the idea of a modern mythology was notoriously labile: once historical change

[7] The formulation stems from a note titled "Perception and Body," which the editors of the *Gesammelte Schriften* date to the period 1918–20/21; it was one of Benjamin's first efforts at developing a philosophical anthropology, some elements of which are discussed in Chapter 4, Section 3.

[8] This formulation stems from the introduction to the second, French-language version (1939) of his exposé for the "Arcades" project.

and progress have been exposed as illusions, the temptation to affirm archaic forces as the only true reality becomes difficult to resist. Benjamin found himself forced to search for a way of immunizing the surrealists' vision against this danger without abandoning its insights. His method was to reconstruct the surrealist vision of a modern mythology, incorporating it into his own theory of *historical* illumination. In what follows, I focus on this central theme in Benjamin's encounter with surrealism—its effect on his way of thinking about history. It was in the course of this encounter that his antinomial conception of history and tradition began to emerge in full force.

2. "Dreamkitsch"

Benjamin's first commentary on surrealism was a cryptic text he titled "Dreamkitsch," probably composed at the end of 1925. It is a dense yet wide-ranging meditation on three products of the surrealist movement's early phase: Paul Eluard and Max Ernst's little-known *Repetitions* (1922), an experiment in coupling pictures with captions; André Breton's first "Manifesto of Surrealism" (1924); and Louis Aragon's *Wave of Dreams* (1924), an account of the surrealists' activities during the previous two years. Benjamin's "Dreamkitsch" has all the earmarks of his most private, esoteric, "difficult" texts. It was both a sympathetic response to surrealism and a productive venture in its own right. Considering how early he wrote it—at the very beginning of his intensive appropriation of modernist culture—it provides a remarkable anticipation of how he would later adapt surrealism for his own purposes. The ideas first formulated in "Dreamkitsch" supplied the germ for Benjamin's "Arcades" project, and he was to spend the next decade pursuing their implications. On close scrutiny, the impressionistic surface of this literary gloss gives way to reveal a dense, carefully constructed network of argument.

The overarching theme of "Dreamkitsch" unmistakably bears Benjamin's own stamp, the possibility of a liberation from the unrecognized compulsions of mythic forces. By exposing the latent presence of the "thicket of primeval history [*Urgeschichte*]"[9] in the modern world one could "strike a decisive blow" at "the superstition of ensnarement in nature" (II 622, 620). Benjamin himself had sought to do just that for

---

[9] Benjamin's usage of the term *Urgeschichte* was to change later in the 1920s. Here *Urgeschichte* still simply designates archaic forces. Only later—in the first notes for the "Arcades" project—did he develop the distinctive conception of an *Urgeschichte* of the nineteenth century. I have therefore rendered *Urgeschichte* as "primeval history" here, whereas later this translation would be misleading.

the virtual world of a literary work, Goethe's *Elective Affinities*. But to treat the surrealists' productions as works of art would have been to miss the point. For the surrealists proclaimed that art was at an end and turned toward the forms of experience themselves, without regard to the "literary precipitates" of that experience (II 296). In "Dream-kitsch" Benjamin accepted their premises and developed three lines of response. The first was the conception of dreamkitsch itself: dream images and ornamental kitsch provided models for detecting the latent presence of archaic forces in modern experience. The second was a brief diagnosis of contemporary changes in the structure of perception and experience. Finally, Benjamin now began to address the issue of liquidating the mythic substrate of those concrete modes of experience predominant in his own era. In "Dreamkitsch" he set up "historical illumination" as a weapon against mythic ensnarement in nature.

The surrealists' fascination with dreams provided Benjamin with a new point of access to his old concerns. He began the piece by propos-ing a history of the dream (II 620). Dreaming, he suggested, is not an unalterable, natural given of human nature but a historically con-structed form of experience. The telling contrast was provided by the romantics' experience of dreams as enticements to unreachable ideals. Dreams no longer opened a view into the exotic distance, as the "blue flower" once had when dreamed of by the protagonist of Novalis's *Heinrich von Ofterdingen;* "whoever wakes up these days as Heinrich von Ofterdingen must have overslept." In the meantime, dreams had become grey and dusty, pointing the way to "banality," the world of everyday things. And kitsch was the quintessence of that banality.

In fact, the connection between dreams and the everyday world runs both ways in "Dreamkitsch." The kitsch of his parents' world, the material culture that surrounded him in childhood, had defined the forms in which ordinary objects had entered the dreams of his genera-tion. That made dreaming on the threshold of the twentieth century something it could never have been to the romantics. But kitsch itself is also literally nightmarish, a projection of unconscious fantasies and dark compulsions. That is the central insight captured in the double meaning of Benjamin's enigmatic title: just as kitsch has penetrated into dreams, so "real" kitsch in the everyday world can be regarded as the product of a dreamlike state. Statements about what appears in dreams turn out to concern the waking world as well. And what we usually consider to be the waking world, consciously and purposively produced, turns out to be a realm of unconscious, involuntary projec-tions. The idea of dreamkitsch thus recalls what Freud called the psy-chopathology of everyday life. But whereas Freud traced this psychopathology in marginalia such as slips of the tongue—cracks in the façade of purposive rationality—Benjamin suggested that the entire surface of the everyday world was a conduit for unconscious projections and delusions.

Benjamin also took issue with Freud's conception of what is enacted in dreams. He credited psychoanalysis with discovering that the schema of dreamwork is the rebus: dream images are picture puzzles whose manifest content must be deciphered. But Freud ultimately regarded the dream's manifest content as a mere vehicle for expressing a latent psychic content. Benjamin, however, preferred one of the surrealists' variations on the psychoanalytic doctrine of dreams. Among the quintessential surrealist experiences was the perception that certain objects, configurations, and places in the waking world sometimes appear to be surrounded by a mysterious shimmer, a haunting quality that hints at a deeper reality, a "sur-reality." They entice us to decipher them, just as do certain images in our dreams. Yet in pursuing such experiences, Benjamin asserted, the surrealists were "following the traces not so much of the soul as of things" themselves (II 621–622). Benjamin clearly did wish to maintain the two levels of the psychoanalytic model of dreams as rebuses: manifest and latent content, surface delusion and hidden significance. Yet he denied that the sensually experienced material world was merely an inessential surface, beneath which the essential, psychic message lay hidden. Paradoxical though it may sound, he looked to the surrealists for a nonpsychological concept of dreamwork. In Benjamin's conception, dreams were not keys to individual psychic conflicts; rather, they were a medium in which an essential dimension of the transpersonal human relationship to the object world was enacted.

Benjamin's kitsch was the degraded form in which his generation had experienced that object world in childhood. Kitsch might be defined as that peculiar mixture of bad taste and bad design produced by embellishing an object with a decorative form inappropriate to its function. He stressed this ornamental face of kitsch, the tangle of "most inward entwinements" into which it led. By extension, kitsch reared its head in any modern phenomenon that betrayed an ornamental face, from the overstuffed bourgeois interior where it held sway to the sentimentality and verbosity of the conversations that filled out the little remaining space. For Benjamin, these things offered "the most matter-of-fact picture of our way of feeling" (II 621). The stifling atmosphere they exuded was all too familiar from his own childhood: "Pale light breaks through heavily draped windows into the interior of those chaotic rooms crammed with furniture where we, as children, were often close to suffocating—as if in the entrails of a reptile" (IV 478).[10] But if ornamental kitsch had so permeated his generation's childhood, then it could not be lightly dismissed as escapist trash or "mere" dreaming. Its riddles would have to be puzzled out in order to distill the true image of their way of feeling.

With "Dreamkitsch" Benjamin also offered one of his first, suggestive sketches of what he saw as a fundamental shift in the human mode of relating to the object world. The very structure of experience, the texture and rhythm of perception were changing. Here, perhaps for the first time, he identified the immediate cause as technology: "Technology is cashing in the external image of things which, like banknotes soon to be invalidated, are never to be seen again" (II 620). The pace of technological change was accelerating the process by which objects and forms of experience become obsolete. He likened this process to the cancellation of banknotes, an image that evokes the runaway German inflation of 1923. The hyperinflation provided the schema for a wholesale liquidation of all that had been handed down, assets both financial and cultural. In the end, the medium of circulation itself had been liquidated, suggesting that technology too might be transforming experience so drastically as to cause a rupture in historical development.

This dissolution of forms included violations of the distance between percipient and perceived, a distance essential to all contemplative modes of perception. "What we have called art first begins two meters away from the body"; that is, art depended on a certain detachment or distance he would later call auratic. "But now, in kitsch, the object world comes right up to us" (II 622).[11] Benjamin's unstated postulate here is a phenomenology of dream experience elaborated in the philosophical anthropology of Ludwig Klages.[12] Klages identified perceptual distance as the essential feature of what he called dream consciousness. Benjamin accepted this characterization, but only after historicizing it: dreams—romantic dreams—indeed had once "opened up a blue distance," but they no longer did so. And because the connection between dreams and the waking world ran both ways for

[10] This passage is from a description of James Ensor's paintings in "Furniture and Masks," Benjamin's report on an exhibition of his work in 1926. See also "Hiding Places" in *Berlin Childhood around 1900,* which describes the gloomy apartment of his childhood fears as an "arsenal of masks" (IV 253–254).

[11] In German: the object world *rückt . . . auf den Menschen zu.* Later, in the notes for "Paris Arcades," he used the verb *zustoßen* in the same sense (V 1009).

[12] Benjamin's notes on "Closeness and Distance" (1922/23) in connection with Klages's theories are an important source for an examination of his encounter with surrealism (VI 83–87). On Klages's phenomenology of dreams and Benjamin's critical transformation of it in the first version of the "Arcades" project, see the final two sections of this chapter.

Benjamin, Klages's phenomenology of dream consciousness could be read as an inverted commentary on the modern *waking* world. Banal, everyday experience, Benjamin felt, was taking on the quality of those dreams in which objects "lunge at us," impervious to our attempts to hold them at arm's length or control their rhythms. The surrealists were receptive to this epochal shift in the modes of perception because they had given up trying to make the kind of art that demands contemplative distance. At first, they believed the "mania for dreaming" that seized them in the early 1920s to be a source of artistic inspiration. But then, "in fact, they shut poetry off, like all the most intensive forces of this time" (II 621). In effect, Benjamin was suggesting that the surrealists' experiments were so fruitful because dreams provided another channel to crucial aspects of modern experience—the accelerating liquidation of forms and the new relationship between perceptual distance and closeness—which had been anticipated in the medium of art.[13] The true point of the surrealists' venture was, not to create art, but to reckon with the consequences of this changing human relationship to the object world.

The reckoning that was due concerned both the recent and the remote past. The two were entwined in the proposal for a historical illumination of dreaming that forms a third motif in "Dreamkitsch." Through their explorations of childhood, the surrealists were taking leave of "an environment from the second half of the nineteenth century" whose familiar forms were rapidly disappearing, "never to be seen again." Leave-taking meant drawing those forms close once more, bringing them into tactile proximity, as if for a farewell caress: "Now, in dreams, the hand once again grasps their image and takes its leave by tracing familiar contours" (II 620). Kitsch itself was undoubtedly a historically specific phenomenon from the near past, the world in which Benjamin himself had grown up. The sources of its power, however, lay much farther back in human history. For him, kitsch was the trace of a far more distant, literally primordial experience. It was at once historically specific and atavistic, for it also had roots in "the thicket of prehistory." Kitsch masked objects in ornamental forms; it was "the uppermost, very last mask" of the "totem pole of objects." A shading in his language reflects the duality precisely: the resonance between penetrating "to the heart of things obsolete [*abgeschafft*]" (the specific world of the recent past) and encountering "the forces of an extinct

---

[13] Later, in the "Work of Art" theses, he would find the same process taking place in the social world. Weaving Brechtian and surrealist idioms, he suggested that the shock effect of film montage corresponded to a broader social trend: audiences needed to "bring objects closer" and subject them to optical tests, thereby violating their auratic sanctity.

[*ausgestorben*] world of things" (a prehistoric realm whose primal forces, however, have lived on). Venturing into the tangled world of the nineteenth-century bourgeois interior led one back into this "thicket of primeval history" with its unmastered, indeed unrecognized mythic compulsions.

Benjamin left no room for doubt that the point of this encounter with the object world was to bring about a release from the nightmarish power of a world of degraded things. The leave-taking he envisioned would be anything but a nostalgic transfiguration, for it had to "push through to the heart." An encounter with that rapidly vanishing world of forms would aim to free us from its stifling, oppressive power, not to linger over it sentimentally. But he also insisted on the liberating potential of an *immersion* in that object world. In fact, this was the only way to the goal:

> Kitsch . . . is the last mask of banality, which we don in dreams and in conversation in order to absorb the forces of an extinct world of things . . . . Now, in kitsch, the object world . . . surrenders to our tentative grasp and, finally, forms figures in our interior. The new humanity [*der neue Mensch*] has the whole quintessence of the old forms within itself, and the being that is formed in the confrontation with an environment from the second half of the nineteenth century . . . might well be called the "furnished person [*der möblierte Mensch*]." (II 622)

Taking leave of the old forms meant penetrating to their heart, but also absorbing them into our interior. To extricate ourselves from the thicket of prehistory, we must risk the plunge back into it and even don the "very last mask" of the totem pole in order to perceive what threatened us in the first place.

In fact, Benjamin's conception of mythic forms of experience was already marked by a peculiar ambivalence that his categories seemed to deny. In his *Elective Affinities* essay he spoke of the realms of truth and myth as being mutually and radically exclusive. Yet his own exploration of the novel's mythic forms implied that the struggle for release from ensnarement begins from within the mythic realm. Now, in "Dreamkitsch," he frankly stated that an immersion in the forms of mythic consciousness was necessary—precisely so as to get free of them. The ambiguities of this undertaking were to mark the rest of his work.[14] One such ambiguity can be stated in historical terms, as Benjamin himself did in the closing passages of the piece. The notion that social and cultural upheaval were producing a radically new humanity—*der neue Mensch*—recurs in countless variations in interwar cultural criticism. Benjamin had imbibed it even before the war, in the youth

---

[14] I return to this issue in Chapter 7, Section 3.

movement. But the paradoxical insistence that this radically new humanity could be forged only with the "whole quintessence" of the old forms within it was one of the hallmarks of his thinking.

The notion of a historical illumination of dreaming invoked at the beginning of the piece links all these themes. Benjamin did not say so explicitly, but the kind of historical elucidation he was proposing had three distinct dimensions. The first was the history of the dream. Dreaming is not a timeless, natural phenomenon, he suggested, for its form, content, and function differ according to the historical period in which it is embedded. He illustrated this idea only in passing, by pointing out how untimely romantic reveries of a "blue distance" had become. Benjamin's point would seem to rest on a slim reed, unsupported by any evidence of what actually happens in dreams; his comments about the romantics and the surrealists address only the literary image of dreaming. Though that may be an interesting observation in itself, it falls short of what he seems to be claiming. Yet this gap in the argument is not as damaging as it appears. In fact, Benjamin was only indirectly concerned with the history of what happens during sleep. What really mattered to him was that the waking world might be read as a product of unconscious, dreamlike projections. The sense in which such dreams have a history was undoubtedly susceptible of demonstration, and that was one of the tasks the "Arcades" project would address.

The second dimension of Benjamin's historical illumination was the constellation he constructed between a specific, recent past—the second half of the nineteenth century—and the remote past of primeval history, or *Urgeschichte*. The implicit link between them, so crucial to his argument, is a certain conception of childhood. Benjamin assumed that ontogeny repeats phylogeny: childhood experience recapitulates earlier stages in the development of the human species.[15] This notion was a commonplace of scientific and pseudo-scientific evolutionary speculation in the nineteenth and early twentieth centuries. He casually alluded to animism, totemism, magic, and myth without any great precision. But this eclecticism is a clue to the unconventional use to which he put these allusions. Benjamin was utterly uninterested in evolutionary theories built on ethnological findings. The virtue of his eclecticism was a healthy disrespect for constructing rigid stages of development. He drew on the discourse about ontogeny and phylogeny to *confound* simpleminded evolutionary thinking and make the historical regressions of "advanced" societies visible. The kind of his-

[15] This figure of thought appears in several of the pieces in *Berlin Childhood around 1900*, including "Butterfly Hunt" and "Hiding Places" (IV 244–245, 253–254). Anna Stüssi, *Erinnerungen an die Zukunft: Walter Benjamins "Berliner Kindheit um 1900*," provides a richly detailed commentary on the *Berlin Childhood*.

torical illumination he had in mind, therefore, could succeed only by uncovering what had *not* undergone historical modulation. Similarly, a release from the oppressive weight of nineteenth-century culture necessarily meant shaking off a nightmare whose origins lay farther back, beyond history, in the realm of archaic compulsions.

Finally, there was a third dimension to Benjamin's idea of historical illumination, an emphatic concept of the present. A specific historical locus, a particular constellation of forces in the historical present, had opened the way for insight into these aspects of the past. In "Dreamkitsch" Benjamin cited the accelerating breakdown of the old modes of perception: by "cashing in the external image of things" and disrupting the perceptual distance constitutive of art, technology was teaching the surrealists a new way of seeing. As he put it soon afterward in the notes for "Paris Arcades," describing his own historical optic,

> The dialectical method is said to aim at doing justice to the concrete, historical situation of its object at every moment. But that is not enough. For it is just as concerned with doing justice to the concrete, historical situation of the *interest* in its object. (V 1026)

Benjamin was challenging the conventional understanding of historical context. The historicity of images meant not only that they belonged to a certain time but that they first became legible from the perspective of certain later situations. As we have seen, his own historical studies had operated on this assumption from the very beginning, only without stating it. Early romanticism and baroque allegory resonated with his sense of his own times—and taught him things about his own age—in a way that classicist cultures did not. Historical truth, in other words was generated by contact between the present and specific moments or conjunctures in the past. The dense, evocative formulations of "Dreamkitsch" represent a watershed in Benjamin's historical orientation. The constellation between the latter half of the nineteenth century and his own time became the central axis of his work from this point on. And, along with it, the need to define one's perspective point in the present now became an explicit issue in Benjamin's conception of historical illumination.

3. Surrealism as "The Last Snapshot of the European Intelligentsia"

The subtitle of Benjamin's 1929 essay "Surrealism: The Last Snapshot of the European Intelligentsia" already suggests the distance he had traveled since the composition of "Dreamkitsch." "Dreamkitsch" testified to his discovery of affinities with the early works of the French surrealists. It was his first attempt to appropriate surrealist figures of thought for his own purposes and even, perhaps, to fuse his intentions with theirs. In the 1929 essay, however, he dealt with surrealism as a movement whose trajectory could now be gauged. Thus his snapshot: snapshots capture the peculiar aura of the transitory, and his subtitle proclaims surrealism to be the last image of something that was about to vanish, the European intelligentsia. But snapshots are also stop-action photos; by fixing what is in motion they make it possible to analyze the components of movement which, to the naked eye, appears as a blur. Benjamin considered the surrealist movement to be transitional phenomenon, the temporary appearance of the intelligentsia en route from its traditional role to a working alliance with the forces of revolution. What was "the path that surrealism had to follow from its origins to its politicization" (II 303)? And what could be learned from surrealism about the crisis of the intelligentsia, about the right and wrong ways to steer toward the necessary transformation of the traditional intelligentsia and its culture? Those were the questions the 1929 essay on surrealism set out to answer.

An essential part of Benjamin's critical apparatus in the essay was a rough historical sketch of French cultural politics from the mid-nineteenth century to the 1920s. The intellectual orthodoxy in nineteenth-century France was set by the what he referred to as its humanistic intelligentsia, characterized by a liberal idea of freedom and uneasy coexistence with Catholicism.[16] The significant challenges to this orthodoxy, in Benjamin's view, had been mounted by two revolts. One was aestheticism, which, under the banner of art-for-art's-sake, elevated beauty above morality. Some aesthetes went farther and flaunted a satanism, a cult of evil that served as a "device, however romantic, to disinfect and insulate against all moralizing dilettantism" (II 304). The second revolt was explicitly political—the uncompromising anarchism exemplified by Bakunin's "radical concept of freedom" (II 306). Benjamin saw the bond between these revolts in their "revolutionary nihilism" (II 299): both were oriented toward a realm of ecstatic, unconditional freedom unreachable through practical action within the prevailing order. He argued that the surrealists' task could be defined by the lines of conflict established between these forces. The heir to the humanistic intelligentsia was the "so-called well-meaning left-wing bourgeois intelligentsia" of the 1920s. Its idea of freedom had become "sclerotic," as shown by its "hopeless coupling of idealistic morality with political practice." These were the straw men of Benjamin's polemics, on

---

[16] Benjamin did not define the relationship carefully; remarkably, the pitched conflict between the two currents is passed over in silence.

whom he poured a stream of violent abuse: "It is typical of this left-wing French intelligentsia—just as it is of their Russian counterparts—that its positive function proceeds entirely from a feeling of obligation, not to the revolution, but to the inherited culture. Its collective achievement, insofar as it is positive, amounts to that of conservators. But politically and economically they must always be reckoned with as a potential source of sabotage" (II 304). The locus of surrealism could be defined "by contrast with the helpless compromises of 'sentiment' " made by these "conservators."[17] If the left-wing bourgeois intellectuals were the heirs of nineteenth-century humanism, then the surrealists were heirs to both nihilist revolts against it—to aestheticism and to anarchism. Their task was to distill what was valid in these revolts and turn it to productive, political, revolutionary purposes.

The point of Benjamin's historical construction was not to provide surrealism with a respectable genealogy but to diagnose the critical juncture the movement had reached in the course of its own development. The first, heroic phase of inspiration in which "everything seemed to integrate itself"—the phase he had dealt with in "Dream-kitsch"—was now over. Surrealism had entered a phase of transformation; it had come to a crossroads, "a moment at which the original tension of a secret society must either explode into a matter-of-fact, profane struggle for power and domination or else decay as a public demonstration" (II 296). In posing this alternative, he was following the lead provided by Pierre Naville, a former member of Breton's circle, in *The Revolution and the Intellectuals* (1927). Naville accused the surrealists of drifting away from the political goals they professed and toward the self-indulgent pleasures of spectacles and scandals staged for their own sake. Their love of provocation showed that they appreciated the "radical concept of freedom" inherent in the spirit of revolt. The question—and here Benjamin concurred fully with Naville—was whether they could manage "to weld this experience of freedom to the other revolutionary experience . . . to the constructive, dictatorial moment in revolution? In short: to bind revolt to revolution." (II 307). The surrealists were in danger of being seduced by their own aestheticist legacy, of mistaking the ecstasy of revolt for genuine political action. This problem was not peculiarly French, for in Benjamin's view the surrealists' "highly exposed position between anarchistic *fronde* and

---

[17] Benjamin's tough talk here might seem to suggest Brecht's influence: the forces capable of shaking off the existing order of things were to be found in the disreputable morality of marginal types rather than the upright moral sentiments of petit bourgeois intellectuals. But the "Surrealism" essay was written before Benjamin's association with Brecht. Moreover, Brecht by no means shared Benjamin's interest in redeeming certain elements of the aestheticist tradition, as can be seen from their differences of opinion over such figures as George and Baudelaire.

revolutionary discipline" was typical of the politicized intelligentsia as such (II 295).

But Benjamin was not suggesting that the surrealists simply sacrifice the ecstatic spirit of revolt. The choice was not "spontaneity or discipline," "intoxication or political action." Rather—and here he went beyond Naville—Benjamin proposed that a closer look at the nature of surrealistic experiences would make it possible to bring surrealism *into* the revolution:

> To win the energies of intoxication for the revolution: this is the project about which surrealism circles in all its books and enterprises. . . . For the surrealists it is not enough that, as we know, an ecstatic component lives in every revolutionary act. This component is identical with the anarchic. But to place the accent exclusively on it would be to subordinate the methodical and disciplinary preparation for revolution completely to a praxis that oscillates between training and celebrating in advance. (II 307)

"To win the energies of intoxication for the revolution": for Benjamin, the real problem was not the surrealists' refusal to sacrifice the "radical idea of freedom" but their "inadequate, undialectical view of the nature of intoxication." In other words, one had to unearth the ambiguities already latent in the heroic phase of the movement, the discovery of intoxication and revolt. Only thus could one reverse the drift into aestheticism that was threatening to derail the surrealists' experiment. Yet the subtext of Benjamin's argument was equally important: only by redeeming the legacy of revolt could one hope to prevent the revolution, with its "constructive, dictatorial" side, from being stillborn. And only the surrealists seemed to be in a position to do so. In any case, Benjamin was sure that they had no choice. Their only viable option was to preside over the disappearance of the intelligentsia in its traditional form, just as their experiments in automatic writing and collage had exemplified the end of the work of art in *its* traditional form. If they proved unequal to their own insights, they would degenerate into the clique of literati their uncomprehending critics took them to be.

The German observer, Benjamin asserted, was in the best of positions to appreciate this. The extreme politicization of Weimar intellectual culture and the effects of inflation had driven the crisis of the intelligentsia and its humanistic concept of freedom to lengths as yet unknown in France. German intellectuals therefore had "no excuse for taking the movement for the 'artistic', 'poetic' one it so superficially appears to be" (II 295). Precisely the two essential features Benjamin ascribed to surrealism—its liquidation of art and its way of wrestling with the politicization of the intellectuals—should be the first things to strike them. Benjamin's appeal to his readers was not meant to be flattering, however. He drove it home with a wry description of an intellectual gradient between France and Germany: "Intellectual currents can generate a sufficient head of water for the critic to install his power station on them. The necessary gradient, in the case of surrealism, is produced by the difference in level between France and Germany. . . . The German observer is not standing at the source. That is his opportunity. He is standing down in the valley" (II 295). Benjamin's intervention at this critical juncture in the development of the surrealist movement was not really directed at the French; that had been Naville's business, and Benjamin had no French readers in any case. His remarks were meant for a home audience. Hence the vehemence of his polemics: behind France's so-called well-meaning left-wing bourgeois intelligentsia stood the world of Berlin's left-wing literary intellectuals—of Kästner, Tucholsky, and Hiller, of activism, expressionism, and Neue Sachlichkeit. They certainly meant to politicize culture but, Benjamin felt, in the wrong way. To him, politicization did not mean using the channels of the existing culture to broadcast "correct" messages; it meant working to help the forms of the new culture itself emerge. Actually, his assertion that the German observer held an advantageous position was a ruse: what upset him was that, in his view, German intellectuals still had not taken the full measure of the collapse of traditional culture. They stood not at the heights but down in the valley. By contrast, the problems confronting the surrealists provided a clear image of the issues facing the European intelligentsia as a whole.

Within the framework of this argument about the surrealist movement, Benjamin conducted his examination of surrealism itself through a critique of aestheticism. His first tack was to challenge the received wisdom about aestheticism. He argued that nineteenth-century aestheticism had been more than political escapism. Even its own proponents had often misunderstood it: " 'Art-for-art's-sake' was hardly ever to be taken literally; it was almost always a flag under which sailed a cargo that could not be declared because it still lacked a name" (II 301). Aestheticism, as a revolt against bourgeois complacency, had misunderstood its own true nature and goals because it was premature. The missing name, Benjamin implied, was "surrealism," for in surrealism the true, political implications of aestheticism were finally emerging. The same held for that more drastic aesthetic affectation known as satanism. In Rimbaud and Lautréamont, satanism was more than just another item in the "inventory of snobbism." For, "if one resolves to open up this romantic dummy, one finds something usable inside: the cult of evil as a political device, however romantic, to disinfect and insulate against all moralizing dilettantism" (II 304). The cult of evil had been a necessary provocation in a culture so saturated with Catholicism: "Rimbaud is indeed a Catholic but, by his own account, in the most wretched part of himself, which he never tires of denouncing . . . the part that forces him to confess that he does not understand revolt" (II 306). Both aesthetic revolts, the cult of art and the cult of evil, remained ensnared in pernicious romantic prejudices; both were romantic dummies that had to be dismantled to extract what was usable in them. But both, like romanticism itself, had nonetheless been implicitly political. The surrealists' invaluable service, in Benjamin's eyes, was to bring this political potential to light.

Yet, as the heirs of aestheticism, the surrealists had also inherited its ambiguities. And they had already proved themselves vulnerable to its temptations. The difficulties began with their discovery of revolt: "Right from the beginning, Breton declared his intention of breaking with the practice of presenting the public with the literary precipitates of a particular form of existence while withholding that form of existence itself. Stated more briefly and dialectically: here the realm of poetry was exploded from within by a closely knit circle of people who pushed 'the poetic life' to the utmost limits of possibility" (II 295–296). So stated, the surrealists' venture still remained ambiguous. Did it necessarily mean abandoning the making of art in order to reveal unconscious energies and change life directly? Or did it still amount to regarding life itself as the ultimate work of art, an aesthetic spectacle beyond compare? "Anyone who has recognized that the writings of this circle are not literature but something else—demonstrations, watchwords, documents, bluffs, forgeries if you will, only certainly not literature—will also know, for the same reason, that they are concerned quite literally with experiences, not with theories, and still less with phantasms" (II 297). Benjamin's rhetorical maneuver here silenced the reader's objections, but it begged the very question his essay so insistently posed: did the surrealists themselves always know the difference? Or had they reentered the realm of art through the back door of an aestheticized life?

Benjamin found the core of the problem in the cult of intoxication (*Rausch*).[18] The surrealists were devotees of all imaginable states of

---

[18] *Rausch* is far more suggestive than the English equivalent "intoxication": it quite naturally bears the connotations of such overwhelming feelings as exhilaration, ecstasy, euphoria, rapture, and passion; its onomatopoetic qualities have an equivalent in the slang term "rush." "Intoxication" is the only real option for rendering *Rausch* in English, but its strong associations with alcohol and toxicity can be misleading. Benjamin uses it to refer to various states of transport, providing a bridge to Klages's theories of dream consciousness and "cosmogonic eros".

rapture and ecstasy: dreams, hypnotic trances, narcotic transports, and occult and telepathic phenomena; Louis Aragon even defined images as intoxicants.[19] The common feature of all these quintessentially surreal experiences is a "loosening of the self." And as the borders of the self loosen, the world seems to "integrate itself": the everyday "threshold between waking and sleep" gets "worn away, as if by the steps of multitudinous images flooding back and forth"; language dissociates as sounds and images associate "with automatic precision and such felicity that no chink remains for the penny-in-the-slot called 'meaning' " (II 296). Intoxication was a means of losing oneself, yet the question remained: to what end? To lose oneself in the spectacle of dreams and uncontrolled projections could only lead to "the muggy backroom of spiritualism" (II 298). Benjamin accused the surrealists of harboring "an entirely inadequate, undialectical conception of the nature of intoxication." Intoxication was another of those romantic dummies that must be broken open, for "a histrionic or fanatical stress on the mysterious side of the mysterious gets us no farther" (II 307); simply confusing dreams with reality brings nothing in exchange for the sacrifice of self. In fact, the abuse of intoxication does not really bring about a loss of individuality, for the self returns, unrecognized, after having been projected onto reality. The dreamer remains trapped in a spell that Benjamin called the "charmed circle of intoxication [*Bannkreis des Rausches*]" (II 297).

The problem was that the surrealists had not reflected soberly enough on the experience of intoxication. If anything, Benjamin proposed taking the liquidation of subjectivity even more seriously: "In the structure of the world, the dream loosens individuality like a hollow tooth. This loosening of the self by intoxication is, at the same time, precisely the fruitful, living experience that allowed these people to step outside the charmed circle of intoxication" (II 297). The point was not to revel in the ecstasy of a complementary world but to return with a sharpened sense for the realities of the world that lies *this* side of the charmed circle. Benjamin proposed the term "profane illumination" as a touchstone for assessing the experience of intoxication. It was understandable that the aesthetes' "bitter, passionate revolt against Catholicism" had led them to champion the ecstasies of drugs against those of religion. But "the true, creative overcoming of religious illumination certainly does not lie in narcotics. It lies in a *profane illumination*, a materialistic, anthropological inspiration to which hashish, opium, and whatever else can give an introductory lesson. (But a dangerous one. And the religious one is stricter)" (II 297).

[19] Aragon, *Paris Peasant*, 78–79.

"Profane illumination" is an oxymoron. Like religious illumination, it suggests the sudden insight that reveals the true face of worldly affairs. Yet profane illumination was to be "materialistic," or "anthropological." There could be no recourse to an outside standpoint such as the authority of revelation. And in this sense a rigorously conceived religious experience—one capable of defining just where its recourse to revelation begins—would provide a more stringent guide than narcotic ecstasies ever could.

"Profane" meant not only "worldly" but "mundane." Not just the nature of the illumination but its objects as well would have to be profane. To Benjamin's way of thinking, the surrealists' fixation on states of extremity was another of their romantic prejudices. He argued that the catalogue of surrealistic experiences could be extended without limit—not by opening up ever more distant, exotic realms but by turning to what was right at hand: "We penetrate mystery only to the degree that we recognize it in the everyday realm, by virtue of a dialectical optic that perceives the everyday as impenetrable, the impenetrable as everyday. . . . The reader, the thinker, the one who is waiting, the flaneur: all are just as much types of illuminati as the opium eater, the dreamer, the entranced one" (II 307–308). The point of Benjamin's dialectical optic was not to envelop banal things and experiences in an impenetrable aura of wonder but to expose the impenetrability they retain despite their appearance of banality. The everyday world was never disenchanted in the first place (therein lay the problem) and so there could be no question of a need to reenchant it. To penetrate and dispel the mystery, however, one must first make it visible. Everyday things must be estranged precisely in order to bring them back. The risk involved in profane illumination was that of losing oneself halfway—of entering but not emerging from the charmed circle of rapture.

Benjamin did provide a series of tantalizing hints at what the kind of profane illumination he envisaged might involve concretely, but in the 1929 essay the idea remained elusive. As "Dreamkitsch" leads us to expect, the surrealists' exploration of the material remains of the nineteenth century continued to exercise a particular fascination on him. Its innermost chamber was once again "the impoverishment of the interior, enslaved and enslaving objects" in which social poverty found its "architectonic" counterpart (II 299). Yet here Benjamin mentioned the ornamental face of that world only in passing, and kitsch not at all. Instead, he now emphasized the surrealists' discovery of "the revolutionary energies that appear in the 'outmoded'":

> In the first iron constructions, the first factory buildings, the earliest photos, in objects that are beginning to become extinct, grand pianos for the

drawing room, the dresses of five years ago, fashionable gathering places when the vogue has begun to ebb from them . . . everything we have experienced on melancholy railroad journeys (the railroads are beginning to age), on godforsaken Sunday afternoons in the proletarian quarters of the big cities, in the first gaze through the rain-blurred window of a new apartment. . . . They bring the tremendous forces of "atmosphere" hidden in these things to the point of explosion. (II 299–300)

This catalogue does not make much sense at first glance. A careful reader of "Dreamkitsch" might have noticed his allusion to a resonance between things extinct and things recently become outmoded. Now, however, the focus was not on the riddles posed by ornamental configurations within the nineteenth-century object world but on the quintessential expression of the accelerating estrangement between that world and the times in which Benjamin was writing: fashion. And "the trick by which this world of things is mastered . . . consists in exchanging the historical view of what has been for a political one" (II 300).

But in what could the political, much less revolutionary, potential of the outmoded consist? If anything, the discovery of beauty in transience and dilapidation—a latter-day version of the romantic fascination with the picturesque—testifies to a highly developed sense of the world as an aesthetic spectacle. The atmosphere that envelops such things does not concentrate energies to the point of "explosion" but, on the contrary, tends to diffuse them into a soft, nostalgic glow. To be sure, Benjamin evoked the surrealists' sense of the accumulated weight of the past exploding in the present. He cited a mock summons to the souls of all times to judgment: " 'Open, ye graves, you dead of the picture galleries, corpses behind paravents, in palaces, castles, and monasteries, here stands the fabulous keeper of the keys, holding a ring with the keys to all times in his hands, who knows how to spring the most cunning of locks and bids you to step into the midst of the world today" (II 300).[20] But not all apocalypses are political, and chiliastic expectations are as likely to foster quietism as political activism. Benjamin's use of the epithet "revolutionary" has a hollow ring, for he did not really explain how the reversal of aestheticism into political action was supposed to take place.

Part of this obscurity derives from a wariness about tipping his hand too far. In 1927 he had begun work on his own exploration of the

---

[20] According to Benjamin, the words had been attributed to Apollinaire. Benjamin read them as a provocation directed at Catholicism's claim to be the keeper of the keys to the past. They also capture the early romantics' messianic idea of the past being culminated and liquidated in the present.

culture of the nineteenth-century Parisian arcades. Benjamin characterized the 1929 essay on surrealism as "an opaque paravent in front of
the 'Arcades' project" (B 489). But the screen he set up was not quite
opaque; many of the cloudy points in the 1929 essay turn out to be
unexplained hints at the "Arcades" project. His references to the significance of iron construction and glass houses, for instance, make
sense only in the context of the theory of modern architecture he was
developing on the basis of the arcades. And behind the ideas of profane illumination and a dialectical optic waited the emerging theory of
modes of perception based on perceptual distance and closeness. Only
on that basis could he unfold a dialectical conception of the nature of
intoxication, one that would show both why it was necessary to enter
its charmed circle and how it was possible to step back out again.

4. Modern Mythology and Dream Consciousness

From mid-1927 until the end of 1929, Benjamin collected notes and
reflections for what he planned as an article-length essay under the
provisional title "Paris Arcades: A Dialectical Enchantment." His ambition was to read the arcades as a phantasmagorical image, "the hollow
mold from which the image of the 'modern' was cast" (V 1045). The
notes he made show its core to be an appropriation and stringent
critique of the surrealists' notion of dream images.[21] From "Dreamkitsch" came the idea of reading the material remains of the nineteenth
century as dream images, and along with it a conception of historical
illumination that sought to unmask the return of archaic forces in
modern culture. On the other hand, the 1929 "Surrealism" essay indicated Benjamin's dissatisfactions with the surrealists' theory of images,
which remained ensnared in pernicious romantic prejudices that left
them prey to the mythic forces they had discovered.

Decisive impulses for the "Arcades" project came from other sources
as well. In choosing the arcades as the central figure of his study, for
instance, he took their architectural form far more seriously than Aragon had. For Benjamin, architecture was the most important testimony
of a latent mythology in the nineteenth century (V 1002). His understanding of that architecture was deeply indebted to Sigfried Giedion's

---

[21] A first, surrealistic conception of the project (1927–1929) has sometimes been contrasted with a second, materialistic phase after the resumption of work in 1934. This
distinction is useful, but if taken too literally it distorts Benjamin's intentions on both
sides of the divide. The early notes and texts are by no means naively rhapsodic, and the
exposés composed in 1935 and 1939 were still decisively shaped by the surrealistic
conception of phantasmagoria.

Building in France.[22] Giedion's conception of architecture enabled Benjamin to transpose the idea of dream images from the interior, where he had housed it in "Dreamkitsch," onto the city outside. The "masks" created by historicist architecture were dreamkitsch writ large, evidence of archaic fears and irrational projections. The architectural form of the arcades was complemented by the specific form of urban experience represented by the flaneur, whose origins were also in nineteenth-century Paris. Here, too, Benjamin drew decisive impulses from outside surrealism. His exemplary modern flaneur was not Aragon but his friend Franz Hessel. It was Hessel who initiated him into the secrets of the Parisian cityscape in the late 1920s, and it was from Hessel that he learned to regard flanerie as more than reliving the dandy's self-indulgent experience of the city as an aesthetic spectacle. Hessel's flaneur undertook a journey into the city's past (III 194). The intoxication that "comes over one who roams the streets for a long time with no definite goal" was an anamnestic rush, an exercise in remembrance. It fixed on the traces past life has inscribed on the physical forms of the city—on historical experience transposed, as it were, into space (V 1053). Yet Hessel's anamnestic flanerie was not simply an attempt to flee from the present into the spectacle of the past. His *Spazieren in Berlin* (Afoot in Berlin) shows him to have been equally devoted to the new constructive architecture and its ideals of transparency. For him there was no building more beautiful than Behrens's turbine factory, a "monumental hall of glass and ferroconcrete"; "entire houses are already being created with a view to how light articulates the body of the building."[23] The interplay of these two sides of Hessel's flaneur was what captivated Benjamin's attention. As he wrote in his 1929 review of *Spazieren in Berlin*, "only a man in whom the new, however quietly, so clearly announces itself can throw such an original and early gaze on what has just become old" (III 197). With those words he provided both a description of Hessel and a maxim to guide his own work.

The germ from which Benjamin's "Arcades" project grew, however, was his reading of Aragon's surrealist narrative *Paris Peasant* (1926). Aragon had explored two shady, marginal places in the city: one was the Opera Arcade (*passage de l'Opéra*) shortly before it was demolished to complete the inner ring of boulevards planned by Baron Haussmann in the nineteenth century; the other was a park, the Buttes de Chaumont, where Aragon pursued the "feeling for nature" in the modern city. The nature he meant, however, had little to do with the pockets of green within the city's tangle of streets. Aragon equated nature with

[22] See the discussion of Giedion in Chapter 4, Section 3.
[23] Hessel, *Ein Flaneur in Berlin* (new title of a republication of *Spazieren in Berlin*), 21, 14.

both the external world as a whole and the unconscious. His proposition, therefore, was that ancient myths of nature and the mythic sense might still be present in the modern city.[24] The surrealists had stammered out a variety of names for what lay behind their "sense of the marvellous suffusing everyday existence," ranging from objective chance and the infinite through the unconscious and the irrational. Aragon now added another: he was pursuing the traces of a "modern mythology."[25] That opened doors for Benjamin, whose own conception of myth had been a nodal point in his previous work. *Paris Peasant* also served him as a test case, enabling his to mark the limits of his appropriation of surrealism.[26] And with this critique of surrealism he developed fresh antitoxins against the vitalist strains of romanticism.

Paris Peasant does not recount a story about a peasant in Paris. Rather, Aragon's title suggests the kind of juxtaposition needed to make a modern mythology visible: the peasant's life is usually embedded in the natural landscape; suppose, however, one were to regard modern Paris—an eminently social and historical product—as a natural landscape invested by its inhabitants with mythic powers. In fact, nothing at all "takes place" in this tale; the Opera Arcade and the Buttes de Chaumont are not so much the setting as the subject of the book. Aragon called them "sacral places," where he had caught fleeting glimpses of the city's hidden mythic face.[27] Why these particular places? Both had been created in the burst of expansion and planning as Paris grew in the nineteenth century—the arcade as a mecca for fashionable shopping, the park as a refuge for healthful recreation. Both were deteriorating and run down, having meanwhile fallen by the wayside of progress. But now that they had ceased to serve ostensibly rational purposes, their unconscious, projective side was coming to light. Decay had made them into twilight zones where they city's shady underside made it home. This shadiness was partly moral: the arcade was now a seamy mecca of prostitution, the park a refuge for suicides. But even the light in them was ambiguous. The glass roof of the arcade bathed its inhabitants in a "glaucous gleam"; Aragon called

---

[24] Aragon, *Paris Peasant*, 136–141.

[25] Ibid., 19; see also 130. Aragon's equation of nature with the unconscious suggests the influence of Schelling's version of German idealism, as does the idea of a new, modern mythology. These connections are discussed by Hans Freier, "Odyssee eines Pariser Bauern: Aragon's 'mythologie moderne' und der Deutsche Idealismus."

[26] The early "Arcades" notes make it clear that Benjamin had already discovered these limits before breaking off work on the project in late 1929. The suggestion that he first became aware of dangers of a rhapsodic form of presentation through his encounter with historical materialism is misleading (see, for instance Tiedemann, "Einleitung des Herausgebers," V 23–24).

[27] Aragon, *Paris Peasant*, 180.

it a "human aquarium."[28] The park's light, too, confused the senses: its cold, white illumination after dark was cast by lanterns, not stars, just as the torrential roar in one's ears came not from the waterfall but the elevated streetcar whose course ran behind it.

These "dimly-lit zones of human activity" where nothing was quite what it seemed to be (or had once been meant to be) were Aragon's "secret repositories of modern myths."[29] He did not use the terms "myth" and "mythology" in a clear, unequivocal sense, however, and the ambiguities in his usage are revealing. In a basic, neutral sense, he used them descriptively. After discarding conscious control and immersing himself in the flow of sensations, he noticed that his attention tended to become fixed on certain objects. He refers to these fixations as the figurative quality of myth:

> I had not understood that myth is above all a reality, and a spiritual necessity, that it is the path of the conscious, its conveyor belt. . . . The intimate relationship I thus discovered, in a hundred circumstances, between the figurative and metaphysical activities of my mind . . . induced me to reconsider those mythical creations which I had previously condemned rather summarily. I soon became aware that the distinctive nature of my thought . . . was a mechanism in every respect analogous to the genesis of myth, and it would certainly not have surprised me if my mind had suddenly fashioned a god for itself.[30]

The idea of myth as the conveyor belt of consciousness was not uncommon among ethnologists at the time. Instead of simply dismissing myths as prescientific delusions, they saw mythic thinking as a phase in the evolution of human consciousness. Mythic and premythic thought were seen to halt the flow of sensation and concentrate it on certain objects; these objects, lifted out of the chaos surrounding them by virtue of their stability, seemed divine. In this sense, "myth" is an epistemological term: it refers to the origins of forms of knowledge in prereligious consciousness.[31]

The shimmer of mystery surrounding ordinary objects and places as the surrealists experienced them, Aragon implied, was a modern trace of this archaic form of experience. In rapturous tones, he invoked the "metaphysical entity of places":

[28] Ibid., 28.
[29] Ibid., 28–29.
[30] Ibid., 128, 130.
[31] This view was advocated most clearly by Hermann Usener, whose work Benjamin knew. The tradition was reviewed and critically appropriated by Ernst Cassirer in his *Language and Myth* and *Philosophy of Symbolic Form*, Vol. 2: *Mythic Thought*. Benjamin mentioned both works in his 1935 review "Problems of Sociolinguistics" (III 456–457).

shores of the unknown, sands shivering with anguish or anticipation. . . .
One false step [*faux pas*], one slurred syllable can reveal a man's thoughts.
The disquieting atmosphere of place contains similar locks that cannot be
bolted fast against infinity. Wherever the living pursue particularly ambiguous activities, the inanimate may sometimes take on the reflection of
their most secret motives: and thus our cities are peopled with unrecognized sphinxes.[32]

The disquieting atmosphere of place sensed by the surrealist flaneur
might be considered a trace of an archaic belief in a local guardian
spirit, the *genius loci*. Indeed, in Aragon's account the unconscious
thoughts and secret motives that a slip of the foot can reveal attach to
the place itself, not to the stroller. But just how sober did Aragon
remain about this discovery? On the one hand, the origin of these
unconscious thoughts seemed clear: they are deposited by the living,
who go about their daily business there, perhaps in the form of the
material artifacts they leave behind. Yet two words jar this conjecture:
why did Aragon rhapsodize about traces of infinity? And in what sense
was the spirit of place a metaphysical entity? One suspects that Aragon
purchased his access to an archaic mode of perception at the cost of
succumbing to it.

The same slippage occurs in Aragon's attitude toward his discovery
of myth. Many of his descriptions are laced with a critical undertone
that ranges from gentle, comic debunking to frank horror. Humanity
fancied that it had left the primitive need for idols behind on the march
of progress. Indeed, the churches he passed when driving through the
countryside seemed abandoned; no one had time any longer to con-
template the folds in the robes of the saints. Yet a strange, new statuary
was arising:

great red gods, great yellow gods, great green gods, planted at the edges
of the speculative tracks along which the mind speeds. . . . Scarcely ever
before has man had the pleasure of seeing destiny and force look so
barbaric. . . . These modern idols share a parentage that makes them
doubly redoubtable. Painted brightly with English or invented names,
possessing just one long supple arm, a luminous, faceless head, a single
foot, and a numbered wheel in the belly, the gas pump sometimes takes
on the appearance of those cannibal tribes who worship war and war
alone. O Texaco motor oil, Esso, Shell, great inscriptions of human poten-
tiality, soon we shall cross ourselves before your fountains, and the youngest among us will perish from having contemplated their nymphs in
naphtha.[33]

[32] Aragon, *Paris Peasant*, 27–28.
[33] Ibid., 131–132.

This mock-bombastic description of gas pumps as modern idols is precisely half-serious. But Aragon followed it with an image of terror. The real modern idols were machines that have eluded our control. Machines were invented to tame nature and subdue our fear of it, banishing the ancient myths of nature. Yet we have forgotten that the machines are only "an extension of our own thought process," so that "other blind forces are born to us, other major fears, and thus we end up prostrating ourselves before the machines that are our daughters." The "essentially modern tragic symbol," for Aragon, was a "large wheel that is spinning and is not being steered by a hand."[34] Variations on the sorcerer's apprentice theme were common in interwar culture. Many were far more sinister: in Fritz Lang's *Metropolis*, the protagonist undergoes a delirium in which a machine in the underground city takes on the features of a moloch that devours workers who appear, transfigured, as slaves. Aragon's image points, less melodramatically, to a similar awareness of the dangers of exalting blind forces as divinities.

Yet he repeatedly submitted to this temptation. The vision of a modern mythology restored "coherence" to his world; it transformed even barren landscapes into a wonderland. Blind forces may get the better of us if we seek to deny their presence, but since they are the only reality there can ultimately be no question of deflecting their energies. So there remained only one choice—to recognize them for what they are and embrace them: "O reason, reason, abstract phantom of the waking state, I had already expelled you from my dreams, now I have reached a point where those dreams are about to become fused with apparent realities: now there is only room here for myself. In vain, reason denounces to me the dictatorship of sensuality. In vain it warns me against error crowned queen at last. Enter, Madam, this is my body, this is your throne."[35] Mythic delusions survive despite the apparent rule of the principle of utility in the modern world; but having entered a rapturous state that enables him to trace their figures in the life of the city, Aragon was unable to return. His only regret was that the fleeting glimpses he catches cannot be stabilized, because the ephemeral resists being forged into a new religion. "Preface to a Modern Mythology": Aragon understood not just his foreword but his entire book as a prelude to the reenchantment of the world.

In a letter to Adorno written in May 1935, Benjamin acknowledged the importance of his reading of *Paris Peasant* for the genesis of the "Arcades" project. His initial excitement had been so great that the

---

[34] Ibid., 132–133.
[35] Ibid., 22.

pounding of his heart forced him to lay the book down every two or three pages. In retrospect, however, he recognized that the pounding had also been a warning pointing to the distance he would have to put between himself and that first reading (B 663).[36] But achieving that distance did not take years and years, as the letter suggested. The process was already well under way in the late 1920s, as the "Arcades" notes show. Although he seldom referred to Aragon explicitly, many of his new theoretical formulations can be read as attempts to define the limits of his appropriation of surrealism. The early "Arcades" notes indeed do show us what was going on behind the "opaque paravent" of the 1929 "Surrealism" essay.

That essay accused the surrealists of harboring an inadequate notion of the nature of intoxication. In the "Arcades" notes, Benjamin leveled the accusation directly at Aragon:

> Demarcation of the tendency of this work from Aragon: whereas Aragon persists in lingering in the realm of dreams, here the constellation of awakening is to be found. Whereas an impressionistic element remains in Aragon—the mythology—(and this impressionism is to be held responsible for the many empty "philosophical" observations in the book) here it is a question of dissolving the "mythology" into the space of history [Geschichtsraum]. (V 1014)

Benjamin's demarcation sets up two contrast pairs that mark the border between his intentions and Aragon's: first the realm of dreams versus the constellation of awakening, and then mythology versus the space of history.[37] As we see in the next section, the categories of history and awakening gave Benjamin his critical leverage against the surrealists' failings. But this passage strikes another note as well. In certain respects, Benjamin could not quite take Aragon seriously. He found his attempts at philosophy amateurish and even consigned the

[36] The passage on the pounding of his heart has been cited more often than the reference to the warning he heard in it. Benjamin spoke here of the rhapsodic presentation and the romantic form of the original conception as belonging to a phase of "unperturbed archaic philosophizing, ensnared in nature [naturbefangen]." Such self-criticism seems puzzling given his preoccupation with the romantics and his critical conception of myth. The point of these comments may lie in the fact that, at the time he made them, Benjamin was trying to convince the Institut für Sozialforschung to grant him a regular stipend. The self-deprecating appeal to Adorno seems calculated to suggest that the association would have a favorable influence on his work.

[37] Benjamin's term Geschichtsraum is a remarkable coinage, combining a temporal concept with a spatial image; it suggests that history is something one can break into—or out of. It also recalls his discussions of history "passing into the setting" in baroque allegory and of the aura as "a peculiar weaving together of space and time." In the following argument about Benjamin's reading of Klages I attempt to show why he used such imagery so persistently.

term "mythology" to inverted commas. And it is somewhat puzzling to find Benjamin singling out Aragon's tendency to remain in the thrall of dreams, since *Paris Peasant* so pointedly centers on the notion of a modern mythology. What was the link between dreams and Aragon's "mythic sense"? And might Benjamin's reckoning also have been directed at a figure behind Aragon, one whose philosophy he took more seriously?

That figure was Ludwig Klages. The acuity and depth of Klages's work, Benjamin always insisted, set it apart from run-of-the-mill *Lebensphilosophie* (III 44). Benjamin drew on Klages in formulating his own philosophical anthropology and read him with the greatest of care, as the dream theory developed in the "Arcades" notes shows.[38] Klages was the kind of opponent from whom he could learn. His theory of dream consciousness as the trace of an archaic mode of perception provided the foil against which Benjamin articulated his discontents with the surrealists' cult of intoxication.

Klages set out his phenomenology of dreaming in his 1914 essay "On Dream Consciousness." His primary interest was the form of dreams rather than their content, and particularly the differences between space and time as experienced in dreaming and waking.[39] The space and time of dreams were not merely incidental to their contents, nor were they derivatives of the form they take for the waking subject; dream space and dream time, he argued, have their own specific qualities. He derived a first approximation to the form of dream consciousness from what he called the "dream mood"—the dreamy state in which one sometimes experiences the waking world. Such states of consciousness, he found, have three features in common. First, they involve a special kind of passivity, which he termed pathic passivity.[40] By pathic, he meant the ability to relinquish or abandon oneself to impressions in such a way that the impressions loosen one's urge to act and lull the will to sleep. One becomes immersed or lost in the way something appears, and the greatest happiness is that of self-forgetfulness. Rhythmic phenomena, particularly "the pulsating repetition of similar impressions," seemed to him a particularly good example. The second characteristic of dream moods was a feeling of distance from the appearances that evoke them. Dreamy moods tend to be

---

[38] See the discussion of Klages in Chapter 4, Section 2. Benjamin listed five of Klages's works, including "Vom Traumbewußtsein," in his "Schemata on the Psychophysical Problem" of 1922/23 (VI 84), which includes two sections on the categories of near and far. Werner Fuld, "Walter Benjamins Beziehung zu Ludwig Klages," is marred by speculation about their personal acquaintance and by a narrow approach to Benjamin's "borrowings" from Klages.

[39] Klages, "Vom Traumbewußtsein," 157–158, 160.

[40] Ibid., 162.

dispelled when such things move closer, regardless of whether the approach is actual or only apparent. Klages pointed out certain "atmospheric appearances" promote dream moods by obscuring the clarity of our perception of distance—fog, twilight, and night as opposed to daylight. In a brief aside, he ventured the suggestion that "the degree of affinity for dreams" of "entire epochs" may be judged by the relation of their architecture to light: "It was the Renaissance that first spurned the dusky mood of the interior and brought, finally, the victory of window light, as a prelude to the intellectuality that wages war against dream consciousness to this very day."[41] He also identified affinities between the individual senses and the dreamlike appearance of distance: "Only sight and hearing are far-senses," he judged, whereas "taste and touch are near-senses" and the sense of smell lies somewhere in between.[42] Klages described the third quality of dream moods as a "feeling of fleetingness." This could take two rather different forms. Certain impressions flare up and then flash past almost as if they had been mirages. But the daydreamer, too, may be overcome by the feeling of his or her *own* transience, particularly when lost in the contemplation of ancient monuments that evoke a sense of temporal distance.[43] Passivity, distance, fleetingness: for Klages, these three elements of the dream mood were the traces of dream consciousness that can be experienced within the waking world.

Klages then used these three elements to deduce what he regarded as the form of dream consciousness itself. To begin with, dream consciousness lifts the separation between the subject and object of perception, between the ego and things.[44] The fleetingness of appearances in dream moods corresponds to a "restless mutability of all images" in dreams themselves. Dream reality has a "protean character" similar to the "mythic art of metamorphosis" in which figures flow and blend into one another. The same holds for the other pole of waking consciousness, the ego. In a world where appearances transform themselves so fluidly, the ego cannot perform the mental acts necessary to fix itself as a self-identical point in time and space. This diffusion of the self goes hand in hand with the dissolving of objects into appearances.[45] The other salient feature of dream consciousness

---

[41] Ibid., 163–164. While rejecting Klages's diagnosis, Benjamin varied this theory of modernity, pointing to the ambiguous light in the arcades as a distorted anticipation of the transparency later realized by glass architecture.

[42] In the "Arcades" notes and the "Work of Art" theses, Benjamin similarly contrasted optical (or contemplative) and tactile (or use-oriented) reception.

[43] Klages, "Vom Traumbewußtsein," 164–165.

[44] Ibid., 167–170.

[45] Klages coins the term *Entdinglichung*, or "de-reification," and says that in dreams *die Dinge entgegenständlichen sich*—"things de-objectify themselves" (ibid., 180, 185).

results from the fact that space and time themselves lose the fixed character of objects. As the barriers between subject and object go down, the separation between "here" and "there" in space loses its force along with the distance between "now" and "then" in time. What replaces them is a "perpetual present with a *boundlessly mobile now-point*" and a "*boundlessly mobile 'here'.*"[46] But the emphasis on the here and now is misleading, for spatial and temporal *distance* have absolute priority over nearness for Klages, as his discussion of the feeling of distance in dream moods already shows. The appearance of distance also helps defuse the ego, because "the unreachable" no longer provides a spur to activity. The tension between here and there, now and then, simply dissolves. The ego ceases striving to reach what appears in the distance, letting itself be pulled away into it instead. That is what Klages finds decisive in the end: "life" is "transported out of the ego over to the *location* of the appearance."[47] What appears across this distance is an "image" that "only now completely captivates us." Passive abandonment to a sphere of fleeting images, a loosening of the ego in a state of ecstatic transport: Klages's theory of dream consciousness, organized around the category of distance, provides a phenomenology of the experience being cultivated by the surrealists.

Klages also offered an explicit theory of the connection between dreaming and mythic consciousness. In his view, the dream form was in no way derivative of modern, waking experience. On the contrary, dream consciousness had survived the breakdown of an archaic, "original totality" of experience, "out of which waking consciousness only later crystallized."[48] Primitive peoples did not perceive the object world as moderns do and then superimpose animistic beliefs on it. Rather, the very organization of their perception was different, and the form of their legends and myths presents a picture of the world as they actually experienced it. In fact, Klages suggested, prominent features of "primitive thinking" become readily accessible if thought of in terms of dreaming—the experience of being whisked from place to place in sudden changes of scene, for instance.[49] Conversely, pathic receptivity to appearances of the kind that characterizes dream consciousness opens a view of *Urbilder,* which Klages described as timeless, archaic images of the world hidden to the conscious ego imprisoned by its purposive striving.[50] In the 1920s, Klages went on to elaborate this phenomenology of archaic consciousness in terms of other states of

[46] Ibid., 185.
[47] Ibid., 189: "*das Leben [wird] aus ihm [dem Ich] hinausverlegt an den* Ort *der Erscheinung.*"
[48] Ibid., 160.
[49] Ibid., 158–159.
[50] Ibid., 185.

transport and ecstasy, the best known being his theory of cosmogonic eros.[51] His work culminated in an extreme, Manichean dualism in which history appears as a perpetual struggle between intuitive experience and conceptualizing consciousness, image (*Bild*) and idea, soul and mind. The title of his major, synthetic work, which indicts the mind as the "adversary of the soul," left no doubt about what he saw as the roots of sickness and of health.

Where did this conflict originate? Klages stated his answer most vividly in "Man and Earth": the culprit was "progress"—not a naive faith in progress, not the wrong kind of progress, but progress as such. Its sole principle was that of "increasing power," power over nature that could be had only at the price of severing the bond between "human creation and the earth." Utility, economic development, and culture were no more than pretexts for "the method that lies in the madness of destruction." Capitalism was partly responsible, for it had replaced the awareness of differences in quality with a single, quantitative scale. Behind it, however, lay Christian monotheism, which had replaced the plurality of gods and spirits with a single, spiritual divinity. But even that explanation did not reach back far enough. For Klages, the problem was at the very origins of consciousness: "With the bloody blows man deals to all his fellow creatures he merely completes what he has already inflicted on himself: to sacrifice an *interwovenness* in the imagistic plurality and inexhaustible fullness of *life* for the homeless *standing above things* of a *spirituality* detached from the world. He has brought himself into discord with the planet that bore and nourished him—indeed, with the cyclical course of the stars."[52] Capitalism and Christianity were only the final forms in which a long, aberrant course of development approaches its apocalyptic culmination. The origins of the disease were nowhere within history. Rather, the catastrophe was history itself, the "course" that "leads out of the circular path of events."[53] Redress, therefore, could not be expected

[51] In the very few instances where Benjamin referred to Klages in his published work, he singled out *Vom kosmogonischen Eros* (1922) as representing the productive side of his work (II 229, III 44).

[52] Klages, "Mensch und Erde," 11–12, 22, 25, 33–37. Klages underscores his reference to the planet's bearing and nourishing by describing *Geist* as matricidal (40). Klages was prominent in the attempt to revive Bachofen's theories of archaic matriarchy and put them at the service of an ultrareactionary *Lebensphilosophie*. Benjamin's 1934 essay "Johann Jacob Bachofen" (II 219–233) was a response to this revival; Erich Fromm's 1934 essay "Die sozialpsychologische Bedeutung der Mutterrechtstheorie," which appeared in the *Zeitschrift für Sozialforschung*, addressed the theory of matriarchy more directly.

[53] Klages's critique of technology as an attempt to master nature that rebounds on its perpetrators has romantic origins. His drastic formulations serve as a reminder that the form in which Benjamin (and subsequently Horkheimer and Adorno in *Dialectic of Enlightenment*) adopted it has important affinities to certain kinds of *Lebensphilosophie*. Herbert Schnädelbach underscores this point in *Philosophie in Deutschland*, 172–174.

from anywhere within history. The only hope was to break out of the course of human history entirely, and back into the archaic realm.

Benjamin, however, in his critical comment on Aragon, spoke of doing precisely the opposite—breaking the stranglehold of mythic forces by dissolving them "into the realm of history." We can now see why he needed to draw on both Aragon and Klages to do so. The surrealists did not fall prey to Klages's unconditional rejection of technology and modernity. They provided clues that would help in tracing the "thicket of prehistory" in the objects and forms of experience deposited by the recent past, the outgoing nineteenth century. But Klages provided a phenomenology of mythic consciousness that was rigorous enough to help in decoding the sensual surface of that world and in explaining why the surrealists remained enthralled by the spell of dreams. Of course, Benjamin would have to work against Klages's delusions as well. Klages laid great stress on the virtues of perceptual distance; access to the world of archaic images was provided by ecstatic transports that overcome the oppressive nearness of things. But what if one were to read Klages against the grain and *reverse* his phenomenology of near and far? What would a theory of dream images and a philosophy of history built on the need to bring things *closer* look like? That is the task Benjamin tackled in the early "Arcades" notes.

5. "Paris Arcades: A Dialectical Enchantment"? The Original Conception of the "Arcades" Project

What did Benjamin mean by characterizing the "Arcades" project as a dialectical enchantment (*Feerie*)? In one of the most striking formulations in the early notes, he pictures himself as a militant partisan of enlightenment. Wielding the weapons of reason, he will vanquish delusion and myth: "Clear fields where until now only madness has been rank. Forge ahead with the whetted axe of reason, looking neither left nor right so as not to fall prey to the horror that beckons from depths of the primeval forest [*Urwald*]. All ground must sometime be made arable by reason, cleared of the tangled undergrowth of delusion and myth. This is to be accomplished here for the nineteenth century" (V 1010). The language Benjamin uses in this reminder to himself resonates with his earlier and later work alike. The tangled undergrowth evokes that "thicket of primeval history" whose traces the surrealists pursued in "Dreamkitsch."[54] He emboldens himself to forge through it

---

[54] Benjamin first used the primeval forest imagery with respect to myth in the *Elective Affinities* essay; see Chapter 3, n. 9.

without heeding the beckoning of sirens who would lure him into the depths, like a modern-day urban Odysseus. The imagery seems to leave no room for ambiguity. There is no question of "magic observation" or even of mapping contours; intent on passing through unscathed, he clears space by razing the obstructions in his path.[55]

This forceful image leaves no doubt about Benjamin's sympathies in his encounter with Aragon and Klages. It presents a reassuringly simple alternative: delusion and myth are the antipodes of reason. Yet for that very reason it also misrepresents Benjamin's actual procedure. He had never believed simple faith in reason to be an adequate match for the snares of myth; in all his writings, this was one of the very few times he identified his weapon as reason plain and simple.[56] The image suggests what may have moved him to reach for the "whetted axe" on just this occasion: the threatening proximity of those irrational forces, or at least of their latter-day advocates. Yet Benjamin's answer to Klages and Aragon was not a broadside on behalf of reason, a salvo fired from a safe distance, but a point-for-point inversion of their theories won in hand-to hand struggle. Their collaboration with mythic delusions was to be put at the service of the resistance; their weakness was to accrue to his strength. Benjamin countered their modern mythology with a theory of historical images aimed at "dissolving the 'mythology' into the realm of history," and he replaced their cult of dream consciousness with a theory of awakening from the nightmare of history. In both cases, he reversed Klages's phenomenology of spatial and temporal distance by developing his own "technique of nearness"—a "pathos of nearness," as he called it at one point (V 1015).

In the first place, Benjamin wanted to demonstrate that mythic forms and compulsions had not been banished by reason and progress but held sway with unabated force in modern culture. Regressive forces persisted not only outside the realm of progress or despite its achievements but as a moment within progress itself. The city of Paris, as the pacesetter for all things modern, was therefore an ideal testing ground; and at the center of his attention stood the Parisian arcades. The ar-

---

[55] In an alternate version of "The Destructive Character" (1931), Benjamin wrote: "Clearing away—the destructive character's action can be graphically portrayed under this codeword. . . . for the destroyer every act of clearing away means an enlightenment [Aufklärung], a complete reduction [Reduzierung] of his own condition, and even the extracting of its root [Radizierung]. Such an Apollonian image of the destroyer becomes compelling once one recognizes how enormously the world is simplified when tested with a view to its fitness for destruction" (IV 999). This is the vein of tough talk in Benjamin's work, the liquidationist moment associated with Brecht and with texts like "Experience and Poverty." The note in the early "Arcades" manuscripts shows just how closely it was bound up in Benjamin's theory of images.

[56] In the theological idiom of his early works, Benjamin used the term "logos," as in the Elective Affinities essay (I 163).

cades were speculative ventures that had begun as fashionable meccas for luxury shopping, but by the early twentieth century they had lapsed into the decrepitude in which Aragon found them. In the twilight of this drastic decline in fortune, Benjamin glimpsed an image of the arcades as a "primeval landscape of consumption" (V 993): "A look through the arcades . . . opens up an ideal panorama of a primeval age scarcely gone by. Here dwells Europe's last dinosaur, the consumer. The rank growth of merchandise spreads over these cave walls as age-old flora and enters into the unruliest connections, like tissue does in ulcers. A world of secret affinities . . ." (V 1045). This image of the arcades as enchanted grottoes bears the stamp of Aragon's modern mythology; as a literary conceit, it stands up to anything in *Paris Peasant*. Yet Benjamin took the arcades as an analytical point of departure. Two patterns of perception crossed there in particularly telling fashion: the labyrinthine spatial form of the metropolis, and the temporal form of modernity as dictated by the rhythms of fashion and consumption. Architecture and fashion provided Benjamin's object lessons in reading the traces of a primeval landscape in the modern city.

Arcades, in French and in German, are "passages" (*passages, Passagen*), a term that underscores their spatial dimension. The title of the article Benjamin planned was to be "Paris Passages," and he reminded himself to keep listening for the overtones set up by the word "passage" (V 1007). The arcades were literally passageways, glass-covered tunnels usually constructed so as to link two streets in the city's layout.[57] They therefore contributed to the modern city's development into a labyrinth, an image Benjamin repeatedly used to designate things quintessentially archaic. "Most hidden aspect of the big cities: this historical object, the new metropolis, with its uniform streets and vast rows of houses, has realized the dreamed-of architecture of the ancients: the labyrinth. . . . Completion in the covered corridors of the arcades" (V 1007). Klages's phenomenology suggested what makes labyrinths—whether literal or figurative—into mythic phenomena: the beholder who allows himself to be drawn inside loses himself in a convoluted interior. The arcades were also peculiarly ambiguous spaces, a fact to which Benjamin attached special importance. They were at once exterior and interior, "street and house" (V 1030). Laid out in the space between rows of houses, they were streets, conduits for public traffic. But shielded from the weather by their glass and iron roofs, they were also houses, and thus living spaces. The light in them

---

[57] By providing pedestrians with a shortcut, the arcades—first and foremost commercial ventures—lured customers to browse in the shops. Their economic viability often depended on capturing strategic locations in the city's layout. See J. F. Geist, *Passagen: Ein Bautyp des XIX. Jahrhunderts*, 30–33.

was ambiguous as well. Their glass roofing filtered the natural daylight, producing the glaucous gleam that prompted Aragon to call them human aquariums. And before the days of electric illumination, the flickering light and shadows cast by gas and oil lanterns made them into "fairy palaces" (V 1001). Ambiguous space, Klages had suggested, in which fixed forms dissolve into mutable appearances, was a hallmark of archaic dream consciousness. Ambiguous light, in turn, fostered the dreamlike appearance of perceptual distance. And Klages himself had proposed that an epoch's affinity for dreams could be gauged by its architecture's handling of light.[58] The arcades, as Benjamin read their image, were thus well situated as a proving ground for his recasting of Klages.

Among the few polished texts Benjamin won from these early notes is an extended image of the arcades as passageways that lead to the city's hidden, mythic topography:

> In ancient Greece one pointed out places that led down into the underworld. Our waking existence, too, is a land in which hidden places lead into the underworld, full of inconspicuous sites where dreams flow out. In the daytime we pass them by unsuspectingly, but once sleep comes we swiftly grasp our way back to them and lose ourselves in the dark passageways. The city's labyrinth of houses, by the light of day, is like consciousness; the arcades (those galleries that lead into its past existence) flow out unnoticed into the streets. But at night, beneath the dark masses of houses, their more compact darkness leaps out frighteningly; and the late passer-by hastens past them, unless we have encouraged him to take the journey down the narrow alley. (V 1046)

Benjamin's image moves sequentially through three layers. The first is literally topographic: the ancients believed the landscape they inhabited to rest on a mythic underworld where chthonic forces held sway. The two realms communicated, however, via conduits that led from the light of day down into darkness—and presumably back up again. Benjamin likens this chthonic topography to the landscape of consciousness. Waking consciousness is marked by sites that provide access to the underworld, but these sites are inconspicuous by daylight. What he stresses, however, is the reverse: though we swiftly grasp our way back to them in sleep, we fail to notice how dreams flow out (*münden*) into *waking* consciousness. He then likens the landscape of consciousness to the labyrinthine topography of the city. The passages that lead back to the sources of dream consciousness are overlooked by day, but with the shift of light as darkness descends they leap out and

[58] Klages, "Vom Traumbewußtsein," 164.

frighten us. But what should be frightening if, in dreams, we *hurry* back to "lose ourselves in the dark passageways"? The answer lies in the tacit simile between the first and third levels of the image: the city's unconscious is an archaic netherworld of dark forces. In every case, the point of communication between the worlds is a hidden place, an inconspicuous site, a dark passageway, a gallery—in short, a passage. Moreover, the very idea of "passage" is laden with mythic significance as a transitional zone, hedged by ritual, where the governing powers mark the course of life.[59]

Archaic *temporal* forms, however, were most perfectly represented by the tyranny of fashion in nineteenth-century Paris and revealed more about the nature of these mythic forces. Fashion, for Benjamin, was a mania for novelty—a perpetual pursuit of the appearance of something new in endless recombinations of the same old elements. This compulsive, insatiable striving for "the latest" served an economic rationale; it was becoming a driving force in the circulation of commodities. But to Benjamin it appeared as one of the paradigmatic forms of mythic consciousness, a diabolical variation on the theme of the eternity of punishments in hell:

> The modern: the age of hell. The infernal punishments are the latest thing available at the time. It is not a question of the same thing happening again and again (a fortiori I do not speak of eternal return) but rather that the face of the world, that oversized head, never changes precisely in that which is the latest, that this "latest" is always the same thing through and through. This constitutes the eternity of hell and the sadist's mania for novelty. (V 1010–1011)

Fashion is therefore a regressive phenomenon, a kind of repetition compulsion whose nature is disguised by the illusory appearance of novelty. The mythic nature of this compulsion also shows itself in the peculiar way fashion enthrones the transitory. Having schooled himself in the traditions of baroque allegory, Benjamin was captivated by the association between transience and death. "Fashion was never anything but a parody of the motley corpse, the provocation of death through the female and, between the boisterous, memorized cheers, a bitter, whispered dialogue with putrefaction. That is why it changes so swiftly: it tickles death and is already another, something new, when death looks around to strike it" (V 1055). In this image, the "primeval landscape of consumption" wins a new face. When fashion is read as an allegory of transience, the nineteenth century is exposed as that

---

[59] Menninghaus points out how pervasive the image of the threshold was throughout Benjamin's work in *Schwellenkunde*, 26–59.

petrified primordial landscape that stood for history itself in the *Trauerspiel* study. The temporal rhythm of fashion reveals the true face of modernity to be that of a barren "moor landscape" where "everything remains always new, always the same" (V 1010).

Yet when Benjamin speaks of the latent presence of the archaic in the modern he means something subtly yet crucially different than what the neoromantic mythologists had in mind. Modernity is not simply a recurrence of timeless archetypes; in fact, the dominance of mythic compulsions has become more insidious and total in the nineteenth century than ever before.

> "*Urgeschichte* of the nineteenth century": this would be uninteresting were one to understand it to mean that "prehistoric" forms are to be rediscovered among the inventory of the nineteenth century. Only if the nineteenth century were to be portrayed as the originary form of *Urgeschichte*—as a form in which the *entirety* of prehistory renews itself so that certain traits of prehistory can be recognized as only precursors of this recent time—would the concept of an "*Urgeschichte* of the nineteenth century" have any sense. (V 1034)

The German word *Urgeschichte* is untranslatable here because it refers neither to a period before recorded history (prehistory) nor to the precursors of nineteenth-century phenomena (prehistory of the nineteenth century). Rather, prehistory is only a foretaste of modernity, in which archaic compulsions hold sway with unprecedented force. Benjamin's view of fashion makes his point clear: when the fact of an eternal return—a repetition compulsion—is disguised by the illusion of novelty, the trap is complete. Whereas prehistoric humanity frankly professed its belief in fate, modernity fails to recognize that it is still ruled by compulsions—a recognition that would be a first step toward breaking their spell. Mythic forces return in the modern world with all the vengeance of Freud's return of the repressed. To capture this constellation of myth and modernity for the history of society was the point of Benjamin's concept of *Urgeschichte*.

Klages's phenomenology was therefore invaluable to Benjamin, but he turned it to utterly different purposes. The fruits of technical progress and the modern capitalist economy were not antithetical to the archaic consciousness but evidence that it had returned in disguised, indeed heightened form. Moreover, Benjamin then went farther and reversed the direction of Klages's way of seeing. Instead of dissolving history into a mythology of eternal recurrence, Benjamin aimed at dissolving the mythology into the realm of history. The point was not to dismiss history as an insubstantial phantom but to develop a conception of history resilient enough to resist such erosion. But how was one to perceive this mythic substrate without being taken in by it? Or, in the language of the 1929 "Surrealism" essay, how could one be sure to step back out of the charmed circle of intoxication after giving oneself over to it?

In spatial terms, the trick was to exchange distance for nearness. "We have been schooled in the romantic gaze into the distance of the historical realm," Benjamin observed, and " 'mythology', to use Aragon's term" also "shifts things away from us" (V 998). The "gaze into the distance [*Fernsicht*]" was meant quite literally. Klages described sight as a "far-sense" whereas Benjamin stressed the need for *tactile* nearness: "Concrete, materialistic reflection on the things that are closest is called for." He played out this contrast between tactile, tactical proximity and visual "perspective" in many different ways. The illusionistic character of the arcades, for instance, was inherent in their very construction: "In the arcades, perpective is lastingly preserved as in cathedral naves" (V 1049). Yet Benjamin refused to surrender the field of dreams to Klages's view that perceptual distance plays the constitutive role in dream consciousness. On the contrary, in "Dreamkitsch" Benjamin suggested that the form of dreams was changing: "The dream no longer opens up a blue distance" (II 620). Instead, Benjamin recast Klages's pathic passivity of dreams as an *inability* to maintain perceptual distance: "Were we . . . to live more tranquilly, according to another rhythm, there would be nothing "fixed" for us; rather, everything would happen before our eyes, everything would befall us [*alles stieße uns zu*].[60] But that's just how it is in dreams. In order to understand the arcades from the ground up, we immerse them in the deepest layer of dreaming and speak of them as if they were to befall us" (V 1009). In fact, Benjamin often associated dreaming with haptic experiences: in "Dreamkitsch," "the hand . . . takes its leave by tracing familiar contours" (II 620).[61] The uses of tactile nearness to break the spell cast by visual distance would later be crucial in the theory of aesthetic perception developed in "The Work of Art in the Age of Its Technical Reproducibility." Benjamin's "pathos of nearness," then, had an inextricably spatial and tactile dimension.

[60] The connotations of the German verb *zustoßen* are difficult to render here. Used impersonally and governing an object in the dative case—as it does here—it simply means that something happens to or befalls someone, often a misfortune or an accident. As an intransitive verb, it means "to lunge" or "to strike." The context suggests that Benjamin is trying to find a term for visual perception that stresses the way appearances come at the percipient.

[61] Similarly in the passage cited above: "Once sleep comes we swiftly *grasp* our way back . . . and lose ourselves in the dark passageways" (V 1046, emphasis added). Many of the texts in *One Way Street* and *Berlin Childhood around 1900* play on children's experience of the world through its tactile proximity.

But space often serves as a metaphor for time. Times long past are "far away," whereas the recent past appears "nearer" to us. And when Benjamin spoke of closeness, he meant temporal proximity above all. Rapid change, however, accelerates the speed with which the past appears to recede from us as we move forward. The nineteenth century was just such an era of accelerating change, moving in rhythms set by technological change, the turnover of the commodity economy, and fashion. The romantic gaze into the distance, therefore, is not only the product of an ideology. It is fostered by a changing historical rhythm, by virtue of which even the recent past quickly begins to look like a distant epoch.[62] The romantic gaze poses as an attachment to the past and to tradition, but it is actually something quite different—a symptom of the breakdown of tradition, of the absence of the past in the present, of a failure in cultural transmission. Tradition, in German, is *Überlieferung,* a "handing down" or "delivering over" of something; the image suggests tactile, virtually hand-to-hand contact. "What would the nineteenth century be to us if we were bound to it by tradition?" Benjamin asked (V 998).

The answer could be found only by anchoring the historical perspective point firmly in the present. That meant carrying out what Benjamin called a Copernican reversal in historical perspective. Kant's Copernican revolution in epistemology had aimed to show how theories of knowledge must take the position of the subject into account. Benjamin proposed doing the same for history: "The Copernican turn in the conception of history is this: [formerly] one took 'what has been' as the fixed point toward which present-day knowledge was attempting to grope its way. Now this relationship is to be reversed" (V 1057). "The true method" of evoking the presence of past things was "to imagine them in our space (not us in theirs). . . . We do not transpose ourselves into them: they step into our life" (V 1014–1015). Benjamin saw the false conception of historical understanding embodied in a single word, "empathy." The German term for empathy, *Einfühlung,* literally means to feel one's way into something. And empathy, or past-mindedness, was the methodological credo of the way of thinking about the past known generally as historicism. For thinkers such as Leopold von Ranke, only past-mindedness could provide access to the true image of the past "as it really was." Benjamin therefore began to identify "historicism" as the antipodes of his own way of thinking about the past. The chain of association thus led to what seems like an odd result. Klages, who glorified *Urbilder* and archaic forms of con-

---

[62] In the later "Arcades" notes he also argued that the mythic element in culture became visible more quickly as the tempo of technological change accelerated (V 576).

sciousness, dismissed history as a sinister illusion, whereas historicism—of whatever variety—insisted that truth lies only in historical modulations, never in timeless essences or natural laws. What struck Benjamin, however, was that both assumed that the true image of the past is timelessly accessible—if only one is willing to sacrifice the present. His response, directed at both in equal measure, was to juxtapose "empathy" with "making things present"—*Vergegenwärtigung*—as the cardinal principle of historical understanding (V 1014–1015).

At first glance, Benjamin might seem merely to be trading one blindness for another, rejecting the romantic pathos of distance and past-mindedness only to fall into an extreme, solipsistic present-mindedness. He appears to sacrifice the past instead of the present. But, in fact, he was thinking of a movement in *both* directions (V 1032). His real interest lay in a particular kind of *constellation* of past and present that yields a "higher concretion" than historicism: the dialectical method must do justice to the historical situation of both the object and the present-day interest in it. The relationship must be reciprocal. The "concrete, historical" subject looks into the past and finds itself prefigured or "preformed" in a past object; but this object, in turn, is "raised to a higher concretion" in the present. A philosophy of history that does justice to this phenomenon, Benjamin suggests, "would speak of an increasing concentration (integration) of reality, in which all that is past (in its time) can receive a higher degree of actuality than in the moment at which it exists" (V 1026). Nowhere does he propose simply projecting the self-images of the present onto the past. On the contrary, only by reading the past can the present hope to find its own image at all. He put the point most succinctly in his 1931 review "Literary History and Literary Studies": "The problem is not to portray works of literature in the context of their times but rather to bring the age that recognizes them—which is our age—to representation in the age in which they originated. Literature thereby becomes an organon of history" (III 290).

The analogy between social and cultural images at large and literature as an organon points to the source of this dialectical conception: the early romantics' philosophy of reflection.[63] The process of reflection "unfolds" the forms, "intensifying" the reflection already latent in them. This can be understood from two sides: later stages of reflection already lie preformed in earlier stages; yet the later stages, in which

---

[63] See Chapter 2. In a note from his later work on the "Arcades" project, Benjamin drew the connection explicitly: "Historical 'understanding' is to be conceived fundamentally as an afterlife [*Nachleben*] of that which is understood; and so that which was recognized in analyzing the 'afterlife of works', their 'fame', is to be considered the basis for history as such" (V 574–575).

latent qualities have become explicit, possess "a higher degree of actuality" and "concretion." The true priority, in other words, lies with the later stages. In the "Arcades" notes, Benjamin now translated these early romantic conceptions so as to stress discrete constellations of past and present moments rather than the continuum of reflection. That enabled him to avoid the ideological shoals of two romantic prejudices he had long been steering away from: romantic vitalism of Klages's variety, which saw all development beyond "original" unity as degeneration; and romantic idealism, which mystified the "total" process of historical development.

Benjamin found the surest counter to both in what he now began to call the dialectical image. The formulations one finds in the early "Arcades" notes are still tentative; only in the later manuscripts does the idea take on sharp contours.[64] But its two essential features were already clear to him. He referred to the first as the time differential inherent in the dialectical image (V 1038). A dialectical image is one that results from the reciprocal relationship between two discrete historical moments. The second feature concerns its fleetingness. Since the dialectical image arises from the configuration of two discrete yet shifting historical moments, it is a "*rapid* image" (V 1034). It is not eternally available, for it disappears once the moment of configuration passes by. The measure of time inherent in it is an emphatic *now*—the "now of recognizability [*Jetzt der Erkennbarkeit*]" (V 1038). This emphatic conception of the present is the second defining feature of the dialectical image. The now that arises from the constellation of past and present represents "the innermost image of what has been" (V 1035). Benjamin characterized his idea of perception as a pathos of nearness; one might well think of his view of historical knowledge as a pathos of simultaneity. But it is simultaneity that produces an "explosion" in the present (V 1032), an explosion that Benjamin explicitly linked to political action: "The dialectical interpenetration and making-present of past contexts is the test of the truth of present action" (V 1026–1027). In this sense, the dialectical image represents "dialectics at a standstill" (V 1035). It loads time into itself until the energies generated by the dialectic of recognition produce an irruption of discontinuity. This conception of time set Benjamin off from vitalism, idealism, and historicism alike.

Along with this conception of historical images, Benjamin developed a theory of awakening to counter Aragon's and Klages's cult of dreaming. That which we normally take to be the waking world—here Benjamin could agree with them—is permeated through and through by

---

[64] For a discussion, see Chapter 7, Section 2.

dream consciousness and dream images. Like the dialectical image, the idea of awakening from dreams served as a model for a relationship between past and present that breaks the hold of mythic consciousness:

> Dialectical structure of awakening: remembering and awakening are most intimately related. Awakening, namely, is the dialectical, Copernican turning of remembrance. It is an eminently composed reversal of the world of the dreamer into the world of the waking. . . . The new, dialectical historical method instructs us to work through that which has been with the rapidity and intensity of dreaming in order to experience the present as the waking world to which every dream ultimately refers (V 1058)

This passage constructs parallels between dreaming and awakening, on the one hand, and past and present, on the other. In Benjamin's conception of historical images, moments in the past have an indwelling telos that unfolds in the present; so too, dreams have a telos that unfolds only in awakening. That yields a theory of *historical* awakening: the historian works through the past with the intensity of dream consciousness in order to experience the present as the waking world to which the dreaming past secretly refers. Benjamin calls the result a reversal (*Umschlag*). The moment of awakening represents a break with dream consciousness, and so the present too must understand how to bring about a break with the past. A "genuine release from an era has the structure of awakening . . . from the realm of dreams" (V 1058).

The problem is that Benjamin's accounts of this structure of awakening include two very different moments. At times the idea of a dialectical reversal serves to refute the notion of historical continuity. "Awakening from a dream is the compelling, drastic experience that refutes the coziness of 'becoming' and exposes what seems to be 'development' as a dialectical reversal" (V 1006). He elaborates the point with a striking image of the tension between two rhythms in silent film:

> On the contemporary rhythm that, indeed, determines this work: very characteristic for the cinema is the counterplay between the thoroughly jarring [*stoßweise*] rhythm of the sequence of images, which satisfies this generation's deepest need to see the "flow" of "development" disavowed, and the gliding music. To drive "development" completely out of the image of history . . . is also the tendency of this work. (V 1013–1014)

Benjamin describes the apparent continuity in historical development as an illusion that conceals real discontinuities, just as the flowing musical accompaniment creates the illusion of continuity in a silent film, which has actually been constructed as a montage of discrete images.[65] As with the romantic gaze into the distance, the illusion is not, in the first instance, a product of ideology; it arises directly out of the sensory experience of a technical and social process. The jarring rhythm of such visual images provides an example of the kind of visual perception that befalls or even lunges at the beholder (*stießt ihm zu*).[66] It violates perceptual distance and shakes the viewer out of the narcotic slumber induced by the gliding music of historical continuity.

Yet in other notes Benjamin seems to contravene the idea of a radical discontinuity between dreaming and awakening. Instead, he depicts them as the poles of a continuum: "One of the tacit presuppositions of psychoanalysis is that the posing of waking and sleep as contraries has no validity for the empirical forms of consciousness . . . but rather gives way to [the idea of] an endless variety of states of consciousness, all of which are determined by the gradations of waking in all mental and bodily centers" (V 1012).[67] Dreaming and waking, conscious and unconscious states do not merely interpenetrate, as psychoanalysis had shown. The "fluctuating state of a consciousness that is always split up and distributed at various levels between waking and sleep" eludes classification in terms of any simple dichotomy. Dreaming, for instance, would represent a specific mode of contact between conscious and unconscious wishes rather than the opposite of waking. The idea was eminently surrealist; the surrealists cultivated precisely that variety of states of contact between conscious and unconscious— dreaming, trances, automatic writing, love, intoxication—to the point where the threshold between them was worn away "as if by the steps of multitudinous images flooding back and forth" (II 296). Something of the sort would be necessary if Benjamin wished to insist that awakening is the telos, the indwelling tendency, of dreaming. "In the context of the dream we seek a teleological moment. This moment is that of waiting. The dream waits secretly for the awakening, the sleeper gives himself over to death only until countermand, waiting for the second in which he frees himself, with cunning, from its clutches" (V 1024). The interpretation of dreams cannot be a one-way street: the waking world may provide the key to the significance of dreams, but dreams give us pointers to significant configurations in the waking world that would otherwise go unrecognized.

Benjamin thus alternated between two images of the relationship

---

[65] The sequence of images here would be the montage of sequences from constantly shifting camera positions rather than the optical blending of individual frames into a moving image.

[66] See the discussion of the word *zustoßen* in n. 60.

[67] That Benjamin accepted this idea is indicated by his subsequent remark that it is to be "transposed from the individual to the collective" (V 1012).

between past and present, dreaming and awakening. In one, he stressed their radical discontinuity; with the other, he insisted that they are inextricably entwined. The present may be the waking world that supplies the perspective from which images of the past must be constructed. But the reverse is no less true: we cannot hope to make the present intelligible without bringing the past into it. Benjamin was aware of that. "One can speak of two directions in this work," he noted. "One proceeds from the past into the present, portraying the arcades, etc., as forerunners, and one moves from the present into the past, in order to allow the revolutionary completion [*Vollendung*] of these 'forerunners' to explode in the present" (V 1032). Paradoxically, the present awakening—a *break* with the dreaming past—goes hand in hand with interpreting, that thickening of the mutual *interconnections* between dreaming and awakening, or past and present. The paradox was already inherent in the image of awakening in the early romantics' philosophy of reflection. As Benjamin reconstructed their concept of criticism, the completion and the destruction of the work were inextricably bound together. His own conceptions of the dialectical image and of awakening now transposed that antinomy into explicitly historical terms. The early romantics themselves had stressed the continuum of reflection; in the *Elective Affinities* essay and the *Trauerspiel* study, Benjamin had articulated the neglected moment of discontinuity. Now, in the theoretical armature being developed for the "Arcades" project, the tension between the liquidationist and preservative moments in his thinking began to exert its full force.

Chapter Six

Benjamin and Proust:
Remembering

1. Benjamin's "Image of Proust"

In the opening words of his 1929 essay "The Image of Proust," Benjamin ascribed to Proust's work a list of qualities he might well have wished for his own: "the absorption of a mystic, the art of a prose writer, the verve of a satirist, the erudition of a scholar, and the partiality of a monomaniac" (I 310). The comment strikes a delicate balance between pathos and irony; and, in fact, the entire essay enacts this subtle play of identification and distance. Benjamin's encounter with Proust's works was a formative influence in every way as important as his critical appropriation of surrealist impulses. There is abundant evidence of their affinities. Together with Franz Hessel, Benjamin translated three volumes of *A la recherche du temps perdu* into German during the late 1920s. He complained at the time of suffering from "an inner poisoning" produced by so extensive and intimate an encounter with a body of work whose intentions were closely related to his own (B 431).[1] Indeed, the theme of memory came to play a central role in Benjamin's work in the 1930s, taking a place alongside the conceptions of phantasmagoria and *Urgeschichte* that developed from his critique of surrealism. That was true, first of all, for his way of thinking about the

---

[1] Adorno later reported that Benjamin "wanted not to read a single line more of Proust than he had to translate, for otherwise he would slide into an addictive dependence that would hinder . . . his own production" (cited at II 1047). Peter Szondi sets these remarks in the proper light by pointing out the differences in their "search for lost time" that become clear in the texts of *Berlin Childhood around 1900*. What Benjamin actually feared was that "in his fascination with a work only apparently similar to his own, he risked becoming alienated from his innermost intention" ("Hope in the Past: On Walter Benjamin," 496). Nevertheless, Benjamin articulated his distinctive conceptions of time and memory through an immanent critique of Proust.

transformation of perception and experience. The phenomenology of perceptual distance first elaborated in the early "Arcades" notes was gradually supplemented by the idea of a dissociation of modern memory. The consequences for Benjamin's theory of criticism were equally important, for he increasingly drew on the doctrine of involuntary memory to develop the temporal inflection of his idea of dialectical images. But Benjamin's encounter with Proust was more than a matter of identification, and he by no means simply borrowed doctrines he found preformulated in Proust's work. Rather, his approach to Proust was guided by the long-term critical strategies underlying his intellectual project, strategies we have seen at work in his encounters with baroque allegory and surrealism. The immanent critique of romanticism begun in the dissertation had long since developed beyond its initial formulation. Yet the coordinates it established and the issues it highlighted continued to guide his critical project.

Benjamin himself characterized his 1929 essay on Proust as a complement to the piece on surrealism, which he had published shortly before (B 496). Both dealt with what he described as an "irresistibly growing discrepancy between literature and life," but they approached the problem from opposite directions. The surrealists were attempting to "shut off poetry, like all the most intensive forces of the times." They took the break with the traditions of autonomous art to be an accomplished and irreversible fact; their response was "to explode the sphere of poetry" by releasing its energies into "life" and practice. Proust, however, had still held fast to the attempt to produce a literary work: "The outstanding literary achievement of our time is assigned a place in the heart of the impossible . . . which marks this great realization of a 'lifework' as the last for a long time. The image of Proust is the highest physiognomic expression the irresistibly growing discrepancy between literature and life could assume. That is the lesson that justifies the attempt to evoke this image" (II 310–311). Proust's procedure might be called conservative by contrast with that of the surrealists. For what Benjamin emphasized was not so much the discrepancy between the two spheres as Proust's precarious attempt to hold the center. Benjamin suggested his own distance from the idea of a lifework by setting the term off in inverted commas. Proust had succeeded in fulfilling his synthetic ambitions—but only just. For Benjamin, this precarious success—"the last for a long time"—provided an object lesson in the growing difficulties involved. Like the surrealists, therefore, Proust had ended by "exploding" the traditional forms of expression. But he did so from within them, by holding to narrative form and demonstrating the extraordinary exertions necessary if literature were to achieve coherence under the new conditions of experience.

An essential part of Benjamin's interest in Proust's work was thus its symptomatic value. His diagnostic method, in turn, was shaped by the early romantics' theory of the novel. What Friedrich Schlegel had called romantic poetry was marked by a certain way of reflecting, combining, and dissolving the classical genres. To Benjamin, that was one of the telling features of Proust's work. "It has rightly been said," he observed, "that all great works of literature found a genre or dissolve one," and Proust's *A la recherche du temps perdu* was "fiction, memoir, and commentary in *one*" (II 310). The remark was actually a self-citation, an allusion to the even stronger claim he had made in the prologue to the *Trauerspiel* study: "Precisely the significant works . . . fall outside the limits of genre. A major work will either establish a genre or abolish it [*hebt sie auf*], and a perfect work will do both at once" (I 225). Benjamin might have had difficulty in naming such a perfect work in 1924; the idea was an abstract locus defined by the premises of the romantic theory of genre. The exceptional status he now claimed for Proust's work, long before its critical acceptance was secure, thus rested on more than a personal affinity. It was grounded in an understanding of literary form derived from the philosophy of reflection in Schlegel and Novalis. The romantic theory of forms provided a framework of expectations that made him sure of Proust's symptomatic significance.

Benjamin's reading of Proust was also guided by the early romantics' shift of attention from the reflecting subject to the medium of reflection. He insisted that Proust's texts, like those of the symbolist poets, dissolved the individual poetic voice and the self into the structures of language. The contemporary French emphasis on Proust's virtues as a psychologist was misguided, he argued (B 486): "The important thing for the remembering author is not what he experienced but the weaving of his memory. . . . Only the *actus purus* of recollection itself constitutes the unity of the text—not the person of the author, much less the plot. One may even say that the intermittences of author and plot are only the reverse of the continuum of remembering, the pattern on the back side of the tapestry" (II 311–312). Memory was "not the source but the muse" for Proust's work (III 194).[2] At times, Benjamin came close to reading him as a forerunner of deconstructive literary crit-

---

[2] This comment (which also dates to 1929) was actually made about the "anamnestic intoxication" of Franz Hessel's flaneur. In Hessel's case, however, Benjamin stressed that the anamnesis was both autobiographical and impersonal: "It leads down . . . into a past that can be all the more captivating to the extent that it is *not only* the author's own, private past. . . . The city, as a mnemonic device of the solitary stroller, calls up more than his childhood and youth, more than its own history" (III 194, emphases added).

icism.[3] "Proust was insatiable when it came to emptying that dummy, the ego [das Ich], in order to keep garnering . . . that which satisfied his curiosity—no, assuaged his homesickness: the image" (II 314). The self was an "intermittence," an incidental by-product of the form-giving impulse, not a unifying force that stood behind the work. The dismantling of the self was also a major theme in Benjamin's concurrent examination of surrealism. There were thus actually two schemas for the "loosening of individuality" in his work. One was the dissolving of subjectivity into the structures of literary form he had explored in the dissertation, an idea characteristic of certain forms of philosophical idealism; the other was the dissolution of the self in the experience of intoxication as conceived by the various forms of vitalism and Lebensphilosophie. Benjamin found that Proust's work demonstrated the virtues and dangers of both in an exemplary fashion.

Finally, the problematic nature of the romantic legacy also showed itself in Proust's work, particularly in his aestheticism. In his essay on the surrealists, Benjamin defined the crucial issues facing them in terms of ambiguities already inherent in aestheticism. He sharply criticized their weakness for the narcissistic pleasures of revolt for revolt's sake, but he was equally concerned to see that they redeem the ecstatic moment in aestheticism. Proust presented the ambiguities of aestheticism from another side, however, for unlike the surrealists he made not the slightest pretense of rebelling against the social milieu in which it was most at home. Benjamin flatly stated that "the conditions underlying his work were unhealthy to an extreme degree" (II 310–311). The young Proust was an "insignificant snob, a frivolous, played-out salon lion" whose complicity with the circles in which he moved seemed complete. He "did not tire of the training that moving in aristocratic circles required. Assiduously and without having to force himself much, he made himself pliant, becoming impenetrable and resourceful, submissive and difficult." Eventually, "this mystification and ceremoniousness became so much a part of him" that he seemed to have taken on the features of his environment like a chameleon (II 314, 316). While conceding all this, Benjamin nevertheless insisted that Proust's works contained a moment of subversive social criticism. His was "not a model life in every respect, but everything about it is exemplary" (II

[3] That is how Benjamin's reading of Proust is construed by Carol Jacobs in *The Dissimulating Harmony: The Image of Interpretation in Nietzsche, Rilke, Artaud, and Benjamin*. But see Wohlfarth's intricate and convincing refutation of Jacobs' reading, "Walter Benjamin's Image of Interpretation." The problem involves not only Proust but the larger issue of Benjamin's affinities with poststructuralism, which derive from his reading of the early romantics' philosophy of reflection. I agree with Wohlfarth's contention that Benjamin restates "the classic Western dream about the origin and goal of language and history" (73).

311). What was this productive discrepancy between Proust's life and work?[4]

Benjamin found a concealed sociological theme in *A la recherche du temps perdu*. Proust, he claimed, had unmasked the upper bourgeoisie by constructing "the entire inner structure of high society as a physiology of chatter. In the treasury of its prejudices and maxims there is not one that is not annihilated by a dangerous comic element. . . . The pretensions of the bourgeoisie are shattered by laughter. Their flight and reassimilation by the aristocracy is the sociological theme of the work" (II 315–316). The ideological point of the upper bourgeoisie's fawning assimilation to the aristocracy, for Benjamin, was to mystify the bases of its power in the sphere of production. Proust portrayed the "upper ten thousand" as

> a clan of criminals . . . the Camorra of consumers. It excludes from its world everything that has a part in production. . . . Proust's analysis of snobbery, which is far more important than his apotheosis of art, represents the high point of his social criticism. For the posture of the snob is nothing but the consequential, organized, hardened view of life from the chemically pure standpoint of the consumer. . . . Proust portrays a class dedicated in all points to camouflaging its material basis, and therefore attached to a feudalism whose lack of intrinsic economic significance makes it all the more serviceable as a mask for the upper bourgeoisie. (II 319)

The argument hinges on its claim about Proust's "analysis of snobbery." On the one hand, Benjamin identified snobbery as an exquisitely refined version of consumption, enabling him to point out that "the pure consumer is the pure exploiter" who, nevertheless, escapes appearing as such because his ties to production remain hidden. On the other hand, snobbery was intimately connected with Proust's "apotheosis of art" as well. Aestheticism in the broadest sense is also a form of consumption, a standpoint from which the world appears as a palette of delectable pleasures, where the only standards are those of taste. In the Proust essay, Benjamin came very close to explaining aestheticism functionally, as a form of class ideology.

---

[4] Benjamin had already discussed the problem of relating life and work in his essay on Goethe's *Elective Affinities*. "The only rational connection between the creator and the work," he argued, "consists in the testimony that the latter gives about the former" (I 155); that is, the work itself constitutes an irreducible source for understanding the life, rather than vice versa. In practice, however, his references to a work's "intentions" are often ambiguous. He frequently refers to Proust without making it clear whether the author, the narrator, or the work is at issue. One thing is certain: Benjamin always firmly rejected the notion that the author's opinions about his or her works provide a definitive standard of interpretation.

But what was Proust's own position? Benjamin wanted to have it both ways. He granted that Proust had offered an apotheosis of art, but this—so Benjamin claimed—was far less important than his analysis of snobbery. Yet the distinction was difficult to maintain, since he was also arguing that snobbery and aestheticism were intimately connected. One way of escaping the dilemma would have been to concede that Proust, too, had been blinded by class ideology. At one point, Benjamin did just that: "This disillusioned, merciless demystifier of the ego, love, and morality—for that is how Proust wished to see himself—makes his entire, boundless art into a veil for this one, vitally important mystery of his class: its economic aspect" (II 319). He even ventured to interpret Proust's homosexuality as a token of the same mystifying impulse to banish all traces of the "productive forces of nature." Not only did Benjamin concede Proust's complicity with his milieu, he went out of his way to stress that Proust had cultivated the vices of flattery and servility to an almost "theological" degree. In another attempt to solve the problem, he distinguished between Proust's opinions and the unintended effects of his art: in his comic debunking it was not Proust who spoke but "the hardness of his works, the intransigence of the man who is ahead of his class" (II 1067).[5] The distinction may have been valid in principle, but it hardly resolved the dilemma. For it was precisely the inherent aestheticism of Proust's works that was at issue, not their author's opinions.

Yet Benjamin was ultimately unwilling to surrender Proust to the forces of transfiguration. What was the moment in his aestheticism that Benjamin was at pains to redeem? For the answer, we must look beyond the 1929 essay. In a brief note on Proust written in July 1932, Benjamin addressed the issue of Proust's hedonism. Proust's real aim, he now claimed, was to vindicate the rights of "enjoyment" (*Genuß*). That meant both the rights of "all" to pleasure—including "the poor and disinherited in enjoyment"—and the right to experience pleasure "in every point and in everything for which it can be vindicated." And the issue of hedonism was not to be separated from Proust's analysis of society. In fact, it was at the heart of his social criticism: "The unconditional intention of redeeming enjoyment . . . is a passion of Proust's

---

[5] Unfortunately, the English translation of the text omits the word "not," entirely distorting the sense of the passage—the contrast between Proust and the hardness of his works (*Illuminations*, 210). In any case, it is interesting to note that Benjamin toned down this passage considerably when he revised the manuscript in 1934. In 1929 he had spoken of Proust's hardness and intransigence; "what he accomplishes, he accomplishes as [the] master" of his class (II 1067). The revised wording is far more restrained, and thus less emphatic about Proust's social insight: "He is only ahead of his class. What it lives already begins to become intelligible in him" (II 319).

that goes far deeper . . . than his disillusioning analyses. Thus, too, his particular fixation on snobbery, in which he wants to get hold of that part of it in which genuine enjoyment lies. Of course, to him the members of high society seem least of all capable of salvaging that treasure" (II 1064–1065). Benjamin thereby reversed his judgment on the significance of Proust's "disillusioning analyses" of high society and even of snobbery. Snobbery now appeared as the refuge—however imperfect—of a legitimate claim to pleasure, not as the precious, mystifying device of a devious elite. The essentially functional analysis of snobbery put forward in 1929 now gave way to an acknowledgment of the valid moment in aestheticism—a moment that Proust, he suggested, had also sought to justify. In fact, Benjamin had indeed spoken of Proust's "blind, senseless, frenzied quest for happiness" in the 1929 essay, but without connecting it to the sociological themes of his work (II 312).

Could it be that Proust's version of the quest for happiness itself had two sides—one that led to the "satanic enchantment" (II 319) of pure consumption and formed the basis for Benjamin's negative verdict and another that vindicated a legitimate form of fulfillment? Proust's image of happiness was inseparable from his doctrine of memory. For him, happiness could only lie in somehow recapturing the past. To explain Benjamin's dilemma about Proust's aestheticism, therefore, we must explore his critical reconstruction of Proust's doctrine of memory.

2. Involuntary Memory

The sociological theme of Proust's work occupied only the central section of three in "The Image of Proust." Its dominant theme, the concern of its opening and closing movements, was Proust's doctine of involuntary remembering, *mémoire involontaire*. The subject of *A la recherche du temps perdu*, Benjamin insisted, was not the narrator's life "as it really was," nor even as he remembered it, but rather "the weaving of memory" itself. Memory is indeed the redeeming experience in Proust's novel; it enables the narrator to overcome dissipation and disillusionment, to recapture the past and, in the end, to conceive the vocation of writing the work that lies in the reader's hands. The hallmark of Proust's involuntary remembering is the fleeting correspondence through which a present sensation evokes an earlier, lost experience. The adult narrator's chance encounter with the taste of a madeleine conjures up the entire world of his childhood in Combray, which suddenly seems to blossom forth from the cup of tea into which it was dipped. The novel threads it way through a sequence of such experiences; each is marked by a moment of bliss, a sensual pleasure that betokens its hidden significance.

Benjamin underscored the distinctive nature of this experience of memory by rendering the term with an unconventional equivalent in German—*unwillkürliches Eingedenken*. The term *Eingedenken* is a coinage; it suggests a kind of memory that involves both remembrance and mindfulness.[6] The compound formed by adding *unwillkürlich* (involuntary) combines this intent quality of remembrance with the unintentional moment of the involuntary. The result is that Benjamin's formulations have a paradoxical ring absent from the original French *mémoire involontaire* or its direct English equivalent, "involuntary memory." The term itself thus alerts us to differences between Benjamin's and Proust's doctrines of memory. Benjamin singled out four distinctive features of Proust's method of retrieving the past. First, involuntary recall takes place spontaneously. Its promptings escape the grasp of deliberate, purposive action, which is goal-bound—*zweckgebunden* or, stronger, *zweckverhaftet* (II 311). Instead, it demands a special kind of receptivity or attentiveness. Second, its occasions are often trivial. It attaches not to the memorable, exalted moments one normally heeds but rather to the most banal and fleeting of everyday experiences (II 312). The third aspect is the measure of time proper to involuntary recollections. Their elusive quality is also due to the fact that they appear unexpectedly as sudden, instantaneous flashes (II 320). Finally, the most potent manifestations of involuntary memory elude our deliberate grasp because they arise from a layer of preverbal, sensory experience: "No one who knows the particular tenacity with which memories are preserved in the sense of smell (but smells not at all in memory!) could call Proust's sensitivity to smells accidental" (II 323). Anchored as they are in the body, sensory and kinaesthetic memories may be amorphous; but for that very reason they retain a rich, vivid quality denied to the deliberate recall of discrete images.

"What was it that Proust sought so frenetically" in the promptings of involuntary memory (II 312)? Benjamin's answer was deceptively simple: happiness, a happiness that would relieve his desperate feelings of homesickness (II 314). For Proust, the image of happiness was indissolubly bound to those of childhood. "Proust, that aged child, allowed

---

[6] The word *Eingedenken* as such exists as neither noun nor verb in German. It plays on the words *gedenken* and *eingedenk*. *Gedenken* (verb or noun) means "thinking of" something or someone, often in a commemorative or memorial sense; *eingedenk* (a predicative adjective that governs the genitive case) means to remember something in the sense of "bearing it in mind."

himself to slump back, tired to the core, on the bosom of nature" (II 322). Involuntary memory had to be sensory and kinaesthetic if it was to retrieve preverbal experiences of childhood bliss. Proust's conceptions of time, memory, and happiness converge in this idea of restoring a lost state. What he sought, for Benjamin, was "the eternal 'once more', the eternal restoration of the original, the first happiness." Proust's vision of happiness was essentially "elegiac"—"one might also call it Eleatic" (II 313). The rhapsodic, sympathetic tone of Benjamin's response makes it easy to overhear the subtle but firm note with which he distanced himself in these words. For Benjamin, Proust's image of happiness was marked by the mythic compulsion to repeat. The fervent wish to recapture the past left him trapped in a charmed circle of eternal recurrence. Benjamin pointed this out by drawing on one of his most potent metaphors for enchantment: "Proust transforms existence into an enchanted forest [Bannwald] of memory."[7] The allusion to an Eleatic idea of happiness closed the circle by evoking the pre-Socratic idealism of Parmenides and his school. The Eleatics' doctrine was an extreme, archetypal version of philosophical idealism; they conceived of the world as a perpetually undifferentiated whole and dismissed change, in all its forms, as an illusion. This association of philosophical idealism with ensnarement in myth is a persistent figure of thought in Benjamin's works.

What Proust had made of involuntary memory was therefore unacceptable to Benjamin. Proust found the eternity he sought in a kind of timelessness—"fragments of existence withdrawn from time."[8] But Benjamin rejected timelessness in all its forms, whether the stabilized eternity of ideas, Klages's schauendes Bewußtsein, or historicism's faith in the timeless accessibility of all moments in the past.[9] Proust did not so much capture time as annihilate it, attempting to flee from the consequences of transience.[10] Nowhere, however, did Benjamin criticize this flight openly. Unwilling to surrender the image of Proust, he disarmed him from within instead. "There may be rudiments of a vestigial ide-

---

[7] Benjamin repeatedly used spell (Bann) and forest (Wald) imagery to evoke mythic phenomena. In the surrealism essay he spoke of a "charmed circle [Bannkreis] of intoxication" (II 297); and, as we have seen, the forest imagery runs back through the early "Arcades" notes and the "thicket of primeval history" in "Dreamkitsch" to the Elective Affinities essay.

[8] Proust, The Past Recaptured, 136.

[9] On various occasions, Benjamin contrasted his conception of time with all three: in "The Image of Proust" (1929) he singled out idealism; in "On Some Motifs in Baudelaire" (1939), it was Bergson's philosophy of the durée (I 637); and in "On the Concept of History" (1940), historicism provided his foil (I 694–695).

[10] Szondi, "Hope in the Past," 497, 499.

alism in Proust," he conceded, "but they are not what determine the significance of this work" (II 320). Instead, he let him down gently:

> There is, however, a dual will to happiness, a dialectic of happiness: a hymnic and an elegiac figure. The one is the unheard-of, the unprecedented, the peak of bliss; the other, the eternal "once again," the eternal restoration of the first, original happiness. (II 313)

Proust had seized on one essential moment of this dual will, but only together—not in isolation—could they produce a happiness free of the mythic compulsion to repeat. Happiness lay in a rhythmic counterplay (*Widerspiel*) of the two moments (II 320). Benjamin's emended doctrine of involuntary remembrance thus preserved the moment of eternity. But it was a different eternity than that intended by Proust, an eternity of "convoluted, not boundless, time." "An experienced event is finite, at least when confined in the single sphere of immediate experience [*des Erlebens*]; a remembered event is boundless, because it is only a key to all that came before and after it" (II 312). True eternity resulted not from lifting an event out of time but from tracing its entwinement with other events. That also distinguished it from the perpetual present of immediate, living experience (*Erlebnis*). Memory consisted neither in recalling discrete moments whose entire significance was given in the instant of their occurrence nor in freeing them from time. Rather, memory was "the ability to interpolate endlessly in what has been" (VI 476).

Benjamin's point can be understood if we keep in mind the way the significance of an event is often revealed by the things that happen subsequently. We have all made decisions that later turned out to have been loaded with unexpected consequences. There are various ways of explaining this process. One is to assume that the consequences were already latent in the choice, but that we failed to foresee them because the decision was guided by unconscious motives. In retrospect, however, subsequent events helped to show us what we "really" wanted (without knowing it) from the very beginning. Another account might emphasize exogenous factors that were decisive in shaping the course of events. The outcome was not at all what we really wanted at the time of the decision. Nonetheless, now that events have run their course, those factors have assigned it a new significance; in a sense, their meaning has been created retroactively. In the former case, the "true" significance of the decision was present all along, whereas in the latter it arose only in the course of events. But in both cases meaning emerges retrospectively, as a function of time and remembering. Moreover, the significance of past events may continue to change as long as the story goes on. New perspectives will continue to emerge from the vantage point of a constantly changing present moment. For a life (or a society) whose future has not been foreclosed, the past can never become a closed book.[11] It will always be subject to revision, in principle, from the standpoint of the present.

We can now begin to see why Benjamin insisted on a counterplay of moments in the dialectic of memory. The retrieval of the past is necessary, of course; that is the role played by recall or, as Benjamin referred to it, restoration. But the significance it has acquired is something new that arises in the moment of recognition. It is there for the first time— hence the element of the unheard-of, the unprecedented, which Benjamin called the hymnic moment. And that also helps to explain the significance of the peculiar variety of memory that Proust, and Benjamin following him, described as involuntary. The moments that must be recalled will tend to be those whose significance was still concealed when they occurred, so that we failed to pay deliberate attention to them.

The moment that is missing from Proust's restorative conception of memory, in other words, is the present moment. Terrified by transience, he sought to flee from "the incurable imperfection in the very essence of the present" (II 312). For Benjamin, however, the present constituted the indispensable point of reference, the vantage point from which the past first begins to achieve its true significance. Instead of declaring their differences openly, however, he attributed his own view to Proust: "Not reflection but making things present [*Vergegenwärtigung*] is Proust's procedure" (II 320). Like Proust, he described memory as the only force that provides a match for "the inexorable process of aging," but the reasons he gave were unmistakably his own: "His true interest is in the course of time in its most real form—its convoluted [*verschränkt*] form, which holds sway nowhere more undistortedly than in remembering, within, and aging, without. To pursue the counterplay of aging and remembering is to penetrate to the heart of Proust's world, to the universe of convolution [*Verschränkung*]. (II 320). For Proust, the process of aging is a catastrophe, for it inexorably increases our distance from an original state of bliss that is to be restored. For Benjamin, however, aging creates meaning by multiplying the "convolutions" of past and present, making fresh interpolations into the past possible. The counterplay of aging and remembering therefore represents an equivalent of the dual rhythm of happiness. "*A la recherche du temps perdu* is the incessant attempt to charge an entire life with the utmost presence of mind [*Geistesgegenwart*]." This kind of presence of mind has nothing to do with attempt-

---

[11] See the discussion in the final section of this chapter.

ing to live as fully as possible in the the pure, immediate present. The mindfulness Benjamin meant was inextricably entwined with remembrance. On the one hand, it involves retrospectively charging the remembered past with significance. But the converse is equally important: involuntary remembering charges the present moment because alertness *activates* corresponding moments from the past.

The prototype of this dual rhythm of memory can be found in Benjamin's earlier work—in the concept of origin (*Ursprung*) formulated in the prologue to the *Trauerspiel* study.[12] There Benjamin had historicized the doctrine of ideas so as to stress that they are never fully present in any particular incarnation. The point, at the time, was to define an alternative to the idealist concept of the aesthetic symbol. Ideas do indeed "deploy themselves" in the phenomenal world in Benjamin's recasting of idealism. But they can be represented only indirectly, through a critical construction of what he called the prehistory and posthistory of a phenomenon (I 226). Insight into any particular "originary phenomenon" therefore depends on a dual insight into its rhythm: "It must be recognized on the one hand as a restoration, a reestablishing, yet precisely in this as something incomplete and unfinished, on the other. . . . The guidelines of philosophical contemplation are recorded in this dialectic inherent in the origin. It shows uniqueness [*Einmaligkeit*] and repetition to be mutually conditioned in all that is essential" (I 226). In the Proust essay, Benjamin invoked the same dual rhythm of uniqueness and repetition to revise the doctrine of involuntary memory. Now, however, he shifted his emphasis, defining memory images as constellations of past and present instead of stressing the "eternal constellations" of ideas.[13] But he was also shifting the locus of the process. The *Trauerspiel* prologue is a theory of knowledge; the task of representing ideas falls to the philosophical critic. The doctrine of memory in the Proust essay, however, is offered as a theory of experience. Memory images arise within the living process of history itself, whether autobiographical or collective; they therefore depend neither on literature nor on philosophical criticism. Therein lay a further reason why Benjamin rejected Proust's "apotheosis of art." The culmination of *A la recherche du temps perdu* comes with the narrator's decision to compose the novel; only art can hope to capture and stabilize the fleeting epiphanies of involuntary memory. Benjamin was suggesting that, though involuntary memory may be subject to historical variation, it does not ultimately depend on

---

[12] See the discussion in Chapter 3, Section 5.

[13] In Chapter 3 I argue that this historical conception better reflects Benjamin's own critical practice, even at the time of the *Trauerspiel* study. In effect, his conception of criticism was catching up with what he was really doing.

the survival of an autonomous aesthetic sphere. This distinction is important for an understanding of the tensions in his work in the 1930s. As long as it seemed plausible, he could sustain his belief that, at least in principle, a real, liberating potential was present within the course of history. When it began to lack plausibility, however, he was subject to the undertow—to which he refused to surrender, unless this is how one understands his suicide—of the lonely fear that "there is boundless hope—only not for us" (B 764).

A final difference between Benjamin and Proust arises from the fact that Benjamin's dialectic of memory addressed a different type of experience than that which Proust sought. It aimed at the redemption of lost and missed opportunities, of unrecognized, unacknowledged, and unfulfilled wishes. Benjamin was ultimately concerned with experiences of imperfection, which is why restoration alone would not do: "He is permeated with the insight that none of us has time to live the true dramas of the existence that is destined for us. That is what ages us. Nothing else. The wrinkles and creases in our faces are the inscriptions of the great passions, vices, and insights that called on us—but we, the masters, were not at home" (II 321). The "he" at the beginning of the passage refers to Proust. But clearly Benjamin was ascribing his own revision of Proust to Proust himself. A passage from the notes he made for the essay underscores the point. Proust was the first

> who was able to break open the secret drawer of "mood" and appropriate for himself what lay within: that disorderly heap that we ourselves, having faithfully mislaid it there, had forgotten and that now simply overwhelms the one who stands before it—as happens to a man at the sight of a drawer stuffed to the brim with useless, forgotten toys. This playing away [*Verspieltheit*] of true life, which only memory tells us of—that must be sought in Proust and made the pivotal point of reflection. (II 1057)

Memory throws open the overpowering sight of a forgotten, disorderly heap of moments at which true life has been missed. The imagery resonates with two decisive moments in Benjamin's earlier work. One is the historical vision implicit in baroque allegory, which piles ruin upon ruin in order to express the experience of the untimely, sorrowful, and unsuccessful. Behind the study of allegory, in turn, is the prologue to "The Life of Students" written in the first months of the war. In the face of the youth movement's collapse, Benjamin had professed loyalty to "the most endangered, most defamed and derided creations and thoughts"; they, more than anything else, embody the "immanent state of perfection" that lies "deeply embedded in every present." In recasting Proust's doctrine of involuntary memory, Benjamin was continuing to search for more resilient ways to keep faith with the intentions that had guided him ever since.

3. The Bridge between Memory and Dream

Readings of Benjamin's Proust essay have tended to focus almost exclusively on the doctrine of involuntary memory and the sociological theme he found in *A la recherche du temps perdu*. Interlaced with these issues, however, was a third concern with establishing a link between memory and dream images. The "bridge to the dream" as Benjamin called it, was the point to which "any synthetic interpretation of Proust must connect" (II 313).[14] Both memory and dreaming were crucial for the genesis of Benjamin's own theory of dialectical images. These two strands have often come unraveled in the minds of his readers, a tendency encouraged by the publication history of his texts. It once appeared that a long-term shift from dream to memory images had taken place in the course of his work during the 1930s: the 1935 exposé for the "Arcades" project is constructed around the concept of dreamlike phantasmagoria, whereas the 1940 "On the Concept of History" appeals exclusively to the idea of remembrance.[15] Yet the early notes for the "Arcades" project show that the two strands were inextricably entwined in Benjamin's thinking from the beginning. In the formula he used there, "awakening is the exemplary case of remembering . . . namely, the dialectical, Copernican turning of remembrance [*Eingedenken*]" (V 1057–1058). Just how did Benjamin go about constructing this bridge in the Proust essay?

Proust's work itself helped set the tone for his reflections. As Benjamin pointed out, the opening meditation on involuntary remembering in *A la recherche du temps perdu* begins "with a depiction of the room of one who is awakening [*Raum des Erwachenden*] (V 1012). The narrator, an insomniac tottering on the threshold between sleep and waking, finds himself buffeted by the "shifting and confused gusts of memory." Benjamin began his own meditation by dislodging commonsense associations through a series of plays on the ideas of dreaming and remembering. The first linkage was their involuntary character. Involuntary memory has nothing to do with deliberate recall, which is simply a

---

[14] The English translation in *Illuminations* dilutes this statement by rendering it in the negative: "No synthetic interpretation can disregard it" (*Illuminations,* 204).

[15] Adorno accused Benjamin of a tendency to psychologize the theory of dialectical images by modeling them on dream images (V 1129). His hostility to the surrealist elements in Benjamin's work helps explain the circumspection with which Benjamin invoked the theme after 1935.

special case of purposive action. Involuntary memory images retrieve experiences that remain impervious to voluntary recollection, never having entered consciousness in the first place. Dreams, too, are involuntarily recalled images whose content is not accessible (or perhaps, on a psychoanalytic reading, not permissible) to waking consciousness. Benjamin saw Proust's working method as a tacit acknowledgment of this connection: shutting himself in a darkened room in order to work by artificial light, "he ended by turning his days into nights" (II 311). Paradoxically, the presence of mind required to snatch the fleeting images of involuntary memory could best be cultivated by simulating the insomniac's bored, restless distraction.

The second arch of the bridge was anchored in the similarity of both dreaming and involuntary memory to forgetting. For "is not . . . Proust's *mémoire involontaire* much closer to forgetting than to what is usually called memory?" (II 311). The willfulness of this paradox quickly eases if we consider what Freudian miscues involve. "Absentmindedly," in moments of apparent forgetfulness, we betray things that often reveal more of ourselves than we could bring forth by trying. Dreaming too involves forgetting in a similar fashion: for hours we "forget" our daytime preoccupations; yet dreaming is also a deeper kind of remembering, for dream images represent complexes and conflicts that originate in past, forgotten experiences. When we wake up, we reconstruct our everyday circumstances by remembering where we left off the night before, but the "few fringes" of the "tapestry of lived existence that forgetting has woven in us" once again fall from our hands (II 311). "Forgetful" dreaming may be memory's richest resource.

Metaphorically, Benjamin bound memory-, dream-, and text-work together in the image of weaving. The Latin word for "text" (*textum*) means "something woven," and memory—not plot or personality—had issued the "strict weaving regulations" that guided Proust's work. Benjamin characterized dream and memory images as the woven ornaments of forgetting or as intricate, entangled arabesques. He captured the connection between all three in the image of a "Penelope-work of remembrance" (II 311). In Homer's *Odyssey*, Penelope is Odysseus' faithful wife who, while waiting for his return, holds an unwanted suitor at bay with the excuse of weaving a garment. To continue forestalling the suitor, each night she secretly undoes what she has woven during the day and begins reweaving it the following morning. Penelope's work is a thus a form of *Eingedenken*, an exercise in keeping faith with one who is absent. It enables her to ward off an ever-threatening catastrophe, the advances of the suitor, and to preserve a wish that still awaits fulfillment. Yet in one respect, Benjamin notes, the weaving of involuntary memory inverts the image of Penelope. For, as in dreams, "the day unravels what the *night* has woven" (emphasis added). Again and again, the pursuit of purposeful activity undoes the ornaments of spontaneous, involuntary remembering.

Suggestive as it is, this image nevertheless generates an unstated, unresolved puzzle. There is a peculiar impotence to Penelope's work; it is a Sisyphean task, condemned to futility, which can only be endlessly repeated. Why is she unable to take matters into her own hands? To speak in Benjamin's idiom, she seems to be ensnared in a mythic compulsion to repeat. In other words, do the implications of the Penelope image undercut the sense he seems to have intended?

The answer, I suggest, depends on appreciating the ambivalence in Benjamin's relationship to Proust, an ambivalence whose traces the essay tends to conceal. As long as day and night—dream consciousness and waking activity, forgetting and remembering—simply alternate, the task must indeed remain Sisyphean. Benjamin worked against the mythic futility implicit in Proustian memory in three ways. The first was to recast Proust's conception of memory so that it would not be a deluded attempt to restore a lost wholeness of meaning. As we have already seen, Benjamin did not simply adopt Proust's doctrine but developed it further through immanent critique. Arguing against Proust's fatalistic belief in "the incurable imperfection in the very essence of the present moment," he stressed the technique of *Vergegenwärtigung*, "making things present." But taken on its own, that solution was not without its pitfalls. Benjamin could not let the argument rest at the discovery of a "true art of memory," an esoteric doctrine that dedicated adepts (or critics) could master. For that would have exposed him to the very accusation he leveled at aestheticism—the charge of tending an elitist cult of genius, something entirely like Stefan George's "priestly doctrine of poetry" (II 623). The redemption of unfulfilled hopes would be reduced to a private show for the few.[16] His second line of response provides a possible answer to this unacceptable outcome: Benjamin attempted to identify the underlying causes of this dissociation of memory. He postulated that memory, like dreaming, is a historically mutable faculty rather than a permanent, natural given of human nature. The increasing atrophy of experience might therefore be traced to social change and this process, in turn, might be susceptible to control. "The inner concerns of the person do not have this issueless private character by nature," he suggested. Rather, the prob-

---

[16] Benjamin underscored the point in his 1939 essay "On Some Motifs in Baudelaire" with the ironic remark that Proust reveals the atrophy of experience precisely in the way he succeeds: "There is nothing more ingenious or more loyal than the way he nonchalantly and constantly strives to make the reader aware that 'redemption is my private show'" (I 643).

lem was the steadily increasing mutual exclusivity of voluntary and involuntary memory (I 610–611). The hypothesis that the dissociation of memory is rooted in social processes had unmistakably progressive bearings, and it became a prominent theme in Benjamin's essays of the 1930s. He used it to help ward off the possible conservative implications of his own doctrines, implications he would certainly have considered misunderstandings.[17]

There is, finally, a third possible line of response. The futility of the alternation is also due to Benjamin's own construction of a polar opposition between mythic restoration and hymnic liberation. Might it be possible to attenuate the tension between the polar forms of remembering? The charge of the polarity would be reduced if the restorative, "elegiac," "mythic" impulse itself turned out to have redeeming features. Such features might be found by reconsidering the perceptual faculty on which both dreaming and memory were based, in Benjamin's view—the ability to perceive and produce "similarities," or "correspondences." Beneath the playful paradoxes of forgetting and the suggestive imagery of weaving, he anchored the bridge between memory and dreams in what he called the mimetic ability.[18]

For Benjamin, the "heart of the Proustian world" could be found in the elusive, intangible resonance between a present moment and one from the past, a resonance that made it possible for memory to associate moments removed from one another in time. Here too Proust's working method provided an important clue—his "frenetic study, his passionate cult of resemblances" in gesture, posture, physiognomy, speech mannerisms, and so on. But the true signs of the "hegemony" of resemblances were to be found at a deeper layer: "The similarity of one thing with another which we rely on, which occupies us in the waking state, only plays on the deeper sort of similarity in the dream world, where whatever goes on emerges in a form that is never identical but similar: opaquely similar to itself [sich selber undurchschaubar ähnlich]" (II 314). The ability to perceive similarities is bound up with the ability to produce them, for that is what makes it possible to generate dream images. The form similarity assumes in dreaming and involuntary remembering is somehow deeper than its manifestations in

[17] That was the spirit of a reminder to himself he included in the later "Arcades" notes: "The pathos of this work: there are no eras of decay" (V 571), a reminder that must be balanced against the fact that he was entirely willing to speak of an atrophy of experience (I 611).

[18] The following discussion is informed by two fragmentary, private texts from 1933, the "Doctrine of the Similar" (II 204–210) and a variant, "On the Mimetic Ability" (II 210–213). Benjamin spoke of his doctrine of mimesis as a foundation stone for a theory of language, and that is how it has most often been read; but his conceptions of memory and dreaming were equally bound up with it.

waking consciousness. Where does this dimension of depth lead? It leads, first of all, back into childhood. As Benjamin stressed here and elsewhere, children at play constantly perceive and enact similarities of the most surprising sort. "A child plays not only sales clerk or teacher but windmill and railway as well" (II 205). Parallel to this ontogenetic plane runs a phylogenetic level. For Benjamin, the ability to perceive similarities derived from an essentially archaic form of consciousness. Baudelaire and the romantics had rooted correspondences in the perception of nature, but Proust was the first to bring them forth "in our lived lives" (II 320).[19]

Here too Benjamin left a telling clue in words that, for him, were always charged with the archaic: the experience of the world "in a state of similarity" is "rapturous" (rauschhaft). Like the rebuses of dream-kitsch, memory images take an ornamental form. They are entangled arabesques, and time itself assumes a convoluted form in involuntary remembering. The images of convolution, ornament, and arabesque are all variations on the underlying pattern of the labyrinth which, for Benjamin, was the paradigm of mythic spatial forms. The evocation of correspondences, in turn, explicitly refers to Baudelaire's "forest of symbols": "The pillars of nature's temple are alive/and sometimes yield perplexing messages;/forests of symbols between us and the shrine/remark our passage with accustomed eyes./. . . the sounds, the scents, the colors correspond."[20] This chain of association leads through the primeval forest imagery in Benjamin's work back to the same destination in mythic consciousness.[21] The entire complex of images helps to illuminate Benjamin's account of Proust's behavior in high-society circles. Proust put his talent for flattery and mimicry at the service of his curiosity. That was essential to his success in insinuating himself among aristocratic circles; at the same time, it was among the secrets of his work. "His passion for the vegetative cannot be taken seriously enough. Ortega y Gasset was the first to draw attention to the vegetative existence of Proust's characters, who are so firmly planted in their social habitat, bent toward the position of the sun of aristocratic favor . . . and impenetrably, inextricably entwined with one another in the thicket of their fate. It is these circles of life that give rise to the poet's method of mimicry" (II 317). The complicity of mimicry with this vegetative if not parasitic social environment seems clear. Yet, as culti-

[19] Or rather—to vary Benjamin's observation in his own spirit—he brought them out in the play of remembrance on those lives in the reflection of those who have lived them.
[20] Baudelaire, "Correspondences"; I cite from Richard Howard's translation of Les fleurs du mal, 15.
[21] In turn, all these associations would eventually run together in the complex image of the aura.

vated by Proust, the art of mimicry produced startling results. For his was not a servile mimicry that remained identical with the forces of that world but the subtle, ironic variation that results in devastating parody. "Mimic and critical behavior can no longer be separated here," as Benjamin put it in his notes for the essay (II 1050).[22]

It is difficult to define Benjamin's concept of similarity with any precision. He used its suggestive qualities in much the same way he used the conception of the aura, as a junction at which connections between apparently disparate cultural and social phenomena could be traced.[23] The concept's function in the Proust essay can be understood only if one keeps in mind that similarity involves resemblance rather than identity or strict homology. The distinction is important, for its implications lead in two rather different directions. On the one hand, the perception and production of similarities result in distortion. For instance, what happens in dreams is "opaque" or "inscrutable to itself" (*sich selber undurchschaubar*). So too, memory images—like the sensations and objects that bear them—may flash by without being recognized. They appear in a form that veils what lies within them, and therein lurks a hazard: the traces they preserve may go unnoticed and vanish irretrievably. In Proust's own words, the past is "hidden . . . in some material object (or the sensation that such an object arouses in us) but we have no suspicion which one it could be. It depends entirely on chance [*hasard*] whether we come upon that object before we die or whether we never encounter it."[24] It is undeniable that the element of distortion produced by similarities is at least partly responsible for this danger. Yet such distortion also has a redeeming feature. Since all experience must pass through the filter of similarity in dreaming and remembering, no recapturing of the past can ever really be a restoration.[25] Similarity ensures that the hymnic moment of memory and happiness will always get its due. The restorative wish is not so much a false kind of remembering as a delusion about the nature of memory.

In other words, both moments of the dual will can ultimately be

[22] In 1929 Benjamin still spoke of mimic rather than mimetic behavior, as he would in 1933. Nevertheless, the notes for the Proust essay are a source of Benjamin's reflections on mimesis as important as the 1916 text "On Language as Such and on Human Language."

[23] The ambivalences involved in both are analogous as well. Unlike the conception of aura, however, the doctrine of the similar took on a decidedly utopian cast in Benjamin's usage.

[24] Proust, *Swann's Way*, 34. Benjamin transcribed this passage in the "Arcades" notes (V 509), calling it Proust's classical formulation of involuntary memory. He later cited it in the 1939 essay "On Some Motifs in Baudelaire" (I 610). I use Proust's own words because Benjamin's translation embellishes them and steers their sense.

[25] Compare Borges's ingenious demonstration of this point in "Pierre Menard, Author of the *Quixote*," in *Labyrinths*.

traced back to similarity and the mimetic ability to perceive and produce it. Benjamin's own argument thus implies that the redeeming force of involuntary memory is inextricable from the archaic forms of consciousness he often characterizes as mythic. The forces that work to free memory from the perils of ensnarement in myth are not antithetical to it in any simple sense; rather, they draw on energies already present within the mythic form of consciousness. In effect, Benjamin was beginning to work with a more differentiated conception of myth. The result was to attenuate the tension of the polar opposition between myth and freedom constructed in his early thinking. We have seen the same tendency emerging from his encounter with surrealism. The counterposition of dreaming and waking gives way to a conception in which they serve as poles of a continuum. Benjamin by no means surrendered the idea that awakening represents a radical discontinuity with dreaming, but he also pointed to their reciprocity. The doctrine of involuntary remembering brings the temporal implications of this ambivalence into the open. In effect, Benjamin was beginning to think in terms of both a liquidation and a redemption of mythic consciousness. Yet here too his programmatic statements never quite acknowledged what he had actually begun doing.

4. The Doctrine of Memory in Benjamin's Later Work

The cluster of issues surrounding the doctrine of involuntary memory became central to Benjamin's work throughout the 1930s. Its further development can be traced along two branches, following his own distinction between the theory of knowledge and the theory of perception (VI 85). On the one hand, Benjamin wove the idea of involuntary memory into a more encompassing theory of experience. He began to work with a distinction between two fundamentally different kinds of experience—*Erlebnis*, "immediate," "living" experience, and *Erfahrung*, an accumulating stock of integrated, "lived" experience. The atrophy of modern experience could then be characterized as a shift from *Erfahrung* to *Erlebnis* and diagnosed in terms of an increasing dissociation of memory. Benjamin pursued these themes in his essayistic work; in this section I provide a brief, necessarily schematic assessment of the course he took.[26] The second branch of development concerns the

---

[26] An excellent, evocative synthesis of these themes is provided by Wohlfarth, "On the Messianic Structure of Benjamin's Last Reflections," 148–166. My ambitions here are more limited in scope but also more analytical. Wohlfarth treats texts from 1929 to 1940 as a simultaneous whole, reconstructing a coherent doctrine, whereas I separate various layers and raise questions about how they articulate.

theory of knowledge or critique. The doctrine of involuntary memory provided the groundwork for elaborating the conception of dialectical images. These reflections played only an indirect role in his published essays, but they formed a central axis in the theoretical armature of the "Arcades" project, as the manuscripts and the notes for "On the Concept of History" clearly show. I return to this theme in the closing reflections of Chapter 7.

Among Benjamin's manuscripts is a fragmentary note titled "From a Small Talk on Proust, Held on My Fortieth Birthday," that is, July 1932. A brief reformulation of the idea of involuntary memory,[27] it adds several new dimensions to those developed in 1929:

> On the knowledge of the *mémoire involontaire:* not only do its images come unsummoned, but it is a matter of images we never saw before remembering them. That is clearest for those images in which we . . . ourselves can be seen. . . . And precisely the most important images—those developed in the darkroom of the lived moment—are the ones we get to see. One could say that a little image [*Bildchen*], a photo of ourselves comes along with our deepest moments. . . . And that "entire life" that is often said to pass before the eyes of the dying, or of those hovering in danger of dying, is composed of precisely these little images. (II 1064)

Here the salient feature of involuntary memory is not so much spontaneous, unintentional recall as the nature of the images it makes accessible, "images we never saw before remembering them." Benjamin puts the point more explicitly in a later context: "Only what has not been consciously and explicitly experienced, what has not happened to the subject as a 'living experience' [*Erlebnis*], can become a component of the *mémoire involontaire*" (I 613).[28] On the contrary, the most important images are those that "develop" later, in the photochemical sense; and the darkroom where this process takes place is that of our subsequent life. The medium in which these images develop is experience in the cumulative, integrative sense that Benjamin termed *Erfahrung*. Finally, he names one moment that has a privileged status among those that call forth such earlier images—the moment of death, or the imminent threat of death. It is not only the entire life of the dying person that passes before his or her eyes, as an old belief would have it, but the true image of that life as it has never been seen before.

But why should it be impossible to experience the full meaning of a moment as it occurs? In other words, just what is actually responsible

[27] The second of its two paragraphs, in which he reconsiders the significance of Proust's hedonism, is discussed in Section 1.

[28] He made a note to the same effect in a list of corrections to the published text of the Proust essay (II 1066).

for the mutual exclusivity of *Erlebnis* and *Erfahrung?* Benjamin did not pose this question explicitly, but his explorations of memory imply several possible answers whose implications point in rather different directions. One complex of responses can be found in the explorations of his own memories in his *Berlin Childhood around 1900*, the first pieces of which likewise stem from 1932.[29] Peter Szondi has pointed out the wealth of images in which Benjamin sought out moments in his childhood that turned out to prefigure later experiences—"omens and traces of his later life." What Benjamin listened for were "the first notes of a future which has meanwhile become the past."[30] Such moments could not have been experienced in their fullness of meaning as they transpired, since that meaning accrued to them only when that which they prefigured later came to pass. In his autobiographical reflections, Benjamin played the role of Friedrich Schlegel's historian as a "prophet facing backward." As Benjamin himself had already put it in *One Way Street,* "memory, like ultraviolet rays, shows each of us the writing in the book of life that invisibly glossed the text as prophecy" (IV 142). But as Szondi stresses, it was not the already-completed past that so fascinated him. Rather, such closed arcs served as models in his search for a past "which is open, not completed," and which still "promises the future." Benjamin sought not to discover the omens of ineluctable fate but to fan the flames of "hope in the past."

But, on the whole, Benjamin's *Berlin Childhood* by no means presents images of childhood fulfillment. On the contrary, as Burkhardt Lindner has shown, it is most deeply marked by the experience of unfulfilled hopes—"helplessness, distortion, clumsiness, waiting, forgetting, and solitariness."[31] The key to these experiences is often a wish. The distortion of experience results, in many instances, from wishes that go unfulfilled or are simply forgotten. Benjamin captured this in a fairy tale image of his own: "The fairy who grants a wish actually exists for everyone. But only a few can recall the wish they made; and thus there are few who later recognize its fulfillment in their own lives" (IV 247). The ground for failure, here, as Benjamin described it, is that the

---

[29] Thematically, the fragment on Proust discussed above hangs together closely with the composition of the *Berlin Childhood*. We know that Benjamin came close to committing suicide in the summer of 1932, and it seems likely that these first brief texts correspond to those images that flash in review before the eyes of one who is threatened with death. Moreover, the *Berlin Childhood* consists of a series of short, separate, "discontinuous" texts—*Bildchen*—like those spoken of in the Proust fragment, and this image itself figures in its concluding piece, "The Little Hunchback" (IV 304). In this it differs markedly from both Proust's rambling reflections and the more loquacious, ruminating reflections of Benjamin's *Berlin Chronicle*, a study for the *Berlin Childhood*.

[30] Peter Szondi, "Hope in the Past," 498–499.

[31] Burkhardt Lindner, "Das 'Passagen-Werk', die 'Berliner Kindheit', und die Archäologie des 'Jüngstvergangenen'," 29.

memory of this wish does not get handed down to one's own later experience. The act of wishing itself remains imprisoned in the sphere of immediate experience (*Erlebnis*), so the awareness of fulfillment is precluded. But there is another side to the process—a side Benjamin did not speak of, although it is implied by his own reflections on *Erlebnis* and *Erfahrung*. Wishes are not necessarily recognized as such in the moment one makes them. On the contrary, often it is the experience of fulfillment itself that first makes it clear what one's wishes were to begin with. In this case it is not the forgetting of the wish that robs one of the experience of fulfillment but the failure to recognize it in the first place. In fact, both of these moments are bound together in Freud's conception of dreams as disguised fulfillments of repressed wishes. Psychoanalytic doctrine highlights the fact that neither the wish nor its fulfillment is necessarily transparent. To translate that insight back into Benjamin's terms, "wishing . . . belongs . . . to the realm of experience [*Erfahrung*]," and the "fulfilled wish is the crowning that is granted to experience" (I 636). In other words, a second explanation of the exclusivity of *Erlebnis* and *Erfahrung* can be found in the nature of wishing.

Benjamin suggested a further complex of answers in "The Storyteller" (1935).[32] Storytelling, as he depicts it, is a medium for exchanging and transmitting experiences, and he therefore traces the disappearance of the living figure of the storyteller to an increasing atrophy of experience itself (II 439). On close reading, three distinct moments in his explanation of this process emerge. The one that has most often attracted his readers' attention links the decay of experience to an underlying change in the structure of the labor process. Benjamin characterizes storytelling itself as a skilled craft, "in effect an artisanal form of communication": "the traces of the storyteller cling to the story the way the traces of the potter's hand cling to the clay vessel." It thrives in setting where the rhythms of work permit relaxed reception and therefore a process of assimilation into the storyteller's memory. He finds the classical locus of the storyteller in the artisanal milieu, in which resident master craftsmen—who know the lore of the local past—exchange experiences with traveling journeymen, who bring tales of faraway places. But factory work and street life foster a very different structure of experience, organized around the parrying of shocks, which favors a quick-wittedness that seals off that "process of assimilation in the depths" on which integrated memory and storytelling depend. Similarly, modern forms of communication broadcast dis-

---

[32] Many central points from "The Storyteller" were adopted in the 1939 essay "On Some Motifs in Baudelaire"; my exposition here sometimes cites formulations from the later piece.

crete items of information, but the demands of "freshness, brevity," and prompt consumption work against their assimilation. As a result, *Erlebnis* thrives at the expense of *Erfahrung*. In other words, the exclusivity of the two sorts of experience is socially constructed and historically variable, not a flaw built into the nature of things. Some forms of social organization facilitate a fusion of the two, whereas others encourage fission.

A second explanation in "The Storyteller" has to do with the logic of narrative form. Whether or not stories may be said to have a single, unified meaning, the very issue of authoritative meanings can be raised only once the end of the story is known. With a novel, for instance, it is only at the end that one can tell the adumbrations from the false leads; things fall into place in retrospect. And from an autobiographical perspective, the end of the story is the subject's own death. Benjamin makes the point as follows:

> "A man who dies at the age of thirty-five," said Moritz Heimann once, "is at every point of his life a man who dies at the age of thirty-five." Nothing is more dubious than this proposition—but for the sole reason that it chooses the wrong tense. A man who died at thirty-five—so runs the truth that was meant here—will appear *to remembrance* [*dem Eingedenken*] at every point in his life as a man who died at thirty-five. In other words, the statement that makes no sense for real life becomes indisputable for remembered life. (II 456)

Heimann's error might also be described in terms of the *Erlebnis*/*Erfahrung* distinction. There is only one fleeting moment at which the man who dies at thirty-five can possibly experience *all* his life as one that ends prematurely, the very instant of his death. It is in this sense that Benjamin notes that "death is the sanction of all the storyteller can tell" (II 450).[33]

But Benjamin does not use the occasion to lament a flaw in the structure of time that keeps ultimate meanings beyond our horizon. On the contrary, he points out that attitudes toward death are socially conditioned and historically variable. And he discerns a growing tendency in the nineteenth century to repress the consciousness of death. Dying was once a "public process" or at least an event that transpired in the spaces of everyday life. "There used to be no house, hardly a

---

[33] It should be remembered that this example presumes an autobiographical perspective; Benjamin was not making a general argument for closed, definitive narrative meaning. Indeed, he had argued against Horkheimer that it is precisely in the light of remembrance that the past always remains fundamentally open (V 588–589). Similarly, he found that the concentrated form of the story makes it perpetually capable of unfolding new meanings and of arousing astonishment and reflection (II 446).

room, in which someone had not once died. . . . Today people live in rooms that have never been touched by death, dry dwellers of eternity, and when their end approaches their heirs stow them away in sanatoria or hospitals" (II 449). To shy away from the face of death, as bourgeois society was doing, is to defraud oneself of the moment of experience in which its authority is grounded.

Finally, these reflections on the privacy of death point to the third explanation in "The Storyteller" for the dissociation of meaning, which has to do with the increasingly private nature of experience in nineteenth-century bourgeois society. The oral culture of storytelling is also a form of sociability; its resource is "experience that is passed from mouth to mouth." The telltale sign of its decline is the rise of the novel, a print medium intended for solitary consumption. "The novelist has secluded himself. The birth chamber of the novel is the solitary individual" (II 442–443). This literary process is not so much the cause of the problem as a symptom of a more general transformation, the "manifold isolation of the private individual."

> Where experience [*Erfahrung*] in the strict sense prevails, certain contents of the individual past combine with those of the collective past. Cults, with their ceremonies and festivals . . . carried out an amalgamation of these two materials of memory again and again. They stimulated remembrance [*Eingedenken*] at certain times and remained handles of memory throughout a lifetime. In this way, voluntary and involuntary memory lost their mutual exclusiveness. (I 611)

Here Benjamin links the mutual exclusiveness of voluntary and involuntary memory—the key to the atrophy of experience—to a bifurcation of individual and collective memory. Whereas nineteenth-century bourgeois society drove a wedge between them, other forms of social organization regularly bring them together. It is interesting that here Benjamin unabashedly invokes the archaic social forms of cult, ceremonial, and festival. Although that surely cannot be taken as a plea simply to reinstate them, it does accord with his conviction that the decay of experience cannot be countered with palliatives for the solitary individual. Rather, new structures of collective experience are required.

Broadly speaking, Benjamin's explanations for the mutual exclusivity of *Erlebnis* and *Erfahrung* fall into two groups. The first consists of those invariable factors that seem built into the structure of time, the logic of narrative form, or the nature of human wishing. If one heeds these, it becomes clear that despite his denials Benjamin indeed did respond sympathetically to Proust's despair over "the incurable imperfection in the very essence of the present moment." The second complex of explanations cites a variety of social factors in order to explain historical variations in the structure of experience. Of course, these two accounts do not necessarily contradict one another. One might imagine an argument that acknowledges both and points out that some forms of social organization do better than others at coping with the intractabilities of time, wishing, and memory. But that is not the tenor of Benjamin's account. Just as he failed to distinguish these two complexes of explanations, so he spoke as if all flaws in the structure of experience can be overcome. For instance, in the last passage cited above he did not simply suggest that the bifurcation of voluntary and involuntary memory could be eased; he made the much stronger claim that they would "lose" their mutual exclusivity. In a similar vein, he spoke of glimpsing the "true" image of the past, however fleetingly. Benjamin perceptively criticized abuses of the pathos of a lost wholeness of meaning. But he himself did not surrender that pathos entirely.

The two lines of argument did converge in one salient point, Benjamin's critique of Bergson's vitalist conception of experience. In his 1939 essay "On Some Motifs in Baudelaire," Benjamin returned once more to his argument that the extraordinary exertions involved in Proust's "synthetic" feat had symptomatic significance. This time, the polemical target was not idealism but what he considered to be the most distinguished exposition of a philosophy of *Erlebnis*.[34] Benjamin argues that the problem with the philosophy of the *durée* is Bergson's failure to undertake a "historical specification of memory" and experience (I 608). The objection means two distinct things. In the first place, Bergson's explanation ignores historical factors, which makes it a false diagnosis of the decay of modern memory. The real problem is not the absence of a will to "actualize" the *durée* but the social changes that undermine the structure of experience. But "historical specification" also refers to the temporal structure of memory itself. For Benjamin, genuine memory and experience are inherently time-laden or "historical"; both involve a certain kind of articulated time. Bergson's glorification of the *durée* is therefore also a false *characterization* of experience, "the quintessence of *Erlebnis* strutting around in the borrowed garments of *Erfahrung*" (I 643). The true contrast is not between the mechanical and the living but between the timeless and the historical: the perpetual present of the *durée*, bereft of the requisites of remembrance,

---

[34] Here, for the first time, he explicitly and unconditionally condemned Klages by locating him in a tradition that ended with him and with "Jung, who has made common cause with fascism" (I 608).

"precludes the possibility of bringing tradition into it [*die Tradition in sie einzubringen*]" (I 643).

The term *einbringen* is a spatial correlate of Benjamin's temporal term *Vergegenwärtigung*, "making things present." For him, there could be no question: there must be a meltdown of the past in the present. It is the image of the *present* that must be saved. Artificial attempts to prolong the life of archaic, auratic forms of consciousness would lead to deplorable consequences in any case. But making things present in Benjamin's sense presupposed a structure of experience that was still more or less intact, and there lay the practical crux of the antinomy.

Chapter Seven

The Antinomies of Tradition: Historical
Rhythms in Benjamin's Late Works

1. "Paris, Capital of the Nineteenth Century"

In 1934, Benjamin resumed work on the "Arcades" project he had put aside in 1929. He now expanded the planned article into a full-scale undertaking that became the master matrix for his work until his death in 1940. As his letters explain, he understood virtually all his major projects of the 1930s as pieces broken out of it. " 'Paris Arcades' . . . to tell the truth it is the theater of all my battles and all my ideas": these words, already addressed to Scholem in 1930, proved to have an unhappily prophetic value (B 506). The Benjamin who began gathering citations in the Bibliothèque Nationale was an exile who had lost his political theater of operations with the demise of the Weimar Republic. From now on, Paris would be both his new base of operations and an object of historical exploration.

With the "Arcades" project Benjamin shifted his focus from literary history and criticism to the larger field of social and cultural history. His models for understanding those larger processes drew on concepts derived from his literary studies, and one of the themes that continued to fascinate him was the effect of capitalist industry and urbanization on inherited cultural forms. But he also began to range more freely onto a broader terrain of social experience. He assembled his copious notes in bundles whose headings range from the material culture of the nineteenth century (arcades, fashion, iron construction, interiors, railroads, panoramas, photography, world exposition halls) to forms of experience (boredom, collecting, flanerie, prostitution, gambling), individual writers and artists (Baudelaire, Grandville, Fourier, Marx, Blanqui, Saint-Simon), and constructive principles (epistemological notes, critiques of historicism and the idea of progress, observations on dreaming and awakening) (V 81–82). The master matrix itself was never completed. Benjamin did, however, leave various guides to his maze of material. One is an intricate system of thirty-two different markings in various colors and shapes appended to many of the passages (V 1262–1277), a private system of cross-references whose purpose, it now appears, was to mine his material for purposes of writing the first Baudelaire essay (VII 872). The other guide is provided by two condensed exposés, composed in 1935 and 1939 (V 43–77). Neither of these is a full or definitive blueprint, not even for the time of its composition, but they do afford an overview of both the project's theoretical construction and Benjamin's plans for mobilizing the mass of material he was gathering.[1]

The project's ambitions are best conveyed by the new title assigned to it by these exposés: "Paris Arcades: A Dialectical Enchantment" now became "Paris, Capital of the Nineteenth Century." Benjamin sought to construct dialectical images of emergent capitalist modernity in what he considered to be its classical locus, Paris under the July monarchy and Second Empire. As we have seen in his encounter with surrealism and Proust, Benjamin's use of the term "image" (Bild) had nothing impressionistic about it. Dialectical images were to be analytical constructions, meant to lay bare both the regressive element and the utopian potential in modern culture. The constructive framework of the project rested on the unusual concept of historical illumination he had been developing. As it is usually understood, historical analysis refutes claims that phenomena are timeless, natural, or inevitable by demonstrating that they are historically conditioned and, in varying degrees, socially constructed. This originally romantic assumption underlay the work of the German Historical School in the nineteenth century, but it was also used by Marx in his critique of the "natural laws" of the capitalist economy. Benjamin, too, drew on it in proposing that dreams and memory have a history. He was, however, also convinced that blind faith in historical progress was making it impossible to perceive the historical regressions that take place beneath the dazzling appearance of change and progress. In a sense, therefore, he also inverted historical thinking, seeking to unearth the dominance of natural compulsions in the allegedly historical. The cutting edge of his view was its implicit reference to the rise of fascism and National Socialism. As Benjamin saw it, fascism was not an abrupt regression, a sudden relapse into barbarism; it had been prepared by the unrecognized return of archaic compulsions in the "advanced" culture of high cap-

---

[1] Buck-Morss makes an effective case for the multilayered, multivalent structure of the project throughout the 1930s in *Dialectics of Seeing*, 49–55.

italism in the nineteenth century. "The germ of today's barbarism already lies enfolded in it. . . . National Socialism casts a harsh light on the latter half of the century" (III 574).[2] World War I had done much the same, and so Benjamin's "Arcades" project can be seen as addressing a concern that had preoccupied him since the collapse of the youth movement: to show that mythic compulsions recur *in* modernity, progress, and instrumental rationality, not despite them—that they hold sway not only at the margins but at the very center, the "capital" of the century.

Benjamin's single most concise statement of this guiding idea was his declaration that "capitalism was a phenomenon of nature [*Naturerscheinung*] whereby Europe once again fell asleep and began dreaming—bringing a reactivation of mythic forces" (V 494). This formulation interweaves conceptual motifs and images from all periods of his work. As in his early writings, he described Europe as being subject to the hold of the mythic forces of a compulsion to repeat and a belief in fate, or the determining influence of objective powers. In the language of the *Trauerspiel* study, history had fallen back into nature. That was the point of the conception of *Urgeschichte* developed in the early "Arcades" notes. The reference to sleep and dreaming, motifs from his recasting of surrealism, points to his model for the delusionary transfiguration of appearances resulting from this regression. Finally, in this formulation he attributed the specifically modern form of regression to capitalism, a conviction he adopted in the years around 1930 and maintained throughout his late work. He agreed with Marx that the laws believed to govern capitalist society had taken on the appearance (*Erscheinung*) of natural phenomena (*Naturerscheinungen*). Or, as Lukács had put it in *History and Class Consciousness,* a book Benjamin knew and praised, cultural and historical phenomena appear as a "second nature" in capitalist society. Reification, to use Lukács' term, was that peculiar sort of illusion in which human relations are projected onto the objective sphere and accepted as natural and inevitable. Marx himself had spoken of the phantasmagoria of commodity fetishism, a term that struck a deep resonance with Benjamin's own idiom of mythos.

In fact, the phantasmagoria produced by historical regression appear in two closely related but crucially different forms in the "Arcades" project. One was captured in the idea of constructing an "*Urgeschichte* of the nineteenth century" which would show that archetypal forms had not only recurred but had taken on an appearance of novelty that made their hold all the more complete (V 579). Fashion provided the

---

[2] Benjamin's statement concerns the Second Empire in Germany, but he understood it to apply to the French Second Empire as well.

paradigm for this figure of thought in the early "Arcades" notes, and in the second version it was assigned an even more important role in the construction of the whole. With the accelerating pace of change being dictated by fashion, the demands of the commodity economy, and technology, the "archaic countenance" of things rapidly being made obsolete showed itself all the more quickly (V 576; see also I 1235–1236). When read with an eye schooled in the forms of baroque allegory, fashion and the commodity appeared as enthronements of the transitory and thus allegories of death. Modernity itself was a "petrified primordial landscape" (I 343).

But Benjamin's *Urgeschichte* of modernity was not only to have been a depiction of a hellish landscape, for there was a second dimension to his characterization of this historical relapse. In calling the images produced by the culture of high capitalism phantasmagoria, he had more in mind than the delusional reifications described by Marx and Lukács. He was interested in learning to decode and interpret what he called the expressive character of phantasmagoria as well (V 574). He contrasted his conception with the orthodox model of base and superstructure, and not only on the issue of the relative autonomy of culture:

> The question is this: if the base determines the superstructure in what might be called the material of thought and experience, but this determination is not simply a mirroring, then how—quite apart from the question of its originating causes—is it to be characterized? As its expression [*Ausdruck*]. The superstructure is the expression of the base . . . just as for the sleeper a full stomach is not mirrored but expressed by the dream content, although the stomach may causally "determine" that content. At first the collective expresses its conditions of life. Those conditions find their expression in dreaming and in awakening their interpretation. (V 495–496)

From the surrealists, Benjamin had learned that the products of conscious, purposive-rational activity could be read as hieroglyphs of unconscious, irrational projections. The teeming proliferation of images in nineteenth-century culture testified to an unleashing of uncontrolled, archaic impulses, but at the same time it provided clues to genuine, unfulfilled wishes and strivings. Phantasmagoria, like the manifest content of dreams, could be understood as rebuses and deciphered to reveal their latent content. If phantasmagoria could be read, then they could not be dismissed as nonsense or mere escapism. For they were also expressions of repressed wishes, and therefore keys to uncovering the nature of those wishes. They were delusions, but not pure delusions; they had both regressive and utopian moments. "Ambiguity," as Benjamin put it, "is the pictorial appearance [*bildliche*

Erscheinung] of the dialectic" (V 55). As political dream interpreters, historians immerse themselves in such ambiguity in order to separate truth from delusion.

The point of exploring phantasmagoria, therefore, was not to revel in the inspirations of the adept who thinks that life is a dream but to awaken from the nightmare that history had become in the nineteenth century. Jung celebrated the persistence of archaic consciousness, Klages despaired over the persistence of its suppression by the forces of spirit, and Aragon hailed the emergence of a modern mythology. Benjamin, working from surrealist and Proustian images, developed two models for breaking the hold of myth: awakening and remembering, which the "Arcades" notes translate into conceptions of the historical process. In the 1935 précis, he crowned the theory of phantasmagoria with a concept of awakening: "The utilization of dream elements in awakening is the textbook case of dialectical thinking. For this reason, dialectical thinking is the organ of historical awakening. Each epoch not only dreams the next but also, in dreaming, strives toward the moment of waking. It bears its end within itself and unfolds it—as Hegel already saw—with cunning" (V 59). A subversive moment lies in wait within the world of delusionary appearances, an idea Benjamin likened to an ambush: "The coming awakening stands like the Greeks' wooden horse in the Troy of the dream" (V 495). Awakening breaks with the state of dreaming; it therefore represents a moment of discontinuity. Yet, in order to awaken, one must search out the teleological elements *within* dream consciousness, those that strive toward "the coming awakening," and attack it from within its fortifications. Benjamin characterized the "Arcades" project itself as "an experiment in the technique of awakening" (V 490), and dialectical images were to be the organon of this process. Its temporal dimension was captured more directly in the language of remembrance. The dialectical image is not only a dream image but an involuntary memory image as well, transposed to the collective: "The dialectical image is to be defined as the involuntary remembering of a redeemed humanity" (I 1233). And as Benjamin conceived it, involuntary memory also bears a duality within it: whereas it retrieves a moment of the past, the emphasis is on the present and the "presence of mind" (*Geistesgegenwart*) that makes it possible. We might say that dialectical images are images that suddenly become "legible" when, at some later, corresponding point in time, their utopian meaning can be unfolded and their hold as phantasmagoria can be broken.

Benjamin's illustrations help to make this clear. The first four sections of the 1935 précis present four phantasmagoria: decorative architecture, exemplified by the "masking" of glass and iron construction in the arcades; the panoramas, those peculiar attempts to construct an interior space that creates the illusion of an exterior landscape with a perspective into the distance; the world expositions, whose halls were "the site of pilgrimages to the commodity fetish"; and the bourgeois interior, which was "not only the universe but also the etui of the private man." The arcades served as his paradigm of the entwinement of regressive and utopian moments in phantasmagoria and of the historical dialectic through which they become visible. As we have seen, in the early notes he read their ambiguous spatial form—simultaneously interior and exterior—as evidence of what Klages called dream consciousness. Yet that very ambiguity held a concealed, utopian dimension as well, for the streets in fact served as the living space of "the dreaming collective":

> Streets are the apartment [*Wohnung*] of the collective. The collective is a perpetually restless, perpetually turbulent being that lives through, experiences, recognizes, and thinks out as much between the walls of houses as individuals in the shelter of their four walls. For this collective, the gleaming enameled shop signs are a wall decoration as good as or better than an oil painting for the bourgeois, walls with their "Post No Bills!" are its writing desk, newsstands its libraries . . . benches its bedroom furnishings . . . and arched driveway tunnels . . . are long corridors, . . . access to the city's inner chambers. Among these chambers, the arcade was the parlor. Here more than anywhere else, the street can be recognized as the furnished, lived-in interior of the masses. (V 533)

The entire image might be a fata morgana that appeared to a flaneur—a bourgeois individual who also, though by choice, inhabits the street—in a hashish trance. Yet it suggests how forms of collective experience are latent within those of the private individual, almost as a parody of them. In the image of the street as a living space, the rigid distinction between the public and private in bourgeois society is lifted—for Benjamin, a utopian anticipation of transparency. In such images, regressive and utopian traits thus fluctuate like the two faces of a gestalt figure (V 526). It was no accident, he suggested, that Fourier had chosen the arcade as the architectural model for his phalansteries. For Fourier's utopia also had two faces: the image of a classless society that dispenses with compulsion and lives in harmony with nature, and the nightmarish vision of a perfectly meshed system of complementary passions, which was nothing less than "a machine made of people" (V 47).

What is more, the latent utopian potential of this phantasmagoria was emerging as the image became readable in Benjamin's own time. "The rapturous interpenetration of street and living space that takes place in nineteenth-century Paris—and especially in the experience of the flaneur—has prophetic value. For the new architecture makes this interpenetration into sober reality" (V 534). In the nineteenth century, glass and iron construction had been concealed in decorative forms and historicizing masks; in the arcades and the world exposition halls, it had been put at the service of commodity turnover; at best, it was confined to locations marked by transience, such as railway terminals, harbors, and warehouses. But now the modern movement in architecture was finally bringing construction itself into its own. Le Corbusier, the Bauhaus architects, and others applied its principles to living spaces, while left-wing constructivists associated it with revolutionary, self-organizing social forces; Benjamin himself read the ideal of transparency as a counter to the impenetrability of the aura. From the perspective of the present, one could see how "the development of the forces of production [had] freed the forms of design from art" in the course of the nineteenth century (V 59, 1236). Phantasmagoria from the past were being banished by a sober awakening in the present. And, in the process, a suppressed tradition was becoming visible.

In the two final sections of the 1935 exposé, Benjamin provided glimpses of the tentative beginnings of the process of awakening during the nineteenth century. The first of these stirrings took place in the medium of "high" literary culture. "Baudelaire, or the Streets of Paris" characterizes Baudelaire's poetry as an allegorical vision of the "deathly idyll" of Parisian modernity. *The Flowers of Evil* represents a form of experience that both participates in the phantasmagoric spectacle of flanerie and begins to transcend it by constructing allegorical images of the constellation of prehistory and modernity. Although undoubtedly at home "in the enemy camp" of bourgeois culture, Baudelaire provided evidence of "the secret dissatisfaction of his class with its own domination" (I 1161). The sixth section, entitled "Haussmann, or the Barricades," evokes a collective stirring to political action. It too presents a Janus-headed image of the Parisian streets: Haussmann had used the city itself as material on which to project the phantasmagoric vision of perspectives that draw the viewer into the distance; his practical purpose, however, was to make the building of barricades impossible. Benjamin presented the uprising of the Commune as a response to both these schemes, a tremor of awakening that ran through the Parisian working class whose historical calling was to abolish the bourgeois world of phantasmagoria.

The conjunction of these final two sections of the précis is important, for it expressed Benjamin's own hope that the venture of constructing dialectical images of the nineteenth century corresponded to an awakening in the realm of collective history. His point of reference was his own presence as an exile in the Paris of the 1930s: the conjunction between the gaze of the bourgeois allegorist and the stirrings of collective action might adumbrate a political possibility in his own time. If Benjamin had had no illusions about the immediate political efficacy of his work as a relatively successful critic in the Weimar Republic, then he was even less prone to them now. But he could hope that the preconditions for his success were the same as those of a revolutionary alternative to fascism; that is, the fact that dialectical images of the nineteenth century were becoming legible helped make it plausible to believe that there was still a real possibility of defeating the regressive forces of fascism. In the language of "On the Concept of History," failed movements for liberation in the past have a claim on the present. The present, in turn, possesses a weak messianic force with which it can redeem the past's unfulfilled hopes—a weak force because it can hope to redeem only the hopes of a specific generation, not those of the past as a whole (I 694). But the past's claim on the present in no way diminishes it, for in making good on those claims the present can catch its own image and thus redeem *itself*. The "hope in the past" that Benjamin had sought on the level of autobiography in *A Berlin Childhood around 1900* was now to be found in the realm of collective history. Yet Benjamin's image of Paris as "capital of the nineteenth century" itself had two faces: Paris was both the capital of revolution and the capital of phantasmagoria.[3] And his hope-against-hope shrank to a desperately small remnant after the signing of the Hitler-Stalin pact, which was certainly among the last possible stops on the way to catastrophe.

2. Dialectical Images

Benjamin's conception of dialectical images, which he spelled out in fragmentary form in the "Arcades" notes as well as "On the Concept of History," forms the junction through which the lines of his historical thinking run. In his theory of dialectical images, he sought a higher concretion than that afforded by the available conceptions of history. We can distinguish two aspects of the kind of concretion he had in mind. One concerns the particular way dialectical images are laden with time: Benjamin spoke of them as fleeting images, sudden constellations of past and present. The other is captured in the idea of phantasmagoria. He wanted to show how the perceived world is "sen-

---

[3] Ivernel, "Paris, Hauptstadt der Volksfront," 116–117.

sually 'transfigured' in its immediate presence," an undertaking that was guided by his assumption that historical truth lies somewhere within those delusionary appearances, in however distorted a form (V 61, 1256). These two dimensions of the dialectical image converge in Benjamin's attacks on what he referred to as historicism. Part of the difficulty in unraveling his theory results from the fact that he used the term to designate two related but distinct kinds of historicism. Most often, he meant the conception of historical methodology typically captured in Ranke's dictum that the historian's task is to depict the past "as it really was"; this view was the target of his reflections on the temporal structure of dialectical images. The second, however, was architectural historicism, the imitative and eclectic building style that had dominated the latter half of the nineteenth century: "This is the point from which the 'critique' of the nineteenth century is to begin. Not from its mechanism and machinism but its narcotic historicism, its craving for masks [*Maskensucht*] in which, all the same, a signal of true historical existence is hidden, a signal the surrealists were the first to pick up. To decipher this signal is the point of the present experiment" (V 493). These references to narcotic effects and an addiction or craving (*Sucht*) for masks show how Benjamin linked the ideas of historicism and phantasmagoria. The two varieties of historicism were in fact related: the application of historicist principles to the study of architectural history provided models for practicing architects, and the design culture based on this donning of masks from the past was indeed essential in transfiguring the material culture of the nineteenth century. Benjamin was not the first to make the linkage. Nietzsche had pioneered the criticism of both as expressions of an inauthentic, disoriented culture; but whereas he saw them as evidence of a culture adrift from its mythic moorings, Benjamin took them as testimony of the recurrence of myth. For purposes of analysis it is helpful to examine the two aspects of Benjamin's theory of dialectical images separately.

Historicism had not always supplied the foil for Benjamin's conception of history. In his encounter with surrealism, the implicit target had been the archaic orientation of *Lebensphilosophie*; in recasting Proust's doctrine of memory, he sought to cleanse it of idealist and vitalist implications alike. But through the 1930s, historicism and the conception of history as progress moved to the center of his attention. In the course of the nineteenth century, historicism had developed into a complex doctrine and spread beyond the discipline of history itself to become a core assumption of all the cultural and social sciences, particularly in Germany. Benjamin's attacks on it cut across conventional fronts in the philosophy of history. Just what was he arguing against? He saw the earmarks of historicism in the ideas of continuity and progress as assumptions about the course of history, and past-mindedness and empathy (*Einfühlung*) as instruments of historical understanding. Considering the development of German historical thinking in the nineteenth century, this is an odd characterization. On the one hand, key features of German historicism are absent from his account—the principle of organic "individualities" as the subjects of history, for instance, or the statist dogma of the primacy of foreign relations over domestic politics and social history. On the other hand, it is strange to find him citing progress as a cardinal principle, since historicism had originated in part as a German reaction against the French Enlightenment's doctrine of progress.[4]

What, then, really bothered Benjamin about the amalgam of doctrines he referred to as historicism? To begin with, he acknowledged that the idea of progress had once had a critical edge: "In Turgot, the concept of progress still served a critical function. Above all, it made it possible to direct people's attention toward retrogressive tendencies in history" (V 596). One of Benjamin's concerns was the complacency bred by the notion that progress was automatic. The form this complacency took among social democrats was particularly debilitating. Defying mandarin professors and prophets of cultural pessimism who preached against the decadence of industrial capitalist society, they had backed into the opposite error—a simpleminded belief that material progress automatically leads to social progress. The result was to "cut the sinews of [their] greatest strength," paralyzing the will to action (I 700).[5] Benjamin ascribed the same effect to the dictum of past-mindedness: "History that shows things 'as they really were' was the most potent narcotic of the century" (V 578). The methodological principle of empathy implied transporting the subject of historical knowledge into the past rather than bringing the past into the present. Although it looked like a method of retrieval, it actually served to insulate the present against the influence of the past. The references to empathy and narcotic qualities lead us to the source of Benjamin's objections: in effect, historicism was a witting or unwitting variant of Klages's exaltation of mythic consciousness. To Benjamin's way of thinking, historicism and *Lebensphilosophie* both ultimately fell victim to the same self-sacrificing evacuation of time.

Benjamin's alternative was that Copernican turn in historical think-

---

[4] "Pure" historicism had, in fact, become tinged with ideas of progress in the course of the nineteenth century. The German Historical School was afflicted with a statist bias from the start, and after the founding of the empire in 1871 nationalistic German historians could hardly resist the inference that the emergence of a German national state showed that there was progress in history after all.

[5] This criticism of historical knowledge has an unmistakably Nietzschean ring; in fact, Benjamin headed the section of "On the Concept of History" in which it appears with a citation from Nietzsche's *Use and Abuse of History*. But Benjamin stressed that the only real alternative was a *proper* conception of historical existence.

ing he had first proposed in the early "Arcades" notes. Not the past but the present was the point of reference for historical knowledge; not empathy but "making things present"—*Vergegenwärtigung*—was its methodological principle. He now spoke of a historical index intrinsic to images:

> The historical index of images says not only that they belong to a particular time, it says above all that they only attain legibility [*Lesbarkeit*] at a particular time. And this "reaching legibility" is a particular, critical point in the motion within them. Every present is determined by those images that are synchronic with it: every now is the now of a particular recognizability [*Erkennbarkeit*]. In it, truth is loaded with time to the bursting point. (V 577–578)

The historical index of an image consists in the correspondence between the context of its origin and the moment at which it becomes legible; Benjamin had developed the model for such constellations in his recasting of Proust's involuntary memory. In a citation he copied into the "Arcades" notes, he compared them with the images deposited on a photosensitive plate: "Only the future has developers at its disposal that are strong enough to bring forth the image in all its details" (V 603–604, I 1238).[6] In this respect, Benjamin's dialectic of historical interpretation resembles Gadamer's hermeneutics: reception involves contact between the present and specific moments of the past which are not always equally accessible; and reception is never just passive acceptance but always creation anew. In his essay on Proust, Benjamin had insisted that presence of mind is the indispensible precondition of autobiographical memory; in the notes for the "Arcades" project, he extended the argument for present-mindedness to history as such. In one of his most provocative formulations, he declared that the Copernican revolution in historical perspective meant that "politics receives primacy over history" (V 491). For him, that meant that the present interests of the true subject of history, "the oppressed," set the terms of historical perspective (I 1244).

But was Benjamin really the thoroughgoing historical relativist this appears to make him? For all his condemnations of past-mindedness, he also issued a telling reminder to himself in which, knowingly or not, he echoed one of historicism's cardinal principles: "The pathos of this work: there are no periods of decay. Attempt to consider the nine-

---

[6] As we have seen in Benjamin's readings of the surrealists and Proust, these conceptual motifs can be traced back to his reworking of the early romantic philosophy of reflection. The idea of unfolding recurs here in the reference to a motion within the image; the moment of discontinuity the *Trauerspiel* prologue stresses now appears as the bursting of the continuity of development.

teenth century as thoroughly positively as I tried to see the seven-teenth in the study on baroque *Trauerspiel*. No belief in periods of decay" (V 571). Among the guiding maxims of historicism was the principle that all eras are "equally close to God." This was an admoni-tion to the historian—observed more in the breach than in the prac-tice—not to intrude his or her own evaluations into the account. And one of the hallmarks of Benjamin's vision was the ability to discern coherence and the emergence of the new in what were otherwise seen as periods of decay. His model was the work of Alois Riegl, who had detected the emergence of a new organization of perception in the ornamental forms of late Roman art and decoration, a style that had previously been treated as a degeneration from classical ideals. Ben-jamin had done something analogous for baroque allegory. Although he undoutedly did believe in certain kinds of decay—witness his theo-ry of the atrophy of experience—his reminder to himself suggested a kind of regulative objectivity. In fact, his alternative to past-minded-ness was not so much present-mindedness as reciprocal illumination: "It is not that the past casts its light on the present or the present casts its light on the past; rather, an image is that in which what has been flashes together into a constellation with the now" (V 576, 578).

The appearance of relativism in Benjamin's conception of history is thus ultimately deceptive. For, in a different way than Gadamer's no-tion of an ongoing dialogue with the past, Benjamin's image of awakening holds out for the idea that in the synchronicity of historical moments the true image of the past can be glimpsed. Here, too, lies an unsuspected correspondence between Benjamin and the historicist tra-dition he adamantly condemned. The admonition to consider all eras equally close to God was more than a methodological reminder. It was also a philosophical assumption that served to ease anxieties about the implications of relativism. Since all individualities were ultimately em-anations of God, the historian could confidently explore their develop-ment in their own terms, dispensing with universal standards of judg-ment; his accounts would still be objective, in the only possible sense. Something analogous was true for Benjamin: however decidedly he took leave of the idea of timeless truth, he did not surrender the idea of objectivity along with it. Truth is "loaded with time to the bursting point"; it is "bound to a temporal core that lies in both the known and the knower" (V 578). "The true image of the past *whisks* by" (I 695). But it is nevertheless the *true* image. Benjamin's own arguments about the logic of narrative form in "The Storyteller" imply that such truth is subject to constant revision as the story proceeds. But one of the mod-els on which Benjamin formed his theories of storytelling and dialec-tical images suggests why he nevertheless held to his idea of the true image. In the images that are said to flash before the eyes of one who is dying, their "whole life" passes in review—from the definitive perspective of its end. And Benjamin defined the dialectical image too as one that "flashes up in a moment of danger" (I 695). For him, the only element of relativity had to do with how much of the past is available at any given time. "Only for a redeemed humankind has its past become citable in each of its moments" (I 694)—that is, only from the messianic perspective of the end of the history which, though we can and must listen for adumbrations of it, remains unavailable.

Whereas the temporal dimension of dialectical images shows the influence of Benjamin's encounter with Proust's work, their phantasmagoric aspect can be traced to his critique of surrealism. In the "Arcades" project, the original conception of dreamkitsch gradually developed into the idea of reading cultural images as configurations of utopian wishes and regressive distortion. The 1939 précis does not surrender this "surrealistic" moment but reaffirms it in the statement that "humanity will continue to be at the mercy of mythic fears as long as phantasmagoria have a place in it" (V 61, 1256).[7] Benjamin did once liken phantasmagoria to what Lukács called false consciousness (III 223). But whereas Lukács simply juxtaposed false with "imputed," appropriate class consciousness, Benjamin sought a method of deciphering phantasmagoria. He compared their role in social consciousness to that of symptoms in the psychic economy of a mentally disturbed individual. They were "wish images," products of repressed wishes and of traumas—or, in the case of society, of "the inchoateness of the social product as well as the deficiencies of the social system of production" (V 46–47). And "according to the law of repression," the more thoroughly such experiences are repressed, the more productive of images—phantasmagoria—a society will become (III 223). Like the manifest content of dreams, phantasmagoria conceal a latent content whose expression is permitted only in distorted form. Society is dreaming a nightmare from which it is trying to awake—that is, its wishes seek expression, recognition, and fulfillment.

The psychological idiom Benjamin used in such formulations does not seem traceable to any clear source. In particular, his contact with psychoanalysis was indirect; there is no evidence that he ever really considered a sustained exploration of psychoanalytic theory, and he made scarcely any use of specifically psychoanalytic insights.[8] Yet cer-

---

[7] Buck-Morss, *Dialectics of Seeing*, 279–284, provides an extended argument for the persistence of the dream theory in the later versions of the "Arcades" project.

[8] A notable exception is "On Some Motifs in Baudelaire," in which Benjamin drew on Freud's observations on the function of consciousness as a protective shield against traumatic shocks and the repercussions of this for memory (I 612–614).

tain comparisons of Benjamin and Freud provide systematic insights that throw important features of his conceptions into relief. In the first place, Benjamin's concept of phantasmagoria is driven by the same fundamental ambivalence as the psychoanalytic idea of wish fulfillment. Dreams, like any symptoms, are compromises: they express a wish and, in so doing, attempt to fulfill it—but only at the price of distorting it almost beyond recognition. Benjamin's phantasmagoria are wish images in the same sense. In their moment of distortion, they reveal a compulsion to repress and disguise; nevertheless, they express genuine wishes in the only way possible at the time, short of the overthrow of the system—psychic or social—of which they are part. For Freud, dreams represent compromises between unconscious wishes and defense mechanisms; for Benjamin, however, the terms of the compromise are different. The ambiguity of phantasmagoria lies in the tension between their regressive and utopian coordinates: regressive, because they express the ensnarement of history in *Urgeschichte;* utopian, because they preserve the messianic promise of fulfillment. Phantasmagoria can be read as traces of attempts simultaneously to "overcome and transfigure the deficiencies of social reality" (V 46–47). Moreover, what Benjamin regarded as the ever-present threat of a resurgence of mythic forces corresponds to a motif deeply embedded in Freud's thought. According to Freud, the historical world remains perpetually subject to the threat of primordial forces by virtue of the fact that its children are raised in families. He identified the paradigm of all psychic complexes with a name, Oedipus, from antique tragedy. For Benjamin too, ancient tragedy represents a first victory for humanity over the forces of myth, a victory that must always be won anew. Finally, many of Benjamin's descriptions of mythic forces call to mind Freud's accounts of the price to be paid for failing to master conflicts successfully. Fundamental conflicts that have not been successfully resolved are doomed to be repeated; in his pessimistic old age, Freud tended to generalize the principle of repetition compulsion to the life of the instincts as such. Benjamin also saw "the essence of the mythic process as recurrence." In a passage that playfully divests the idea of the pathos he usually lent it, he likened such compelled repetition to a familiar childhood torment: "The eternal return is a projection onto the cosmos of the punishment of staying after school: humanity must copy over its text in countless repetitions" (I 1234).[9]

Yet the differences go as deep as the similarities. They begin with Benjamin's attacks on the categories of subjectivity, personality, and

---

[9] The reference to the eternal return points to Nietzsche and to Auguste Blanqui's pessimistic cosmological fantasy *L'éternité par les astres* rather than to Freud.

interiority, a theme he sounded from the days of the youth movement onward. The rebuses that interested Freud, however much they may be based on structures common to the species, were products of the individual psyche and clues to its constitutive experiences. Benjamin offered two alternatives to this view, very different not only from Freud's image of the psyche but also from one another. In the notes for the "Arcades" project, he sometimes spoke of simply "transposing" psychoanalytic concepts "from the individual to the collectivity" (V 492). Whereas the notes usually posit a "dreaming collectivity," the 1935 précis slips into references to "the collective's unconscious," drawing Adorno's fire in an extended critical reply.[10] In fact, Benjamin did not stake out a clear position between rejecting methodological individualism and hypostatizing a collective subject. The critique of Jung and Klages he planned, but unfortunately never pursued, would have helped clarify his position. That he continued to believe in the emergence of a latent collective subject is shown by notes that identify "the subject of history" as "the oppressed, not humanity" (I 1244). But in other formulations he attacked the category of subjectivity as such, not just an exaggerated individualism or the excesses of interiority. His interest in a philosophy that dispenses with the subject-object distinction altogether goes back to his reading of the early romantics' philosophy of reflection as a corrective to Kant and Fichte alike. Benjamin sometimes seemed to locate the unconscious in the material world itself. He observed that the surrealists, unlike psychoanalysis, tracked down "the traces not so much of the soul as of things" (II 621). Or, as he described the figure of the collector: "The decisive thing about collecting is that the object is released from all its functions in order to enter into the closest possible relations with that which is similar. This is the diametrical opposite of usefulness. . . . Here we constitute an alarm clock that calls the kitsch of the previous century to 'assembly'" (V 271). The collector thus performs a modest dress rehearsal for a messiah who will come, not to destroy, but to rearrange a world that instrumental rationality has degraded into a chaos of objects imprisoned in "the drudgery of being useful" (V 53). The tragedy of modern culture is not—in Simmel's Hegelian terms—that objective culture threatens to overwhelm subjective cultivation but that it rests on the unrestricted domination of nature by humanity. Benjamin never resolved the conflict between his conception of a dreaming or oppressed collectivity as the true subject of history and his rejection of the category of subjectivity as such.

In any case, the tenor of Benjamin's messianism also separates him

[10] Adorno's letter and the ensuing exchange are reprinted at V 1127–1144; commentaries can be found in works on the Adorno-Benjamin debates cited in n. 4 of the Introduction.

fundamentally from the founder of psychoanalysis. Freud, who professed the classical Enlightenment faith in science, was as confident of its ability to guarantee gradual progress as he was wary of ultimate solutions. By contrast, Benjamin espoused a messianic creed of radical historical discontinuity, of awakening and a liquidation of mythic forces. Their ways of understanding the temporal relationship between dreams and the waking world differed accordingly. In psychoanalysis, the meaning of dreams and symptoms indeed refers to truths about the waking world, but these lie in past conflicts. For Benjamin, however, this meaning was ultimately to be revealed in the light of a future moment of awakening. Freud came to believe that any release from the compulsions of the past remains tentative, fragile, and conditional. For Benjamin, the ties of historical continuity were already being irrevocably broken; this rupture was a social given, a point of departure rather than a willful act of psychic repression. He may have sought out moments of tentative awakening in the past. But he felt sure that if the relationship between past and present was to become anything more than the permanence of a catastrophe, it would have to take the form of a break or reversal as dramatic as waking up from sleep.

3. The Antinomies of Tradition

Benjamin's notes for "On the Concept of History" include the following observation under the heading "Problem of Tradition": "Fundamental aporia: 'Tradition as the discontinuum of what has been as opposed to history [*Historie*] as the continuum of events'. . . . 'The history [*Geschichte*] of the oppressed is a discontinuum'.—'The task of history is to get hold of the tradition of the oppressed' "(V 1236). These words show how aware Benjamin had become of the intextricable entwinement of elements of continuity and discontinuity in his conceptions of tradition and history. His fundamental aporia is what we have described as an antinomy—the particular kind of conundrum that results from the conflict between inferences drawn from two equally necessary and convincing principles. Their common premise, in this case, was an interest in redeeming what he now called the tradition of the oppressed. These oppressed were the final incarnation of a long line of figures whose history could be traced back through his own work as well: those "most endangered, most defamed and derided creations and thoughts" in the preamble to "The Life of Students"; the historical experience of "all that is untimely, sorrowful, and unsuccessful" in the *Trauerspiel* study; and the unfulfilled promise of happiness in his own "Berlin childhood around 1900." Benjamin held to both branches of the antinomy to the last, surrendering neither the idea of tradition nor the necessity of breaking with the past: "The idea of discontinuity is the foundation of genuine tradition. The connection between the feeling of beginning anew and tradition must be pointed out" (I 1242).

The origins of this antinomial figure of thought go as far back in his thinking as those figures of the oppressed. The motifs of awakening and remembering make it clear why, for Benjamin, the present must not lose contact with the past: the true image of the present is locked up somewhere within it. Yet there could be no question of timelessly conserving the past, or simply continuing it, for the images it bears are ridden with distortion. Benjamin attempted to encompass both these moments in the idea of the dialectical image as a constellation between the present and a particular moment in the past. "Every present is determined by those images that are synchronic with it: every now is the now of a particular recognizability" (V 578). This emphatic conception of the now (*Jetzt*) was crucial for Benjamin. The "dialectical penetration" of past contexts meant actualizing them, making them present (*Vergegenwärtigung*); the indwelling *telos* of the dream would be realized in the moment of awakening (V 495). He thought of such time-laden constellations as crystallizing the motion of time for a fleeting instant, breaking the continuum of development: "In other words: an image is dialectics at a standstill" (V 578). All these conceptions can be traced back to an early romantic motif he had constructed in his dissertation: the unfolding continuum of reflection culminates in a reversal; poetic ecstasy reverses into prosaic sobriety. In the prologue to the *Trauerspiel* study he underscored this moment of discontinuity as a corrective to the notion that absolute ideas can ever be fully immanent and stabilized in any particular. After 1925 he extended these reflections in part by broadening his focus from a theory of knowledge, which concerned the synthetic construction and redemption of images of truth by the critic, to a theory of perception and an attempt to work out how such images might be seized by social forces at large.

Benjamin's idea of temporal constellations made a paradoxical conjunction of continuity and discontinuity possible; dialectical images represent one of his resolutions of the antinomy of tradition. A second, equally important resolution was the theory of reception he was beginning to develop in his late works.[11] A work of art, Benjamin argues—

---

[11] The following account draws together the pieces of a theory of reception in "Eduard Fuchs" (II 465–478); a methodological preface to his incomplete study of Baudelaire, the so-called *Methodenfragment* (I 1160–1167); Konvolut N of the "Arcades" notes; and the notes to "On the Concept of History" (I 1229–1246). A study of Benjamin's reception theory that comes to similar conclusions through a brilliant extended reading of the *Methodenfragment* is Kaulen, *Rettung und Destruktion*.

and, by extension, any given "historical state of affairs" (V 587)—can be seen as integrating or crystallizing a constellation he calls its prehistory and posthistory (II 467). This constellation of pre- and posthistory is the key to any full appreciation of both the social function and the meaning of a work or event. In his 1937 essay "Eduard Fuchs, Collector and Historian," he cited his own conception of the work as an originary phenomenon (*Ursprungsphänomen*) from the *Trauerspiel* preface as the source of this conception (II 468).[12] Now this concept came into its own, although with significant new inflections. What the work crystallizes is no longer described as an idea but as a force field subject to constant change. In fact, Benjamin says almost nothing about the prehistory of works; rather, he emphasizes their posthistory, which continues into present: "It is the present that polarizes events into pre- and posthistory" (V 588). Present-day interests disclose those aspects of the past that speak uniquely to us; or, as Benjamin earlier put it, "the innermost structures of the past are illuminated for each present only in the light generated by the incandescence of their actuality" (III 97).[13]

In Benjamin's version of reception history, hermeneutics moves in two directions. The first works from the past into present. Historical understanding is "the afterlife [*Nachleben*] of the object" itself, "whose pulsation can be traced into the present." But now this afterlife, a conception that goes back to the romantics' unfolding medium of reflection, is construed in a concrete, social sense as the process of transmission.[14] In the process of transmission a work acquires functions and meanings that leave behind both the author's intention and the reception of the work by contemporaries in its original context (II 467, 469). These new meanings and functions are not a mere encrustation that must be stripped away to get at the object itself; on the contrary, they have become indispensible to our own understanding of the work. This interest in the interpreter in turn points to the second direction of historical understanding, which also works from the present back into the past by inquiring into the interest in the object. If the work's reception is comparable to a continuous stream of transmission, the critical historian soberly appraises the forces that govern the course of this stream. Shifting from organic to constructive metaphors, Benjamin asks "Whose mills does this stream drive? who makes use of its gra-

---

[12] See Chapter 3, Section 5.

[13] This passage stems from his 1928 review of Eva Fiesel's *Die Sprachphilosophie der deutschen Romantik*; in fact, some elements of Benjamin's theory of reception were formulated and practiced in his reviews of the late 1920s and early 1930s.

[14] Kaulen, *Rettung und Destruktion*, 94, traces the term itself directly to "The Task of the Translator."

dient? who dammed it up?" (I 1161). This sort of historical understanding entails a complex procedure, he admits, but impatient attempts to address a work directly forfeit much of the essential testimony to its social function as well as its meaning. Finally, the complementarity of these two motions of understanding ensures that a critical history of receptions does not imply license simply to construct the object to the specifications of present-day interests. The study of effects and receptions must ultimately uncover hidden relationships in the object itself and, in the case of a work of art, must ensure "that it becomes more transparent to us as a *work of art*" (II 469). Benjamin's reception theory thus avoids both conservative preservation and narrow presentism alike.

He sets particular store by the processual character of tradition. The changing conditions of present-day interest, or *Aktualität*, guarantee that "a historical state of affairs constantly polarizies into pre- and posthistory anew, never in the same way" (V 587). The past is therefore fundamentally incomplete, leaving tradition open to startling revisions. Benjamin makes an emphatic plea against reifying the past as if it were a matter of "goods" that could be securely possessed. "The work of the past [*das Werk der Vergangenheit*] is . . . not complete"— neither past works themselves nor the working of the past (II 477).[15] If this is an indictment of a degraded conception of the canonical tradition, it deserves no less to become a guiding principle of the tradition of the oppressed. Tradition is never a secure "inheritance," and the sort of transmission that treats it as such has catastrophic effects (I 1242, V 591). Revising his own formulation, Benjamin thus reminds himself that "history must not only get hold of the tradition of the oppressed but found [*stiften*] it as well" (I 1246). The goal is not simply to replace one entrenched, affirmative canon with another but to open the traditioning process to ceaseless contestation. The tradition of the oppressed is to be both a different tradition and a different kind of tradition.

Up to this point, Benjamin's account seems to aim at tending or restoring historical continuity—tracing "pulses," recovering, renewing, even founding traditions. But this is only half the story, for Benjamin also implants a potent moment of discontinuity in his reception theory. "The idea of discontinuity is the foundation of genuine tradition," he asserts, for two distinct but related reasons. The first results from the social basis of the process of transmission, which is implicated in a larger context of injustice and exploitation. Art and learning owe

---

[15] See the discussion of his disagreement with Horkheimer over the closure of the past (V 588–589) at the end of Chapter 4, Section 4.

their existence "not only to the efforts of the great geniuses who created them but also to the anonymous toil of their contemporaries. There is no document of culture that is not at the same time a document of barbarism" (I 696; see also II 476–477).[16] The tradition of the oppressed necessarily strives to rupture the unbroken continuity of history in the sense of putting an end to the unjust social practices within which culture and tradition have always been embedded. These social and ideological considerations in turn suggest the second rationale for discontinuity. The ideological construction and transmission of culture has been selective: entire movements, particular authors, individual works, and, not least, moments *within* canonical works have been systematically ignored or suppressed and thus have not entered into tradition. The cardinal example examined in this study is the *Frühromantik;* by now perhaps the best-known case in Benjamin's work is his revision of the image of Baudelaire, showing him as an urban poet whose work bears the stigmata of the social and political experience of his times rather than as a "pure" poet or an adept of mysticism.[17] But the genuine conception of tradition does not seek restitution by reincorporating what has been lost into a seamless continuum. Instead, it presents the suppressed or neglected as a "witness against the transmission" (I 1166). The critical historian does not seek to swim with the stream of tradition. For just those places where transmission "breaks off" are the most revealing; tradition is more like a wall with rough and jagged spots that provide the critical historian with a foothold that helps in getting over it (V 592, I 1242).

As with the dialectical image, the entwinement of continuity and discontinuity in Benjamin's concept of reception history mobilizes the antinomial tensions in his thinking successfully and productively. Like Gadamer's conception of "effective history" and the positive role of "prejudices" in historical understanding, it captures the mutual implication of interpreter and object. By contrast with Gadamer, however, Benjamin explicitly rejects the presumption that the effective history of a work represents a more or less adequate unfolding of it. He presumes, instead, that the interests that guide the traditioning process tend to distort the work, systematically and tendentiously. At the same time, Benjamin does not take this principle so far as to suggest

---

[16] Benjamin's point echoes Brecht's "Questions of a Worker Who Reads" (1935): "Who built the Thebes of seven gates? / In the books stand the names of kings. / Did the kings haul the stones? / . . . Every page a victory. / Who cooked the victory feast? / Every ten years another great man. / Who paid the bills? / So many reports. / So many questions" (Brecht, *Die Gedichte von Bertolt Brecht in einem Band,* 656–657).

[17] For another such recovery of a moment excluded from tradition, see the treatment of Benjamin's response to the Enlightenment, and especially of Carl Gustav Jochmann, in my Conclusion.

that either the structure of works or their reception consigns them to a history of disparate (much less contingent) effects. On the contrary, a critique of the reception and a reading that redeems suppressed elements of a work do, ultimately, converge. He makes this argument explicitly for the case of Baudelaire: "In the reading of Baudelaire . . . bourgeois society has given us a course of historical instruction. This course of instruction can never be ignored. A critical reading of Baudelaire and a critical revision of this course of instruction are one and the same" (I 1161). Here Benjamin lodges a claim for congruence between the structure of the work and its reception in the strongest of terms: they are—at least in their *critical* versions—"one and the same." Once more, Benjamin's and Gadamer's hermeneutics seem to converge. The interpreter's "anticipation of completeness," which has been seen as an indication of conservatism in Gadamer's views, has its counterpart in Benjamin. But for Benjamin such completeness is not an enabling assumption that makes interpretation possible but the result of subjecting a tradition to critical revision. Benjamin's conception is nonetheless backed by an implicitly idealistic view of the congruence of the structure of the work and its posthistory, an assumption that can be traced to the concept of the *Ursprungsphänomen* in the *Trauerspiel* preface and, ultimately, to the romantic philosophy of reflection. For all its critical thrust and incorporation of discontinuity, Benjamin's conception of tradition stops well short of yielding to historical contingency.[18]

It is in the realm of social history and collective action, into which Benjamin translated this conception of tradition based on literary models, that his paradoxical conjoining of continuity and discontinuity creates unresolved difficulties. There is a sequence of notes in the manuscripts for "On the Concept of History" in which his reasoning leads him to the verge of addressing these difficulties but then breaks off. In the moment of action, he suggests, revolutionary actors are peculiarly aware of historical discontinuity; indeed, they are involved in creating it. Yet this feeling goes together with a sense of intimate connection between their acts and their conceptions of past history (I 1236, 1241). The contradiction between these two circumstances, Benjamin claims, is only apparent. For revolutionary actors characteristically reach back over the recent past to draw images and legitimations from ancient

---

[18] Kaulen, *Rettung und Destruktion*, 178–193, provides an illuminating comparison of Benjamin's views with other versions of reception aesthetics and history. He draws a favorable contrast between the "dialectical unity" of effective history and analysis of works in Benjamin's reception theory and H. R. Jauß's reception theory, which dissociates them and, as he sees it, "fetishizes" empirical evidence about the reception. But he does not demonstrate that Jauß's charge of a latent metaphysics in Benjamin's views is unjustified.

precedents; Benjamin refers to the French Revolution's citation of the Roman republic. But in the case of the modern proletariat, he notes, the impulse to action has not been accompanied by any such historical correspondence: "No remembrance took place." The reference to memory is worth noting, because it signals a crucial difference between collective memory and the critic's construction of dialectical images. Unlike the critic, whose procedures are synthetic, revolutionary actors must be able to draw on and activate living, collective remembrance. Benjamin's compressed and fragmentary reflections do not explain why he thought "no remembrance took place." He briefly notes the failure of the Social Democrats' attempts to foster such historical remembrance artificially, but he does not ask whether this resulted from faulty organizing strategies or from some other cause. This other cause might well have been the atrophy of experience diagnosed in his works, an atrophy that strikes directly at the bonds of memory. *This* sort of discontinuity would not enable collective action but, on the contrary, would undermine it. The problem is that Benjamin's striking dictum that "the continuum is that of the oppressors" turns out to be a half-truth (I 1244). His own postulation of a link between revolutionary action and collective remembrance means that there is also a continuity that works in favor of the oppressed. Benjamin's denial to the contrary, therefore, this antinomy in his work remains a contradiction.

The question is why he failed to take the full measure of the consequences of this contradiction. Part of the reason may hide in the subtle equivocation that had developed in his conception of mythic forms of consciousness.[19] In his early work, Benjamin had posited a strict polarity between the realms of myth and truth, which he insisted were mutually exclusive (I 162). But in the theory of experience he then went on to develop he argued that memory depends on faculties originally entwined with mythic forms of consciousness. In this conception, truth and myth come mixed: "The separation of the true from the false is not the point of departure but the goal of the materialist method. That means that it starts out from an object permeated with error and doxa. The distinctions it undertakes . . . are distinctions within this thoroughly mixed object itself" (I 1160). This maxim held not only for historical evidence but for human faculties themselves. The production of memory images and phantasmagoria, and their retrieval and *deciphering* as well, ultimately depended on the persistence of a faculty with roots in an archaic form of consciousness—what he called the mimetic ability to perceive and produce similarities, or correspondences. "'Every epoch dreams the following'. Nothing new arises

[19] See Chapter 6, Section 3.

without this phantasmic, anticipatory form in dream consciousness" (I 1236) and, he might have added, without the power of collective remembrance to summon up corresponding images of past injustice. Had Benjamin done justice to this implicit shift in his thinking, he more likely would have recognized the problematic consequences of a rupture in the continuity of remembrance.

A second possible explanation has to do with an ambiguity of the term "image." In Benjamin's usage, it could refer to the order of either knowledge or perception. In some important instances, it appears to refer to both at once: thus, in a late note, "the dialectical image is to be defined as the involuntary remembering of humanity" (I 1233). One might argue that a decay of tradition—which would result from changes in the structure of perception—need not undermine the possibility of *knowledge* of the past. Historians might still be able to construct the true image of the past synthetically. But to cite the words with which he characterized Proust's "synthetic achievement" in 1939, Benjamin was not content with the kind of redemption that remains a "private show" (I 643). His ambiguous use of the term "image" was therefore also a gesture of hope: it implied that there could ultimately be no gap between the knowledge available to the historian and the perceptions actually taking shape in the real, historical world. His late work provides a striking example of this linkage. In a note for the "Arcades" project, he spoke of the "historical index" inherent in images, an index that provided the key to the possibility of reading the past in a moment of danger. In "On the Concept of History," however, he spoke not of an index but of a "secret *appointment* between past *generations* and our own" (I 694; emphases added). The "Arcades" project, I suggest, was guided by Benjamin's hope that images could become legible for the historian only if an actual historical awakening was still possible. But what if it turned out that the two did not unfold together after all? What if the historian recognized opportunities to redeem lost chances, but those engaged in the real-life struggle lost to the forces of regression? Of course, Benjamin's entire view of history was attuned to the retrieval and redemption of lost chances. But neither he nor his work were immune to the consequences of such failure.

His vulnerability showed itself in an oscillation between two modes of thinking. On the one hand, Benjamin was capable at times of an extraordinary immersion in the world of appearances, even appearances of the most delusionary sort; at others, however, he seemed to back away from them in horror. A willingness to lose himself in the "forest of symbols" alternated with a grasp for the "whetted axe of reason" in order "not to fall prey to the horror that beckons from the depths of the primeval forest." This oscillation can already be seen in the difference between his two major projects of the early 1920s. In the essay on Goethe's *Elective Affinities*, Benjamin sought to provide an exhaustive account of the realia of the work in order to locate the "secret" within the world of delusions—the signs of a struggle for release from mythic forces that takers place *within* their domain. The *Trauerspiel* study presented a very different vision: an image of history lapsed into a state of nature, a world afflicted by transience, ruin, and decay. This world appears not as a forest of symbols but as a "petrified primordial landscape." In the 1930s, his works repeated this eccentric motion. The "Arcades" project was to "decipher the signals of true historical existence" latent in phantasmagoric wish images—configurations of utopian promise and regressive disortion in endless variety. In his final theses "On the Concept of History," however, Benjamin depicted a rather different historical landscape: "His face is turned toward the past. Where a chain of events appears to *us, he* sees a single catastrophe that heaps rubble on rubble and hurls it at his feet. . . . This storm drives him irresistibly into the future, on which he turns his back, while the heap of ruins before him grows toward the heavens. That which we call progress is this storm" (I 697–698). This image of history as a piling up of ruins itself derives from the allegorist's gaze in the *Trauerspiel* study. In the "Arcades" project, Benjamin projected an image of history both rich and threatening. "On the Concept of History," however, tends to level those differences; in the end, each rebus yields the same image: history is simply the dismal permanence of catastrophe. Benjamin himself could be an incisive critic of such distanced, abstract condemnations of history, even in causes he approved of. Ten years earlier, he had taken an author he admired to task for the "absurdity" of a merely negative knowledge of history (*verneinende Geschichtserkenntnis*): "That which we wish to destroy may not stand before us as an abstract negative, a counterexample. It can only appear that way momentarily, in the illuminating flash of hate. One must not only know that which one wants to destroy; to do the job thoroughly, one must also have felt it" (III 265).[20] These words might have stood as a reminder to himself as well.

We should bear in mind, however, that the alternation between these two attitudes toward history was not only a matter of Benjamin's temperament. By the end of the 1930s, the course of history itself decreed that the difference between wandering through tangled thickets of delusion and gazing on "the bleak confusion of a charnel house" no longer represented much of a choice.

---

[20] The writer was Werner Hegemann, a left "outsider" whom Benjamin admired (VI 183); in "A Contemporary Jacobin," a review of Hegemann's study of Berlin as "the greatest rent-barrack city in the world," Benjamin praised him as a "fanatical democrat" but lamented the lack of a physiognomic sense in his work (III 263–265).

Conclusion

Benjamin's Recasting of the German Intellectual Tradition

While working out a critical conception of tradition, Benjamin also developed a thoroughgoing, substantive revision of the traditions of German intellectual culture. He did not live to spell out what he meant by the "tradition of the oppressed" invoked in the notes to "On the Concept of History." The idea implies two distinct though compatible possibilities. One would be rooted directly in the history of those whose anonymous toil supports a culture whose products have always also been "documents of barbarism." The tradition of the oppressed, in this sense, would be an alternate tradition of those excluded from the canons of "high" culture, and those who set out to recuperate it might undertake the sort of politically engaged social and cultural history represented by the work of historians such as E. P. Thompson. In fact, Benjamin's language and the Brechtian strain of plebeian radicalism in his work of the 1930s resonate with the words of Thompson's famous preface to *The Making of the English Working Class,* in which he declared his intention to rescue the "casualties" of history from "the enormous condescension of posterity."[1] Benjamin's book reviews from the late 1920s and early 1930s sometimes propose such a shift of focus from high to popular culture,[2] but under the conditions of exile his pointer was bound to remain a gesture.

Benjamin always spoke of *the* tradition of the oppressed in the singular and specified its bearer as an oppressed *class*. This perspective accorded with his attempt in "Eduard Fuchs," "On the Concept of History," and elsewhere to ally his distinctive sense of history with the

[1] E. P. Thompson, *The Making of the English Working Class,* 12–13.
[2] See especially his 1931 review "How Can Highly Successful Books Be Explained?" (III 294–300).

fortunes of historical materialism. Characteristically, however, he did not so much propose an alliance as declare one by fiat: the historical materialist, he asserted, "is aware of" the weak messianic power with which every generation is endowed, the need to brush history against the grain, and so on, though none of these things was intrinsically linked to historical materialism as it had previously been understood. The same holds for Benjamin's identification of the subject of tradition as a singular, oppressed class: nothing in his theory requires that this subject be either singular or a class; this is to say that he might well be claimed as a precursor of a radically pluralist, engaged social history.

Benjamin's idea of a tradition of the oppressed can also be read less literally. In most of his work he operated on the terrain of the canonical tradition, unearthing the critical resources of high culture. In this sense, the tradition of the oppressed would encompass not only those excluded from such culture but the suppressed, subversive moments within it as well.[3] We have seen how far-reaching Benjamin's recasting of the German tradition was, and how his implicit agenda was set by the choices he made in breaking with the youth movement. His immanent critique of German intellectual culture recovered and mobilized the resources of the *Frühromantik*, of baroque allegory, and of aestheticism. In his mature work, he brought these resources from the tradition to bear in a distinctive philosophical anthropology he referred to as anthropological materialism, "real humanism," or a "new barbarism." His position in the intellectual field also explains his persistent, intimate enmity with German radical conservatism as well as the decisionist moment that remained so deeply ingrained in his thinking, however carefully he sought to frame it. Finally, along with other members of the German-Jewish generation of 1914, he infused his critique with the idiom of Jewish messianism. Yet it is not enough, I have argued, to treat the Jewish motifs in his work simply as an external influence. Benjamin's affinity for the messianic impulse, his reasons for appealing to it, and the fecundity of his work with it all need to be explained in terms of the dominant intellectual field and his long-term

---

[3] Benjamin tacitly assumed a natural, unproblematic alliance between the two. But contemporary German radical conservatives were also suspicious of securely transmitted traditions, which they, much like Benjamin, saw as corrupted by the dominant culture of the German empire. Adorno once aptly described their awareness of the discontinuity this entailed as a conservatism of distance ("Über Tradition," 35–36. Adorno also discussed how the decay of tradition creates a dilemma—which he called a contradiction or, at one point, an antinomy—which is closely related to the issues considered in this study). But the discontinuous history of lost or suppressed moments the radical conservatives sought to recuperate had little to do with the interests of those Benjamin had in mind. See also Norbert Altenhofer, "Die zerstörte Überlieferung: Geschichtsphilosophie der Diskontinuität und Traditionsbewußtsein zwischen Anarchismus und konservativer Revolution."

intellectual strategies. The persistence with which he pursued those strategies should not be taken as a lack of flexibility. As we have also seen, the strategies themselves continued to evolve, and to the end of his life Benjamin remained remarkably open to new contexts and influences. In fact, perhaps his most surprising revision of the German tradition was his appeal in the 1930s to another of its submerged utopian resources—to the radical Enlightenment and the lost democratic traditions of the German bourgeoisie.[4]

Benjamin's relationship to the Enlightenment tradition remains among the most persistently misconstrued aspects of his work. The prevailing assumption has been that he rejected it root and branch. The evidence usually cited is his critical commentary on Kant in his 1917 essay "On the Program of the Coming Philosophy." Kant's conception of knowledge, Benjamin argued, with its fixation on the certainty of the natural sciences, was restricted to "a reality of a low, perhaps the lowest, order" and therefore could produce only a conception of "experience reduced virtually to zero, to a minimum of significance" (I 158–159). But even these strictures were ambiguous. It is certainly true that Benjamin saw scientific and instrumental conceptions of knowledge, language, and action as degraded. The metaphysical pathos of his early work led him to envision "a new and higher kind of experience yet to come" (I 160). Yet an essential condition of such higher experience, for Benjamin, was a prior, radical reduction of mythic complexity. Kant's stringency appealed to the liquidationist strain in Benjamin's temperament. His observation that Kant had provided "the map of paths [*Wegekarte*] through the barren forest of reality" was certainly meant as an indictment of the barrenness of modern experience (I 126). But the image also adumbrates his later description of the destructive character who "reduces the existing to rubble, not for the sake of the rubble but of the path [*Weg*] that leads through it" (IV 398). Even in his early work, Benjamin resisted·the ideological simplicities of idealist and vitalist calls to overcome the shallowness of the Enlightenment.

In his later work, this ambivalence toward the figure of Kant was played out in his attitude toward the history of the German bourgeoisie. Benjamin argued that, since the founding of the empire, the bourgeoisie had betrayed the ideals and interests it once represented, defending the positions it had conquered while surrendering the spirit in which it had done so (IV 151). This view was widely held on the left (and not only on the left) during the interwar years. But Benjamin gave

---

[4] A notable exception to the neglect of these themes in Benjamin's work is the reminder provided by Klaus Garber in *Rezeption und Rettung*, 44–52.

it a particular turn. From exile he published a collection of little-known German letters spanning the century from 1783 to 1883 under the title *Deutsche Menschen*, in which he evoked the specific qualities he prized.[5] Few of the letters he selected discuss public affairs or literary and philosophical issues; rather, he meant to show how the virtues of early bourgeois humanism expressed themselves in the private sphere (IV 956). Benjamin's description of these virtues is disarmingly simple. He invokes not so much ideas or principles as a bearing (*Haltung*)—a bearing of straitened, yet dignified humanity:

> If the way that a meagre, straitened existence and true humanity are dependent on one another shows itself nowhere more clearly than in Kant, . . . then this letter by his brother shows how deeply rooted in the people was the sense of life that is formulated in the philosopher's works. In short, wherever humanity is at issue, one should not forget the confines of the bourgeois rooms [*die Enge der Bürgerstube*] into which the Enlightenment cast its light. (IV 157)

In these forgotten circumstances Benjamin found a laconic reliability that was still "unspent and unaffected by the overexploitation" to which the "classics" had been subjected in the nineteenth century (IV 153). His eye for these virtues was sharpened, of course, by his own experience of the straitened circumstances of exile. *Deutsche Menschen* was not an exercise in nostalgia but an understated, yet potent indictment of a bourgeoisie that had betrayed its own tradition of avowing the poverty of experience.

Perhaps Benjamin's most moving appeal to German traditions of Enlightenment and radical democracy was his preface to Carl Gustav Jochmann's "Regression of Poetry." Jochmann was an early nineteenth-century bourgeois radical from Riga whose reputation had dwindled to little more than his name.[6] Benjamin pointed out that the oblivion to which his memory had been consigned was anything but accidental. Retracing Jochmann's links to progressive movements in the Baltic

[5] *Deutsche Menschen* appeared under the pseudonym Detlev Holz in Switzerland; Benjamin told Scholem and Horkheimer that the title was meant as camouflage, which he hoped would enable it to escape the attention of Nazi censorship and circulate in Germany (Benjamin and Scholem, *Briefwechsel*, 228; IV 948); see also Albrecht Schöne, " 'Diese nach jüdischem Vorbild erbaute Arche': Walter Benjamins *Deutsche Menschen*." Benjamin constructed similar histories of the German bourgeoisie in two other, smaller collections of texts, "From Cosmopolitan to Bourgeois" (in collaboration with Willy Haas) (IV 815–862), and "Germans of 1789" (IV 863–880).

[6] The publication of Jochmann's essay and Benjamin's preface in the *Zeitschrift für Sozialforschung* in 1939 set off an acrimonious dispute with Werner Kraft, who accused Benjamin of attempting to steal the claim to rediscovering Jochmann. The issues are discussed by the editors of the *Gesammelte Schriften* (II 1397–1403); see Kraft, *Carl Gustav Jochmann und sein Kreis*.

states as well as to German Jacobin circles in revolutionary and postrevolutionary Paris, he argued that Jochmann's exclusion from tradition was politically motivated. The circles in which Jochmann moved were not those of the celebrated luminaries of German culture. But this did not diminish their stature in Benjamin's eyes. Rather, they were the sort of "men, limited in their productive talents yet so important in the economy of world history, whose straightforwardness and fidelity to their convictions provided the indispensible, unappreciated basis for the farther-reaching, yet all the more cautious revolutionary formulations of a Kant or a Schiller" (II 576). Notably, Benjamin now contrasted their humane, political reliability with the unsteadiness of early romantics, whose humanistic enthusiasm had collapsed into a mystification of medievalism and a "hunt for false riches," cavalierly ignoring the implication of culture in social injustice (II 581).

Benjamin's pointer to Jochmann did not signal a new identification with the Enlightenment on his part or any wholesale rehabilitation of it. In fact, this was just what made Jochmann such an apt figure for his purposes: even as one of the "dispersed and scattered advance party of the bourgeoisie" in eighteenth-century Germany, he was "isolated among the dispersed" (II 578–579). A German scholar taking refuge among left-wing emigré circles in Paris, a revolutionary in a reactionary age, Jochmann was untimely, falling between the defeat of German Jacobinism and the progressive resurgence of the Vormärz. Politically steadfast, like his democratic associates, he nevertheless held views of language, culture, and nature richer than those of most Enlightenment thinkers—views that placed him closer, in fact, to those authentic intentions of early romanticism that Benjamin had been at pains to recover. Jochmann was therefore the perfect figure to indicate the position Benjamin himself sought to maintain on the left. His essay on Jochmann also provides eloquent testimony to how much he had learned, since his early work, about the importance of "the question of neighborhoods." It was not that Benjamin's view of the heritage of the Enlightenment had changed fundamentally; he remained ambivalent about it. But now he was clearer about the less conspicuous virtues of its "real humanism," and clearheaded enough to recognize their timeliness.

Bibliography

Works by Benjamin

Briefe. Edited and with an introduction by Theodor W. Adorno and Gershom Scholem. Frankfurt: Suhrkamp, 1966.

Briefe an Siegfried Kracauer. Marbach am Neckar: Deutsche Schillergesellschaft, 1987.

Briefwechsel 1933–1940 [with Gershom Scholem]. Edited by Gershom Scholem. Frankfurt: Suhrkamp, 1980.

Gesammelte Schriften. Edited by Rolf Tiedemann and Hermann Schweppenhäuser. Frankfurt: Suhrkamp, 1972–1989.

   Volume I: *Abhandlungen*. Edited by Rolf Tiedemann and Hermann Schweppenhäuser. 1974.

   Volume II: *Essays, Vorträge*. Edited by Rolf Tiedemann and Hermann Schweppenhäuser. 1977.

   Volume III: *Kritiken und Rezensionen*. Edited by Hella Tiedemann-Barthels. 1972.

   Volume IV: *Kleine Prosa, Baudelaire-Übertragungen*. Edited by Tillman Rexroth. 1972.

   Volume V: *Das Passagen-Werk*. Edited by Rolf Tiedemann. 1982.

   Volume VI: *Fragmente vermischten Inhalts, Autobiographische Schriften*. Edited by Rolf Tiedemann and Hermann Schweppenhäuser. 1985.

   Volume VII: *Nachträge*. Edited by Rolf Tiedemann and Hermann Schweppenhäuser, assisted by Christoph Gödde, Henri Lonitz, and Gary Smith. 1989.

English-Language Translations of Benjamin's Works

The following list includes published translations of Benjamin's texts relevant to the argument here. A comprehensive bibliography of English-language translations, which includes alternate versions of some texts, has been compiled by Gary Smith, "Walter Benjamin in English: A Bibliography of Translations," in G. Smith, ed., *Walter Benjamin: Philosophy, History, and Aesthetics* (Chicago: 1989), 260–263. An extensive selection of Benjamin's works in English translation is being prepared by Harvard University Press.

"Central Park." *New German Critique* 34 (Winter 1985), 32–58.
Charles Baudelaire: A Lyric Poet in the Age of High Capitalism. London: 1973. Includes "The Paris of the Second Empire in Baudelaire"; "Some Motifs in Baudelaire"; "Paris, the Capital of the Nineteenth Century."
The Correspondence of Walter Benjamin and Gershom Scholem, 1932–1940. Edited by Gershom Scholem. New York: 1989.
"Doctrine of the Similar." *New German Critique* 17 (Spring 1979), 65–69.
"Eduard Fuchs: Collector and Historian." *New German Critique* 5 (Spring 1975), 27–58.
Illuminations. Edited by Hannah Arendt. New York: 1968. Includes "Unpacking My Library"; "The Task of the Translator"; "The Storyteller"; "Franz Kafka"; "Some Reflections on Kafka"; "What Is Epic Theater?"; "On Some Motifs in Baudelaire"; "The Image of Proust"; "The Work of Art in the Age of Mechanical Reproduction"; "Theses on the Philosophy of History."
"Left Wing Melancholy (On Erich Kästner's New Book of Poems)". *Screen* 15 (Summer 1974), 28–32.
Moscow Diary. Cambridge, Mass.: 1986. Also includes "Russian Toys" and several letters from 1926/27.
"N [Re the Theory of Knowledge, Theory of Progress]." In G. Smith, ed., *Walter Benjamin: Philosophy, History, and Aesthetics*. Chicago: 1989. 43–83. A crucial group of notes from the "Arcades" project.
One-Way Street and Other Writings. London: 1979. Includes all of *Reflections* plus "A Small History of Photography," "Eduard Fuchs, Collector and Historian," and an unabridged version of *One-Way Street*.
The Origin of German Tragic Drama. London: 1977.
"Program of the Coming Philosophy." In G. Smith, ed., *Walter Benjamin: Philosophy, History, and Aesthetics*. Chicago: 1989. 1–12.
"A Radio Talk on Brecht." *New Left Review* 123 (September/October 1980), 92–96.
Reflections: Essays, Aphorisms, Autobiographical Writings. Edited by Peter Demetz. New York: 1978. Includes "A Berlin Chronicle"; "One-Way Street" (selections); "Moscow"; "Marseilles"; "Hashish in Marseilles"; "Paris, Capital of the Nineteenth Century"; "Naples"; "Surrealism"; "Brecht's *Threepenny Novel*"; "Conversations with Brecht"; "The Author as Producer"; "Karl Kraus"; "Critique of Violence"; "The Destructive Character"; "Fate and Character"; "Theologico-Political Fragment"; "On Language as Such and on the Language of Man"; "On the Mimetic Faculty."
"Reply" (letter of December 9, 1938, to Adorno). In Perry Anderson, Ronald Taylor, et al., eds., *Aesthetics and Politics*. London: 1977. 134–141. Benjamin's response to Adorno's critique of "The Paris of the Second Empire in Baudelaire," the first version of the Baudelaire essay.
"Rigorous Study of Art." *October* 47 (Winter 1988), 84–90.
"Socrates." *The Philosophical Forum* 15 (Winter/Spring 1983/84), 52–54.

"Theories of German Fascism." *New German Critique* 17 (Spring 1979), 120–128.
Understanding Brecht. London: 1973. Includes "What Is Epic Theater?" (first version); "What Is Epic Theater?" (second version); "From the Brecht Commentary"; "A Family Drama in the Epic Theatre"; "The Country Where It Is Forbidden to Mention the Proletariat"; "Commentaries on Poems by Brecht"; "Brecht's *Threepenny Novel*"; "The Author as Producer"; "Conversations with Brecht."

Works on Benjamin and Other Works Consulted

Adorno, Theodor W. "Die Idee der Naturgeschichte." In Adorno, *Gesammelte Schriften,* vol. 1. Frankfurt: 1973.
——. "A Portrait of Walter Benjamin." In Adorno, *Prisms.* London: 1967. 227–241.
——. "Rückblickend auf den Surrealismus." In Adorno, *Gesammelte Schriften,* vol. 11: *Noten zur Literatur.* Frankfurt: 1974. 101–105.
——. "Über Tradition." In Adorno, *Ohne Leitbild: Parva Aesthetica.* Frankfurt: 1967. 29–41.
——. *Über Walter Benjamin.* Frankfurt: 1970.
——, Ernst Bloch, Ernst Fischer, et al. *Über Walter Benjamin.* Frankfurt: 1968.
Altenhofer, Norbert. "Die zerstörte Überlieferung: Geschichtsphilosophie der Diskontinuität und Traditionsbewußtsein zwischen Anarchismus und konservativer Revolution." In Thomas Kroebner, ed., *Weimars Ende.* Frankfurt: 1982. 330–347.
Alter, Robert. "Walter Benjamin." *Commentary* 48, no. 3 (1969), 4–6.
Aragon, Louis. *Paris Peasant.* Translated by Simon Watson Taylor. London: 1980.
Arendt, Hannah. "Bertolt Brecht, 1898–1956." In Arendt, *Men in Dark Times.* New York: 1968. 207–249.
——. "Walter Benjamin, 1892–1940." In Walter Benjamin, *Illuminations.* Edited and with an Introduction by Hannah Arendt. New York: 1969.
Aufmuth, Ulrich. *Die deutsche Wandervogelbewegung unter soziologischem Aspekt.* Göttingen: 1979.
Baudelaire, Charles. *Les fleurs du mal.* Translated by Richard Howard. Brighton: 1982.
Behne, Adolf. *Neues Wohnen—neues Bauen.* Leipzig: 1927.
Belmore, Herbert W. "Walter Benjamin." *German Life and Letters* 15 (1962), 309–313.
Bergson, Henri. *Materie und Gedächtnis.* Frankfurt: 1982.
Bernoulli, Carl Albrecht. *Johann Jacob Bachofen und das Natursymbol.* Basel: 1924.
Biale, David. *Gershom Scholem: Kabbalah and Counter-History.* 2d ed. Cambridge, Mass.: 1982.
Bloch, Ernst. "Hieroglyphen des XIX. Jahrhunderts." In Bloch, *Erbschaft dieser Zeit.* Frankfurt: 1962. 381–386.
——. "Revueform in der Philosophie." In Bloch, *Erbschaft dieser Zeit.* Frankfurt: 1962. 368–371.

Bohrer, Karl-Heinz. *Die Kritik der Romantik: Der Verdacht der Philosophie gegen die literarische Moderne.* Frankfurt: 1989.

Boie, Bernhild. "Dichtung als Ritual der Erlösung: Zu den wiedergefundenen Sonetten von Walter Benjamin." *Akzente* 31 (1984), 23–39.

Bolz, Norbert W. "Einleitung: Walter Benjamin und seine Totengräber." In N. Bolz and R. Faber, eds., *Walter Benjamin: Profane Erleuchtung und rettende Kritik.* Würzburg: 1982. 7–35.

Borges, Jorge Luis. *Labyrinths.* New York: 1964.

Bourdieu, Pierre. "The Genesis of the Concepts of Habitus and of Field." *Sociocriticism* 2 (1985), 11–24.

———. "Intellectual Field and Creative Project." *Social Science Information* 8 (April 1969), 89–119.

———. *Outline of a Theory of Practice.* Cambridge: 1977.

Bradbury, Malcolm, and James McFarlane, eds. *Modernism, 1890–1930.* Harmondsworth: 1976.

Brecht, Bertolt. *Arbeitsjournal: Erster Band, 1938 bis 1942.* Edited by Walter Hecht. Frankfurt: 1973.

———. *Die Gedichte von Bertolt Brecht in einem Band.* Frankfurt: 1981.

Breton, André. *Nadja.* Paris: 1964.

Brodersen, Momme. *Spinne im eigenen Netz: Walter Benjamin, Leben und Werk.* Bühl-Moos: 1990.

Bruford, W. H. *Germany in the Eighteenth Century: The Social Background of the Literary Revival.* Cambridge: 1935.

Buber, Martin. *Drei Reden über das Judentum.* Frankfurt: 1911.

Buci-Glucksmann, Christine. "Catastrophic Utopia: The Feminine as Allegory of the Modern." In Catherine Gallagher and Thomas Laqueur, eds. *The Making of the Modern Body: Sexuality and Society in the Nineteenth Century.* Berkeley: 1987.

———. *Walter Benjamin und die Utopie des Weiblichen.* Hamburg: 1984.

Buck-Morss, Susan. *The Dialectics of Seeing.* Cambridge, Mass.: 1989.

———. *The Origin of Negative Dialectics: Theodor W. Adorno, Walter Benjamin, and the Frankfurt Institute.* New York: 1977.

Bullock, Marcus. *Marxism and Romanticism: The Philosophical Development of Literary Theory and Literary History in Walter Benjamin and Friedrich Schlegel.* New York: 1987.

Bulthaup, Peter, ed. *Materialien zu Benjamins Thesen "Über den Begriff der Geschichte."* Frankfurt: 1975.

Bürger, Peter. "Benjamins 'rettende Kritik'. Vorüberlegungen zum Entwurf einer kritischen Hermeneutik." In Bürger, *Vermittlung—Rezeption—Funktion: Ästhetische Theorie und Methodologie der Literaturwissenschaft.* Frankfurt: 1979. 160–172.

———. *Der französische Surrealismus: Studien zum Problem der avantgardistischen Literatur.* Frankfurt: 1971.

———. "Literaturwissenschaft heute." In Jürgen Habermas, ed., *Stichworte zur "Geistigen Situation der Zeit."* Frankfurt: 1980. 781–795.

———. *Theorie der Avantgarde.* Frankfurt: 1974. English translation: *Theory of the Avant-Garde.* Minneapolis: 1984.

Butler, E. M. *The Tyranny of Greece over Germany.* Cambridge: 1935.

Cassirer, Ernst. "Hermann Cohen, 1842–1918." *Social Research* 10 (1943), 219–232.
———. *Language and Myth*. New York: 1946 (originally 1925).
———. *The Philosophy of the Enlightenment*. Princeton: 1951.
———. *The Philosophy of Symbolic Forms*. 3 volumes. New Haven: 1953–57 (originally 1923–29).
Chow, Rey. "Walter Benjamin's Love Affair with Death." *New German Critique* 48 (Fall 1989), 63–86.
Cohen, Hermann. "Religion und Sittlichkeit." In *Jüdische Schriften*, vol. 3: *Zur jüdischen Religionsphilosophie und ihrer Geschichte*. Berlin: 1924. 98–168.
Cowan, Bainard. "Walter Benjamin's Theory of Allegory." *New German Critique* 22 (Winter 1981), 109–122.
Crois, John Michael. *Cassirer: Symbolic Forms and History*. New Haven: 1987.
David, Claude. *Stefan George: Sein dichterisches Werk*. Munich: 1967.
Deak, Istvan. *Weimar Germany's Left-Wing Intellectuals: A Political History of the Weltbühne and Its Circle*. Berkeley: 1968.
Eichner, Hans. *Friedrich Schlegel*. New York: 1970.
Ermarth, Michael. *Wilhelm Dilthey: The Critique of Historical Reason*. Chicago: 1978.
Espagne, Michael, and Michael Werner. "Vom Passagen-Projekt zum 'Baudelaire': Neue Handschriften zum Spätwerk Walter Benjamins." *Deutsche Vierteljahresschrift für Literaturwissenschaft und Geistesgeschichte* 4 (1984), 593–657.
Fletcher, Angus. *Allegory: The Theory of a Symbolic Mode*. Ithaca: 1964.
Freier, Hans. "Odyssee eines Pariser Bauern: Aragons 'mythologie moderne' und der Deutsche Idealismus." In Karl-Heinz Bohrer, ed., *Mythos und Moderne*. Frankfurt: 1983. 157–193.
Fügen, Hans Norbert. "Der George-Kreis in der 'dritten Generation'." In Wolfgang Rothe, ed., *Die deutsche Literatur in der Weimarer Republik*. Stuttgart: 1974.
Fuld, Werner. "Die Aura: Zur Geschichte eines Begriffs bei Benjamin." *Akzente* 26 (1979), 352–370.
———. *Walter Benjamin: Zwischen den Stühlen. Eine Biographie*. Munich: 1979.
———. "Walter Benjamins Beziehung zu Ludwig Klages." *Akzente* 28 (1971), 274–286.
Gadamer, Hans-Georg. *Wahrheit und Methode: Grundzüge einer philosophischen Hermeneutik*. Tübingen: 1975. English translation: *Truth and Method*. 2d. rev. ed. New York: 1989.
Gallas, Helga. *Marxistische Literaturtheorie: Kontroversen im Bund proletarisch-revolutionärer Schriftsteller*. Neuwied: 1971.
Garber, Klaus. *Rezeption und Rettung: Drei Studien zu Walter Benjamin*. Tübingen: 1987.
Gay, Peter. *Weimar Culture: The Outsider as Insider*. New York: 1968.
Geist, J. F. *Passagen: Ein Bautyp des XIX. Jahrhunderts*. Munich: 1979.
Georgiadis, Sokratis. *Sigfried Giedion, eine intellektuelle Biographie*. Zurich: 1989.
Giedion, Sigfried. *Bauen in Frankreich: Eisen, Eisenbeton*. Leipzig: 1927.
Gluck, Mary. "Toward a Historical Definition of Modernism: Georg Lukács and the Avant-Garde." *Journal of Modern History* 58 (December 1986), 845–882.

Goethe, Johann Wolfgang. *Die Wahlverwandtschaften*. Frankfurt: 1955.

Goldstein, Moritz. "Deutsch-jüdischer Parnaß." *Der Kunstwart* 25, no. 11 (1912), 281–294.

Greiffenhagen, Martin. *Das Dilemma des Konservatismus in Deutschland*. Frankfurt: 1986.

Habermas, Jürgen. "Bewußtmachende oder rettende Kritik? Die Aktualität Walter Benjamins." In Siegfried Unseld, ed., *Zur Aktualität Walter Benjamins*. Frankfurt: 1972. English: "Consciousness-Raising or Redemptive Criticism: The Contemporaneity of Walter Benjamin." *New German Critique* 17 (Spring 1979), 30–59.

———. "Die deutschen Mandarine." In Habermas, *Philosophisch-politische Profile*. 3d ed. Frankfurt: 1981. 458–468.

———. *Der philosophische Diskurs der Moderne*. Frankfurt: 1985.

———. "Technology and Science as 'Ideology'." In Habermas, *Toward a Rational Society: Student Protest, Science, and Politics*. Boston: 1970.

Harlan, David. "Intellectual History and the Return of Literature." *American Historical Review* 94 (June 1989), 581–609.

Henkel, Arthur, and Albrecht Schöne. *Emblemata: Handbuch zur Sinnbildkunst des XVI. und XVII. Jahrhunderts*. Stuttgart: 1967.

Herf, Jeffrey. *Reactionary Modernism*. Cambridge: 1984.

Hermand, Jost, and Frank Trommler. *Die Kultur der Weimarer Republik*. Munich: 1978.

Hermann, Ulrich. "Die Jugendkulturbewegung: Der Kampf um die höhere Schule." In T. Koebner, R.-P. Janz, and F. Trommler, eds., *"Mit uns zieht die neue Zeit": Der Mythos Jugend*. Frankfurt: 1985. 224–244.

Hessel, Franz. *Ein Flaneur in Berlin* (altered title of a republication of *Spazieren in Berlin*). Berlin: 1984.

Hillach, Ansgar. "'Ästhetisierung des politischen Lebens': Benjamins faschismustheoretischer Ansatz—eine Rekonstruktion." In Burkhardt Lindner, ed., *"Links hatte noch alles sich zu enträtseln": Walter Benjamin im Kontext*. Frankfurt: 1978. 127–167.

———. "Walter Benjamin: Korrektiv Kritischer Theorie oder revolutionäre Handhabe? Zur Rezeption Benjamins durch die Studentenbewegung." In W. Martin Lüdke, ed., *Literatur und Studentenbewegung*. Opladen: 1977.

Hiller, Kurt, ed. *Das Ziel: Aufrufe zu tätigem Geist*. Munich: 1916.

Hofmannsthal, Hugo von. "Das Schrifttum als geistiger Raum der Nation." In Hofmannsthal, *Gesammelte Werke*, vol. 4: *Prosa*. Frankfurt: 1955.

Hohendahl, Peter Uwe, ed. *A History of German Literary Criticism, 1730–1980*. Lincoln: 1988.

Holborn, Hajo. "Der deutsche Idealismus in sozialgeschichtlicher Beleuchtung." *Historische Zeitschrift* 174 (October 1952), 359–384.

Hollinger, David. "The Return of the Prodigal: The Persistence of Historical Knowing." *American Historical Review* 94 (June 1989), 581–609.

Hörisch, Jochen. "Herrscherwort, Geld, und geltende Sätze: Adornos Aktualisierung der Frühromantik und ihre Affinität zur poststrukturalistischen Kritik des Subjekts." In Burkhardt Lindner and W. Martin Lüdke, eds., *Materialien zur ästhetischen Theorie Th. W. Adornos: Konstruktionen der Moderne*. Frankfurt: 1979. 397–414.

Horkheimer, Max, and Theodor W. Adorno. *Dialektik der Aufklärung*. Frankfurt: 1969.

Huyssen, Andreas. "The Cultural Politics of Pop." In Huyssen, *After the Great Divide: Modernism, Mass Culture, Postmodernism*. Bloomington, Ind.: 1986. 141–159.

Iggers, Georg. *New Directions in European Historiography*. Middletown, Conn.: 1975.

Ivernel, Philippe. "Paris, Hauptstadt der Volksfront oder das postume Leben des 19. Jahrhunderts." In N. Bolz and B. Witte, eds., *Passagen: Walter Benjamins Urgeschichte des XIX. Jahrhunderts*. Munich: 1984. 114–135.

Jacobs, Carol. *The Dissimulating Harmony: The Image of Interpretation in Nietzsche, Rilke, Artaud, and Benjamin*. Baltimore: 1978.

——. "Walter Benjamin's Image of Proust." *Modern Language Notes* 86 (1971), 910–943.

Janik, Allan, and Stephen Toulmin. *Wittgenstein's Vienna*. New York: 1973.

Janz, Rolf-Peter. "Mythos und Moderne bei Walter Benjamin." In Karl-Heinz Bohrer, ed., *Mythos und Moderne*. Frankfurt: 1983. 363–381.

Jauß, Hans-Robert. "Literarische Tradition und gegenwärtiges Bewußtsein der Modernität." In Jauß, *Literaturgeschichte als Provocation*. Frankfurt: 1970. 11–66.

——. "Schlegels und Schillers Replik auf die 'Querelle des Anciens et des Modernes'." In Jauß, *Literaturgeschichte als Provocation*. Frankfurt: 1970. 67–106.

Jay, Martin. *Adorno*. Cambridge, Mass: 1984.

——. *The Dialectical Imagination: A History of the Frankfurt School and the Institute of Social Research, 1923–1950*. Boston: 1973.

——. "The Frankfurt School's Critique of Karl Mannheim and the Sociology of Knowledge." In Jay, *Permanent Exiles: Essays on the Intellectual Migration from Germany to America*. New York: 1985. 62–78.

Jennings, Michael. "Benjamin as a Reader of Hölderlin: The Origins of Benjamin's Theory of Literary Criticism." *German Quarterly* 56 (1983), 544–562.

——. *Dialectical Images: Walter Benjamin's Theory of Literary Criticism*. Ithaca: 1987.

——. "The Mortification of the Text: The Development of Walter Benjamin's Literary Criticism, 1912–1924." Ph.D. diss., University of Virginia, 1981.

Kambas, Chryssoula. *Walter Benjamin im Exil: Zum Verhältnis von Literaturpolitik und Ästhetik*. Tübingen: 1987.

——. "Walter Benjamins Verarbeitung der deutschen Frühromantik." In Giesela Dischner und Richard Faber, eds., *Romantische Utopie—utopische Romantik*. Hildesheim: 1979. 187–221.

Kaulen, Heinrich. *Rettung und Destruktion: Untersuchungen zur Hermeneutik Walter Benjamins*. Tübingen: 1987.

Kemp, Wolfgang. "Fernbilder: Benjamin und die Kunstwissenschaft." In Burkhardt Lindner, ed., " 'Links hatte noch alles sich zu enträtseln.' Walter Benjamin im Kontext. Frankfurt: 1978. 224–257.

Kindt, Werner, ed. *Grundschriften der deutschen Jugendbewegung*. Düsseldorf: 1963.

_____, ed. *Die Wandervogelzeit: Quellenschriften zur deutschen Jugendbewegung, 1896–1917.* Düsseldorf: 1968.

Klages, Ludwig. *Der Geist als Widersacher der Seele.* Bonn: 1960.

_____. "Mensch und Erde." In Klages, *Mensch und Erde.* Jena: 1920. 13–45.

_____. *Vom kosmogonischen Eros.* Jena: 1926.

_____. "Vom Traumbewußtsein." In Klages, *Sämtliche Werke,* vol. 3: *Philosophie III (Philosophische Schriften).* Bonn: 1974. 157–189.

Kloppenberg, James. "Deconstruction and Hermeneutic Strategies for Intellectual History: The Recent Work of Dominick LaCapra and David Hollinger." *Intellectual History Newsletter* 9 (1987), 3–22.

Kracauer, Siegfried. *Die Angestellten: Aus dem neuesten Deutschland.* Frankfurt: 1971.

_____. *Das Ornament der Masse.* Frankfurt: 1977.

Kraft, Werner. *Carl Gustav Jochmann und sein Kreis.* Munich: 1972.

Kupffer, Heinrich. *Gustav Wyneken.* Stuttgart: 1970.

LaCapra, Dominick, and Steven L. Kaplan. *European Intellectual History: Reappraisals and New Perspectives.* Ithaca: 1982.

Lacoue-Labarthe, Philippe, and Jean-Luc Nancy. *The Literary Absolute: The Theory of Literature in German Romanticism.* Albany: 1988.

Laermann, Klaus. "Der Skandal um den *Anfang:* Ein Versuch jugendlicher Gegenöffentlichkeit im Kaiserreich." In T. Koebner, R.-P. Janz, and F. Trommler, eds., *"Mit uns zieht die neue Zeit": Der Mythos Jugend.* Frankfurt: 1985. 360–381.

Laqueur, Walter. *Weimar: A Cultural History, 1918–1933.* New York: 1974.

_____. *Young Germany.* New York: 1962.

Lebovics, Hermann. *Social Conservatism and the Middle Classes in Germany, 1914–1933.* Princeton: 1969.

Lehmann, Hans-Thiess, "Portrait Bertolt Brechts." In Horst Albert Glaser, ed. *Deutsche Literatur: Eine Sozialgeschichte,* vol. 9: *Weimarer Republik—Drittes Reich.* Reinbek bei Hamburg: 1983. 273–282.

Lepenies, Wolf. *Die drei Kulturen: Soziologie zwischen Literatur und Wissenschaft.* Munich: 1985.

Lethen, Helmut. "Neue Sachlichkeit." In Horst Albert Glaser, ed. *Deutsche Literatur: Eine Sozialgeschichte,* vol. 9: *Weimarer Republik—Drittes Reich.* Reinbek bei Hamburg: 1983. 168–179.

_____. *Neue Sachlichkeit (1924–1932): Studien zur Literatur des "Weissen Sozialismus."* 2d ed. Stuttgart: 1975.

Lindner, Burkhardt. "Benjamin-Bibliographie (1971–1978)". In H. L. Arnold, ed., *Text und Kritik 31/32: Sonderband Walter Benjamin.* 2d ed. Munich: 1979. 114–120.

_____. "Brecht/Benjamin/Adorno: Über Veränderungen der Kunstproduktion im wissenschaftlich-technischen Zeitalter." In H. L. Arnold, ed., *Text und Kritik: Sonderband Bertolt Brecht I.* Munich: 1972. 13–26.

_____. "Goethes 'Wahlverwandtschaften' und die Kritik der mythischen Verfassung der bürgerlichen Gesellschaft." In N. Bolz, ed., *Goethes "Wahlverwandtschaften": Kritische Modelle und Diskursanalysen zum Mythos Literatur.* Hildesheim: 1981. 23–44.

_____. "Habilitationsakte Benjamin: Über ein 'akademisches Trauerspiel' und über ein Vorkapitel der 'Frankfurter Schule' (Horkheimer, Adorno)." *LiLi:*

Zeitschrift für Literaturwissenschaft und Linguistik, 14, nos. 53/54 (1984), 147–165.

———. "Das 'Passagen-Werk', die 'Berliner Kindheit', und die Archäologie des 'Jüngstvergangenen'." In N. Bolz and B. Witte, eds., *Passagen: Walter Benjamins Urgeschichte des XIX. Jahrhunderts.* Munich: 1984. 27–48.

———. "Positives Barbarentum—aktualisierte Vergangenheit: Über einige Widersprüche Benjamins." *alternative* 23 (June/August 1980), 130–139.

———. "Satire und Allegorie in Jean Pauls Werk: Zur Konstitution des Allegorischen." *Jahrbuch der Jean-Paul Gesellschaft* 5 (1970).

———. "Werkbiographie und kommentierte Bibliographie (bis 1970)." In H. L. Arnold, ed., *Text und Kritik 31/32: Sonderband Walter Benjamin.* 2d ed. Munich: 1979. 103–113.

Linse, Ulrich. "Die Jugendkulturbewegung." In Klaus Vondung, ed., *Das wilhelminische Bildungsbürgertum.* Göttingen: 1976. 119–137.

Lönker, Fred. "Benjamins Darstellungstheorie: Zur Erkenntniskritische Vorrede zum *Ursprung des deutschen Trauerspiels.*" In F. Kittler and H. Turk, eds., *Urszenen: Literaturwissenschaft als Diskursanalyse und Diskurskritik.* Frankfurt: 1977. 293–322.

Löwy, Michael. "Jewish Messianism and Libertarian Utopia in Central Europe (1900–1933)." *New German Critique* 20 (Spring/Summer 1980), 105–115.

———. "Revolution against 'Progress': Walter Benjamin's Romantic Anarchism." *New Left Review* 152 (July/August 1985), 42–59.

Lüdke, W. Martin, ed. *"Theorie der Avantgarde": Antworten auf Peter Bürgers Bestimmung von Kunst und bürgerlicher Gesellschaft.* Frankfurt: 1976.

Lunn, Eugene. *Marxism and Modernism: An Historical Study of Lukács, Brecht, Benjamin, and Adorno.* Berkeley: 1982.

McCole, John. "Benjamin's *Passagen-Werk:* A Guide to the Labyrinth." *Theory and Society* 14 (1985), 497–509.

Maier, Charles. "Between Taylorism and Technocracy: European Ideologies and the Vision of Industrial Productivity in the 1920's." In Maier, *In Search of Stability: Explorations in Historical Political Economy.* Cambridge: 1987. 22–53.

Makkreel, Rudolf. *Dilthey: Philosopher of the Human Sciences.* Princeton: 1975.

Mattenklott, Gert. "'Nicht durch Kampfesmacht und nicht durch Körperkraft. . .': Alternativen Jüdischer Jugendbewegung in Deutschland vom *Anfang* bis 1933." In T. Koebner, R.-P. Janz, and F. Trommler, eds., *"Mit uns zieht die neue Zeit": Der Mythos Jugend.* Frankfurt: 1985. 338–359.

Mayer, Hans "Bertolt Brecht und die Tradition." In Mayer, *Brecht in der Geschichte: Drei Versuche.* Frankfurt: 1971. 7–159.

Meier-Cronemeyer, Hermann. "Jüdische Jugendbewegung." *Germania Judaica* 8 (new series 27/28) (1969), 1–122.

Mendes-Flohr, Paul. *From Mysticism to Dialogue: Martin Buber's Transformation of German Social Thought.* Detroit: 1989.

Menninghaus, Winfried. *Schwellenkunde: Walter Benjamins Passage des Mythos.* Frankfurt: 1986.

———. *Unendliche Verdoppelung: Die frühromantische Grundlegung der Kunsttheorie im Begriff absoluter Selbstreflexion.* Frankfurt: 1987.

———. "Walter Benjamins romantische Idee des Kunstwerks und seiner Kritik." *Poetica* 12 (1980), 421–442.

———. *Walter Benjamins Theorie der Sprachmagie.* Frankfurt: 1980.

Merker, Nicolao. *Die Aufklärung in Deutschland*. Munich: 1982.

Mogge, Winfried. "Wandervogel, Freideutsche Jugend und Bünde: Zum Jugendbild der bürgerlichen Jugendbewegung." In T. Koebner, R.-P. Janz, and F. Trommler, eds., *"Mit uns zieht die neue Zeit"*: *Der Mythos Jugend*. Frankfurt: 1985. 174–198.

Mohler, Armin. *Die konservative Revolution in Deutschland, 1918–1932: Ein Handbuch*. Darmstadt: 1972.

Mohr, Christoph, and Michael Müller. *Funktionalität und Moderne: Das neue Frankfurt und seine Bauten, 1925–1933*. Frankfurt: 1984.

Mommsen, Hans. "Generationskonflikt und Jugendrevolte in der Weimarer Republik." In T. Koebner, R.-P. Janz, and F. Trommler, eds., *"Mit uns zieht die neue Zeit"*: *Der Mythos Jugend*. Frankfurt: 1985. 50–67.

Mosse, George. *Germans and Jews*. New York: 1970.

Müller, Michael. "Architektur für das 'schlechte Neue'," in Müller, *Architektur und Avantgarde: Ein vergessenes Projekt der Moderne?* Frankfurt: 1984.

_____. *Die Verdrängung des Ornaments*. Frankfurt: 1977.

Nadeau, Maurice. *The History of Surrealism*. New York: 1985.

Nägele, Rainer. *Theater, Theory, Speculation: Walter Benjamin and the Scenes of Modernity*. Baltimore: 1981.

_____, ed. *Benjamin's Ground: New Readings of Walter Benjamin*. Detroit: 1988.

Neuloh, Otto, and Wilhelm Zilius. *Die Wandervögel: Eine empirisch-soziologische Untersuchung der frühen deutschen Jugendbewegung*. Göttingen: 1982.

Noeggerath, Felix. "Synthesis und Systembegriff in der Philosophie: Ein Beitrag zur Kritik des Antirationalismus." Ph.D., Erlangen, 1916 (also listed as 1930).

Noll, Monika. "Walter Benjamin und die revolutionäre Position in der modernen französichen Literatur." *Deutsch-französisches Jahrbuch* 1 (1981), 41–58.

Oehler, Dolf. "Charisma des Nicht-Identischen, Ohnmacht des Aparten: Adorno und Benjamin als Literaturkritiker, am Beispiel Proust." In Heinz Ludwig Arnold, ed., *Text und Kritik, Sonderheft Adorno*. Munich: 1977. 150–158.

Oettermann, Stephan. *Panorama: Die Geschichte eines Massenmediums*. Frankfurt: 1980.

Olenhusen, Irmtraud, and Götz von Albrecht. "Walter Benjamin, Gustav Wyneken und die Freistudenten vor dem Ersten Weltkrieg: Bemerkungen zu zwei Briefen Benjamins an Wyneken." *Jahrbuch des Archivs der Deutschen Jugendbewegung* 13 (1981), 98–128.

Ollig, Hans-Ludwig. *Der Neukantianismus*. Stuttgart: 1979.

Panofsky, Erwin, and Fritz Saxl. *Dürers 'Melencholia I'*. Leipzig: 1923.

Peter, Klaus. "Einleitung." In Peter, ed., *Romantikforschung seit 1945*. Königstein/Ts.: 1980.

_____. *Friedrich Schlegel*. Stuttgart: 1978.

_____. *Idealismus als Kritik: Friedrich Schlegels Philosophie der unvollendeten Welt*. Stuttgart: 1973.

Pocock, J. G. A. *Virtue, Commerce, and History*. Cambridge: 1985.

Proust, Marcel. *The Past Recaptured*. Translated by Andreas Mayor. New York: 1970.

_____. *Swann's Way*. Translated by C. K. Scott Moncrieff. New York: 1970.

Rabinbach, Anson. "Between Enlightenment and Apocalypse: Benjamin,

Bloch, and Modern German Jewish Messianism." *New German Critique* 34 (Winter 1985), 78–124.

Radnoti, Sandor. "Benjamin's Politics." *Telos* 37 (1978), 63–81.

Ringer, Fritz. *The Decline of the German Mandarins: The German Academic Community, 1890–1933.* Cambridge, Mass.: 1969.

——. "Differences and Cross-National Similarities among Mandarins." *Comparative Studies in Society and History* 28 (January 1986), 145–164.

——. *Fields of Knowledge: French Academic Culture in Comparative Perspective, 1890–1920.* Cambridge: 1992.

——. "The German Mandarins Reconsidered." Unpublished manuscript, personal copy.

——. "The Intellectual Field, Intellectual History, and the Sociology of Knowledge." *Theory and Society* 19 (1990), 269–294.

Roberts, Julian. *Walter Benjamin.* London: 1982.

Rosen, Charles. "The Origins of Walter Benjamin." *New York Review of Books* 24 (November 10, 1977), 30–38.

——. "The Ruins of Walter Benjamin." *New York Review of Books* 24 (October 27, 1977), 31–40.

Rüegg, Walter, ed. *Kulturkritik und Jugendkult.* Frankfurt: 1984.

Rumpf, Michael. "Faszination und Distanz: Zu Benjamins George-Rezeption." In P. Gebhardt, M. Grzimek, D. Harth, M. Rumpf, U. Schödelbauer, and B. Witte, *Walter Benjamin: Zeitgenosse der Moderne.* Kronberg/Ts.: 1976. 51–70.

Scheerbart, Paul. *Lesabéndio: Ein Asteroïden-Roman.* Munich: 1913.

Schivelbusch, Wolfgang. *Intellektuellendämmerung: Zur Lage der Frankfurter Intelligenz in den zwanziger Jahren.* Frankfurt: 1982.

Schlegel, Friedrich. *Kritische Friedrich Schlegel Ausgabe.* Edited by Ernst Behler, with Jean-Jacques Anstett and Hans Eichner. Munich: 1958–. Vol. 2: *Charakteristiken und Kritiken I (1796–1801).* 1967.

Schnädelbach, Herbert. *Philosophie in Deutschland, 1831–1933.* Frankfurt: 1983. English translation: *Philosophy in Germany, 1831–1933.* Cambridge: 1984.

Scholem, Gershom. *On Jews and Judaism in Crisis: Selected Essays.* Edited by Werner J. Dannhauser. New York: 1976.

——. *The Messianic Idea in Judaism and Other Essays on Jewish Spirituality.* New York: 1971.

——. *Von Berlin nach Jerusalem: Jugenderinnerungen.* Frankfurt: 1977.

——. *Walter Benjamin: Die Geschichte einer Freundschaft.* Frankfurt: 1975.

——. "Walter Benjamin und Felix Noeggerath." *Merkur* 35 (February 1981), 134–169.

——. "Walter Benjamin und sein Engel". In Siegfried Unseld, ed., *Zur Aktualität Walter Benjamins.* Frankfurt: 1972. 87–138.

——. *Walter Benjamin und sein Engel.* Frankfurt: 1984.

Schonauer, Franz. *Stefan George.* Reinbek bei Hamburg: 1960.

Schöne, Albrecht. " 'Diese nach jüdischem Vorbild erbaute Arche': Walter Benjamins *Deutsche Menschen.*" In Stéphane Moses and Albrecht Schöne, eds., *Juden in der deutschen Literatur: Ein deutsch-israelisches Symposion.* Frankfurt: 1986. 350–365.

——. *Emblematik und Drama im Zeitalter des Barock.* München: 1964.

Schorske, Carl. *Fin-de-siècle Vienna: Politics and Culture.* New York: 1980.

Schulte-Sasse, Jochen. "Theory of Modernism versus Theory of the Avant-Garde." Foreword to Peter Bürger, *Theory of the Avant-Garde*. Minneapolis: 1984. vii–xlvii.

Shattuck, Roger. *The Banquet Years: The Origins of the Avant-Garde in France, 1885 to World War I*. New York: 1968.

———. *Proust's Binoculars*. New York: 1962.

Simmel, Georg. *Philosophische Kultur*. Leipzig: 1919.

Sontag, Susan. "Under the Sign of Saturn." In Sontag, *Under the Sign of Saturn*. New York: 1980. 109–134. Originally, "The Last Intellectual." *New York Review of Books*, October 12, 1978.

———. "Writing Itself: On Roland Barthes." In S. Sontag, ed., *A Barthes Reader*. London: 1982. vii–xxxviii.

Spencer, Lloyd. "Allegory in the World of the Commodity." *New German Critique* 34 (Winter 1985), 59–77.

Stachura, Peter D. *The German Youth Movement, 1900–1945*. London: 1981.

Stark, Gary D. *Entrepreneurs of Ideology: Neoconservative Publishers in Germany, 1890–1933*. Chapel Hill: 1981.

Stern, Howard. "Gegenbild, Reihenfolge, Sprung: An Essay on Related Figures of Argument in Walter Benjamin." Ph.D. Diss., Yale University, 1978.

Stoessel, Marlene. *Aura: Das vergessene Menschliche. Zu Sprache und Erfahrung bei Walter Benjamin*. Munich: 1983.

Stüssi, Anna. *Erinnerungen an die Zukunft: Walter Benjamins "Berliner Kindheit um 1900."* Göttingen: 1977.

Szondi, Peter. "Hope in the Past: On Walter Benjamin." *Critical Inquiry* 4 (Spring 1978), 491–506.

———. "Die Städtebilder Walter Benjamins." *Der Monat* 14 (July 1962), 55–62.

Thompson, E. P. *The Making of the English Working Class*. New York: 1963.

Tiedemann, Rolf. *Dialektik im Stillstand*. Frankfurt: 1984.

———. "Historischer Materialismus oder Politischer Messianismus? Politische Gehalte in der Geschichtsphilosophie Walter Benjamins." In Peter Bulthaup, ed., *Materialien zu Benjamins Thesen "Über den Begriff der Geschichte."* Frankfurt: 1975. 77–121.

———. " 'Die Kunst, in anderer Leute Köpfe zu denken': Brecht—kommentiert von Benjamin." In Walter Benjamin, *Versuche über Brecht*. 2d. ed. Frankfurt: 1978. 173–208.

———. *Studien zur Philosophie Walter Benjamins*. Frankfurt: 1965.

Unger, Peter. *Walter Benjamin als Rezensent: Die Reflexion eines Intellektuellen auf die zeitgeschichtliche Situation*. Frankfurt: 1978.

Utley, Philip Lee. "Radical Youth: Generational Conflict in the *Anfang* Movement, 1912–January 1914." *History of Education Quarterly* 19 (1979), 207–227.

———. "Siegfried Bernfeld: Left-Wing Youth Leader, Psychoanalyst, and Zionist, 1910–1918." Ph.D. diss., University of Wisconsin, 1975.

Vietta, Silvio. "Frühromantik und Aufklärung." In S. Vietta, ed., *Die literarische Frühromantik*. Göttingen: 1983. 7–84.

Volkmann-Schluck, Karl Heinz. "Novalis' magischer Idealismus." In Hans Steffen, ed., *Die deutsche Romantik: Poetik, Formen und Motive*. Göttingen: 1967. 45–53.

Wawrzyn, Lienhard. *Walter Benjamins Kunsttheorie: Kritik einer Rezeption*. Darmstadt: 1973.

Wellek, René. "The Early Literary Criticism of Walter Benjamin." *Rice University Studies* 57 (1971), 123–134.

Willett, John. *Art and Politics in the Weimar Period: The New Sobriety, 1917–1933.* New York: 1978.

Winkler, Michael. *George-Kreis.* Stuttgart: 1972.

_____. "Der Jugendbegriff im George-Kreis." In T. Koebner, R.-P. Janz, and F. Trommler, eds., *"Mit uns zieht die neue Zeit": Der Mythos Jugend.* Frankfurt: 1985. 479–499.

Wismann, Heinz, ed. *Walter Benjamin et Paris: Colloque international, 27–29 juin 1983.* Paris: 1986.

Witte, Bernd. *Walter Benjamin.* Reinbek bei Hamburg: 1985.

_____. *Walter Benjamin: Der Intellektuelle als Kritiker.* Stuttgart: 1976.

Wohl, Robert. *The Generation of 1914.* Cambridge, Mass.: 1979.

Wohlfarth, Irving. " 'Die eigene, bis zum Verschwinden reife Einsamkeit': Zu Walter Benjamins Briefwechsel mit Gershom Scholem." *Merkur* 35 (February 1981), 170–191.

_____. "Et cetera? Der Historiker als Lumpensammler." In N. Bolz und B. Witte, eds. *Passagen: Walter Benjamins Urgeschichte des XIX. Jahrhunderts.* München: 1984. 70–95.

_____. "History, Literature, and the Text: The Case of Walter Benjamin." *MLN* 97 (1981), 1002–14.

_____. "Hors d'Oeuvre." In Walter Benjamin, *Origine du Drame Baroque Allemand.* Paris: 1985. 7–21.

_____. " 'Immer radikal, niemals konsequent . . .': Zur theologisch-politischen Standortsbestimmung Walter Benjamins." In N. Bolz and R. Faber, eds., *Antike und Moderne: Zu Walter Benjamins "Passagen."* Würzburg: 1986. 116–137.

_____. "No-Man's-Land: On Walter Benjamin's 'Destructive Character'." *Diacritics*, June 1978, 47–65. German version: "Der 'Destruktive Charakter': Benjamin zwischen den Fronten." In B. Lindner, ed., *'Links hatte noch alles sich zu enträtseln': Walter Benjamin im Kontext.* Frankfurt: 1978. 65–99.

_____. "On Some Jewish Motifs in Benjamin," in Andrew Benjamin, ed., *Problems of Modernity.* London: 1989. 157–215.

_____. "On the Messianic Structure of Benjamin's Last Reflections." *Glyph* 3 (1979), 148–212.

_____. "The Politics of Prose and the Art of Awakening: Walter Benjamin's Version of a German Romantic Motif." *Glyph* 7 (1980), 131–148.

_____. "Re-Fusing Theology: Some First Responses to Walter Benjamin's Arcades Project." *New German Critique* 39 (Fall 1986), 3–24.

_____. "Resentment Begins at Home: Nietzsche, Benjamin, and the University." In Gary Smith, ed., *On Walter Benjamin: Critical Essays and Recollections.* Cambridge: 1988. 224–259.

_____. "Walter Benjamin's Image of Interpretation." *New German Critique* 17 (Spring 1979), 70–98.

Wolin, Richard. *Walter Benjamin: An Aesthetic of Redemption.* New York: 1982.

Wurgaft, Lewis D. *The Activists: Kurt Hiller and the Politics of Action on the German Left, 1914–1933.* Philadelphia: 1977.

Wuthenow, Ralph-Rainer, ed. *Stefan George in seiner Zeit: Dokumente zur Wirkungsgeschichte,* vol. 1. Stuttgart: 1980.

Wyneken, Gustav. *Schule und Jugendkultur*. Jena: 1913.
_____. *Was ist "Jugendkultur"?* Munich: 1913.
Yates, Frances. *Giordano Bruno and the Hermetic Tradition*. New York: 1964.
_____. *The Occult Philosophy in the Elizabethan Age*. London. 1979.
Zerner, Henri. "Alois Riegl: Art, Value, Historicism." *Daedalus* 105 (Winter 1976), 177–188.

Index

Library of Congress Cataloging-in-Publication Data

McCole, John (John Joseph), 1954–
    Walter Benjamin and the antinomies of tradition / John McCole.
        p.   cm.
    Includes bibliographical references and index.
    ISBN 0-8014-2465-8 (cloth : alk. paper) — ISBN 0-8014-9711-6 (paper : alk. paper)
    1. Benjamin, Walter, 1892–1940—Criticism and interpretation. 2. Tradition (Philoso-
phy) 3. Modernism (Aesthetics) 4. Europe—Intellectual life—20th century. I. Title.
PT2603.E455Z7335   1993
838'.91209—dc20   92-21431